D1408525

East Asian Regionalism

East Asia is a region that holds much fascination for many people. It is one of the world's most dynamic and diverse regions and is also becoming an increasingly coherent region through the interplay of various integrative economic, political and socio-cultural processes. Such a development is generally referred to as 'regionalism', which itself has become a defining feature of the contemporary international system, and this book explores the various ways in which East Asian regionalism continues to deepen.

Focusing on the main themes of the East Asia region and the study of regionalism, economic regionalism and East Asia's new economic geography, Southeast Asia and the Association of Southeast Asian Nations (ASEAN), trans-regionalism, East Asia's new free trade agreement trends and key transnational issues in East Asia such as international migration and energy security, *East Asian Regionalism* will be an essential text for courses on East Asian regionalism, Asian politics and Asian economics.

Key pedagogical features include:

- end of chapter 'study questions';
- 'case studies' that discuss topical issues with study questions also provided;
- useful tables and figures which illustrate key regional trends in East Asia;
- extensive summary conclusions covering the chapter's main findings from different international political economy perspectives.

Christopher M. Dent is Reader in East Asia's International Political Economy at the University of Leeds, UK.

East Asian Regionalism

Christopher M. Dent

Routledge
Taylor & Francis Group

LONDON AND NEW YORK

First published 2008
by Routledge
2 Park Square, Milton Park, Abingdon, Oxon
OX14 4RN

Simultaneously published in the USA and Canada
by Routledge
270 Madison Ave, New York, NY 10016

Transferred to Digital Printing 2009

*Routledge is an imprint of the Taylor & Francis
Group, an informa business*

© 2008 Christopher M. Dent

Typeset in Century School Book by Keyword
Group Ltd
Printed and bound in Great Britain by
TJI Digital, Padstow, Cornwall

British Library Cataloguing in Publication Data
A catalogue record for this book is available from
the British Library

*Library of Congress Cataloging in Publication
Data*
Dent, Christopher M., 1965-
East Asian regionalism / Christopher M. Dent.
    p. cm.
Includes bibliographical references and index.
ISBN 978-0-415-43483-6 (hbk.) — ISBN 978-0-
415-43484-3 (pbk.) — ISBN 978-0-203-94642-8
(ebook) 1. East Asia—Economic policy. 2.
Regionalism—East Asia. I. Title.
HC460.5.D45 2008
337.1'5—dc22   007033033

ISBN10: 0-415-43483-1 (hbk)
ISBN10: 0-415-43484-X (pbk)
ISBN10: 0-203-94642-1 (ebk)

ISBN13: 978-0-415-43483-6 (hbk)
ISBN13: 978-0-415-43484-3 (pbk)
ISBN13: 978-0-203-94642-8 (ebk)

To the Aldersea Family and memories of Bela House. For the fun, the music and the laughter.

Contents

List of Tables and Figures

Tables

Figures

Abbreviations

ABAC	APEC Business Advisory Council
ABMI	Asian Bond Market Initiative
ACD	Asia Co-operation Dialogue
ACFTA	ASEAN–China Free Trade Agreement
ACU	Asian Currency Unit
ADB	Asian Development Bank
AEC	ASEAN Economic Community
AEMM	ASEAN Economic Ministerial Meeting
AFAS	ASEAN Framework Agreement on Services
AFC	ASEAN Finance Corporation
AFTA	ASEAN Free Trade Area
AIA	ASEAN Investment Area
AICO	ASEAN Industrial Co-operation
AIJV	ASEAN Industrial Joint Venture
AIP	ASEAN Industrial Projects
AMF	Asian Monetary Fund
AMMH	ASEAN Ministerial Meeting on Haze
APAEC	ASEAN Plan of Action on Energy Co-operation
APEC	Asia-Pacific Economic Co-operation forum
APT	ASEAN Plus Three
ARF	ASEAN Regional Forum
ASA	ASEAN Swap Agreement
ASC	ASEAN Security Community
ASCC	ASEAN Socio-Cultural Community
ASCOPE	ASEAN Council on Petroleum
ASEAN	Association of Southeast Asian Nations
ASEM	Asia-Europe Meeting
ASOEN	ASEAN Senior Officials on Environment meeting
BCSA	bilateral currency swap agreement
BIMP-EAGA	Brunei–Indonesia–Malaysia–Philippines East ASEAN Growth Area

BIMSTEC	Bay of Bengal Initiative for Multi-Sectoral Technical and Economic Co-operation
CACM	Central America Common Market
CAN	Andean Community of Nations
CARICOM	Caribbean Community
CEMAC	Economic and Monetary Community of Central Africa
CEPA	Closer Economic Partnership Arrangement
CEPEA	Comprehensive Economic Partnership in East Asia
CEPT	Common Effective Preferential Tariff
CER	Closer Economic Relations (between Australia and New Zealand)
CET	common external tariff
CISFTA	Commonwealth of Independent States Free Trade Area
CLMV	Cambodia, Laos, Myanmar and Vietnam
CMI	Chiang Mai Initiative
COMESA	Common Market for Eastern and Southern Africa
CSCAP	Council for Security Co-operation in the Asia-Pacific
EAC	East African Community
EAEC	East Asian Economic Caucus
EAEG	East Asian Economic Grouping
EAERR	East Asia Emergency Rice Reserve
EAFTA	East Asia Free Trade Area
EALAF	East Asia–Latin America Forum
EAS	East Asia Summit
EASG	East Asia Study Group
EAVG	East Asia Vision Group
EEA	European Economic Area
EEC	Eurasian Economic Community
EFTA	European Free Trade Area/Association
EHP	Early Harvest Programme
EMEAP	Executives' Meeting of East Asian Central Banks
ENSO	El Niño-Southern Oscillation
EPA	Economic Partnership Agreement
EPG	Eminent Persons Group
ESI	Energy Security Initiative (of APEC)
EU	European Union
EVSL	Early Voluntary Sectoral Liberalisation scheme
FDI	foreign direct investment
FELDA	Federal Land Development Authority (of Malaysia)
FTA	free trade agreement
FTAA	Free Trade Area of the Americas
FTAAP	Free Trade Area of the Asia-Pacific
GAFTA	Greater Arab Free Trade Area
GATS	General Agreement on Trade in Services
GATT	General Agreement on Tariffs and Trade
GCC	Gulf Co-operation Council

GDP	gross domestic product
GMS	Greater Mekong Sub-region
GPN	global production network
GW	gigawatt
HDD	hard disk drive
HPA	Hanoi Plan of Action
HRD	human resource development
HTTF	(ASEAN) Haze Technical Task Force
IAI	Initiative for ASEAN Integration
IAPs	Individual Action Plans
ICT	information and communication technology
ILM	international labour migration
IMF	International Monetary Fund
IMSGT	Indonesia–Malaysia–Singapore Growth Triangle
IMTGT	Indonesia–Malaysia–Thailand Growth Triangle
IMV	Innovative International Multi-purpose Vehicle
IPE	international political economy
IPN	international production network
IPR	intellectual property rights
JACEP	Japan–ASEAN Comprehensive Economic Partnership
JAFTA	Japan–ASEAN Free Trade Agreement
JERC	Japan Economic Research Centre
JSEPA	Japan–Singapore Economic Partnership Agreement
KAFTA	South Korea–ASEAN FTA
KEDO	Korea Peninsula Energy Development Organisation
LDC	less developed country
LNG	liquefied natural gas
LWR	light water reactor
MAPA	Manila Action Plan
Mercosur	Southern Common Market
MFN	Most Favoured Nation
MNE	multinational enterprise
MTI	Ministry of Trade and Industry (Singapore)
MW	megawatt
NAFTA	North American Free Trade Agreement
NEAT	Network of East Asia Think Tanks
NGO	non-governmental organisation
NMI	New Miyazawa Initiative
NRT	new regionalism theory
NTB	non-tariff barrier
ODA	overseas development assistance
OECD	Organisation for Economic Co-operation and Development
OPEC	Organisation of Petroleum Exporting Countries
PACER	Pacific Agreement on Closer Economic Relations
PAFTA	Pacific Free Trade Area

PAFTAD	Pacific Trade and Development conference
PBEC	Pacific Basin Economic Council
PECC	Pacific Economic Co-operation Council
PICTA	Pacific Island Countries Trade Agreement
PTA	Preferential Trading Arrangement
RHAP	Regional Haze Action Plan
RoO	rules of origin
RPN	regional production network
SACU	South African Customs Union
SADC	South African Development Community
SAARC	South Asian Association for Regional Co-operation
SAR	Special Administrative Region
SCO	Shanghai Co-operation Organisation
SCSGT	South China Sea Growth Triangle
SEACEN	Southeast Asian Central Banks
SEANWFZ	Southeast Asia Nuclear Weapon-Free Zone
SEANZA	Southeast Asia, New Zealand, Australia
SME	small and medium-sized enterprise
STAR	Secure Trade in the APEC Region
STEER	Singapore–Thailand Enhanced Economic Relationship
SUVs	sports utility vehicles
TAGP	Trans-ASEAN Gas Pipeline
TAR	Trans-Asian Railway
TPSEPA	Trans-Pacific Strategic Economic Partnership Agreement
TRADP	Tumen River Area Development Programme
UN	United Nations
UNDP	United Nations Development Programme
UNESCAP	United Nations Economic and Social Commission for Asia and the Pacific
WAEMU	West African Economic and Monetary Union
WTO	World Trade Organisation
ZOPFAN	Zone of Peace, Freedom and Neutrality

Preface

East Asia is a region that holds much fascination to many. It is one of the world's most dynamic and diverse regions. East Asia is also becoming an increasingly coherent region through the interplay of various integrative economic, political and socio-cultural processes. Such a development is generally referred to as 'regionalism', and this book explores the various ways in which East Asian regionalism has deepened, and continues to do so. The book has been designed with both tutors and students in mind, providing comprehensive overviews of the key themes from the multi-disciplinary perspectives of international political economy, or IPE. Thus, it primarily blends the analytical elements of international relations, political science and economics related studies. The IPE approach often draws upon other relevant disciplines – for example, sociology, business studies, history and geography – and these too have been utilised in certain chapters to provide further insights into the development of East Asian regionalism. Particular features of this book especially intended for tutor/student study include:

- End of chapter 'study questions' on all the themes covered by the text, which may be used as a basis for class discussions.
- 'Case studies' in most chapters that discuss topical issues with study questions provided at the end of each study.
- Useful illustrative tables and figures, the latter especially conveying key regional trends in East Asia in a helpful graphic snapshot form.
- Extensive summary conclusions that overview the chapter's main findings from four different IPE theoretical perspectives, namely neo-realism, neo-liberalism (institutionalism), social constructivism and Marxism-structuralism.

The book is structured along the following lines. Chapter 1 provides a general introduction to the East Asia region and the study of regionalism generally. It also discusses the analytical virtues of studying East Asian regionalism from an international political economy perspective.

Chapter 2 examines the nature of East Asian regionalisation and the new economic geography of the region, focusing on how business activities and economic linkages are integrating the region closer together at the micro-level. It starts by discussing the historic dimension to East Asia's regionalisation, looking at the long-term development of regional trading systems and then recent trade trends. A substantive study is thereafter made of the rise of international production networks in East Asia and how we may understand their differentiated integrative effects within the region. Links between these networks and zones of concentrated economic activity in East Asia are then examined in an economic geography context. This includes an examination of the emergence of sub-regional 'growth polygons' that have been another special feature of East Asia's regionalisation.

Chapters 3, 4 and 5 all centre their analysis on the main regional organisations and frameworks to which East Asian countries are party. Chapter 3 looks at the Association of Southeast Asian Nations (ASEAN) and the development of regionalism in Southeast Asia, its analysis being structured by examining ASEAN main regional integrative projects, namely ASEAN Free Trade Area (AFTA), the Initiative for ASEAN Integration (IAI), and ASEAN Economic Community (AEC). In Chapter 4, we look at the development of trans-regional community building in Asia-Pacific and the contribution made here by the Asia-Pacific Economic Co-operation (APEC) forum. As is argued in this chapter, the relationship between East Asian countries and APEC has often been problematic, primarily because of the challenges APEC faces in having to accommodate a wide diversity of politico-economic interests and cultures from around the Pacific trans-region.

Chapter 5 looks at the development of East Asia's newest regional group frameworks, namely ASEAN Plus Three (APT) and East Asia Summit (EAS), the basis of the former being established in 1997 and the latter in 2005. Largely because it emerged in the wake of the 1997/8 East Asian financial crisis, much of the APT framework's achievements have been made in the area of regional financial governance, as previously indicated. In Chapter 5, we look at how the yet undefined relationship between the APT and EAS frameworks in many respects is connected with reconciling the region-centred interests of China and Japan. This is followed by Chapter 6's study of East Asia's new bilateral free trade agreement (FTA) trend, and particularly explores whether bilateral FTAs are making a positive contribution or not to regional community-building in East Asia.

Chapter 7 makes a study on three key transnational issues affecting the East Asia region, these being transboundary 'haze' pollution, international migration and energy security. In all three cases, the challenges and problems presented by these transnational issues have generated tensions amongst countries in the region as well as requiring them to work more closely together to address these challenges and problems. These studies reveal different kinds of linkages developing within the region, and therein further perspectives on regionalism and regionalisation in East Asia.

Finally, the concluding Chapter 8 draws together the main findings of preceding chapters within a newly developed analytical framework devised to further deepen our understanding of East Asian regionalism, and the nature of regionalism generally in the international system.

I would like to express my special thanks to a number of people. John McCauley at Routledge kindly provided me with various map templates on which many of the book's figures are based. Stephan Beckert at Telegeography kindly sent me the raw data sets that formed the basis of Chapter 2's figures on intra-regional telecoms traffic in East Asia. I am also very grateful to Ying Meng at the University of Leeds for finding important research materials that were extensively used in Chapter 7. A big thank you too to Stephanie Rogers at Routledge for her cheerful help and encouragement through the book project's development. In addition, I would like to acknowledge the extremely useful advice provided by three anonymous reviewers on how to improve the book's structure and content. Thanks too to all my colleagues in the Department of East Asian Studies at the University of Leeds, and the new White Rose East Asia Centre. Finally, an extra special thanks to all my family for their love, patience and support. This book is dedicated to my dear friends, the Aldersea Family, for all the fun times we have shared together over the past 20 or so years. Your love and friendship has meant so much to me, and always will.

Chapter 1

East Asia and regionalism

An introduction

1.1 East Asia: an emerging region within the global system

East Asia has achieved one of the most profound economic transformations in recorded history. In the 1950s and 1960s, it was a relatively poor developing part of the world, with countries such as Korea having comparable income per capita and development levels on par with many sub-Saharan African states. The region accounted for only 4 per cent of world gross domestic product (GDP) in 1960. By the 1990s, East Asia had become one of three core economic regions (along with Europe and North America) that together dominated the world economy, accounting for 25 per cent of world GDP by 1995. East Asia had become the new workshop of the world, the location of fast emerging markets, and a new financial power in the making. Japan had first spearheaded East Asia's economic rise up to the 1990s, and now China has become a major force behind the region's economic momentum. These two countries are amongst the world's four largest national economies, but East Asia is also host to the highest concentration of newly industrialised economies (e.g. South Korea, Taiwan, Singapore, Thailand, Malaysia) found anywhere in the world. The trade and financial surpluses generated by East Asian countries are second to none. The region accounts for just over a quarter of world trade, production, new technology patents and gross domestic product. It is also the home of some of the world's largest banks and multinational enterprises.

It could even be argued that the very concept of an 'East Asia' region principally derived from burgeoning studies on its growing prominence in the international economic system. In the 1980s and 1990s, scholars gradually began to ditch the antiquated, Western-centric referent 'Far East' for the region, and the distinction between 'East Asia' and 'Asia' was increasingly used to specify where exactly on the vast continent the profound economic transformation was actually occurring on a specific regional (rather than continental) scale. Moreover, East Asia's economic advance was in many ways founded on certain regional dynamics, and this explains why we often talk of the East Asian 'economic miracle' or the East Asian development model, and hence a particular coherence to East Asia's regional economic development. For example, many countries in the region emulated Japan's developmental state paradigm of state-business partnered capitalism and export-oriented industrialisation with generally successful effect.

East Asian countries learned from each other's lessons of development and implemented many similar policies, leading to some extent to a shared development experience. Also, Japanese firms played an initially crucial role in helping integrate the East Asian regional economy through networked trade and investment. American companies too contributed to this process through foreign investments made across the region. In addition, after many of East Asia's less developed countries had graduated to newly industrialised, middle income economy status they began to trade and invest more with each other. This further deepened East Asia's regional economic interdependence. While the export-oriented nature of East Asia's economic development made it highly dependent on global markets, countries in the region had become increasingly beholden to each other. The region's 1997/8 financial crisis clearly revealed the inter-linkages that bound together East Asia's economies in ways that were arguably then not fully appreciated. Various integrative forces continue to bind the region together at the economic, political, social and other levels, although these processes were also constituent to wider global-scale integrative developments commonly referred to as globalisation.

A comprehensive study of East Asia as an 'economic region' requires us to extend beyond the disciplinary focus of economics to include many other fields, especially international relations, security studies, political science, history, business, geography and sociology. As we later discuss in more detail, the *international political economy approach* with its emphasis on multi-disciplinarity is able to embrace these different fields and offer valuable holistic perspectives on the study of regionalism. This book's study on East Asian regionalism is hence a work of international political economy analysis. Its main objective is to consider to what extent East Asia is becoming, and will become an increasingly coherent (economic) region within the structure of the international or global system.

There appear, however, to be various factors stacked against the deepening of East Asian regionalism. East Asia is probably the most diverse region in the world in terms of economic development asymmetry, mix of political regimes and socio-religious traditions and characteristics (Table 1.1). Moreover, it is a region marked by historic animosities between rival nations, where conflicts still persist between old and new states alike, and where nationalism remains a potent force in many countries of the region. East Asia therefore would seem to face a special set of challenges in the endeavour of regional community-building. And yet East Asia does appear to exhibit signs of strengthening integration and coherence as a regional entity. This is evident in terms of deepening region-wide economic exchange (e.g. trade, investment, financial flows), transnational business operations, cross-border infrastructural linkages, international policy co-operation and co-ordination (including regional organisation development), social movements, shared popular culture, and various socialisation processes occurring amongst the peoples and societies of East Asia. There has been a significant expansion of intra-regional contacts in East Asia through improved transportation and communication technologies, tourism, migration, television and satellite broadcasts (Cohen 2002). A growing density of social communications within a region can engender a sense of shared identity and community amongst the involved participants (Deutsch 1957, 1966, Pempel 2005a).

At the same time as East Asia is regionally integrating, there remains some debate concerning what we actually mean by 'East Asia' in geographic terms. For example, from looking at a map it would seem that the Russian Far East should be included in the region (Figure 1.1), but invariably it is not considered part of the East Asia regional community. This may be because it is a peripheral sub-national region within an essentially Eurocentric country, Russia, and also because of its marginal, at best,

Table 1.1 East Asia: a diverse region

	GDP (US$bn, 2004)	Population (millions, 2004)	Per capita GDP (US$, 2004)	Area (000 sq. kms)	Main economic governance and development paradigm	Political system and government	Main religion(s)
Japan	4622.8	127.8	36,170	378	Developmental statism-mixed economy, services/manufacturing predominant	Democracy (Constitutional Monarchy)	Shinto, Buddhism
China	1931.7	1313.3	1,470	9,561	Planned/socialist market economy-manufacturing predominant	Communist (Socialist Republic)	Atheism, Taoism
South Korea	679.7	48.0	14,610	99	Developmental statism-mixed economy, services/manufacturing predominant	Democracy (Presidential Republic)	Buddhism, Christianity
Taiwan	305.3	22.7	13,450	36	Developmental statism-mixed economy, services/manufacturing predominant	Democracy (Presidential Republic)	Buddhism, Taoism
Indonesia	257.6	222.6	1,160	1,904	Predatory/developmental statism-mixed economy, services/manufacturing predominant	Democracy (Presidential Republic)	Islam
Hong Kong	163.0	7.1	22,960	1	Market liberal-market economy, services predominant	Special Administrative Region (of China)	Buddhism, Taoism, Christianity
Thailand	161.7	63.5	2,550	513	Predatory/developmental statism-mixed economy, services/manufacturing predominant	Democracy (Constitutional Monarchy) / Military Junta (from September 2006)	Buddhism
Malaysia	118.3	24.9	4,750	333	Predatory/developmental statism-mixed economy, services/manufacturing predominant	Semi-Democracy (Federal Constitutional Monarchy)	Islam
Singapore	106.8	4.3	24,840	1	Developmental statism-mixed economy, services/manufacturing predominant	Semi-Democracy (Parliamentary Republic)	Taoism, Buddhism, Islam
Philippines	84.6	81.4	1,040	300	Predatory/developmental statism-mixed economy, services/manufacturing predominant	Democracy (Presidential Republic)	Christianity
Vietnam	45.2	82.5	550	331	Planned/socialist market economy-manufacturing predominant	Communist (Socialist Republic)	Buddhism
North Korea	40.0	22.8	1,750	120	Planned economy/Juche (autarky) system-military sector predominant economy	Communist (Juche State)	Repressed
Myanmar	8.0	50.1	160	678	Predatory capitalist-military sector/agriculture predominant	Military Junta	Buddhism
Brunei	6.8	0.4	18,690	6	Oil sheikdom/oil-based economy	Absolute Monarchy	Islam
Cambodia	4.9	14.5	338	181	Predatory capitalist-mixed economy, agriculture predominant	Democracy (Constitutional Monarchy)	Buddhism
Macao	6.8	0.4	14,140	0.02	Market liberal-market economy, services predominant	Special Administrative Region (of China)	Buddhism
Laos	2.5	5.8	431	236	Planned/socialist market economy-agriculture predominant	Communist (Socialist Republic)	Buddhism
East Timor	1.7	1.0	980	15	Agriculture predominant economy	Democracy (UN Protected Republic)	Christianity
Mongolia	1.6	2.6	615	1,565	Ex-planned now mixed economy-agriculture and mining predominant	Parliamentary Democracy	Buddhism, Shamanism

Sources: Economist Intelligence Unit, Beeson (2007)

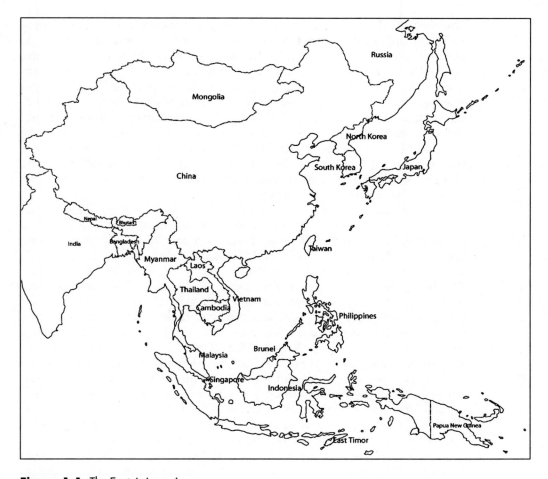

Figure 1.1 The East Asia region

Note: Countries denoted in a smaller font size have not usually been considered part of the East Asia region but rather part of other regions, n.b. India, Nepal, Bhutan and Bangladesh (South Asia), Papua New Guinea (Oceania).

engagement in East Asia's regional economic dynamic and integrational processes. This latter point is also relevant to explaining why Mongolia is so often overlooked as a constituent East Asian nation in regional groupings and regional organisation membership. One could even argue that for the Russian Far East and Mongolia to be more readily acknowledged as part of East Asia they need to appear more clearly on the regional economic radar.

In addition, some observers prefer to distinguish Southeast Asia as a distinctly separate entity to East Asia, and in this geographic division East Asia becomes what others would normally refer to as Northeast Asia.[1] The definitional parameters of regions often seem in a constant state of flux, as especially revealed in debates over country eligibility to regional organisation membership. This has long been the case in Europe regarding

European Union membership (e.g. Turkey's accession), and it has become an increasingly relevant issue for East Asia. For example, the East Asia Summit process that was initiated in December 2005 includes India (normally grouped with South Asia), Australia and New Zealand, two countries usually classified as belonging to the Oceania region. As Chapter 5 discusses, there were political motives behind Japan's advocacy of incorporating these three countries, which was at first opposed by China and others, but the main point here is that one person's East Asia may be different to another's. Hettne (2005:2) even goes so far as to argue that, 'there are no "natural" regions: definitions of a "region" vary according to the particular problem or question under investigation'. Thus, what we mean by particular regions can be highly contested.

For the purposes of clarity, however, this book will refer to East Asia as a composite of two sub-regional elements, namely: *Southeast Asia* – Brunei, Cambodia, East Timor, Indonesia, Laos, Malaysia, Myanmar, Philippines, Singapore, Thailand, Vietnam; and *Northeast Asia* – Japan, China, South Korea, North Korea, Hong Kong SAR, Macau SAR, Mongolia and Taiwan. This being said, our analysis of East Asian regionalism will show that extra-regional factors (e.g. third countries, transnational business, global-level issues) are also highly relevant. Much attention, for instance, is paid in the regionalism literature to the importance of the United States in East Asia's regional political economy (Beeson 2006a, 2006b). East Asia is itself part of a wider Asia-Pacific trans-region that incorporates Pacific coast America (North and Latin elements) and Oceania. Studies of East Asia are often situated in an Asia-Pacific context mainly owing to strengthening trans-regional economic links across the Pacific (Ariff 1991, Garnaut and Drysdale 1994, Islam and Chowdhury 1997, Lee 2002, Zhang 2003). Furthermore, the transnational business activities integrating East Asia together at a micro-level are often part of global production and distribution networks of firms that originate from outside the region. These linkages give East Asian regionalism an *extra-dimensional* aspect, and studying it thus requires us to consider related developments occurring at the wider international or global level. The extra-dimensional nature of East Asian regionalism is a core theme of the concluding Chapter 8.

1.2 Regionalism: key concepts and definitions

Regionalism is one of the key defining features of the contemporary international system. We increasingly talk of 'East Asia', 'Europe' and 'Latin America' and so on as distinctive regions or regional communities that are elemental parts of world society. Indeed, it has been argued that we now live in a world of regions, and an international system increasingly defined by interactions between regions and regional powers (Buzan and Waever 2003, Katzenstein 2005). Thus, the study of regionalism is now a crucial element of studying the international system generally. Moreover, understanding how regionalism has developed in East Asia – one of the world's most important and powerful regions – is also critically important.

Regionalism is, of course, not a wholly new phenomenon, but it has become an important discourse in the study of international relations and international political economy for the above reasons. Regionalism is also a contested concept, not least because regionalism manifests itself in different ways in different parts of the world. In broad terms, we may refer to regionalism as the *structures, processes and arrangements that are working towards greater coherence within a specific international region in terms of economic, political, security, socio-cultural and other kinds of linkages.* These may arise either as a result of:

1) micro-level processes that stem from regional concentrations of interconnecting private or civil sector activities, and this may be specifically referred to as *regionalisation*; or

2) public policy initiatives, such as a free trade agreement or other state-led projects of economic co-operation and integration that originate from inter-governmental dialogues and treaties, which may be specifically referred to as *regionalism* when contrasted to regionalisation.

In this context, regionalism is thus more of a policy-driven, top-down process while regionalisation is more of a societal-driven, bottom-up process. Various levels of interaction exist between both processes. For example, a motive behind the regionalist policy initiatives of governments is to further exploit the prosperity-generating potential of regionalisation, and these policy initiatives may not be formulated in the first place without there being a sufficient level of regionalisation in which to ground them. Regionalisation may in turn be enhanced by state-led regionalism projects. To many observers, *regionalism* and *regionalisation* are synonymous terms, but it is often the case that 'regionalism' is used as the generic referent for both processes.

Many if not the majority of studies on regionalism focus primarily on its economic dimension. This is because *economic regionalism* is by and large the most pronounced and well known form within the international system. Commonly cited manifestations of economic regionalism are the European Union's 'Single Market' and 'euro zone', the North American Free Trade Agreement (NAFTA), Mercosur (in South America), the South African Customs Union, the Gulf Co-operation Council (in the Middle East), ASEAN's Free Trade Area, and the Asia-Pacific Economic Co-operation forum. Whereas economic regionalism is mainly concerned with regional level trade, investment and financial inter-linkages, *political regionalism* generally refers to integral formations in the region's political community, involving the development of transnational policy-networks, the expression of shared political interests amongst the region's leaders, advancements in policy-co-ordination and common policy enterprises, and the creation of region-level institutions to manage any common 'political space' formed between the region's nation-states.

The European Union (EU) exhibits by far the most advanced levels of political regionalism in the international system. *Security regionalism* can to some extent be expressed in political terms, especially if traditional politico-military notions of security are upheld. More generally, security regionalism refers to the growing commitment between a region's military powers to form common security arrangements that assure peace for the region as a whole. This can entail non-aggression pacts, alliance partnerships and various co-operative activities in the security domain. We may also talk about *socio-cultural regionalism* in relation to how a region's society may develop its own sense of common identity. Underlying this is how we may consider regions as being socio-culturally or socio-politically constructed, and this is discussed later when we consider social constructivist perspectives on regionalism.

Economic regionalism – the principal focus of this book – strongly overlaps and inter-connects with these other domains of regionalism. For example, regional political frameworks (e.g. policy co-operation mechanisms) are required for East Asia's regional economic projects to function properly. The progress of economic regionalism in East Asia may be hindered whilst security tensions persist and a region-wide sense of social and political community remains weak. Conversely, a growing economic interdependence between the East Asian states can lend great imperative to forging closer political and security ties between them: a stronger coherence experienced in one domain can help build coherence in others. For example, market-driven processes that increasingly link the economies of East Asia together could provide the spur to closer policy, and hence political co-operation given the need to manage this emerging interdependence.

Moreover, stronger security co-operation may be deemed necessary to ensure a more stable environment for economic regionalism to maintain both its momentum and its flow of associated benefits captured by the regional community. From a slightly different but related perspective, Hettne (2005) argues that regionalism develops via various forms of cohesiveness, these primarily being of a *social* (ethnicity, race, language, religion, culture, history, consciousness of a common heritage), *economic* (trade, investment, finance linkages), *political* (regime type, shared ideology) and *organisational* (regional institutions, etc.) nature. Overall, we can say that there is a mutual reinforcement process involved amongst the different domains of regionalism's development, and it will be shown throughout this book.

1.3 Studying regionalism: classic regionalism and new regionalism theories

The study of regionalism has changed significantly over time. A prime reason for this is that different forms of regionalism have evolved in response to changing conditions and developments within the international system, e.g. globalising processes. 'Classic' or traditional theories of regionalism arose out of scholarly work of the 1950s and 1960s, with Europe being the principal basis for empirical studies. Viner (1950) is acknowledged as the original theorist in this area, and his work was later refined and built upon by Meade (1955), Gehrels (1956), Lipsey (1970), Balassa (1961), Michaely (1965) and others. Their empirical and theoretical work was largely preoccupied with how regional integration can progress in a generally linear fashion over five different levels or stages. These are outlined in order below:

- *Free trade area or agreement (FTA)*: this involves the mutual removal of all tariff, quota and other trade restrictions between or amongst the agreement's members. Each member, however, retains the ability to formulate its own trade policy towards non-members.
- *Customs union*: extends an FTA arrangement to include the adoption of a common external tariff (CET), and thus the basis of a common trade policy. All members apply the same CETs upon non-member imports entering the customs union.
- *Common or internal markets*: extends a customs union to involve the elimination of the barriers that impede the free movement of goods, services, people and capital.
- *Economic and monetary union*: extends a common or internal market by its members adopting a common currency. Monetary union requires members to collaborate more closely on a variety of economic policies, e.g. on fiscal, social and industrial policies. This is because with monetary union the spillovers from one policy domain into others become more extensive, e.g. between monetary policy and tax policy.
- *Economic and political union*: the ultimate stage of regional integration. Members embrace federal union, essentially becoming a unified state. The United States and Germany are important historical examples of such a union.

Of those listed above, FTAs are by far the most common form of economic integration in the world, and a number of customs unions have been established (Figure 1.2). While some regional groupings such as Mercosur have aspired to a common market, only the EU has a robust common or 'single' market in place. Furthermore, the EU is the only regional group in modern times that has established a comprehensively functioning economic and monetary union, although various regional currency arrangements exist such as the CFA franc currency system[2] in West and Central Africa, and East Asia's network of bilateral currency swap arrangements under the Chiang Mai Initiative (see Chapter 5). Regional groups often adopt a 'multispeed' approach to integration in accordance with factors such as development asymmetry, length of regional group membership, etc. For example, the less developed members of ASEAN (Cambodia, Laos, Myanmar and Vietnam) have longer to remove their trade barriers within the AFTA

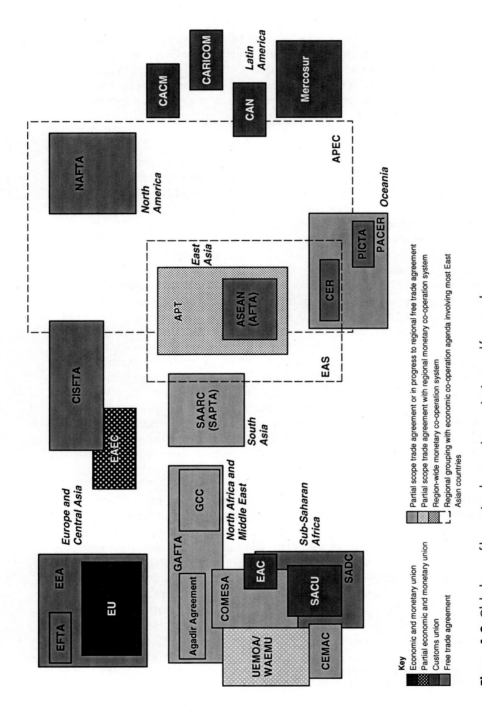

Figure 1.2 Global map of key regional economic organisations and frameworks

Notes: See Table 1.2 for abbreviations of regional organisations and agreements and their constituent membership.
Source: WTO and author's own research.

schedule of trade liberalisation. This is because they have higher tariff rates, partly used to help protect the development of their infant industries.

For much of the Cold War period, Euro-centric theories (e.g. functionalism, neo-functionalism, neo-federalism, inter-governmentalism) and empirics on regionalism dominated the field. Other regions invariably looked to Europe as the model on which to develop their own regionalist projects, primarily because the EU and its antecedents (e.g. the European Community) remained by some considerable degree the world's most comprehensive and sophisticated form of regionalism. The EU has been a long-standing pathfinder in regional integration, particularly with regard to institution-building and treaty-based aspects of this process. However, as regionalism became a more widespread and salient feature of the international system, scholars increasingly began to question the usefulness of Euro-biased classic integration theory (Fawcett and Hurrell 1995, Gamble and Payne 1996, Hettne et al. 1999, Katzenstein 2000, Poon 2001).

It was evident that regionalism was evolving in different ways around the world for two main reasons. First, the development of regionalism was a highly endogenous process, being shaped by various economic, socio-cultural, political and historic path dependent factors that are locally situated or embedded, which therefore did not lend to a uniformity of experience (Hettne and Soderbaum 2000, Wallace 1994). In other words, the nature of regionalism varied depending on where you found it. Second, the world was a different place to when the fundamentals of classic integration theory were first developed. Major structural transformations in the international system have occurred since, especially from after the end of the Cold Were, and this presented opportunities for new innovative forms of regionalism to emerge (Milner 1992). Perhaps most importantly on this point, globalisation has led to a shift away from the past emphasis on introverted, defensive regional blocs during the Cold War bipolarity period to more outward-looking and flexible forms of regional co-operation and integration in a world where trade and other economic barriers between global or macro-regions (e.g. Europe, East Asia, Latin America) are diminishing whilst global systems of connectivity between them are strengthening. The 'open regionalism' principles on which the APEC forum is based (see Chapter 4, Case Study 4.1, see p. 129) arose in this context.

Thus, classic integration theory has gradually given way to new regionalism theory (NRT), especially outside the mainstream economics field (Boas et al. 2005, Fawcett and Hurrell 1995, Gamble and Payne 1996, Hettne 2005, Hettne and Inotai 1994, Hettne et al. 1999, Larner and Walters 2002, MacLeod 2001, Mansfield and Milner 1999, Storper 1997). Many disciplinary fields have contributed to NRT's development, most importantly international political economy, political science, international relations, sociology and economic geography. This more multi-disciplinary approach has enabled us to move well beyond the narrow economistic approach of classic integration theory and its limitations in understanding the fuller political, social and other causes and consequences of economic regionalism (Mansfield and Milner 1999). From a more political science perspective, European regional integration also became less of a model and more of a benchmark for particular institutionalised paths of regionalism (Dieter 2006).

Moreover, NRT does not deny the importance of institutions in advancing regional integration and co-operation, but rather takes a much broader view on their role here. Dieter (2006) reminds us that institutions help reduce transaction costs, lower uncertainty amongst agents, facilitate deal-making, ensure compliance, are vehicles for learning and socialisation, and help shape collective identities with regard to developing regionalist projects. Furthermore, new regionalism theorists have sought to broaden our understanding of what we mean by 'region'. Rafael (1999:1208) for instance suggests that a region may 'alternately or simultaneously appear in various guises: politically as an administrative unit, culturally as an ethnic enclave or linguistic community, economically as zones of production and exchange'.

Economic geographers have particularly highlighted how the transnational business activities and systems are creating new regional (or subregional) economic spaces that cut across national economies (Borrus et al. 2000, Olds et al. 1999). The business or market-led driving forces behind this trend are perhaps better characterised as regionalisation rather than regionalism, although governments do invariably foster the development of these so called 'growth polygons' (e.g. the Indonesia–Malaysia–Singapore Growth Triangle) that are especially prevalent in East Asia (see Chapter 2). What economic geographers have stressed is to think about regional or subregional economic coalescence in different geo-spatial terms than before: regionalist projects do not always comprise a collection of whole national economies with neatly defined borders. Furthermore, regionalisation tends to involve linkages between particular sub-national and transnational economic zones within a macro-region like East Asia, and therefore patterns of integration within a region can be highly asymmetric (see Chapter 2).

The social construction of regions, and therein regionalism itself, is another distinctive strand to new regionalism theory, although sociological perspectives on regional group development date back a while. For example, during the time of the EEC's emergence, Deutsch (1957) contended that increased communication amongst states and societies can help create a sense of community amongst them by developing trust, establishing mutual interests and an appropriation of 'we-ness'. Wendt (1992), Hurrell (1995) and others have brought new social constructivist ideas and perspectives to the study of regionalism. For Hurrell (1995:72), the study of regionalism entails the method of 'conceptualising the interaction between material incentives, inter-subjective structures, and the identity and interests of the actors' with regard to the region. According to Wendt (1992), growing interdependences within a globalising world are creating new transnational communities of common interest, and a sense of 'regionness' derives from this process where patterns of economic and political transactions and social communications are concentrated within particular regional spaces, that may in turn be differentiated from other regionalised communities.

The idea of *regional community-building* itself may be considered a holistic concept that derives mainly from new regionalism theory (Hettne et al. 1999, Hurrell 1995). It may be broadly conceived as the fostering of closer co-operative relations amongst the region's constituent states, peoples, organisations and other agencies with the aim of developing regional economic, political and social cohesion. Here, community-building and cohesion are inter-determinate terms, both inferring how community members become increasingly beholden to each other. This may arise from the identification or formation of common regional interests (e.g. arising out of revealed or cultivated linkages of interdependence) and due actions taken at the regional level that are intended to best manage or govern those interests. Some kind of regional identity-formation may emerge from this process, yet what is ultimately essential is the substantial development of co-operative and harmonious relations within a regional community, and this is especially important where conflict has been the norm in particular aspects of a region's international relations, as is the case for East Asia. Furthermore, regional community-building should also make positive contributions towards the broader development of international society by regional communities providing more rationalised and integrated building blocs for developing global governance structures and frameworks.

Finally, whereas classic regionalism theory is primarily focused on state actors, new regionalism theory stresses the importance of non-state actors, societal forces and multilateral institutions in the development of regionalism, in its various guises. There is hence corresponding plurality in both the different forms of regionalism and the different stakeholder influences (including norms of behaviour) that can shape its nature and direction (Acharya 2004). In sum, *new regionalism* may be contrasted with classic regionalism theory by its particular emphasis on: multiple and co-existent levels and forms of regional co-operation and integration (e.g. state-driven, market-driven; sub-regional, trans-regional); a less technocratically determined and more socially constructed or ideational view to understanding regional community-building; and the connections between regionalism and extra-regional processes and structures at the global and multilateral levels. New regionalism theory has thus helped open up a wider scholarly debate on different ideas and kinds of regionalism that are emerging in the contemporary world order.

Case Study 1.1 The welfare effects debate in classic regionalism theory

There has been a long-standing debate in 'classic regionalism' theory concerning whether regional trade blocs (e.g. free trade areas, customs unions) have an overall positive or negative impact upon global economic efficiency or welfare. Negative effects generally arise from *trade diversion*, which occurs when efficient non-member country producers are subsequently disadvantaged by relative tariff charges incurred by the trade bloc's internal liberalisation (i.e. free trade) that is not matched by similar external liberalisation. In this scenario, relatively less efficient producers (within the bloc) are able to expand production at the expense of more efficient producers who lie outside the bloc. Using a hypothetical example in relation to the AFTA, suppose that New Zealand before the implementation of AFTA was the largest exporter of dairy products to Indonesia because New Zealand farmers were able to out compete other foreign producers on efficiency and price terms. Let us assume that Indonesia imposed a 25 per cent tariff on all imported dairy products before AFTA, and then reduced this to zero per cent as part of the AFTA programme. This enabled Thai dairy producers to undercut their more efficient New Zealand rivals owing to the zero tariff advantage they now enjoy when exporting to Indonesia, and indeed to other ASEAN markets that New Zealand dairy farmers export to. The latter is still faced with an import tariff rate of 25 per cent in Indonesia and maybe higher tariff rates elsewhere within the ASEAN group. Thus in this situation, efficient production has been displaced by relatively more inefficient production, leading to a negative welfare effect globally because of a worsening in the ratio of required resources per unit of output produced.

The negative welfare effects of trade diversion must be weighed against the positive welfare effects borne from *trade creation*, which arises when the same internal tariff liberalisation allows more competitive regional bloc-based producers to expand their own share of the bloc's markets once held by their less efficient rivals inside the bloc area. It follows that the higher the level of intra-industry trade (i.e. the simultaneous import and export of goods from the same industries) within the regional bloc, the wider the scope for trade creation opportunities. Put alternatively, if regional bloc members possess similar industry sector profiles, this fosters a more intensified engagement of competitive free trade between producers and buyers in the region. On the other hand, differing industrial profiles associated with a pattern of inter-industry trade narrows the scope for potential trade creation. Again taking AFTA by way of general illustrative example, suppose that textile producers in Vietnam are most cost efficient in low-end production (i.e. simple garment manufacture) amongst the ASEAN group. Under AFTA, all countries now have to remove their tariffs on textile imports from other ASEAN countries, thus exposing relatively inefficient low-end textile producers to a new level playing field of competition. Vietnamese producers are thus better able to outcompete the more inefficient producers, say from Malaysia or Indonesia, and expand their efficient production into the

AFTA market. Hence, inefficient production is displaced by more efficient production, leading to a positive economic welfare effect within ASEAN.

With FTAs there is also the particular complication of *trade deflection*, which arises when firms based outside a free trade area seek to route their exports to relatively high *external* tariff countries through relatively low tariff FTA member states. As stated in the main text, in an FTA each member country establishes free trade with the other but sets their own tariff levels and other trade barriers against non-members, i.e. 'external' tariffs and barriers. Suppose that Singapore imposed only a 1 per cent tariff on imported automobile components from outside AFTA but the Philippines maintained a 10 per cent import tariff level. A Japanese automobile component producer now tries to deflect or re-route their exports to the Philippines via Singapore, thus creeping in under a 1 per cent tariff rate instead of a 10 per cent rate. If Philippines customs officials identify these imports as sourced from Singapore rather than from Japan, then the Japanese firm has got away with it. However, most countries will have so-called 'rules of origin' that determine where products have been made, or at least where most of the value-added production (sometimes referred to as 'local content') has occurred (see Chapter 6).

Classic regional integration theory, though, is primarily concerned with the 'one-off' effects produced by regional trade blocs, and therefore constitutes a 'static' form of analysis. Dynamic regional integration theory on the other hand considers the longer-term impact of regional economic integration, concentrating on how productive capacity is subsequently affected, as opposed to the resource allocative efficiency focus of static theory. These advantages are usually borne from the opportunities presented by enlarged markets, a liberalised competitive environment and a widened scope for mutually beneficial inter-firm collaborations. In general terms, these comprise:

- *Economies of scale:* as regional integration deepens, the opportunities to exploit economies of scale become more frequent. The conditions for internal specialisation created within a regional trade bloc will lead to cost efficiencies that in turn yield welfare gains. Each member will specialise further in accordance with their own competitive advantages by expanding production within a larger and more unified market space within the region.
- *Increased competition:* the effective opening up of the regional trade bloc's market will intensify the competitive pressures exerted on domestic producers from their partner equivalents. These pressures should force firms to reduce prices, invest in new technologies and strive to improve efficiency in order to survive and prosper in the new competitive environment.

- *Benefits derived from closer collaboration:* deeper integration leads to greater inter-firm collaboration across national borders in the form of joint ventures and other forms of strategic alliances. This will yield greater transfers of technology and skills across the region, and other positive synergetic effects at the micro-level. At the macro-level, deeper integration requires national governments to collaborate closer together on various policy-related matters that in turn create more efficient policy spaces (e.g. by bloc countries adopting common regulatory practices) in which economic activity takes place.

It should be noted that the wider the membership and the deeper the integration (i.e. free trade area or customs union to common market) then, in theory, the more frequently the above opportunities tend to occur.

Study Questions

1. Why can trade creation and trade diversion outcomes be expected to be more significant in certain industries than in others?
2. Critically assess the limitations of this aspect of classic regionalism theory in evaluating the impact of trade integration within a region.

1.4 Regionalism in the international system

1.4.1 Regionalism and globalisation

Regionalism, or regionalisation is closely linked to the phenomenon of globalisation. If globalisation can be thought about fundamentally as increasing levels of *connectivity*, *integration* and *interdependence* between different parts of the *world economy and society* occurring on a global (i.e. worldwide) scale, then regionalism and regionalisation is about how this is arising on a regional scale.[3] As Hettne (2005) observed, regionalism and globalisation are closely related aspects of contemporary transformations in the world order. Furthermore, in the flux and structural change in the international system brought on by the forces of globalisation, nation-states have often lacked the independent or autonomous resources to sufficiently address the opportunities and threats posed by globalisation. Working together in regional associations and groups has, however, made this more possible based on collectively pooled strengths, resources and preferences (Dent 1997). East Asia's regionalism should, then, be viewed in the context of globalisation-related developments (Beeson 2007).

While some maintain that regionalism is a building bloc of globalisation, others have taken the view that regionalism fragments the international system into separate and disconnected competing blocs – a kind of 'closed regionalism' – and thus works against the development of globalisation and global society. In George Orwell's political novel, *1984*, the world was engaged in constant global conflict between the three dominant regions – Oceania, Eurasia and East Asia! Although not too long ago there were real fears that such a dystopian future may emerge in the early twenty-first century, fortunately this has not transpired. After the 11 September 2001 terrorist attacks on the United States, some academics have warned of inter-civilizational conflict becoming the 'new Cold War', and to some this may convert into inter-regional conflict. Although inter-regional relations (e.g. East Asia and Europe) have become an important new feature of the world system, these have generally helped bridge links between regional communities and made a positive contribution to the development of global society (Dent 2004, Gilson 2002).

1.4.2 Regional economic organisations and frameworks

Studies of regionalism often begin by outlining the spread of regional organi-sations and frameworks around the world by way of demonstrating its global pervasiveness. This is a good entry point for many, and indeed this chapter has already listed a few examples. Figure 1.2 and Table 1.2 map out and detail the world's main regional economic organisations and frameworks that cur-rently exist. Regional 'economic' organisations and frameworks have been chosen because this book is primarily an international political economy based study, and moreover there are still relatively few regional organisations and frameworks in which economic-related matters are not core to their agen-das. For further purposes of clarification, regional economic 'agreements' often derive from regional organisations or frameworks (e.g. AFTA from ASEAN), or may be considered a framework of some kind when they exist in their own right, such as NAFTA. These agreements can, however, mark the progressive integrational development of regional organisations associated with classic regionalism theory noted earlier (e.g. free trade agreements, customs unions) as illustrated in Figure 1.2.

Keeping in mind, then, the aforementioned analytical limitations of classic integration theory, Figure 1.2's global 'mapping' of regionalism pri-marily focuses on state-led or institutionalised regional economic projects. We can see that the levels of integration and co-operation reached amongst the world's regional economic organisations and frameworks vary signifi-cantly. The integrative prominence of the EU was noted earlier, possessing the world's only fully functional economic and monetary union and common market arrangements. Apart from the EU, there are only seven regional customs unions currently in operation, two in Africa (SACU and EAC), one in Central Asia (EAEC) and four in Latin America (CACM, CARICOM, CAN and Mercosur). In addition to these are eight regional free trade area arrangements: SADC in Africa; EFTA and the EEA in Europe; CISFTA in

Table 1.2 Key regional economic organisations and frameworks around the world

Regional economic organisation / framework		Integrational aims and achievements	Current member states
APT	ASEAN Plus Three	Established in 1997 as a regional economic grouping that has primarily focused on regional financial co-operation and integration.	Brunei, Cambodia, China, Indonesia, Japan, Laos, Malaysia, Myanmar, Philippines, Singapore, South Korea, Thailand, Vietnam.
ASEAN	Association of Southeast Asian Nations	Established in 1967. Regional free trade area (AFTA) in place since 2003. Plans to evolve into the ASEAN Economic Community (AEC, a common market) by 2015.	Brunei, Cambodia, Indonesia, Laos, Malaysia, Myanmar, Philippines, Singapore, Thailand, Vietnam.
Agadir Agreement		Since 2004, work in progress towards a sub-regional free trade agreement as part of developing the Euro-Mediterranean Free Trade Area.	Egypt, Jordan, Morocco, Tunesia.
APEC	Asia-Pacific Economic Co-operation forum	Since 1994, work in progress to establish a 'free trade and investment zone' across the Asia-Pacific by 2020 based on the principles of 'open regionalism'.	Australia, Brunei, Canada, Chile, China, Japan, Hong Kong SAR, Indonesia, Malaysia, Mexico, New Zealand, Papua New Guinea, Philippines, Peru, Russia, Singapore, South Korea, Taiwan, Thailand, United States, Vietnam.
CACM	Central American Common Market	Customs union since 1961.	Costa Rica, El Salvador, Guatemala, Honduras, Nicaragua.
CAN	Andean Community of Nations	Customs union since 1998.	Bolivia, Colombia, Ecuador, Peru.
CARICOM	Caribbean Community	Customs union since 1973.	Antigua and Barbuda, Bahamas, Barbados, Belize, Dominica, Grenada, Guyana, Haiti, Jamaica, Monserrat, Trinidad & Tobago, St. Kitts & Nevis, St. Lucia, St. Vincent & the Grenadines, Surinam.
CEMAC	Economic and Monetary Community of Central Africa	Partial scope trade agreement since 1999.	Cameroon, Central African Republic, Chad, Congo, Equatorial Guinea, Gabon.
CER	Closer Economic Relations	Free trade agreement since 1983.	Australia, New Zealand.
CISFTA	Commonwealth of Independent States Free Trade Area	Free trade agreement since 1994.	Armenia, Azerbaijan, Belarus, Georgia, Kazakhstan, Kyrgyzstan, Moldova, Russian Federation, Tajikistan, Ukraine, Uzbekistan.
COMESA	Common Market for Eastern and Southern Africa	Partial scope trade agreement since 1994.	Angola, Burundi, Comoros, Democratic Republic of Conga, Djibouti, Egypt, Eritrea, Ethiopia, Kenya, Libya, Madagascar, Malawi, Mauritius, Rwanda, Seychelles, Sudan, Swaziland, Uganda, Zambia, Zimbabwe.
EAC	East African Community	Customs union since 2005. Plans to establish monetary union based on the East African shilling by 2009.	Kenya, Tanzania, Uganda.
EAEC	Eurasian Economic Community	Customs union since 1995.	Belarus, Kazakhstan, Kyrgyzstan, Russian Federation, Tajikistan, Uzbekistan.
EAS	East Asia Summit	Regional grouping since 2005 mainly focused on economic related issues.	APT members plus Australia, India, New Zealand.
EEA	European Economic Area	Free trade agreement, various forms of policy co-operation and co-ordination, and regulatory conformity.	EU and EFTA member states.
EFTA	European Free Trade Association	Free trade agreement since 1960.	Iceland, Norway, Liechtenstein, Switzerland
EU	European Union	Customs union established in 1968. Common market in 1993. Economic and monetary union in 2002 based on the euro currency. Various common regional policies operated.	Austria, Belgium, Denmark, Finland, France, Germany, Greece, Ireland, Italy, Luxembourg, Netherlands, Portugal, Spain, Sweden, United Kingdom,

Table 1.2 (continued) Key regional economic organisations and frameworks around the world

Regional economic organisation / framework		Integrational aims and achievements	Current member states
GAFTA	Greater Arab Free Trade Area	Since 2005, work in progress to establishing a regional free trade area.	Bahrain, Egypt, Iraq, Jordan, Kuwait, Lebanon, Libya, Morocco, Oman, Palestine, Qatar, Saudi Arabia, Sudan, Syria, Tunesia, United Arab Emirates, Yemen.
GCC	Gulf Co-operation Council	Partial scope trade agreement since 1984. Aim of establishing a common market and monetary union by 2010.	Bahrain, Kuwait, Oman, Qatar, Saudi Arabia, United Arab Emirates.
Mercosur	Southern Common Market	Customs union since 1991.	Argentina, Brazil, Paraguay, Uruguay, Venezuela.
NAFTA	North American Free Trade Agreement	Free trade agreement since 1994.	Canada, Mexico, United States
PACER	Pacific Agreement on Closer Economic Relations	Trade and economic co-operation agreement between CER and PICTA member countries since 2001.	Australia, New Zealand, Cook Islands, Federated States of Micronesia, Fiji, Kiribati, Nauru, Niue, Palau, Papua New Guinea, Marshall Islands, Samoa, Solomon Islands, Tonga, Tuvalu and Vanuatu.
PICTA	Pacific Island Countries Trade Agreement	Free trade agreement since 2001.	Cook Islands, Federated States of Micronesia, Fiji, Kiribati, Nauru, Niue, Palau, Papua New Guinea, Marshall Islands, Samoa, Solomon Islands, Tonga, Tuvalu and Vanuatu.
SACU	South African Customs Union	Customs union since 1970 (revised since first established in 1910)	Botswana, Lesotho, Namibia, South Africa, Swaziland.
SADC	South African Development Community	Free trade agreement since 2000. Various economic, political, social and environmental issues addressed on its regional agenda.	Angola, Botswana, Congo, Lesotho, Malawi, Mauritius, Mozambique, Namibia, Seychelles, South Africa, Swaziland, Tanzania, Zambia, Zimbabwe.
SAARC	South Asian Association for Regional Co-operation	SAARC established in 1985. Partial scope trade agreement (South Asian Preferential Trade Arrangement, SAPTA) since 1995. Progress since 2006 to eventually establish a regional FTA (SAFTA).	Bangladesh, Bhutan, India, Maldives, Nepal, Pakistan, Sri Lanka.
UEMOA / WAEMU	West African Economic and Monetary Union	Partial scope trade agreement since 2000. Monetary union based on the CFA franc currency.	Benin, Burkina Faso, Côte d'Ivoire, Guinea-Bissau, Mali, Niger, Senegal, Togo.

Central Asia; NAFTA in North America; CER and PICTA in Oceania; AFTA in East Asia (see Table 1.2). The CER between Australia and New Zealand is strictly a bilateral rather than a regional FTA. In fact, the vast majority of FTAs are bilateral in nature. From 1997 to 2005, the number of FTAs worldwide had increased from 72 to 153, and nearly 90 per cent of these were bilateral agreements (Dent 2006a, WTO 2005). Some of these involve region-to-country agreements, such as the ASEAN–China FTA and the EFTA–South Korea FTA, and analysis of the relationship between trade bilateralism and regionalism is reserved for Chapter 6. Returning to the map and outline of regional economic organisations and frameworks in Figure 1.2 and corresponding Table 1.2, we can see that a large remainder have only operationalised so called 'partial scope' regional trade agreements. These are essentially sub-FTA arrangements whereby only a selection of product lines are eligible for reciprocated free trade treatment between signatory countries,[4] and Figure 1.2 illustrates how many of Africa's main regional trade frameworks fall into this category (CEMAC, COMESA, UEMOA/WAEMU), while the Agadir Agreement and GCC group have still to implement the core of their respectively planned regional free trade areas.

The actual integrity and effectiveness of a regional economic integration arrangement can also vary considerably for a number of reasons. The first is that developing countries especially often lack the technocratic and institutional capacity to operationalise these arrangements in a meaningful way. If the ensuing regulatory and enforcement gaps are significant, this will lead many to question the usefulness of the agreement concerned. A second problem that also tends to blight developing countries relates to intra-regional trade ratios. These tend to be low for poorer developing country groups in particular because their main trade partners are invariably outside their regional group, mainly owing to income level and industry capacity factors. Many may question the usefulness of a regional trade agreement if intra-regional trade accounts for only a small percentage of the group's total trade. For some developing country regions this ratio may be as low as 5 to 10 per cent, and for Southeast Asia/ASEAN this is only just over 20 per cent. These figures contrast notably with the EU's intra-regional trade ratio of well over 60 per cent. This point overlaps somewhat with the third issue, in that state-led regional economic projects *per se* may mask the lack of regionalised micro-level activities and linkages generally within a region, i.e. regionalisation. Regional economic organisations and frameworks essentially frame the macro-perspective or the institutional architecture of regionalism within the international system. While they are often premised on exploiting deepening regionalised business and other societal activities, regional organisations and frameworks are only able to tell part of the regionalism story. Chapter 2, for example, shows that economic regionalisation in East Asia has developed to a relatively high level in comparison to other regions. This is despite East Asia's latecomer entry into the state-led regionalism trend.

We can adjudge, though, both from mapped patterns of regional economic projects and bilateral FTAs that state-led regional integration has been especially strong in Europe and Latin America. Table 1.2 shows that East Asia is a relative newcomer here, only embarking on this form of regionalism in the 1990s. Most other regions had first initiated regional projects in the 1950s and 1960s (the SACU antecedent even dates back to the 1910s). However, East Asia is fast catching up in many respects and there has been much talk of realising ambitious integrational objectives in the future. The core of the AFTA's agreement was implemented by 2003, and ASEAN is planning to create an AEC by 2015. After less than three years of its inaugural summit meeting, the APT framework had established a regional network of bilateral currency swap agreements – the Chiang Mai Initiative – that was devised to help avert another regional financial crisis. It has since expanded its scope to include more agreements and an over doubling of its collective funds to US$82.5 billion by May 2007. The Chiang Mai Initiative network is set for transformation into a multilateralised system based on a central regional fund. Chapter 5 explores how other efforts to improve regional financial governance in East Asia are occurring through the APT framework in conjunction with the Asian Development Bank (ADB) and national governments, such as the Asian Bond Market Initiative (ABMI). As Amyx (2004:8) observes, these arrangements are 'giving rise to dense networks of communication between central bankers and finance ministers in the region – networks that did not exist at the time of the Asian financial crisis', which has been important from the perspective of policy-maker networking within the region. There have also been proposals for introducing the basis of an Asian Currency Unit and an East Asia Free Trade Area, the latter as a follow through from the spate of bilateral FTA projects weaved across the region.

Dieter (2006) and others have noted that the APT framework's primary focus on regional financial integration presents an alternative path to trade integrational approach of classic regionalism theory. Aspects of 'financial regionalism' are evident in other parts of the world (Fritz and Metzger 2005). For example, UEMOA/WAEMU uses the CFA franc as a basic regional currency unit, the EU has its euro, and the North American Framework Agreement operates a set of bilateral currency swaps amongst the NAFTA member countries of the US, Canada and Mexico (Henning 2002). However, it is the centrality of regional financial governance in the APT framework that makes it somewhat unique. Like ASEAN and the emerging EAS process, the APT's agenda addresses a number of transnational issues that affect the whole region, such as those of a more general economic, social, health-related (e.g. SARS), crime-related (e.g. drug trafficking, piracy) or environmental nature. These make up the broader foundation on which regional community-building can be fostered and developed. Regional organisations (e.g. ASEAN) or frameworks (e.g. APT)[5] rather than 'stand alone' regional agreements tend to have broader transnational issue agendas that focus on enhancing regional co-operation amongst the organisation's member states. Good examples of this are SADC in Southern Africa and Mercosur in Latin America. Regional economic agreements such as NAFTA on the other hand tend to be more commercially oriented, simply concerned with facilitating greater economic transactions within the region, although as noted earlier many of these agreements are embedded within regional organisations (e.g. AFTA and ASEAN) and therefore form part of a wider regional community-building endeavour.

Another recent development worth noting is the involvement of East Asian states in 'overlapping' regional organisations, frameworks and agreements, i.e. with states outside the East Asia region. In 2001, China formed the Shanghai Co-operation Organisation (SCO) with Russia and the Central Asian states of Kazakhstan, Kyrgyzstan, Tajikistan and Uzbekistan, the group's principal aims being to advance co-operation in economic, security and cultural affairs amongst member countries. In 2005, Singapore, Brunei, Chile and New Zealand signed the Trans-Pacific Strategic Economic Partnership Agreement (TPSEPA), a quadrilateral free trade agreement between these East Asian, Oceanic and Latin American states. In the same year, the East Asian and South Asian states of China, Laos, South Korea, Bangladesh, India and Sri Lanka upgraded the Bangkok Agreement (first signed in 1975) to a more substantial 'partial scope' agreement that extended the original tariff liberalisation list from 1,800 to 4,800 products and entailed higher tariff reduction rates than previously agreed.[6] A year earlier in 2004, Thailand signed an enhanced BIMSTEC (Bay of Bengal Initiative for Multi-Sectoral Technical and Economic Co-operation) agreement with Bangladesh, Bhutan, India, Nepal, Myanmar and Sri Lanka that committed these countries to abolish tariffs amongst them by 2017.

In addition to these, East Asian states have been involved in other new wider regional initiatives. The Boao Forum for Asia, modelled on the Davos World Economic Forum, held its first meeting in April 2002 as a non-governmental forum that aims to strengthen economic exchanges and co-operation within the region. Just a couple of months later in June 2002, Thailand hosted the first Asia Co-operation Dialogue (ACD) meeting, involving ministers from most Southeast Asian states (except Myanmar), Japan, China, South Korea, Bangladesh, India, Pakistan and the Middle Eastern states of Bahrain and Qatar. Subsequent annual ACD meetings have focused on economic, social and cultural issues and co-operation in these areas. Its membership has continued to expand, and now also includes Bhutan, Iran, Kazakhstan, Kuwait, Mongolia, Oman, Russia, Saudi Arabia, Sri Lanka, Tajikistan, United Arab Emirates and Uzbekistan.

While these wider regional agreements and frameworks may only be making minor contributions to the development of regionalism, they are nevertheless further evidence of how East Asia is enmeshed in broader processes of international economic integration and co-operation that lie outside the region. Figure 1.3 shows the involvement of East Asian countries in different regional organisations and frameworks, and therein the overlapping and concentric configurations of membership to these organisations and frameworks that can arise. This connects with the issue of how the geo-spatial and other boundaries of regionalism are often contested. Further discussion on this and other extra-dimensional aspects of East Asian regionalism is made in Chapter 8.

1.4.3 The security and geopolitical dimensions of East Asian regionalism

Regional economic organisations and frameworks emerge out of a complex interaction of factors that often extend well beyond economic motivations. Geopolitical and security-related factors have been especially critical determining factors in this process. Chapter 3 discusses how, for example, ASEAN was originally a construct of Cold War geopolitics, initially forged with the guided management of the United States as a bulwark against the advance of communism in Southeast Asia. The EU's earliest antecedent, the European Coal and Steel Community, also originated from security-related imperatives, this being to avert another major conflict ever occurring within the region again. Furthermore, depending on relative configurations of membership, regional security organisations and fora can augment the regional community-building endeavours of their economic

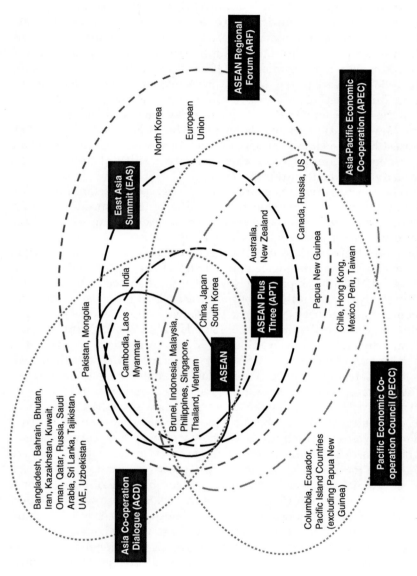

Figure 1.3 Main regional organisations and frameworks involving East Asia

counterparts, or actually originate from the same organisational stem, the ASEAN Regional Forum (ARF) being an instance of this (see Figure 1.3).Regional security arrangements can bring greater stability and trust amongst a regional community of nations, without which economic regionalism may be very difficult to achieve. By the same token, competing security arrangements can have an adverse effect, dividing the region into competing political and economic blocs, as was essentially the case during the Cold War period. American led or supported arrangements such as the Southeast Asian Treaty Organisation (1954–77) and the Asian and Pacific Council (1966–73) were pitted against the security alliances of communist states like China, Vietnam and North Korea, with the Soviet Union always at least in the background in East Asia's security theatre. Regional security relations, however, still remain problematic. The ARF, established in 1994, is the closest East Asia has to a regional security arrangement but its prime emphasis is on dialogue and it has achieved relatively little at addressing the main security issues confronting the region.[7]

Furthermore, cultivating a stronger regional security community will always be undermined somewhat by the US's continued predilection for 'hub-and-spoke' bilateral alliances with certain East Asian states, these being especially strong with Japan, the Philippines, South Korea, Thailand and Singapore. More importantly, there remain considerable differences in the security interests, ideologies and policies of the Asia-Pacific's 'great powers' – the US, China, Japan and Russia – as for instance clearly revealed in the Six Party Talks on nuclear proliferation in the Korean peninsula. Other contentious security issues (e.g. the Taiwan–China question, territorial claims on the Spratly and Paracel Islands in the South China Sea, the territorial dispute between South Korea and Japan over the Dokdo/Takeshima Islands, the US's 'war on terror') also pose their own challenges to fostering closer economic relations amongst East Asian states.

The economics–security nexus in regional organisations can also be quite prominent (Dent 2007a). In Chapter 4, we explore how since the 11 September 2001 terrorist attacks, the US has promoted the incorporation of security-related objectives onto the hitherto primarily economic and trade focused agenda of APEC. Broadening conceptions of 'security' in the contemporary era have led to the incorporation of 'new security' sectors (e.g. environmental, societal, economic) into the analytical frame and practice of international relations (Buzan et al. 1998, Collins 2007, Stares 1998). These sectors connect closely with the aforementioned transnational issues to which regional organisations and frameworks like ASEAN and APT are paying increasing attention. This forms part of the wider holistic approach to regional co-operation and community-building now evident in East Asia and other parts of the world.

There are wider geopolitical debates concerning East Asian regionalism that should also be considered. Let us start with the US, which as we would expect has an obvious strategic interest in promoting the idea of Asia-Pacific rather than East Asian regionalism (Beeson 2006a, Berger 2006). In recent times, APEC has been the main institutional vehicle used by the

United States for this purpose, but it is a regional organisation in relative decline during a period when emerging frameworks like APT and EAS have been in ascendancy (see Chapters 4 and 5). The US remains a crucial economic, political and security partner for many East Asian states. Its social, cultural and ethnic ties with the region are strong. Much of East Asia still looks to the United States for leadership in regional and global affairs (Agnew 2005, Beeson 2006a). And yet the US has been a more or less peripheral player regarding many important new developments in East Asia's regional political economy. This has been in certain cases of Washington's own choosing, such as not ardently pursuing 'observer status' in either the APT or EAS frameworks.

The US has, though, been forced to observe China's increasing centrality in East Asia's regional affairs. China's strategic economic importance to the region, its closer relations cultivated with ASEAN and increasingly with South Korea, and its purposeful engagement with various regional and multilateral institutions are indicative of expectations concerning the country's return to its 'historic position' as East Asia's pre-eminent power (Shambaugh 2004). At the same time, China is constantly compelled to assuage the fears of those both inside and outside the region that she poses a significant economic and security threat. The persistence of such anxiety may have an undermining effect on East Asian regionalism.

Inextricably linked to the above are questions concerning China, Japan and regional hegemony in East Asia (Calder 2006, Drifte 2006, Zhao 2004). This is discussed from different theoretical perspectives of international political economy in the following section, and we have already noted how China and Japan held different political motives concerning EAS group membership. In brief, it is generally believed that Japan advocated the inclusion of Australia, New Zealand and India in the group so as to help counterbalance China's power within the EAS. China on the other hand expressed a preference for an APT-based membership of the group, but it was Japan's view that prevailed. As Chapter 5 discusses in some detail, Sino-Japanese relations are a primary determinant in the future of East Asian regionalism. The two countries dominate the East Asia region to a significant degree with respect to their economic, political and socio-cultural influence.

How China and Japan come to terms with each other is of vital importance to the rest of the region. Will they be able to forge a bilateral axis akin to France and Germany in Europe as the cornerstone foundation on which regional integration and co-operation in East Asia can be built, or is either China or Japan likely to make a sole bid for regional leadership over forthcoming years? The outcome is unlikely to be so clear-cut, but Japan's position in East Asia's regional affairs has been somewhat problematic of late. Other countries in the region continue to harbour a number of concerns regarding Japan, including: a long-standing view held by many Japanese that their country is somehow separate from Asia (akin to Britain's at times rather ambivalent association with 'Europe'); the high priority Japan still affords to its close security and economic relationship with the United States; the apparent indifference of Japan's recent political leaders

(Junichiro Koizumi and Shinzo Abe) to regional sensitivities concerning Japan's wartime record; and how these same leaders have sought to make political capital out of exploiting Japanese nationalism. While Japan remains the region's largest economy, its relative economic position in East Asia is slipping. All these factors pose significant challenges to Japan as to the conduct of its regional diplomacy. Yet the country still has a vitally important role to play in East Asia's regional community-building process.

1.5 International political economy theories and regionalism

1.5.1 The usefulness of international political economy analysis

This book studies East Asian regionalism from an IPE analytical perspective. Our discussions above on the security and geopolitical dimensions to East Asian regionalism drew upon a number of disciplinary perspectives, mainly international relations, politics and economics. The study of international political economy may be primarily considered the fusion of these three core fields into a multi-disciplinary framework. This makes IPE especially useful for analysing regionalism given its multi-faceted nature. In this section, key concepts and theoretical perspectives of IPE are introduced that are most relevant to studying the various themes of East Asian regionalism. These will also provide the main analytical framework for each chapter's concluding section, the main purpose of this exercise being to understand the chapter's subject matter from different theoretical and analytical viewpoints. This will provide the reader with a more critically informed overview of what has been studied in the chapter.

Strange (1994:18) has perhaps offered the best generic definition of IPE, in that it 'concerns the social, political, and economic arrangements affecting the global systems of production, exchange, and distribution and the mix of values reflected therein'. International political economy analysis emerged from the 1970s onwards as a subset discipline of international relations. However, scholars from various fields have been drawn to IPE analysis partly because the analytical tools from their own discipline could not adequately explain certain phenomena arising within the world system. For example, economists using their conventional theoretical and conceptual frameworks could not fully explain the effect of political and social factors in the determination of trade policy formation, patterns of international economic exchange (e.g. trade, foreign investment), multinational enterprise (MNE) behaviour, and so on.

Certain developments in the international arena during the 1970s provided impetus to IPE studies, including the 1973/4 oil shock, stagflation (i.e. high inflation combined with stagnant economic activity) amongst Western countries, Japan's ascendancy as the world's next economic superpower and the growing global impact of the European Community. IPE came increasingly to the fore of international studies with the end of the Cold War and the ensuing shift from politico-ideological competition to economic competition (and from geopolitics to geo-economics) in the 1990s. The integrative forces of globalisation and regionalism strengthened not only material linkages within the world system but also issue-linkage between economic, political, environmental and societal phenomena on increasingly extensive scales. International political economy analysis has proved particularly useful in studying both material and issue-based linkages. Let us demonstrate the usefulness of the IPE analytical approach with two examples. The first concerns how IPE can help us understand issues relating to Japan's persistently large trade surpluses with the United States and the EU:

- *Source of the trade imbalance*: this may be explained by the country's effective trade-industry policies, informal kinds of protectionism in Japan (e.g. economic nationalism), Japanese MNE strategies, issues of relative competitiveness between Japan, the US and EU, e.g. productivity, education and skills levels.
- *Reaction from the US and EU*: how and why have American and European domestic industry groups (e.g. steel, autos) lobbied governments for protectionist counter-measures?
- *Managing the trade diplomacy conflict*: diplomatic measures and strategies deployed by the US and EU in terms of unilateral measures (e.g. tariffs), bilateral diplomacy (i.e. direct negotiation with Japan) and multilateral diplomacy (e.g. WTO) to redress their respective trade imbalances with Japan.

Our second example concerns the ASEAN–China Free Trade Agreement (ACFTA) signed in November 2002. What were the *economic, political* and *security motivations* behind ACFTA? Were any of these motivations more important than the others, and can or should they be disaggregated in the first place? Does ACFTA reflect China's aspirations for regional leadership in East Asia? Even though ASEAN currently has a trade surplus with China, many analysts believe ACFTA will eventually convert this into a trade deficit as increasingly competitive Chinese-made products from a growing range of industries enter tariff-free into Southeast Asia. So what economic motives do ASEAN countries have for promoting ACFTA? Furthermore, how can we explain Japan's reaction to ACFTA with reference to international diplomacy, politics and economics? Finally, the above questions are relevant to consideration of what impact will ACFTA have on East Asian regionalism? These questions are best addressed by IPE analysis.

1.5.2 Applying key IPE theories and concepts to the study of regionalism

There are four main schools of IPE thought or theory, namely: neo-realism, neo-liberal institutionalism, social constructivism and Marxism-structuralism.

In the analysis that follows, we apply these different IPE theoretical perspectives to regionalism in a general introductory manner. As noted earlier, these perspectives will thereafter be applied in the conclusions of subsequent chapters by way of summarising their main findings and arguments.

1.5.2.a Neo-realism

Neo-realism derives from realist theory of international relations, whose historic roots can be found in the writings of Thucydides, Machiavelli, Hobbs and others. It is founded on the realist assumption that nation-states remain the most important IPE actor, and all other actors are essentially subordinate to its power and interests. Moreover, nation-states are essentially competitive power maximisers, leading to inter-state anarchical relations within the international system. The strength of nationalist sentiment and historical mistrust amongst East Asian countries was noted earlier in the chapter, and neo-realists tend to stress how these factors pose significant constraints on regional community-building. While neo-realists accept that inter-state coalitions (e.g. ASEAN) can arise, they argue these only serve to realise various national interests. Thus, according to neo-realists, ventures into regionalism are simply a projection of nation-state interests onto a broader international canvas. For example, Malaysia champions ASEAN as an organisation and its group interests in East Asia and the wider world because it is in Malaysia's interests to do so. Neo-realism suggests that Malaysia has used ASEAN as a vehicle to advance the country's own national position, status and influence in East Asia and on the international stage generally. Similarly, neo-realists would argue that China and Japan's promotion of East Asian regionalism derives from competing interests in leading a future East Asian regional group, such as APT.

Following on from these assumptions concerning nation-state behaviour, neo-realism contends that states have a preference for *relative gains* over other states rather than higher net *absolute gains* achieved from co-operative inter-state actions. We can illustrate this by use of a simple example. Suppose that the current distribution of trading power 'points' between the Northeast Asian states was this: Japan 7, China 6, South Korea 3. The three countries then estimate that after forming a regional free trade area between them the distribution of trading power 'points' would change to: Japan 10, China 11, South Korea 8. Neo-realists suggest that even though Japan stands to realise an absolute gain of 3 points (7 to 10), it will not promote the regional free trade area because its international position relative to China will worsen (+1 to −1). Now suppose if revised estimates on a Northeast Asian FTA's gains suggest the following distribution: Japan 13, China 9, South Korea 6; according to neo-realists Japan now has an incentive to promote the free trade area because its international position relative to China will improve as a consequence (+1 to +4). However, if China's leaders also think along neo-realist lines then they in turn will not promote this regional project based on these revised estimates. The main conclusion here, then, is that when this line of neo-realist thinking is pervasive amongst many states then regional co-operation is more difficult to achieve.

A further premise of neo-realist theory is that while it accepts that international structures can condition the behaviour of nation-states, these in turn are ultimately determined by the interaction of nation-states themselves. So, for example, East Asian countries may act in accordance with WTO or FTA rules on trade policy but at the same time certain countries may have the power and influence to shape those rules to suit their own national interests. Within this theoretical tradition, realists essentially championed the primacy of nation-states whereas neo-realists are also concerned with systemic structure (Gilpin 1984, Waltz 1979). The so called 'English School' of international relations and hegemonic stability theory (HST) are both examples of the latter. English School thinking proposes that nation-states form the basic units of an international society in which countries work together to solve common problems whilst retaining the inviolable rights of national sovereignty. That international society is itself, however, more than the sum of its parts, and state behaviour is subject to the rules, norms, values and institutions that constitute international society generally. The same can apply on a regional scale, and hence this is relevant to the formation of regional organisations and frameworks like ASEAN and APT, yet nation-states nevertheless remain the prime object of analysis to most English School theorists.

HST meanwhile contends that hegemonic states play a stabilising role in an anarchical international economic system (Kindleberger 1973, Krasner 1976, Lake 1991, Milner 1998). Britain is supposed to have played this hegemonic stability role in the nineteenth century, and this onerous responsibility passed onto the United States during the twentieth century. Initially these states underwrite an open trading system from which they benefit, owing to their own competitive advantages they can successfully exploit within that system more than any other nation-state. Owing to this power they are able to compel and pressure others to support them in this task, and here we see the hegemon's exercise of structural power: the ability to influence and shape international structures and the rules of the game that other countries must abide by (Strange 1994, Tuathail and Agnew 1992). However, as the hegemonic state loses its power so it takes increasing recourse to trade protectionism and even refuge in a regional trade bloc, over which it can still exercise effective power and dominance. As other countries retaliate with their own trade protectionism, and also form their own regional trade blocs as a counter-measure, so instability and fragmentation of the international economic system occurs. Hegemonic stability theorists point to the inter-war period (1918–39) when rising protectionism and bloc formation contributed to the outbreak of the Second World War, and also more recently to the US, its creeping trade protectionism and unilateralism (in reaction to a burgeoning trade deficit from the 1970s onwards) and entrenchment within the NAFTA 'bloc'.

While HST can appear somewhat simplistic and over-generalised, it may help explain the rise of regionalism as the world shifted from 'hegemonic stability' to multipolarity. The decision taken by ASEAN states in the early 1990s to form their Free Trade Area was partly based on concerns over the impact that NAFTA and the EU's Single Market programme would have on their trading positions, especially when close industrial rivals such as Mexico and Central and Eastern Europe were expected to gain preferential access to the world's two largest markets. The emergence and development of APT may also be seen as reaction to this general shift to multipolarity, and the sense that East Asia – as one of the world's three prosperous 'triad' regions – does not have its own FTA or single market arrangement yet. In this sense, certain neo-realists may argue that regional trade blocs are merely projections of the competitive power-maximising behaviour of nation-states, working collectively to improve their relative international position over collectives of nation-states. In other words, East Asian states are only collaborating with each other in order to compete more effectively against states from other regions.

1.5.2.b Neo-liberalism, neo-liberal institutionalism

Neo-liberal theories of international political economy are founded on the 'classic' liberal notions of individual self-determination and utility-maximising rationality. From this, for example, derives the *laissez faire* principles of free trade and comparative advantage. Classic liberal theory contends that it is private organisations (i.e. firms) that trade with each other, not nation-states as such, and hence liberals emphasise individuals and private organisations as the most significant actors in the international economic system. This leads to a preoccupation with competition between firms, rather than inter-state competition, and the primacy of markets over states. Indeed, 'state power' (i.e. governments) versus 'market power' (i.e. firms, private capital) has become a core IPE issue in the era of globalisation, especially after the various financial crises that arose during the 1990s (e.g. the EU's Exchange Rate Mechanism crisis in 1992/3, the Mexican peso crisis of 1994/5, and perhaps most importantly the 1997/8 East Asian financial crisis). East Asia's financial crisis clearly revealed how international financiers and currency speculators could prevail over most of the region's central bank authorities who were trying to counteract downward global market pressure on their national currencies. It came down to a question of sheer financial power: private international financiers simply had more money to throw into market interactions than most government's had when attempting to manage an exchange rate policy.

Neo-liberalism extends the theoretical foundations of classic liberal theory. For example, neo-liberalism stresses how non-state actors *per se* (not just individuals and firms) play an increasingly important role in the contemporary international economic order. This can include transnational actors, such as representatives from non-governmental organisations

(NGOs), officials from supranational or international agencies, or MNE business executives. Moreover, even where state-centric negotiations determine actual outcomes, trans-governmental coalitions may evolve between like-minded state officials whose own self-serving interests may not necessarily be aligned to the state they are supposed to represent (Risse-Kappen 1995). For example, trade diplomats from around the East Asian region may have more in common with each other than say their own government colleagues working in domestic-oriented ministries. Some of these trade diplomats will have gone to the same American, European or Asian university for their post-graduate degree, and they may share similar views on how the international system and international relations should be managed. Neo-liberals would suggest it is from such elite policy-maker networks across different governments that the ideas and initiatives for regional economic co-operation and integration can derive. We shall see later how there are links here with social constructivist theory. More generally, neo-liberalism contends that the growth in both the number and scope of international organisations, together with the new inter-linkages forged by globalisation, has broadened the nature of transnational relations and introduced greater complexity to the governance of international economic relations.

While there exists a strong neo-liberal consensus against state intervention, *neo-liberal institutionalists* argue that states need to co-operate to both redress market failure at the international level and jointly provide the public goods required for the international economic system to function in a non-anarchical fashion. This of course applies at various levels, for example at the global-multilateral level such as the Kyoto Protocol on reducing carbon emissions, and at the regional level through the work of regional organisations. Moreover, in contrast to neo-realist theory, neo-liberal institutionalism maintains that while international organisations may owe their origins to hegemonic power, they are not subsequently dependent upon it once they become established. This is partly due to them creating the conditions in the international economic system that help legitimise their own independent *raison d'etre*. Thus, global-multilateral and regional organisations have become more than just the sum of their nation-state members. Some neo-liberals, however, play down the importance of institutionalised co-operation by arguing that 'international organisations are not the causes of co-operation but mechanisms through which co-operation occurs' (Haggard and Moravcsik 1993: 285). Thus, the institutionalist wing of neo-liberal theory has often been treated as a separate theory.

According to neo-liberal institutionalists, then, regional institutions such as ASEAN, APEC and APT are founded on the above premises of co-operative behaviour. Indeed, managing the *complex interdependence* between sets of closely connected nation-states (e.g. within the same region) is a key theme of neo-liberal theory analysis, especially its neo-liberal institutionalist strand. Keohane and Nye (1977) developed the notion of complex interdependence as a critique of the neo-realist worldview that states behave in a largely autonomous manner, proposing instead that independent state strategies are often not viable. This largely derived from the neo-liberal observation that multiple transnational channels connect societies, or sections of societies, across different nation-states and it has become increasingly relevant in the era of globalisation. We can see various instances today where globalisation and our expanding knowledge and observation of transnationalised activities and issues can make it difficult to disaggregate national allegiances, identities and interests. Consider the following examples:

- *Southeast Asia's 'haze' pollution problem*: pollution respects no national boundaries and ASEAN member-states have been compelled to tackle this at a regional level.
- *East Asian financial crisis of 1997/8*: the crisis exposed the lack of regional co-operation mechanisms to address the 'contagion' spread of currency market turmoil from one country to another.
- *SARS virus*[8] *outbreak of 2002/3*: very similar to the above. Again, East Asian countries met soon after the outbreak to formulate regional-level solutions for containing and eradicating the virus.
- *Other 'new' transnational security issues*: including drug-trafficking, economic migration and refugee flows.

It is from such imperatives to co-operate that states within the same region decide to embark upon regionalist endeavours, so neo-liberal institutionalists would argue. The extent to which they decide to co-operate and regionally integrate with each other is another matter.

1.5.2.c Social constructivism

Social constructivism is a relatively new strand of IPE theory that also crosses over into international relations theory more generally. Essentially, it stresses the importance of ideas, values, beliefs, identity-formation in IPE analysis. In this sense it offers non-materialistic perspectives both on why things happen in the international economic system and how we may interpret events and developments within that system. In other words, these may be understood via our 'social' or 'ideational' construction of IPE phenomena, relationships and so on. Moreover, according to social constructivists it is the contestation of ideas rather than that of vested interests that primarily shape today's IPE. As John Maynard Keynes – the greatest economist of the twentieth century – himself famously stated in his highly influential book, *The General Theory*:

> The ideas of economists and political philosophers, both when they are right and when they are wrong, are more powerful than is commonly understood. Indeed the world is ruled by little else. Practical men, who believe themselves to be quite exempt from any intellectual influences, are usually the slaves of some defunct economist.

Madmen in authority, who hear voices in the air, are distilling their frenzy from some academic scribbler of a few years back.

(Keynes 1936: 383)

What Keynes was saying here was that all theories and policies are essentially derivatives of certain ideas or beliefs, whether it is free trade, liberty, democracy, community, individualism and even the idea of a region or 'regionness'. We would not, for instance, be studying East Asian regionalism if ideas of 'East Asia' or 'regionalism' had themselves not been *constructed* over many years and decades of analytical discourse. As Katzenstein (2000) argued, regions are more than the physical flow of goods and people within a defined regional space: regions are also social and cognitive constructs, focusing on how peoples from different nations within a defined geographic space commonly associate around a shared sense of region. To Jayasuriya (1994:412), regionalism

is a set of cognitive practices shaped by language and political discourse, which through the creation of concepts, metaphors, analogies, determine how the region is defined; these serve to define the actors who are included (and excluded) within the region and thereby enable the emergence of a regional entity and identity.

In addition, Hurrell (1995:466) talks about the notion of *regional community* being the development of the region 'into an active subject with a distinct identity, institutionalised or informal actor capability, legitimacy and structure of decision-making in relation with a more or less responsive regional civil society, transcending old state borders'.

In international comparative terms, the sense of 'regionness' is arguably strongest in Europe, especially continental Europe. The creation of the euro has consolidated European regional identity-formation still further. Whilst East Asia remains a highly diverse region, one could argue that the sense of East Asian regionness and regional identity-formation, especially amongst its most educated and travelled peoples, has grown in recent years. This may be viewed from two main phase perspectives. First, the regional economic dynamic experienced by many of the region's states led both East Asians themselves and also those from outside the region to develop holistic explanations of the East Asian economic 'miracle'. In other words, what was it about East Asia as a region and East Asians generally that made it and them so successful in development terms? This helped create a sense of regional cohesion, and to some extent a sense of regional community amongst East Asians themselves, especially amongst the region's elite groups, e.g. policy-makers, business leaders and academics.

Second, one could argue that it was (ironically) the supposed end of East Asia's economic miracle with the arrival of the 1997/8 financial crisis that further consolidated the idea of East Asian regionalism. The financial crisis was an experience shared by many people from the East Asia region, and moreover it clearly revealed that important economic, political and social inter-linkages bound them together in some way. Regional crises, and the shared imperative to avoid another one, can therefore provide the societal or public support needed in the development of new regionalist projects. The origins and development of the European Community/Union may be broadly understood in this way (after two World Wars), and the APT process may also be understood in similar terms (after a significant financial and economic crisis).

Social constructivism also stresses the importance of various societal developments occurring at the micro-level in the 'social construction' of regions, which could be described as socio-cultural regionalisation processes. The emergence of pan-regional social and cultural movements in East Asia is now closely linked to debates concerning regional identity-formation. This relates to various aspects of Asian popular culture, such as Japanese cartoons and karaoke, Korean pop music, Star TV, Chinese and Korean television shows, multinational Asian singing groups, Asian fusion food, and so on. Pempel argues that the growing pan-Asian appeal of these cultural products is creating at least a rudimentary basis of regional popular identity, and moreover observes that, 'From cartoons to karaoke and from pop music to internet sites, such youth-oriented popular culture now bleeds across East Asia's national borders in ways unimaginable two decades ago' (2005b: 24).

Furthermore, intra-regional social and cultural exchange has been gathering momentum in East Asia in terms of movement of people, international student exchange, foreign travel, and trade in cultural goods, e.g. music, film (METI 2005). These developments in regional socialisation all contribute in some way to regional identity-formation in East Asia. Certain social constructivists have also argued that inter-regional links, such as the Asia-Europe Meeting (ASEM) framework and the East Asia–Latin America Forum (EALAF), are based on, and help further define regional identity formation. This is mainly because such interaction develops respective senses of regional 'we-ness' and 'them-ness' (Gilson 2002). According to the social constructivist view, then, the more that East Asia as a region interacts in a collective or coalitional sense with other macro-regions, the more regional identity-formation can be expected to develop.

1.5.2.d Marxism and structuralism

The intellectual origins of Marxism derive from the writings of nineteenth century political economist Karl Marx. Marxist theory postulates that classes are the dominant actors in the world system. Similar to neo-realists, Marxists contend that international economic relations are essentially conflictual in nature because of inherent inter-class frictions that arise between capital and labour, and in particular from the capitalist exploitation of workers. According to Marxist thought, the prevailing hierarchy in the international economic system is determined not by politico-military power, as neo-realists suggest, but rather by the patterns of production and exchange established by the global capitalist system. Globalisation has further enhanced the power of capital, consequently strengthened the influence of firms over state economic policy, a point that neo-liberals would also generally agree on in the context of the 'states versus markets' debate.

Marxist scholars such as Wallerstein (1979) have emphasised the historical perspective on the development of global capitalism when studying contemporary international economic relations. Marx himself wrote much on the relationship between the expansion of internationalised capital interests and imperialism. In the post-colonial era, the Marxist interpretation of transnational class conflict has moved on to place greater emphasis on MNE competition for global market shares, thus branding them as the new imperialist actors or as agents of neo-colonialism. Following on from this argument, Marxists generally contend that state-led regionalist initiatives and frameworks such as ASEAN, APT and APEC are merely attempts by the transnational capital class (e.g. MNE executives, state policy-makers, international financiers) to consolidate or advance capitalist development in accordance with their interests. Free trade agreements are also viewed in the same way as they break down the barriers to the growth and expansion of transnational capitalism.

Marxists take a similar view on regionalisation, emphasising how multinational enterprises use their market power to play off workforces against each other within international production networks so as to drive down labour costs and maximise economic rents, e.g. profits. The so called 'new international division of labour' (NIDL) has been facilitated by two main developments (Frobel et al. 1980). The first relates to advances in transport and communication technologies that have enabled the co-ordinated management of production networks and labour forces across national borders. The second concerns how new process technologies have fragmented and standardised specific tasks that can be more easily contracted out to developing countries with low labour costs. Consequently, greater scope has emerged for competition between workforces from developed and developing country locations, which MNEs exploit to their advantage. Marxists suggest that this can be observed very clearly on a regional scale, and moreover explains patterns of regionalisation in East Asia and elsewhere. As stated earlier in this chapter, *regionalisation* derives from market or business determined interactions within particular regional spaces. In this context, MNEs are exploiting their capital advantages over national borders, and in doing so linking up different parts of the region's economy through various NIDL-based activities. Chapter 2 examines how companies such as Toyota make their products on a regional division of labour involving a number of East Asian countries. For example, large multinationals like Toyota are able to set countries to competitively bid for different sub-contracted production elements in order that the company secures the best terms and conditions, e.g. investment tax-breaks, pre-skilled labour, a more 'flexible' regulatory environment.

Structuralist perspectives and theories on IPE draw upon certain Marxist premises outlined above, as well as dependency theory and world-system theory. Structuralism stresses the importance of economic, political and social structures in explaining the nature of the world economic system (Chase-Dunn 1989, Wallerstein 1978, 1979). In terms of international *economic* structures we particularly mean those of production, finance, technology and knowledge. It shares similarities with the Marxist view of economic history, stressing the particular division of labour that has evolved in the world economy based on the growth of capitalism as the dominant form of production. In analysing the structure of the world economic system, structuralism draws upon dependency theory to explain the persisting gap between developed and developing country areas. This theory states that the *core-periphery* divide between advanced industrialised countries (i.e. the 'core') and under-developed countries (i.e. the 'periphery') is sustained by subservient economic relationships in which the latter remain dependent upon the former for capital, technology, finance and trade. This relationship of 'unequal exchange' endures because it is in the interests of dominant capitalist forces – or transnational capital class as Marxists would more specifically identify – to maintain the status quo. Indeed, the persisting gap between the developed countries (Europe, North America) and developing country regions (Africa, Latin America, Central and South Asia) seems to support the general case for structural rigidity in the international economic system.

In East Asia's case, many newly industrialising economies (e.g. South Korea, Taiwan) have broken out of 'periphery' dependency into what has been called the 'semi-periphery' strata, whereby they offer core-like sources of capital, markets, technology, etc. themselves, whilst remaining partially dependent on core AIEs. Two points follow here in relation to regionalism. First, structuralists would argue that the emergence of East Asia's semi-periphery has helped bind together the regional economy through performing intermediary functions (e.g. investment and trade links) between the region's core and periphery elements. Second, the region's long established 'core' capitalist power itself – Japan – played a key role in cultivating the development of the region's semi-periphery in the first place. Chapter 2 discusses in some detail how Japan's overseas investments and technology transfers dispersed around the region helped neighbouring countries develop (the so called 'flying geese' model). More generally, Japanese companies have been a major driving force in the regionalisation in East Asia through their extension of transnational corporate systems of production and distribution throughout the region. In addition, structuralists may argue that state-sponsored regionalist projects amongst developing, 'periphery' countries, such as AFTA, are essentially attempts to overcome the structural constraints of dependency by constructing a more self-sufficient regional market. Although economic geographers in particular question the usefulness of viewing economic regions as composites of core, semi-periphery and periphery countries (Dicken 2003), these structural divisions may still apply when examining regionalised 'dependency' linkages between different *economic zones* within a region, as discussed in Chapter 2.

1.6 Conclusion

This chapter first looked at the emergence of East Asia as an increasingly important region in the international economic system, and considered questions relating to defining its 'regionness'. It was argued that East Asia's regional coherence has become gradually stronger, despite the various political, socio-cultural, economic and security-related impediments ranged against this. We looked at the key concepts and definitions of regionalism, particularly looking at how we may distinguish some concepts and definitions from others, for example regionalisation from state-led regionalism. The intermeshing of these concepts and definitions (e.g. economic and political regionalism) was also noted. Thereafter, we examined how the study of regionalism has evolved over time from the Euro-centric theories of 'classic regionalism' to the more recently emergent 'new regionalism theory' paradigms, which take into account much broader understandings of how, why and where regionalising processes are formed.

This was followed by a discussion on how regionalism has manifested itself in the international system. We first considered the linkages between regionalism and globalisation, and how they may be thought of as being part of similar integrative processes occurring within the world but on different geo-spatial scales, i.e. regional and global. Second, we examined how regional economic organisations and frameworks have spread and developed within the international system, noting that East Asia is a relative latecomer compared to most other regions in this regard. However, the recent creation of the APT and EAS regional frameworks are important new developments with potentially very significant implications for the wider international community. Third, we looked at the security and geopolitical dimensions of East Asian regionalism, discussing amongst other things the connections between economics and security in regional affairs, as well as issues of regional leadership that took into account the relationship between East Asia's two dominant countries, Japan and China. The chapter concluded by considering the analytical usefulness of IPE concepts and theories in the study of East Asian regionalism. IPE analysis helps us understand why, how and for whom regionalism may occur, and what the implications of regionalism may be for the region itself and the wider international system. Furthermore, the key concepts, ideas and theoretical tools of IPE analysis outlined here will principally frame discussions in each subsequent chapter's concluding section.

Chapter Study Questions

1. Why is regionalism such a contested concept?
2. How and why has regionalism manifested itself in different ways within the international system?
3. Why have many aspects of East Asian regionalism been so slow to develop in comparison to other global regions?
4. What different actors may be involved in East Asian regionalism? Identify what their specific interests and influence are likely to be in regionalist projects.
5. Explain why international political economy (IPE) analysis is so useful when studying East Asian regionalism.

Notes

1   Those who have a preference for this geographic distinction tend to be specialists in either Southeast Asian, Chinese or Japanese studies.

2   CFA is derived from the term *Colonies françaises d'Afrique* ('French colonies of Africa').

3   For Athukorala (2003:1), globalisation essentially concerns 'the deepening structural interdependence of the world economy'. Scholte (2001:14–15) comments that, 'Globalisation refers to processes whereby many social relations become relatively de-linked from territorial geography, so that human lives are increasingly played out in a world as a single place. Social relations – that is, the countless and complex ways that people interact and affect each other – are more and more being conducted and organised on the basis of a planetary unit.'

4   World Trade Organisation rules only permit developing countries to enter into such agreements under the so called 'Enabling Clause'. For a discussion on this, see Dent (2006a).

5   See Chapter 8 for a discussion on the distinctions between regional organisations and frameworks.

6   This mostly related to agricultural, textile and petrochemical sectors. The Bangkok Agreement was originally an initiative of the Economic and Social Commission for Asia and the Pacific (ESCAP), and is Asia's oldest preferential trade agreement. India, Bangladesh, South Korea, Laos and Sri Lanka were the Bangkok Agreement's founding members, with China acceding in 2001.

7   The ARF essentially brings together a number of ASEAN's 'dialogue partners' (the US, Japan, China, Russia, South Korea, Australia, New Zealand, Canada, India and the EU) to discuss security-related issues in general. Its work is augmented by 'track II' arrangements such as CSCAP (Council for Security Co-operation in the Asia-Pacific) meetings and workshops where government officials, other organisational representatives and specialists discuss various security-related issues.

8   SARS stands for 'severe acute respiratory syndrome'.

Chapter 2

East Asia's regionalisation and new economic geography

2.1 Introduction

In Chapter 1, we broadly defined regionalism as the structures, processes and arrangements that are working towards greater coherence within a specific international region in terms of economic, political, security, socio-cultural and other such linkages. It was further noted that *regionalisation* was an important constituent element of this, relating to regional concentrations of inter-connecting private or civil sector activities arising at the micro-level. This chapter first explores the historic roots of East Asia's economic regionalisation before proceeding to outline its main features in the contemporary era, of which there are many aspects to consider. One of the most important concerns the growth and expansion of international production networks (IPNs) in the region, which have been a significant integrative force in the development of the East Asian regional economy. There are geographic factors at play with the formation of IPNs, as with other aspects of East Asia's regionalisation. As is discussed, there are certain spatial or zonal dimensions to networked patterns of regionalised economic activity in East Asia generally. For example, key elements of IPNs are invariably rooted in localised industrial districts or clusters, these being highly concentrated areas of economic development specialising in particular industrial sector operations. In this nexus between the networked and zonal aspects of East Asia's regionalisation, we also examine the critical role played by the region's world cities (e.g. Tokyo, Shanghai, Seoul, Hong Kong, Singapore, Bangkok), for example, as the main nodes in East Asia's regional infrastructure systems. In addition, this chapter makes a study of East Asia's emerging 'growth polygons', these being sub-regional economic zones that involve a number of participant countries in symbiotic development relationships. At the higher geo-spatial scale, we can discern a pan-regional development corridor that represents the prime core of East Asian regional economy. Together, the above developments may be considered the new economic geography of East Asia's regionalisation, and the international political economy analysis of this chapter draws upon the disciplinary perspectives of geography, business studies and economic development, amongst others.

2.2 East Asia's regionalisation in historic context

Like most other regions, the historic development of East Asia's economic regionalisation is founded on its trade networks. The region has always been amongst the world's most important trading zones. The East Asians had extensive and well developed commercial systems long before they were first 'discovered' and 'opened up' by the European powers from the fifteenth century onwards (Sakakibara and Yamakawa 2003). As Chanda (2006:61) argues, the promotion of trade has been a leitmotif in the region. The desire to live better and earn profits has driven Asian traders to risk their lives crossing oceans and in the process created a common economic space from the very beginning of recorded history. Long-distance trading created a cosmopolitanism that laid the foundation for commercial prosperity.

Furthermore, based on the contention that the region's comparatively high population growth figures were indicative of sustained economic development, Frank (1998:174) contends that, 'Asia and various of its regional economies were far more productive and had far and away more weight and influence in the global economy than any or all of the "West" put together until 1800'. China was the world's largest economy until the early nineteenth century, when it was overtaken by Britain – the world's first emerging industrialised nation (Bairoch 1981, Braudel 1992, Pomeranz 2000).

A huge pan-Asian trade network had emerged during the first millennium based on commercial linkages established between China (trading in silk and porcelain products), India (spices, medicinal herbs, precious stones and cotton textiles) and Southeast Asia's producers of rice, teak, nutmeg, cloves and scented wood products (Chanda 2006). These linkages also extended to the Mediterranean and around the Indian Ocean. China was the main centre of East Asia's regional trading system at this time. From the twelfth to early fifteenth centuries, China also dispatched numerous treasure ships on long expeditions to other continents. Thereafter, it focused on a tighter network of closer trade links in the region, and still maintained an extensive tributary trade system that kept other East Asian nations and peoples in China's commercial orbit (Fairbank 1968). China's artisans produced goods at the high value-added end of the market, exporting silk and porcelain products to Asia and Europe, and therein accumulating huge quantities of silver and other precious metals through trade payments made by importing countries.

Japan emerged as a major new Asian maritime power in the fourteenth and fifteenth centuries. Its trade with China and Korea grew significantly from the thirteenth century and by the fifteenth and sixteenth centuries it had expanded its trade network to the Malacca Straits in Southeast Asia. In some ways, Japan was filling the void left by China's aforementioned introversion from the 1430s onwards. Yet China remained ultimately the pre-eminent power, with Japan participating in China's tributary trade from 1404 to 1549. Japan's prime exports to China were silver, copper, sulphur, folding fans, screens and swords, while China mainly exported raw silk, porcelain, paintings, medicines and books to Japan (Hall 1970). In the meantime, Southeast Asia began to participate increasingly in intra-regional trade as a consequence of the commercial expansions of China, India, Japan and Europe from the fifteenth century onwards. Southeast Asia's geographic position, lying between India and China, made the sub-region an important crossroads and conduit for international trade, especially sea-borne trade. By this time Southeast Asia's main exports were spices, aromatic woods, resins, lacquer, tortoise shell, pearls, and sugar. China was by far the most important market for Southeast Asian traders for many centuries. The sub-region's entrepôt centres also played a crucial role in facilitating intra-regional trade. The most important of these was Malacca (on the Malay peninsula), founded in 1403, and which became a vital trading post for Chinese, Japanese, Indian, Arabic, African and Central Asian merchants.

The arrival of the European maritime powers from the late fifteenth century opened up new dimensions to Asia's trading system. Portugal was the pioneering European maritime power, and continued to dominate Euro-Asian trade up to the late sixteenth century. The Dutch and the English, however, increasingly challenged this position from the seventeenth century onwards. A broad network of international trade routes had already been developed within Asia, and European trading companies such as the English East India Company and the Dutch Verenigde Oostindische Compagnie (VOC) extended and developed intra-Asian trade further. Up until the eighteenth century, the VOC's volume of intra-Asian trade was roughly the same as its Euro-Asian inter-regional trade. European traders also invested in developing certain Asian goods, some of which were exchanged for other Asian goods across intra-regional trade networks, and then were exported back to Europe. Asia's long established merchant class provided the 'soft infrastructure' of networked relationships to facilitate this trade. Intra-Asian trade could still at this time be divided into two main spheres. The first centred on the Indian Ocean (India, Central Asia, western parts of Southeast Asia) and the second on China's seaboard (Northeast Asia and eastern parts of Southeast Asia). Trade between these two spheres naturally occurred, much of it sea-borne through Southeast Asia, passing through the Malacca Straits and other routes. This led to the dispersion of mainly Chinese and Indian trading communities throughout Southeast Asia to facilitate this commerce.

During the late nineteenth and early twentieth century, there was a substantial increase in Asia's intra-regional trade. Over 1883 to 1928, intra-Asian export ratio as a percentage of the total rose from 24 per cent to 41 per cent, and for intra-Asian imports from 28 per cent to 44 per cent. According to Sugihara (1990) the development of a modern cotton industry, centred on Japan, was a key driver behind the trend. Japanese textile manufacturers imported primary materials from China and Southeast Asia and then exported finished products to the East Asian regional market and beyond. More broadly, Japan's rapid industrialisation from the late nineteenth century onwards, coupled with its imperial expansion into the region, were the prime factors behind deepening regionalisation of the East Asian economy during this period (Beasley 1987).[1] Another spur to intra-regional trade was the adoption of many East Asian countries of the gold standard (the global currency exchange system) by the end of the nineteenth century, with the prime aim of facilitating the import of manufactured goods, capital and technologies from the West, much of which was used in developing the region's infrastructure.

However, by the late 1930s, intra-regional trade flows slackened. At the global level, the world trading system was breaking down as a result of rising protectionism amongst the Western industrial powers having adverse effects upon East Asian export trade in particular. East Asia's trade was also interrupted by Japan's invasions of other parts of the region, and by the subsequent exploitative imperial division of labour imposed on many East Asian countries under the euphemistically phrased 'Greater East Asia Co-Prosperity Sphere'. During the 1940s and 1950s, East Asia's intra-regional commerce remained generally stagnant. Domestic political turmoil and the rise of nationalism in the post-colonial era turned many of the region's countries inward in their perspective. Japan's newly reconstituted multinational companies, the *keiretsu*, were making only tentative forays into the regional market by the end of this period. On the whole, national rather than regional cohesion had become the prime objective of East Asian states during this period (Hamashita 1997).

2.3 Recent trends in East Asia's regional trade

East Asia's intra-regional trade ratio has gradually increased since the 1960s, and has been especially fast from the 1980s onwards (Das 2004). Its overall intra-regional trade ratio was around 25 per cent in the early 1960s, rising to 35 per cent by 1980, and then to 55 per cent by 2005. This compared to North America's 43 per cent and the EU's 65 per cent in the same year. However, Southeast Asia's intra-regional trade ratio remained quite low at just 22 per cent in 2003 and Northeast Asia's (China, Japan, Korea, Taiwan) ratio was 26 per cent. The significant gaps between East Asia's sub-regional and pan-regional figures suggest extensive trade links between Southeast and Northeast Asia. In many ways, China has now emerged as the key link in East Asia's regional chain of trade. Not only does the country play an important hub function in the region's trade-investment relations (through attracting large amounts of export-oriented inward FDI), but it has also become the largest trading partner for an increasing number of other East Asian countries (Table 2.1). The growth of international production networks in the region is another important contributing factor generally to deepening trade regionalisation in East Asia, as we later analyse in some detail. Electronics, machinery, automobiles, transport equipment, and ICT products together account for the majority share of East Asia's intra-regional trade. These are multi-component goods, and the manufacturing thereof is fragmented into various sub-assembly production operations with production situated in the most advantageous locations around the region.

The growth of component trade is indicative of the extent to which international production network activity has expanded in East Asia (Borrus et al. 2000). Trade in parts and components accounted for around US$140 billion of East Asia's intra-regional trade in 2003. In Southeast Asia, the shares of components in total manufacturing exports have increased

Table 2.1 Intra-regional trade in East Asia, 2004 (US$ millions)

	Brunei	China	Hong Kong	Indonesia	Japan	Macao	Malaysia	Philippines	Singapore	South Korea	Taiwan	Thailand	Vietnam
Brunei		276	62	315	1,920	1	346	5	660	695	15	435	2
China	276		172,456	11,095	168,069	1,882	22,530	9,320	29,144	84,708	78,324	16,316	6,811
Hong Kong	62	172,456		2,258	41,904	1,023	9,693	5,886	20,579	19,992	26,113	6,898	1,714
Indonesia	315	11,095	2,258		24,886	12	5,983	1,391	12,084	8,410	4,094	5,144	1,028
Japan	1,920	168,069	41,904	24,886		249	28,104	16,569	27,461	67,078	58,678	35,138	7,023
Macao	1	1,882	1,023	12	249		27	12	78	74	194	27	15
Malaysia	346	22,530	9,693	5,983	28,104	27		4,404	41,467	9,909	9,846	11,327	1,751
Philippines	5	9,320	5,886	1,391	16,569	12	4,404		7,092	4,676	5,442	3,007	1,136
Singapore	660	29,144	20,579	12,084	27,461	78	41,467	7,092		12,219	17,705	12,821	4,629
South Korea	695	84,708	19,992	8,410	67,078	74	9,909	4,676	12,219		17,156	5,522	4,061
Taiwan	15	78,324	26,113	4,094	58,678	194	9,846	5,442	17,705	17,156		6,583	4,319
Thailand	435	16,316	6,898	5,144	35,138	27	11,327	3,007	12,821	5,522	6,583		2,386
Vietnam	2	6,811	1,714	1,028	7,023	15	1,751	1,136	4,629	4,061	4,319	2,386	

Notes: Figures for total bilateral trade between trade partners. Owing to discrepancies in the trade statistics published by bilateral trade partners concerning the their bilateral trade flows, figures from both partners have been aggregated and then halved.
Source: IMF Direction of Trade Statistics Yearbook 2005.

significantly, to over 50 per cent for Malaysia, the Philippines and Singapore, and 35 per cent for Thailand. Ratios for China and Vietnam are still quite low by comparison (18 and 9 per cent, respectively) but are rising fast. More generally, East Asia is more dependent on assembly trade than any other part of the world, including Europe and North America. The share of components in East Asia's total manufacturing exports was 32 per cent in 2000 compared to 28 per cent for NAFTA and 19 per cent for the EU. Moreover, component trade accounted for 44 per cent of East Asia's export growth over the 1992–2000 period, which again was considerably higher than ratios for North America (30 per cent) and Europe (22 per cent). Similar comparisons could be made for imports: on components' share of total trade, 35 per cent for East Asia, 23 per cent for NAFTA and 20 per cent for the EU. The assembly trade ratios on both exports and imports for Malaysia, Singapore and the Philippines were over 50 per cent. China's ratios, whilst still relatively low in the early 1990s, has risen sharply, from 7 per cent in 1992 to 15 per cent in 2000 for exports, and from 20 per cent to 34 per cent for imports (World Bank 2003a).

Japan is still the most important regional trade partner for around half of all East Asian countries (Table 2.1). Furthermore, it remains an important hub centre for production sharing operations, originating about one-third of all regional exports of components for assembly. Indonesia imports 70 per cent of its component products from Japan; for South Korea, Taiwan and the Philippines this is at least 50 per cent (Ng and Yeats 2003). Of China's top 30 imported products (four–digit HST[2] code level) from other East Asian countries, most were component or material items (the top three in 2003, accounting for 15 per cent of the total, were parts of office machines, electronic microcircuits and parts of telecom equipment), very few were actual 'final products', e.g. jerseys and pullovers. China meanwhile exports a much higher proportion of final products in comparison to other East Asian countries, the top six most important items being children's toys, parts of office machinery, footwear, parts of telecom equipment, jerseys and pullovers, and travel goods. These goods accounted for 22 per cent of China's exports to other East Asian countries in 2003. China accounts for around a quarter of the region's total component trade exports (Sakakibara and Yamakawa 2004).

The expansion of international production network activity in East Asia is one explanation for the growth in intra-regional trade. Gravity theories of trade provide another more generalised explanation, emphasising market size and geographic distance as the main determining factors of international trade and investment flows. These theories contend that trade between countries is proportional to their economy's size, and inversely proportional to the geographic distance between them (Greenaway and Milner 2002). As East Asian economies have grown, so they become more important markets to one another through the exertion of economic gravitational forces. Thus, the rapid development of China as a market and its proximity to a number of other East Asian countries explains its increasing importance to the region's trade, and also to deepening trade regionalisation overall.

2.4 The rise of international production networks in East Asia

2.4.1 What are international production networks (IPNs)?

Regional economic interdependence in East Asia has moved increasingly beyond deepening intra-regional trade. Economic links between East Asian countries at the micro-level have become more *functionally integrative*. By this we mean East Asian regionalisation has become much more than just growing levels of economic exchange (e.g. trade and investment flows) to include the expanding development of regional business systems and operations, mainly through the growth of IPNs. As we shall see, IPNs can differ significantly in terms of their organisational and spatial nature. They are closely associated, or even synonymous with MNE activity, and indeed IPN analysis derives largely from case-study evidence from the literature on multinational enterprises (Dobson and Chia 1997, McKendrick et al. 2000, Naughton 1999). Yun (2003:173) defines an IPN as 'an international division of labour, in which each function or discrete stage of a value chain is spatially or geographically relocated in the most efficient site, and under-taken by different firms including MNEs and local firms'. By *value chain*, we are referring to the different functional activities that 'add value' to the production process, e.g. design, research and development, material processing, supplier logistics, information and communications management, finance, manufacturing, marketing and end-product distribution.

Firms *fragment* the value chain into internationally organised configurations in accordance with the specific locational advantages of the countries involved. These can include human resource factors (low cost or skilled labour), access to materials, utilising specialised production or technological capabilities, government policies aimed at attracting inward foreign investment and market-oriented factors. Configuring the network can entail a combination of *intra-firm* and *inter-firm* linkages, or *service links*. In this process, firms must consider how the marginal cost savings of fragmentation are offset by the service link costs of operating the network (Jones and Kierzkowski 1990). Advances in communication and transportation technologies have, though, both gradually reduced service link costs and enabled firms to more effectively manage IPNs on larger organisational and geographic scales (Luthje 2002).

Improvements in production technology have also enabled an ever finer slicing of the production process into separate blocks or fragments (Athukorala 2003). This has led to wider geographic IPN configurations. For example, when Japanese consumer electronic manufacturers such as Sony, Sharp, Sanyo and Toshiba began to relocate production to other parts of East Asia, they began by transferring the wholesale production of particular products (e.g. video cassette recorders) to more advanced developing economies such as South Korea and Taiwan. Then over time, these firms started to shift certain component production and sub-routine assembly processes from these economies to even lower-cost countries in Southeast Asia, thus fragmenting and further dispersing the international production network (Felker 2004, Giroud 2004). Tachiki (2005) notes that this product segmentation process, or 'move the product, not the factory' strategy, occurred across a number of industries, especially from the 1980s onwards. In addition, the liberalisation of commercial policies (i.e. trade and foreign investment) over recent years has reduced the transaction costs (e.g. import tariffs) of operating IPNs (Arndt 2001). However, restrictive rules of origin (RoO) measures – whether applied in free trade agreements or elsewhere – can cause distortions to IPN trade, and firms may forgo free trade access privileges if restrictive rules (e.g. product-specific RoO) are incommensurate with IPN logistics (Baldwin 2001).

2.4.2 East Asia in focus

Many East Asian countries compete with each other to attract IPN investments made by foreign firms. Increasingly, they compete less on cost considerations and more on skills capability, managerial and technical capacity, supply logistics, infrastructural provision, and providing investor firms with access to world-price inputs and capital factors. Many East Asian governments have implemented 'industrial cluster' policies with this in mind, developing or building upon specialised facilities and capabilities (e.g. pool of skilled labour) located in particular zones or 'industrial districts' within their country. As we later discuss, these 'zones' and 'districts' are hence important nodes in international production networks.

We noted earlier the deep historic roots of East Asia's intra-regional trade networks and the more recent contributive factors to their development. International *production* networks are, however, essentially founded on the trade–investment relationship. Of all the world's regions, East Asia is host to the highest concentration and also greatest variety of IPN activity (Henderson et al. 2002, Kimura and Ando 2004, World Bank 2003a, 2005, Yun 2003, Yusuf et al. 2004). Japan's 'flying geese' model is often cited as the modern antecedent of East Asian IPN development (Peng 2000, Tsui-Auch 1999). This model or theory was first developed by Akamatsu (1935) in the 1930s, who observed that the process of a country's trade development under the Japanese imperial division of labour generally followed three sequential stages: import of new products, import substitution and export. This pattern appeared on a graph in an inverse 'V' shape, hence resembling a flying geese formation. Companies such as Nissan and Mitsubishi constructed production plants across the region, linked together to other plants, both back in Japan and elsewhere. The flying geese concept was revived in the 1960s to explain Japan's re-emergent role in shaping the East Asian regional economy. Liberal economists amalgamated Akamatsu's theory with Vernon's (1966) theory on trade, FDI and 'catching-up' product life cycles (Inoue et al. 1993, Kojima 1977, Ozawa 1991).

During the 1960s, Japanese MNEs began to make substantial investments in other parts of East Asia, first in South Korea and Taiwan, and then into Southeast Asia. This involved the relocation of labour-intensive industries (e.g. textiles, basic electronics) that took advantage of developing East Asia's much lower unit labour costs (Chowdhury and Islam 1993, Mason 1999, Tachiki 2005, Yusuf 2003). By the mid-1970s, Japanese firms accounted for 70 per cent of inward FDI in South Korea, representing an estimated quarter of the host country's economic growth at the time. Japanese trading companies also controlled around half of Taiwan's exports by the late 1970s. In the meantime, American firms were also developing their own overseas investments and basic production networks in East Asia, partly under procurement contracts to support US military operations in the Korean and Vietnam civil wars. American electronics firms started to make significant investments in Singapore during the early 1960s (Yeung 2001). In addition, the US Government's huge aid programmes that operated in South Korea and Taiwan during the early Cold War period helped their economies develop the industrial and infrastructural capacities required to both attract increasingly higher value-added FDI and participate in regional production systems.

As the techno-industrial foundations of East Asia's first generation 'tiger' economies (i.e. Singapore, South Korea, Taiwan, Hong Kong) strengthened, so these in turn evolved into overseas investing countries, joining Japan, the US and also European countries as foreign investors in less developed parts of East Asia. This process was the essence of the flying geese dynamic, based on initial investments from 'leading geese' economies having a positive multiplier effect on regional economic development, with less developed countries following in the slipstream of stronger leading economies. In this respect, the early phase of East Asia's IPN development was founded on the relatively simple principle of relocating labour-intensive component production and assembly to developing countries by vertically integrated processes (Feenstra 1998, Hellenier 1973, Sharpton 1975).

The revaluation of the Japanese yen, as a consequence of the 1985 Plaza Accord between the G7 countries, led to a notable surge of Japanese outward FDI during the late 1980s. The revaluation (the deliberate rising of a currency's exchange rate value) meant not only that Japanese firms relocated more production overseas in East Asia and elsewhere but also that Japan-based firms more widely regionalised their procurement strategies as it become cheaper to import components and other inputs because of the stronger value of the yen. This gave a significant spur to IPN development in East Asia. As the production networks of Japan's *keiretsu* firms (the country's large and often diversified multinationals) extended and deepened across the region in the 1980s and 1990s, many observers commented on the politico-economic dimension of this development. Saravanamuttu (1988:9) noted in the late 1980s that, 'the pattern of Japanese trade, aid and investment in ASEAN reveals an overall Japanese strategy of penetration in the region which generates ever greater economic dependence of ASEAN on Japan'.

For Furuoka (2005), the flying geese model of growing corporate ties was part of a broader development of economic and diplomatic linkages between Japan and a newly industrialising East Asia region. Katzenstein (1997), Pempel (1997) and Yoshimatsu (2003) have all proposed the idea of how Japanese FDI helped extend Japan's distinct form of state-society relations (i.e. developmentalism) across East Asia's national borders. Moreover, this had made the development co-operation aspect of East Asian regionalism stronger over time (Arase 1995, Hatch and Yamamura 1996).[3]

According to Hobday (1995), overseas Chinese firms and American companies also made much overlooked contributions to IPN growth in East Asia from the 1960s onwards. Moreover, the nature of production networks in the region can vary according to the originating nationality of the core firm or firms in the network in terms of its organisational configuration and governance structure (Tsui-Auch 1999, Yun 2003). For example, because they are relatively large, Japanese and Korean firms tend to exert more control from the network centre whereas comparatively smaller scale Chinese family-based businesses may not have a co-ordinating centre as such but rather work more on a common 'neural network' relational basis (Orru et al. 1997, Whitley 1992). More specifically, in Japanese-centred IPNs much of the core network operations (e.g. design, innovation) have tended to remain in the home country, with relatively low value-added activities contracted out to foreign elements of the IPN, in comparison to American and European multinational operations in East Asia (Borrus et al. 2000, Paprzycki 2005). Furthermore, Japanese IPNs are often essentially a regionalisation of their domestic *keiretsu* network system with clustered just-in-time suppliers following the core firm overseas, as Case Study 2.1 on the Thai automotive sector cluster discusses.

2.4.3 Types of IPN in East Asia

There are three main motives for firms to develop IPN operations. First, technological advances and other factors (e.g. government policy) have enabled firms to search for the most *cost-effective* means of producing whole or component elements of products, in the context of more nations competing with each other to attract IPN-based investments. Low cost developing countries possessing suitable levels of industrial capacity have hence been increasingly drawn into regional production networks. Second, MNEs also look to identify the competitive locational advantages of nations in *qualitative* terms, especially regarding their specialist production capabilities, e.g. automobile component production in Thailand. This is an important organising principle of IPNs, and closely relates to the industrial district phenomenon in which nations develop dense supplier network clusters that are geographically concentrated to serve and attract major assembly firms. Third, an IPN's value-chain activities may be dispersed in such a way that helps a firm, or firms *spread corporate risk*. Different value-added functions within the production network may be organised that allow certain parts of the network to easily duplicate the work of another part or parts, which is advantageous when disturbances (e.g. exchange rate movements, labour unrest, a political crisis) occur within one or more countries involved in the production network.

These factors can determine the types of international production that arise within a region, and therein the nature and depth of regionalisation that IPNs bring to East Asia. As we note, some forms of international production can have a much stronger networking and integrative effect than others. Figure 2.1 presents four different types of international production (network) that are explained here in turn:

- *Platform Production for Regional Market (type I)*: this type involves minimal level input from international sources. Value-added activities are concentrated in just one country and served by local suppliers. The main assembly production is likely to be situated in an industrial district that provides the 'platform' from which the assembly or core firm exports to the regional market. This is the most important regional dimension to the firm's operations.
- *International Vertical Production (type II)*: international sourcing occurs but in a mostly uni-directional manner, whereby suppliers of materials and components serve the needs of assembly firms, e.g. automobile and electronics manufacturers. These vertical production links

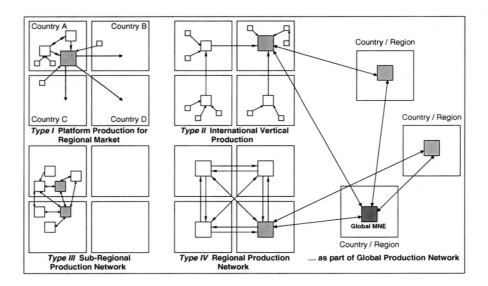

Figure 2.1 Types of international production within a regional economic space
Source: Adapted from Knox and Agnew (1998) and Dicken (2003)
Note: Shaded in areas denote core firms in the regional / global production system.

do not involve mutual exchanges or co-operation between the core firm and its local and international suppliers, or much interaction amongst supplier firms. Both *type I* and *II* international production hence have low network characteristics.

- *Sub-Regional Production Network (type III)*: a high degree of networked activity between a number of firms but geographically concentrated in a particular transborder zone, often involving just two countries or economies. This IPN activity may be based on common socio-cultural links (e.g. Taiwan–China) or exploiting economic complementarities between contiguous border zones. These may be considered small-scale 'growth polygons' or sub-regional economic zones (SREZs, discussed later in the chapter).

- *Regional Production Network (type IV)*: operates on a high level of network interaction between firms from multiple countries across the region. Tends to apply to larger MNE producers in sectors such as electronics, computers, automobiles and machinery industries. Many supplier and other types of associate firms are brought into the network by the core firm. The most regionally integrative of the four types.

These are generalised types of international production that are devised to illustrate key principles and methods on which IPNs can be organised. Not all IPNs neatly fit into this categorisation but rather lie in between types, or have different characteristics from a number of types. For example, there are many IPNs that generally fall into the *type IV* category that only involve two or three countries. There are also sub-regional scale IPNs that are based more on vertical production links (*type II*) than interactive networked links (*type III*). To some extent, the spatial and technological broadening of China's industrial base confers on it an almost independent IPN capacity in an increasing number of sectors. In their study on Southeast Asia and China, Wong and Chan observed that:

> Compared to ASEAN, which generally lacks an adequate base of supporting industries, China has a huge integrated industrial base and is strongly capable of providing auxiliary items like processing equipment, intermediate parts, and electronic components needed for manufacturing. Given its moderately well-developed basic technology industries such as machinery, China has the potential to develop an extensive network, or clusters, of supporting industries. Foreign companies could find it conducive to locate in China and benefit from agglomeration economies generated from being close to those supporting industries.
>
> (2003: 510).

This suggests that production network activity in China could increasingly approximate *type I* integration, although still depending significantly on inward FDI linkages. Moreover, even large dynamic economies such as China cannot develop and maintain dominant competitive advantages across all fields of production. Furthermore, comparative advantage theory suggests that even when one country does have many absolute efficiency advantages over others, it is still beneficial to establish an international division of labour on which to expand trade. This is because such an arrangement allows all countries, including dominant ones, to exploit areas of relative efficiency advantage through further specialisation.

Figure 2.1 also shows how a region's international production networks are often embedded within larger global production networks (GPNs). This represents an important interface between regionalisation and globalisation, and is especially relevant to East Asia given its IPN density. In many ways, IPNs may be considered as essential sinews of globalising business activity, being linked to wider global circuits of capital (Storper 1997). Multinationals originating from outside the region – generally American and European firms – continue to organise production networks in East Asia that are linked to their globalised operations. Coe et al. (2004: 469) suggest that from the GPN perspective, MNEs look to establish a 'strategic coupling' between their global production networks and 'regional assets' (e.g. technological and human resource capabilities) and states work to develop these regional assets in order to attract IPN investment.

From another perspective, we can highlight three common features of IPN development that are distinctive to East Asia (Ando and Kimura 2003, Kimura and Ando 2004, 2005). First, they have become a key element in many East Asian countries' economic development. There is no other global region where this applies more so. As previously noted, many of East Asia's key industries (e.g. electronics, computers, automobiles, industrial machines) are organised along IPN lines. Second, East Asian IPNs tend to involve multiple countries. While relatively high degrees of IPN activity are apparent between Germany and neighbouring East European countries (Czech Republic, Hungary and Poland), and also between the United States and Mexico, such configurations network together only two or three contiguous countries. By contrast, East Asia's development asymmetry, and hence heterogeneity of country competitive advantages, broadens the scope for IPN divisions of labour. Third, East Asian IPNs can comprise sophisticated combinations of inter- and intra-firm networked relationships. They are thus qualitatively different to the horizontal business exchanges observed in Europe, or the more simple cross-border, intra-firm production sharing that is a defining feature of IPNs within North America.

Case Study 2.1 An IPN perspective on Thailand's automotive industry

Thailand is Southeast Asia's largest manufacturer of automobiles and East Asia's third largest exporter of cars, after Japan and South Korea. Its automotive industry is concentrated in the geographic centre of the country, more specifically the Bangkok Metropolitan Area, Samut

Prakarn province, and the eastern seaboard provinces of Chonburi and Rayong (see Figure 2.2). The Thai Government introduced a policy developing an industry cluster for auto components production from the early 1960s in this particular geographic zone. By initially focusing on component manufacturing rather than the 'national car' project approach (as adopted by Malaysia), Thailand was able to attract increasing amounts of foreign investment in the automotive sector based on offering supplier network capability and associated infrastructural provision. Japanese manufacturers have remained the dominant foreign investor presence from the beginning. Nissan established a production plant at Samut Prakarn in 1962, and Toyota in the same province at Samrong Nua in 1964[4], importing completely knocked down (CKD) kits of vehicle parts from Japan for reassembly. Honda Motors also first established a corporate presence (sales operations) in Thailand in 1964, motorcycle production from 1967 and car manufacturing from 1984. Mitsubishi, Isuzu, Mazda and Hino had also established operations in Thailand by the mid-1970s. There are now over 20 foreign automobile manufacturers operating in the area that also hosts over 1,700 auto-parts supplier firms of which around 700 are first-tier suppliers (more than double that for Malaysia and Indonesia, the next largest Southeast Asian automotive producers), and 40 per cent of these are foreign majority-owned (Noppach 2006). There are, for instance, over 100 Japanese auto parts makers operating in the country. Thailand's automotive industry is the country's second largest export sector. In 2006, Thailand exported around US$5 billion worth of auto parts, and also well over a third of the one million cars the country now produces annually.

In 1993, the Thai Board of Investment significantly enhanced its incentive measures programme to foreign investors in the automotive sector. In response, foreign investing firms expanded a range of operations in the supply chain, including raw materials handling, casting and moulding, pressed parts, and other components (Mori 2002). A few years later in 2000, the Thai Government eliminated its local content rules on automotive products. Previously, local content ratios had been gradually raised to between 60–70 per cent for one-ton pickup trucks and 54 per cent for passenger cars. The elimination of these rules gave greater scope for the Thai automotive sector's engagement in IPN activity, as there were now less restrictions on how firms internationally sourced materials and components. This was further helped by the government-funded programmes to expand infrastructural provision and investment incentive measures for the automotive industrial districts in the central and eastern seaboard areas (Doner et al. 2004).

It was noted earlier in this chapter that Japanese firms traditionally tended to exert more direct control over IPN activities within their core supplier network, i.e. vertically integrated *keiretsu*. Hence, Toyota, Nissan and other major assembly firms were followed by many of their

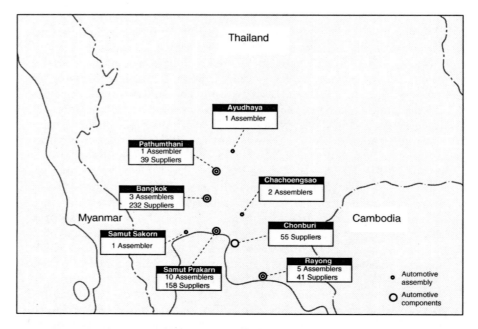

Figure 2.2 Thailand's automotive industry cluster
Source: Thai Automotive Institute.
Notes: Based on 2002 data. Suppliers relate to first-tier type.

first and second tier suppliers that set up plants in close proximity to their core firms. Lecler (2002) observed for example that by the late 1990s, although the bulk of Toyota Motors Thailand's local purchasing was sourced within the country, much of this came from Japanese supplier-firms clustered around Toyota's main assembly operations, and that another high share of sourcing derived from Japanese–Thai joint venture enterprises. Lecler (2002) also concluded that in Toyota's Thailand-based operations a relatively small proportion of inputs were by this time sourced from other Southeast Asian countries. Furthermore, high value-added inputs such as engines were generally imported from Toyota plants based in Japan. Mitsubishi Motors were also found to have pursued a similar procurement strategy with at least 60 per cent of inputs derived from within Thailand and a high percentage of this from Japanese supplier-firms. The pattern of sourcing and exchange outlined above would appear to have many attributes of *type I* internation production. In contrast, American and European automobile manufacturers based in Thailand (e.g. General Motors and BMW) have traditionally sourced more widely from suppliers outside the region (Coe et al. 2004), thus complying with *types II* and *IV* international production networks with GPN linkages.

However, since the early 2000s, Toyota and other Japanese automobile producers have developed more regionally dispersed and integrative production networks in East Asia. This is primarily owing to the increasing participation of China in the company's regional division of labour. Table 2.2 shows for example that from 2000 to 2006, Toyota Motor Corporation established eight new joint-venture enterprises in the country, covering both model assembly and components manufacturing operations, taking the total number of its plants in China to 11 (three components making plants had been established in 1998). The other new plant Toyota Motors established in Asia during the 2000–6 period was in India. These new plants, together with other substantial recent investments made by Toyota in its Asia-based production facilities have significantly extended the company's IPN operations in the region (Figure 2.3).

In 2002, Toyota launched its IMV (Innovative International Multi-purpose Vehicle) project in which a range of its pickup trucks and multi-purpose vehicles would be produced by a global manufacturing and supply system. Thailand was chosen as the location for by far the largest of Toyota's four IMV project assembly plants, others being Indonesia, Argentina and South Africa. The IMV scheme also involved a production network arrangement for major components (diesel engines in Thailand, gasoline engines in Indonesia, and manual transmissions in the Philippines and India), and their supply to the Thailand and other IMV assembly plant countries charged with vehicle production (Automotive World 2006).

More generally, as Figure 2.3 and Table 2.2 indicate, Thailand remains Toyota's prime base in Asia (outside Japan) for production operations, producing 416,300 vehicle units in 2005 from its two assembly plants there. In 2003, the country became the host of one of two new Toyota Technical Centres (TTCs) that operate in continental Asia, the other being at Tianjin, China. The TTCs conduct research and development on product design, testing and evaluation, and also distribute technology-related information through the company's international production networks. In addition, Thailand is party to recently signed, or soon to be signed free trade agreements with China, Japan and India.[5] These are expected to further spur Thailand's IPN linkages with these countries in this sector, thus moving more towards a *type IV* (regional production network) configuration.

In addition, there is evidence of other Japanese automobile producers extending the value-adding nature of their investments in Thailand. For example, Honda – which exported 70,000 vehicle units from Thailand in 2006 – announced its decision in December 2006 to transfer most of its regional production planning and purchasing operations for automobiles from Japan to Thailand.[6] By this time, Thailand had become Honda's hub centre for most of the company's key operations in the Asia-Pacific region, including research and development,

Table 2.2 Toyota's overseas production operations in Asia by 2006

Country	TMC affiliate company	Location	Operations established	Products	No. of employees	Vehicles produced (2005, 1,000 units)
Bangladesh	Aftab Automobiles	Dhaka	1982	Land Cruiser Prado, Hino bus	110	0.1
China	Tianjin Fengjin Auto Parts (TFAP)	Tianjin	1998	Continuous velocity joints, axles	350	–
	Tianjin FAW Toyota Engine (TFTE)	Tianjin	1998	Engines	800	133.8
	Tianjin Toyota Forging (TTFC)	Tianjin	1998	Forging parts	100	–
	Tianjin Toyota Press	Tianjin	2002	Stamping parts	260	–
	Tianjin Toyota Resin	Tianjin	2002	Plastic parts	190	
	Tianjin FAW Toyota Motor (TFTM)	Tianjin	2002	Corolla, Vios, Crown, Reiz	2,310	131.1
	FAW Toyota (Changchun) Engine (FTCE)	Changchun	2004	Engines	250	–
	Toyota FAW (Tianjin) Dies (TFTD)	Tianjin	2004	Stamping dies for vehicles	160	–
	Guangqi Toyota Engine (GTE)	Guangqi	2004	Engines, engine parts (cam shafts, crank shafts)	50	–
	Sichuan FAW Toyota Motor (SFTM)	Chengdu	2000	Coaster, Land Cruiser 100, Prado, Prius	1,800	13.4
	Guangzhou Toyota Motor (GTMC)	Guangzhou	2006	Camry	1,400	–
Taiwan	Kuozui Motors	Taipei	1986	Camry, Corolla, Hiace, Vios, Zace, Wish, Dyna, engines, stamping parts	2,486	139.7
India	Toyota Kirloskar Motor Private (TKM)	Banglaore	1999	Innova, Corolla	2,567	44.5
	Toyota Kirloskar Auto Parts Private (TKAP)	Banglaore	2002	Axles, propeller shafts, transmissions	742	–
Indonesia	PT. Toyota Motor Manufacturing Indonesia	Karawang, Jakarta	1970	Kijang Innova, Kijang P/U, engines	3,949	113.2 (cars) 232.8 (engines)
Malaysia	Assembly Services Sdn. Bhd (ASSB)	Shah Alam, Selangor	1968	Camry, Corolla, Vios, Hiace, Hilux, Innova, Fortuner, engines	3,232	54.5 (cars) 10.5 (engines)
Pakistan	Indus Motor Company	Karachi	1993	Corolla, Hilux, Cuore*[2]	1,651	28.5
Philippines	Toyota Autoparts Philippines (TAP)	Santa Cruz	1992	Transmissions, continuous velocity joints	578	220.7
	Toyota Motor Philippines (TMP)	Paranaque, Metro Manila	1989	Camry, Corolla, Innova	1,289	17.8
Thailand	Siam Toyota Manufacturing	Phanthong, Chonburi	1989	Engines, propeller shafts, casting (block, head)	1,219	403.8
	Toyota Auto Body Thailand	Samut Prakarn	1979	Stamping parts	141	–
	Toyota Motor Thailand (TMT)	Chachoengsao	1964	Camry, Corolla, Vios, Wish, Hilux Vigo, Yaris	6,172	366.9
	Thai Auto Work (TAW)	Samut Prakarn	1988	Fortuner, Hilux, VIGO	477	49.4
Vietnam	Toyota Motor Vietnam	Hanoi	1996	Camry, Corolla, Vios, Hiace, Land Cruiser, Innova	712	13.3

Source: Toyota Motor Corporation (www.toyota.co.jp/en/about_toyota/manufacturing/worldwide.html)

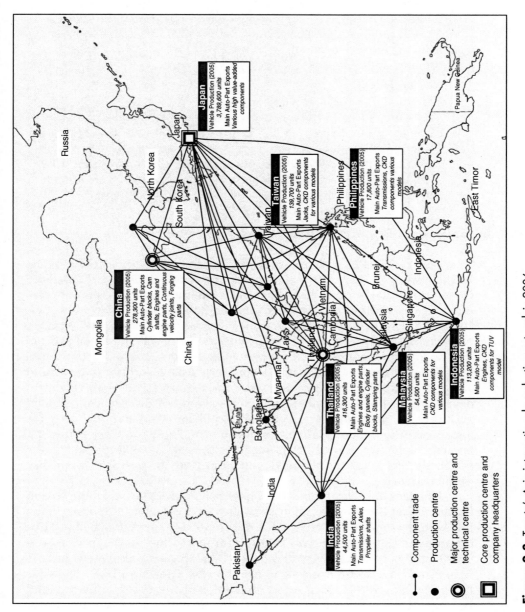

Figure 2.3 Toyota's Asia international production network in 2006

Source: Toyota company data.

Note: CKD stands for 'completely knocked down' kits of auto-part components.

new production engineering, and playing a lead role in improving Honda's quality, cost and delivery processes. In 1998, the company also opened its Asian Parts Centre, a state-of-the-art facility located on the outskirts of Bangkok that also plays a crucial role in the management of Honda's global parts supply network. This is a further example of the global production network dimension to Thailand's automotive industry.

Study Questions

1. How and why has the qualitative nature of Thailand's participation in automotive sector IPN activity changed over time?
2. Why has Toyota dispersed its IPN activities over so many East Asian countries? What different types of functional integrative linkages exist between the different nodes in this international production network?

2.4.4 Industry-specific perspectives

The nature of IPN configuration differs from industry to industry. In their study of East Asia's electronics and automotive parts industries, Doner et al. (2004) found that the former generally consisted of more cost efficient, specialised and broadly interdependent production networks. In contrast, the latter was organised more on a 'hub and spokes' basis consisting of relatively less efficient and more self-contained production arrangements in relatively protected national markets. Furthermore, inter-firm network relations in the automotive parts industry were found to be dominated by a few core firms that maintain relatively greater control over both technology transfers and devolvement of core value-added activities to associate firms, as has traditionally been the case for Japanese automobile producers operating in Thailand. Case Study 2.1 presents evidence, though, that suggests the region's automobile sector generally has recently changed and improved its position somewhat in these areas.

Changes in IPN configurations may occur quite slowly. A main reason for this is that locations (e.g. industrial districts or clusters, discussed in the following section) in the production chain are able to retain a competitive advantage over emerging rival locations for some time. McKendrick et al.'s (2000) study of how the hard disk drive (HDD) industry developed in East Asia provides a useful example to explain this. American HDD producer firms first moved their East Asian production operations to Singapore and Penang (Malaysia) in the 1980s. As the IPN activities in this sector spread, Singapore and Penang were able to retain a substantial degree of value-added production because their untraded interdependency advantages (e.g. skilled labour, technology and knowledge spillovers amongst firms, specialised and extensive infrastructure) remained important as HDD product engineering complexity increased. McKendrick et al. (2000) observed during the late 1990s with regard to Penang's HDD production capability that, 'no other location possessed the same depth of engineering resources to make them', and additionally that,

> Singapore also assumed a more explicit role in developing and managing the regional production network, functioning as a transfer station for the introduction of new products. Finally, the country began to diversify into new niches, including media, drive design, and other branches of data storage.
>
> (McKendrick et al. 2000: 165).

Singapore thus became the test bed of new HDD product manufacture before wider scale production was initiated at other plants in the region. The fundamental strength of Penang's position in this IPN value-chain lay in a broader computer industry cluster development in the location. Many large computer sector firms had moved operations to in and around Penang. These included Komag (wafer disk fabrication), Quantum (hard disc drives), Intel (microchip production and design) and Motorola (software), all of which had made significant new investments during the late 1990s and early 2000s, although Dell, AMD and Read-Rite relocated their Penang-based plants to China and other parts of Southeast Asia during this period (Ernst 2004, 2005). The broader relationship between IPNs and industrial districts such as Penang is discussed in our next section, and also in Case Study 2.2.

2.5 East Asia's regionalisation: zonal–network dimensions

2.5.1 Industrial districts and agglomerated zonal development

In examining the growth of IPNs, we focused on how East Asia's regionalisation had developed through the spread of international networked systems of business activity. This activity, however, is always locally situated because IPNs are ultimately founded on exploiting specialised local economic assets. These assets are often concentrated in *industrial districts*, such as Bangkok Metropolitan Area with regard to Thailand's automotive industry (Figure 2.2, Case Study 2.1). Industrial districts are based on a *cluster* or *agglomeration dynamic* where spatial concentrations of firms and their activities confer particular competitive advantages. Industrial district agglomeration may work for and against IPN fragmentation and development, depending on the nature of the IPN itself (Ando and Kimura 2003).

However, it is not just a matter of the centripetal forces of industrial district agglomeration being ranged against the centrifugal forces of IPN dispersion. Industrial districts can serve as the essential network nodes on which IPNs are geographically rooted. This represents the interface between the networked and zonal development aspects of East Asia's economic regionalisation. At a more general level, agglomeration is an important element of East Asia's new economic geography when considering how economic activity may be defined in *zonal terms*, for example, being concentrated in sub-national, urban-industrial zones, or cutting across national borders in a transnational manner, as we later discuss with regard to East Asia's sub-regional 'growth polygons'.

Various types of industrial districts exist. Some have deep historic roots that derive from a locality's craft traditions and accumulated skills, such as the silverware and kitchenware makers of Tsubame, Japan, and the cane furniture producers of Cebu, Philippines (World Bank 2003b, Yamawaki 2001). Some industrial districts may be based around the core operations of one or two large firms in a particular area (e.g. Toyota and Toyota City in Japan) that is defined by 'hub–spoke' or 'core–ring' networked relations amongst firms in the district. Others may arise from state-developed industrial parks or estates (e.g. Jurong Town Corporation in Singapore, Hsinchu Science Park in Taiwan, various special economic zones in China) that seek to link up domestic with foreign capital (Kim 2005, Kuchiki and Tsuji 2005). Smaller industrial districts tend to have very specific sectoral specialisation (e.g. biotechnology at the Biopolis estate in Singapore) while spatially larger districts are invariably host to a cluster of related and supporting industries, as previously noted with regard to the computer and electronics industry cluster around Penang in Malaysia; and another example being China's main automotive sector clusters located in Tianjin and Guangzhou (see Figure 2.3).

Most industrial districts are located in areas of significant urbanisation because they can draw upon high levels of human, infrastructural and technological resources. For example, a key factor behind the clustering of Japan's many high-tech industrial activities around the Tokyo area is that most of the country's prestigious universities and research institutes are located in the area, and have established strong links with high-tech firms. As the World Bank (2003b:236–7) more generally observed, 'Over time, Tokyo has accumulated a huge amount of intangible capital, including research and production skills; social capital, deriving from business associations and networks; and relationships among firms and service providers such as banks'. Other lower-tech examples of this urban-industrial clustering include Japan's garment and motorcycle industries concentrated around Hamamatsu, and Taiwan's machine tool industry that has traditionally been centred in Taichung City, and which has gradually moved out to the outer semi-suburban ring of Taichung district (Otsuka 2006, Sonobe et al. 2003, Sonobe and Otsuka 2006, Yamamura et al. 2003, 2005).

Case Study 2.2 The Taiwan–China axis in East Asia's computer industry

This case study highlights the importance of specific economic zones in the global production network of East Asia's computer industry, centred on the Taiwan–China axis. A simplified overview of the complex pattern of relationships that exist in this sector has been chosen to explain basic principles. Figure 2.4 shows how the network consists of different kinds of linkages between firms located in particular industrial districts and economic zones. The primary functional relationships in this network are essentially determined by the technological capacities located within these districts or zones themselves. American and Japanese companies such as Dell and Sony – from their respective home bases in Silicon Valley and the Tokyo–Nagoya–Osaka zone – have for some time operated sub-contracted arrangements with Taiwan's computer industry firms, who manufacture and also sometimes help design and develop the subcontractor's products on their behalf (Saxenian 1999). Thus, a Taiwanese company like Quanta will make Dell-branded laptop/notebook computers. This international subcontracting is conducted on a huge scale. In 2004, Dell sourced US$10 billion of products from Taiwanese firms and similarly Hewlett Packard a sum of US$21 billion.[7]

The core of Taiwan's computer industry is centred at Hsinchu Science Park (HSP), just south-west of Taipei and established in 1980 to primarily develop Taiwan's ICT production capacity.[8] Around 400 firms are located in the HSP with combined sales approaching US$30 billion annually. Some of the most important are Quanta (the world's number one laptop/notebook computer manufacturer), TSMC[9] (who operate the world's largest semiconductor factory at Hsinchu), Asustek (who make iPods for Apple), Acer (one of the world's top five computer brands by sales), and UMC[10] (operates the world's second largest semiconductor foundry, also at Hsinchu). The HSP is also host to a dense network of small–medium sized enterprises (SMEs) that specialise in niche production and new technology development. Both small and large firms based at Hsinchu are working at the cutting edge of ICT engineering and production. As a result, Hsinchu-based firms are working in closer research and development collaboration with their Silicon Valley based counterparts.

Together, Taiwanese firms account for substantial world shares of key ICT products, including around 80 per cent of laptop/notebook computers, 65 per cent of scanners, 60 per cent of monitors and 40 per cent of network interface cards. However, an increasing proportion of Taiwanese firm production now takes place in China's coastal provinces (Dent 2005a). China is now the world's second largest manufacturer of ICT products (after the United States) but an estimated

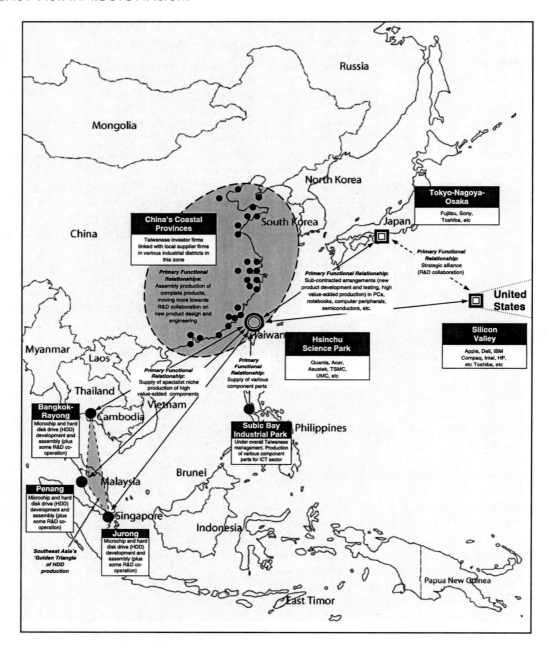

Figure 2.4 The Taiwan–China axis in East Asia's computer industry: international production network and industrial district perspectives (simplified)

40 to 80 per cent of the country's computer hardware goods are made in Taiwanese-owned factories.[11] A number of large-scale investments have been made in China, including TMSC's US$900 million 8-inch silicon wafer chip plant in Shanghai. Over recent years, Taiwan's laptop/notebook computer production has concentrated in the Yangtze River Delta area, incorporating Shanghai, Kunshan, Suzhou and Wujiang (Hu et al. 2005). In this economic zone there are a number of Taiwanese firms (Arima, Asustek, Clevo, Compal, Elite, FIC, Inventec, Mitac, Quanta and Wistron) making products under subcontract with Apple, Dell, Fujitsu-Siemens, Hewlett Packard, NEC, Sony, Toshiba and others. As China's techno-industrial capabilities have improved, so have local Chinese enterprises linked to Taiwanese firms been able to make contributions to new product design and engineering processes. There has thus been a significant evolution in the primary functional relationship in this part of the network.

Many Taiwanese firms have plants in Penang (Malaysia), Jurong (Singapore), Bangkok-Rayong (Thailand) and Subic Bay Industrial Park[12] (Philippines) that primarily act as production nodes in the IPN but also, as previously discussed in Penang and Singapore's case the HDD industry, as contributing to higher value-adding activities within the network. Indeed, by the mid-2000s, Singapore, Thailand (Bangkok-Rayong region) and Malaysia (Penang) formed the so called 'golden triangle' of HDD production in Southeast Asia, accounting for a large proportion of the industry total output (Bowen and Leinbach 2006, Hiratsuka 2006). These kinds of inter-cluster linkages make for more integrative IPNs (i.e. *type IV* international production) and deepening regionalisation generally in East Asia (Kuchiki 2006). In conclusion, we can thus observe from this case study that IPNs are often configured in a pattern of linked up industrial districts or broader economic zones across the region, which in turn entail changing and multiple division of labour relationships amongst firms in the production network.

Study Questions

1. To what extent are Taiwanese firms 'in command' of East Asia's computer industry IPN?
2. 'Taiwan may not be party to East Asia's main regional organisations or free trade agreements, but this does not matter because it is very much engaged in various regionalisation processes occurring within East Asia.' Discuss.

2.5.2 East Asia's world cities, regional infrastructure networks and regionalisation

Many if not most industrial districts do not have well defined spatial boundaries, and moreover dense economic activity may be concentrated in wider urban-industrial zones or conurbations, such as the Tokyo–Nagoya–Osaka in Japan, Taipei-Hsinchu in Taiwan, Seoul-Inchon in South Korea, Manila-Quezon City in the Philippines, and, in China, Beijing-Tianjin, Hong Kong-Guangzhou-Shenzhen (Pearl River Delta zone) and the Yangtze River Delta area (Scott 1998, Smith 2004). On the spatial scale between these conurbation zones and core city areas are metropolitan areas, such Metro Manila, Bangkok Metropolitan Area, Taipei-Keelung, Greater Tokyo Area, Shanghai Municipality Area, Seoul Capital Area, Jabotabek (centred on Jakarta, Indonesia) and Osaka-Kobe-Kyoto metropolitan area (Figure 2.5). Urban-industrial zonal growth has been a key feature of East Asia's dynamic economic development (Fujita 2007).

In addition to being the prime locational nodes of the region's international production networks (see Figure 2.4 and Case Study 2.2), the general commercial interaction amongst urban-industrial zones represents the majority proportion of intra-regional trade, investment, finance and other forms of economic exchange in East Asia. The region's larger and more powerful cities, or 'world cities' have played an important role in East Asia's regional economic integration (Taga 1994, Fujita et al. 1999). As Smith (2004:400) observed generally, such cities perform various co-ordinating and decision-making functions for 'geographically dispersed business networks of finance, manufacturing, retailing, and transport'. Sassen (1991) has also argued that global or world cities serve as the prime 'command and control centres' in the international economy, being the headquartered locations of large powerful firms and also the main infrastructural hubs of the region.

The region's 'world cities' have played an important role in East Asia's regionalisation generally, being also the main centres for international political, social and cultural exchange and interaction within the region. Taylor (2005) notes that the importance of a world city in the global or regional network of cities is broadly determined by two factors, the first being its 'network node' *size* as a measure of the city site, and the second being its importance in terms of *connectivity* as a measure of the city's situation within the network. A world city's network node size and connectivity levels can be judged in relation to specific economic, political, social and cultural activity criteria:

Economic
- Internationalised infrastructural network facilities and linkages
- Industrial district(s) positions in international production networks
- Host to main or regional headquarters of MNEs
- Stock exchange position in the international market
- International corporate services provision, e.g. finance and banking, media, architecture, engineering, accountancy, management consultancy, advertising, law

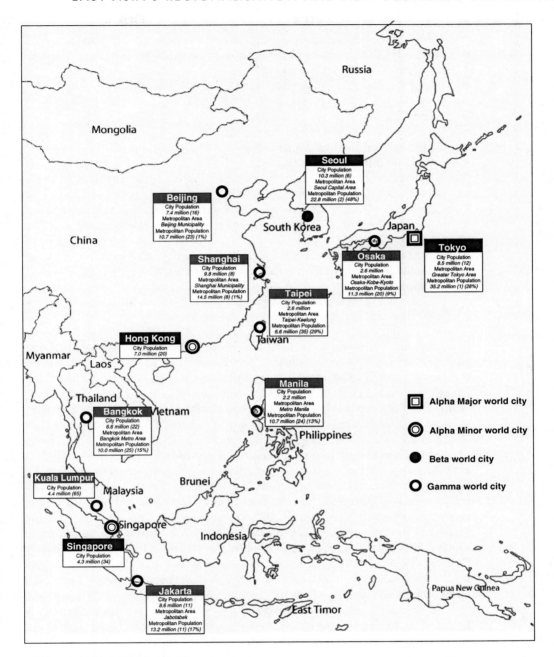

Figure 2.5 East Asia's world cities

Note: World city classifications based on Beaverstock et al. (1999). Figures based on 2005 data. Integer numbers in brackets relate to world rankings for city and metropolitan area populations. Percentage figures in brackets relate to metropolitan area's share of the country's population.

Political
- International organisation headquarters or offices, e.g. UN agencies, ADB
- Global NGO (e.g. humanitarian, environmental, labour) headquarters or offices
- Foreign missions and foreign ambassadorial community

Social and Cultural
- Expatriate/foreign worker community
- International student community
- Centre for international tourism
- Internationalised media and entertainment industries, e.g. newspapers, music, television, film
- Cultural institutions, facilities and events of international renown, e.g. galleries, theatre, museums, arts centres, international music and film festivals
- International sports facilities and community, and hosting of major international sports events, e.g. Asian Games, ASEAN Football Championship
- Significant institutions in the international community, e.g. universities, research institutes, hospitals, medical laboratories

Keeping in mind the general (i.e. network node size and connectivity) and specific (i.e. economic, political, social and cultural activity) criteria, we can classify world cities into certain status levels. Tokyo is the highest-level category of world city in East Asia, being an Alpha Major type, with Hong Kong and Singapore close behind in the Alpha Minor world city category (Figure 2.5). Seoul classifies as a Beta world city and a number of other East Asian cities (Bangkok, Beijing, Jakarta, Kuala Lumpur, Manila, Osaka, Shanghai, Taipei) have been classified as Gamma world cities (Beaverstock et al. 1999). In addition, East Asia's world city metropolitan areas account for large proportions of economic activity in the region. For example, the metropolitan areas of Bangkok, Manila, Seoul, and Taipei account for over 50 per cent of their respective national GDPs. In addition, the cluster of cities around Shanghai in the Yangtze River Delta zone, with a combined population of around 80 million, is thought to account for nearly 40 per cent of China's GDP. As Figure 2.5 also indicates, East Asia has some of the world's largest metropolitan area populations including the first (Greater Tokyo Area, 35.2 million in 2005) and second (Seoul Capital Area, 22.8 million in 2005) largest.

East Asia's regional infrastructure networks are also ultimately founded on various major cities throughout the region. It is through these city-based infrastructural 'hubs' that a great proportion of regionalised economic and social activity occurs in East Asia. As Figure 2.6 indicates, East Asia's cities rank as some of the world's most important transportation hubs. For example, the region has seven of the world's top 10 largest seaports by cargo traffic (Singapore and Shanghai ranked first and second, respectively) and all the world's top six seaports by container traffic

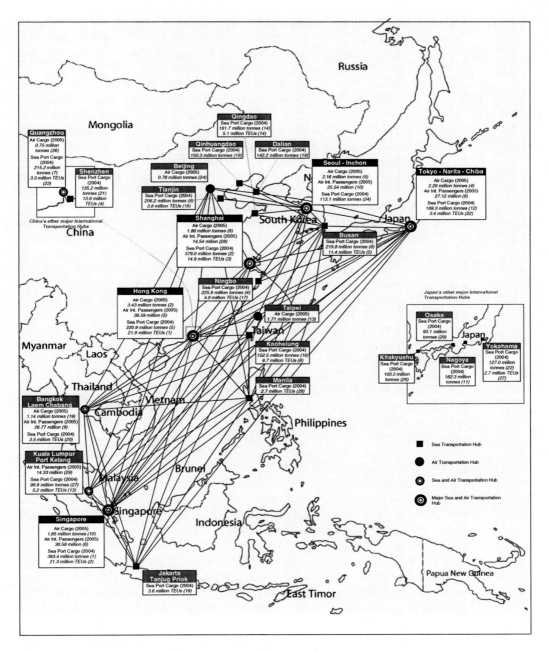

Figure 2.6 East Asia's main regional transportation hubs and corridors

Sources: Airports Council International, American Association of Port Authorities.

Notes: Numbers in brackets relate to world ranking for that transportation volume. Only those East Asian air and sea transportation hubs (i.e. airports and sea ports) that were ranked in to the world top 30 have been included. Port names have been included where these are not the same as the city hub to which they are linked, e.g. Kuala Lumpur and Port Kelang. TEUs (twenty-foot equivalent units) relate to container capacity.

(Hong Kong, Singapore, Shanghai, Shenzhen, Busan and Kaohsiung in respective order). In air transportation, East Asia has five of the world's top 10 both in air cargo traffic (Hong Kong second, Narita-Tokyo fourth and Inchon-Seoul fifth) and on international passenger traffic (Hong Kong fifth, Singapore sixth, Narita-Tokyo eighth, Bangkok ninth and Inchon-Seoul tenth). These high rankings are testament to both intensifying regionalised activity in East Asia and the region's increasingly important position within the global economy. It is interesting to note that China alone has eight of the world's top 20 largest seaports by cargo traffic, which is indicative of its rising prominence in East Asia's regional and global trade.

Recent attempts to advance the development of the Trans-Asian Railway (TAR) network should also be noted. This project, overseen by the United Nations Economic and Social Commission for Asia and the Pacific (UNESCAP) since the 1960s, took a significant step forward in November 2006 when Asian Ministers of Transport signed the 'International Agreement on Trans-Asian Railway Network' in Busan, South Korea. The Agreement committed TAR countries to further develop a more regionally integrated rail network through enhancing network capacity and improve cross-border inter-linkages (see Figure 2.7).[13] The latter is a particular problem in Southeast Asia, mainly because of the different track gauges used by countries in the sub-region. Ambitious plans exist to link up archipelago countries such as Indonesia and Japan to the East Asian landmass by tunnel and bridge building schemes. For example, establishing a link between the Korean peninsula and Japan has been discussed since the 1930s.

Meanwhile, South Korea has been trying to negotiate with North Korea the building of a railway link across their Demilitarised Zone border that would link the South to the TAR network. More interior-located cities and provinces have particularly supported the development of the network, mainly because, as we have seen, much of East Asia's dynamic economic development has occurred in the region's coastal areas. By strengthening the links between the 'dry ports' of interior-located cities and their coastal-located counterparts, the TAR network could help extend the region's development dynamic into hitherto peripheral economic zones. A UNESCAP Asian Highway Network Agreement also came into force in July 2005. Developing more integrated and inter-modal transportation networks across East Asia will be important facilitators of regionalised activity.

Similar developments in the region's communication network infrastructure will have the same effects. Figures 2.8a and 2.8b illustrate the significant intensification of voice telecommunications traffic flows within East Asia over the 2000 to 2005 period. As the figures show, there has been a notable increase in flows reaching above the 100 million minutes threshold between various sets of East Asian countries within these few years, this being indicative of the intensification of communications within the region generally. Furthermore, according to analyst firm Telegeography, East Asia's telecommunications traffic has also recently intensified more in intra-regional terms relative to its extra-regional traffic.[14] Again, East Asia's main 'world'

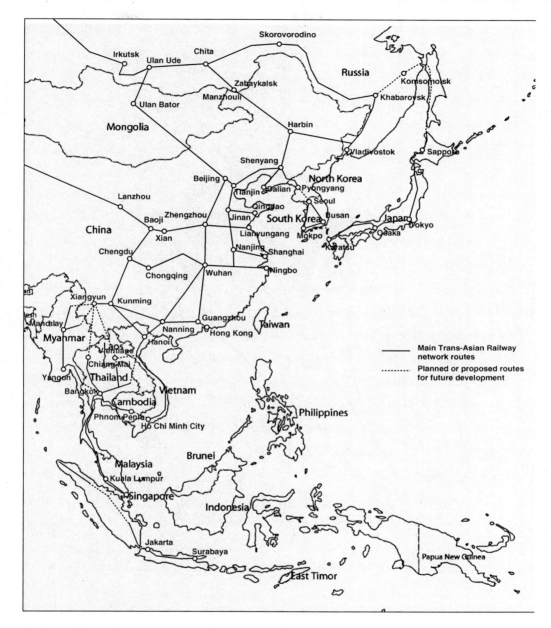

Figure 2.7 Trans-Asian Railway network (East Asia section)

Sources: Based on Schiller Institute, 'Maps of Great Infrastructure Development Projects Around the World' (www.schillerinstitute.org/economy/maps/maps.html), United Nations Economic and Social Commission for Asia and the Pacific, 'Regional Commissions Development Update – 20th Edition' (http://www.un.org/Depts/rcnyo/newsletter/NL20/asian%20railway%20ESCAP.bmp)

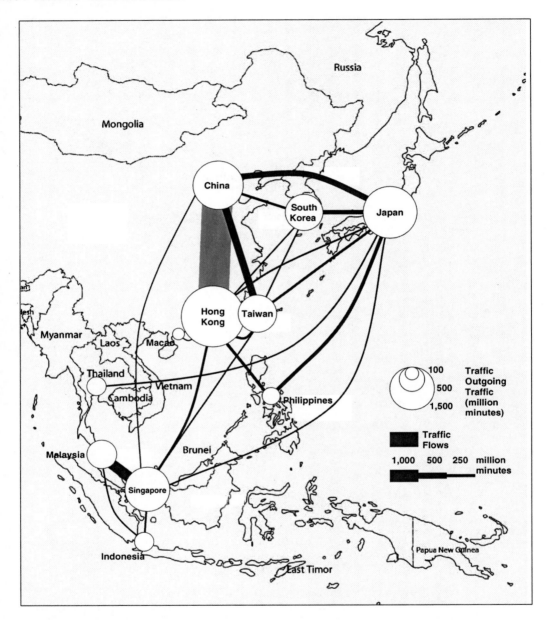

Figure 2.8a Voice telecommunications traffic flows within East Asia (minimum 100 million minutes, 2000)

Source: Based on data provided by Telegeography (http://www.telegeography.com) with kind permission.
Notes: All data is based on millions of minutes of telecommunications traffic for the public telephone network. Traffic flow routes shown are for those with more than 100 million minutes reported by public telephone network operators.

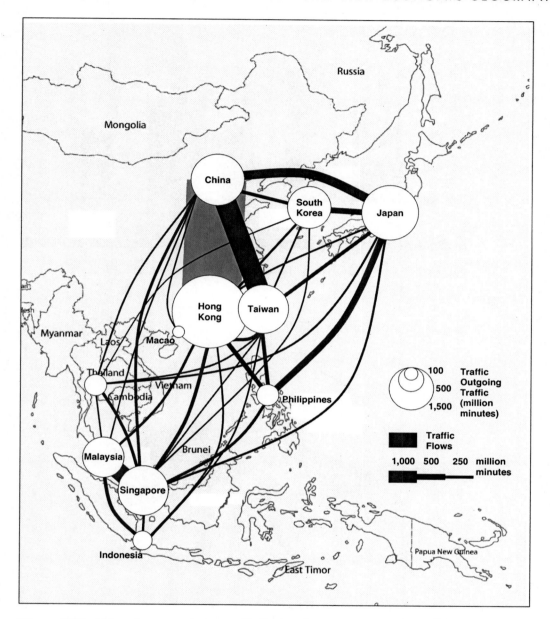

Figure 2.8b Voice telecommunications traffic flows within East Asia (minimum 100 million minutes, 2005)

Source: Based on data provided by Telegeography (http://www.telegeography.com) with kind permission.

Notes: All data is based on millions of minutes of telecommunications traffic for the public telephone network. Traffic flow routes shown are for those with more than 100 million minutes reported by public telephone network operators.

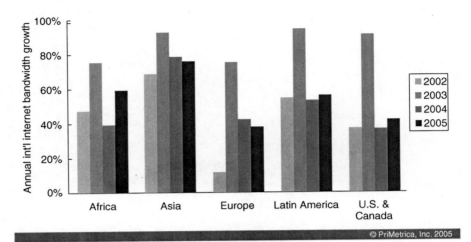

Figure 2.9 International internet bandwidth growth by region, 2002–5
Source: Telegeography

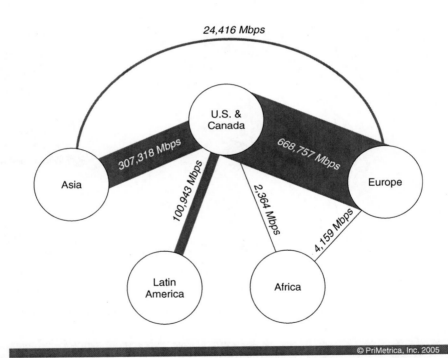

Figure 2.10 Inter-regional internet bandwidth, 2005
Source: Telegeography
Notes: Mbps stands for megabits per second.

cities serve as the principal hub centres for this regional infrastructure network. Figure 2.9 also shows that Asia recorded the highest sustained rates of internet bandwidth growth for any region over the 2002–5 period, from which we can imply further evidence of advancing regionalised connectivity within East Asia. In addition, Figure 2.10 indicates that East Asia has strong inter-regional internet bandwidth links with North America, thus suggesting comparatively high levels of communications flows across the Asia-Pacific trans-region.

In conclusion, the networked links woven over time amongst cities, industrial districts and other forms of economic zones are thus a prime foundation of East Asia's regionalisation, and these links may also be constituent elements of international production networks themselves (Ando and Kimura 2003, Fujita 2007, Sturgeon 2001). We have thus seen how there are important zonal–network connections to consider when studying the development and nature of East Asia's regionalisation.

2.5.3 Growth polygon zones in East Asia

2.5.3.a What are 'growth polygons'?

Another important zonal dimension to East Asia's new economic geography and regionalisation concerns the various 'growth polygons' that have emerged across the region over the last two or three decades (Thant et al. 1995). There are in essence sub-regional economic zones that encompass concentrations of transborder economic relationships and activities, and are hence closely associated with *type III* configurations of international production (Figure 2.1), although they may span a sub-regional group of countries and not just two. In many cases, growth polygons may be considered as, or closely associated with sub-regional production networks. Many are founded on transnationalised production chains within a sub-regional locale that exploit the specific comparative advantages of each participating economic zone. The advance of economic liberalisation – which has broken down international barriers to trade, investment and finance – has assisted this integrative process.

In recognising the emergence of growth polygons, many governments in East Asia have undertaken measures to further assist their development, for example through infrastructure investments (e.g. the construction of new transport links, energy generation provision and communication hubs and networks) and general policy co-operation to manage the economic interdependence between their countries where sub-regional integration is apparent. Many growth polygons are also supported by international agencies such as the ADB. In some cases, they may be considered more as constructs of inter-state development policy rather than dense geographic concentrations of transnationalised business activity. The ADB-sponsored Greater Mekong Sub-region (GMS) is a good example of this (Than 1997).

In general, growth polygons involve contiguous or neighbouring economic zones from different nation-states participating in a symbiotic development relationship. Sometimes they engage whole countries in combination with sub-national territories, as applies in the GMS project. The role of each zone or country will depend upon their comparative level of development, access to factor resources, position in international production networks, and so on. East Asia is host to the world's highest concentration of growth polygon activity. Similar to international production networks, the transborder nature of growth polygons leads us to question the notion that the East Asian regional economy consists simply of a series of unitary nation-state components.

As we have already examined in the preceding analysis on IPNs, particular districts and zones of the East Asian economy are often more integratively linked with districts and zones from other countries than with those inside the same country. The same principle applies to growth triangles that, like IPNs, have created new integrative economic spaces and constitute an important layer to East Asia's regionalisation. Figure 2.11 illustrates where the region's main growth polygons are located. Their constituent geographic elements and other details are as follows:

- *Indonesia–Malaysia–Singapore Growth Triangle (IMSGT)*: linking Singapore to Indonesia's Riau province and Malaysia's Johor province.
- *Greater Mekong Sub-region (GMS)*: Burma (or Myanmar), Cambodia, China (Yunnan Province), Laos, Thailand and Vietnam. Sponsored by the ADB.
- *Brunei–Indonesia–Malaysia–Philippines East ASEAN Growth Area (BIMP–EAGA)*: involving Brunei Darussalam, and Indonesia (Kalimantan, Sulawesi, Maluku and Irian Jaya), Malaysia (Sabah, Sarawak and Labuan), and the Philippines (Mindanao and Palawan). Sponsored by the ADB.
- *Tumen River Area Development Programme (TRADP)*: involving North Korea's Economic and Trade Zones (Kaesong, Rajin-Sonbong), Eastern Mongolia, China's Yanbian Korean Autonomous Prefecture (Jilin Province), the Russian Far East's Primorsky Territory and South Korea.
- *Yellow Sea Rim Sub-region*: coastal Northeast China, South Korea, and southern Japan. Overlaps geographically with the TRADP but based more on a natural density of international business interactions than any joint policy initiative.
- *South China Sea Growth Triangle (SCSGT)*: Chinese business community linkages between southeast coastal China, Taiwan and Hong Kong. The Taiwan–China axis in East Asia's computer industry (Case Study 2.2) is embedded within this growth polygon.
- *Indonesia–Malaysia–Thailand Growth Triangle (IMTGT)*: established in 1993 and centred on the Straits of Malacca zone. This has expanded from an original 10 participating provinces to 25: Indonesia (North Sumatra, Aceh, West Sumatra, South Sumatra, Riau, Bangka Belitung, Jambi and Bengkulu), Thailand (Satun, Songkhla, Patani, Yala, Trang, Phatthalung, Nakhon Si Thammarat and Narathiwat) and Malaysia (Selangor, Penang, Kedah, Perlis, Perak, Melaka, Negri Sembilan and Kelantan). Sponsored by the ADB.

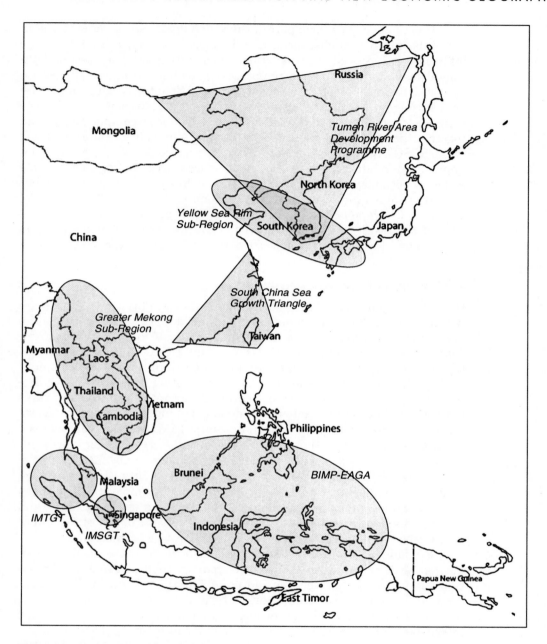

Figure 2.11 East Asia's growth polygon zones

Notes:
BIMP-EAGA: Brunei–Indonesia–Malaysia–Philippines East ASEAN Growth Area
IMSGT: Indonesia–Malaysia–Singapore Growth Triangle
IMTGT: Indonesia–Malaysia–Thailand Growth Triangle.

Growth polygons form part of the *new regionalism* paradigm, and in particular how regionalist forms and linkages may evolve through a more informal, business-led or transnational basis rather than just technocratically-driven, nation-state centred processes, as has been generally associated with European models of regionalism (see Chapter 1). There may even be a strong socio-cultural aspect to this sub-regionalism, such as the Chinese *guanxi* (i.e. social connections) links that commercially bind together the economies of south-east coastal China, Taiwan and Hong Kong in the SCSGT (Chen and Ho 1995). To restate an earlier point, this does not imply a redundant role for government policy or regional economic diplomacy, as both may play an instrumental role in sub-regional development projects (Chen 1995, Rocamora 1994, Thambipillai 1998, Turner 1995). Thus, the development of some growth polygons may be more 'governed' – such as the GMS, IMSGT and TRADP – while the development of others may be almost completely business-led or 'natural', e.g. the SCSGT.

2.5.3.b Types of growth polygons

Growth polygons can be categorised into three broad types in accordance with the particular evolutionary path of their development (Marton et al. 1995, Rimmer 1994, Tan et al. 1995). First, *transborder metropolitan spillovers* centre on an urban growth pole (industrial cities, industrial districts, or city-states like Singapore and Hong Kong) whose development 'spills over' into neighbouring territories from other countries, thus creating a transnational economic space around its core. There are thus links here with the agglomeration growth dynamic of industrial districts. As we examine in more detail, the Singapore-centred IMSGT represents a good example of this type. In such growth polygons, the cross-border movement of capital is driven primarily by economic complementary factors. In the case of the IMSGT, relatively low-tech and labour-intensive production activities in Singapore are gradually relocated to the comparatively low-cost neighbouring economies of Malaysia's Johor Province to the north and Indonesia's Riau province to the south and west of the city-state. There tends to be a strong export-orientation to this growth polygon type.

Second, *joint natural resource-based or infrastructure-based development projects* are concerned with the co-management of a shared transnational resource like a river, the GMS and TRADP being prime examples. This entails developing frameworks of sub-regional diplomacy between involved local and national governments to manage transborder economic interdependence issues, as well as minimise disputes arising from economic activities derived from the common resource or resources concerned. For example, if the Yunnan provincial government in China decides to construct a hydro-electric dam upstream on the Mekong River, how will the electricity generated serve the wider sub-region? Furthermore, what economic and environmental impacts will the dam have for those downstream in other GMS partners? Infrastructure-based growth polygons may develop around a transnational resource like a river (e.g. making more sections of it navigable) or be simply concerned with improving international infrastructural links within a sub-regional locale. The BIMP-EAGA project may be viewed primarily in these terms.

Third, *outgrowth of internationalising, inter-firm networks* type growth polygons most closely corresponds to a sub-regional production network as discussed earlier. At their core are clusters of export-oriented firms within a particular sub-regional locale with generally wide sectoral coverage. These networks are generally founded on cross-border kinship or sociocultural ties, and Chinese *guanxi* connections tend to be especially relevant here. The SCSGT – incorporating southeast coastal China, Hong Kong and Taiwan – is a prime example of this growth polygon type. The concentration of sub-regional commercial activities based on such international inter-firm networks forges a transnational economic space between the constituent economies. The dense pattern of commercial activities between Taiwan and south-eastern coastal China is an important centre of economic gravity in the East Asian regional economy. As with IPNs, each growth polygon may not fall neatly into one of the types above but rather exhibit characteristics from different types.

Case Study 2.3 The Indonesia–Malaysia–Singapore growth triangle (IMSGT)

The IMSGT is arguably East Asia's most developed and formalised growth polygon. It was established by a Singapore Government policy initiative in the late 1980s to assist the techno-industrial restructuring of the city-state's economy (Grundy-Warr et al. 1999, Low 1996, Perry 1991). Singapore is an island territory at the southern end of the Malay Peninsula. Maintaining its position as one of Asia's most advanced regional export production platforms remains a prime developmental objective of the Singapore government. As the economy has moved up the techno-industrial ladder so relatively lower-tech, labour-intensive production (e.g. textiles, basic electronics) has had to make way for higher-tech productive activities (e.g. biotechnology) in the various industrial estates spread across the city-state. This did not necessarily require a MNE's whole operations to be displaced, rather just the lower-tech production processes, i.e. certain fragments of an IPN. The aim of the IMSGT was to relocate these production processes just offshore, to either the Johor province of Malaysia to the north and to the Riau province of Indonesia to the south and west of Singapore (see Figure 2.11). This was a strategy for retaining high value-added MNE investment and productive activities in Singapore rather than the MNE relocating their entire operations to some other East Asian location, such as China.

Malaysia and Indonesia also benefit from the IMSGT arrangement in terms of increased flows of the gradually higher-tech investment being displaced in Singapore. Both Johor and Riau's economic development has improved quite significantly as a consequence. As part of the IMSGT, industrial estates were jointly established by the Singapore Economic Development Board and Indonesian authorities on the Riau Islands of Batam (in 1991) and Bintan (in 1992) to attract 'spill-over' investment from Singapore. Joint infrastructure development projects both here and between Singapore and Johor assisted the parallel development of transnational production and distribution links being forged by MNEs operating in the IMSGT area. Riau and Johor continue to provide a source of low-cost labour and resources, and Singapore continues to act as the core of this transborder sub-regionalised economy.

Whilst the IMSGT may appear to be mainly policy-led, the sub-regional locale is a historic area of international trade that can be traced back to the third century Srivijaya trading empire through to Britain establishing Singapore as a colonial trading post from the early nineteenth century onwards (Dent 2002, Dosch 2003). Hence, the IMSGT could be said to have long-standing commercial foundations. In more recent years, however, it has experienced various problems. The momentum of the IMSGT has gradually slowed since the late 1990s. This could be partly attributed to the extension of the Singapore Government's foreign industrial park policy into the wider Southeast and East Asia region (e.g. with industrial parks set up in China and Vietnam) as part of its 'Regionalisation 2000' strategy, first launched in 1995 (Yeoh and Willis 1997). Many Singapore-based companies have not been lured by the economic advantages and incentives that accompany relocation in Johor and Riau. Other low costs locations, such as China, are proving increasingly more attractive in comparison. In addition, there remain long-standing disputes between Singapore and Malaysia over resource and infrastructure issues, for example concerning the terms and conditions of extending Malaysia's freshwater supply contract with Singapore. The contract runs out in 2061 but Singapore wants to renew this up to 2161. Johor is the providing source of this freshwater, whose own future IMSGT-based economic development will require increasing amounts of this natural resource – an interesting environmental IPE aspect of sub-regionalism that may be applied also to the GMS and TRADP arrangements. Malaysia's plans to develop Johor's Port Klang facilities as a rival trading hub to Singapore is another contentious issue in their bilateral relations. Lastly this 'growth triangle' is actually more bipedal than triangular in nature owing to the still underdeveloped economic linkages between Johor and Riau.

There were signs, however, in 2006 that the IMSGT could be given new impetus from plans to extend the geographic scope of the growth polygon northwards to include the Malaysian peninsula states of

Negeri Sembilan, Melaka and Pahang, and also south and westwards to embrace West Sumatra, South Sumatra, Bengkulu, Jambi, Lampung and West Kalimantan in Indonesia.[15] If realised, the plan would provide a further demonstration of the dynamic and fluid nature of sub-regionalism's development.

Study Questions

1. Why was Singapore the principal instigator of the IMSGT project?
2. To what extent are growth polygon projects like the IMSGT making contributions to the development of East Asian regionalism?

2.5.4 East Asia's pan-regional development corridor

At the highest end of the geo-spatial scale of the zonal dimension of regionalisation are pan-regional 'development corridors'. These generally comprise the densest concentration of infrastructure development, high-tech industry districts, and high-income markets within a macro-region like East Asia. They thus represent the main spine or 'growth axis' of a region's economic development, and generally where regionalised linkages are also the strongest. They can define also where a macro-region's prime core and periphery zones are situated, and thereby we are able to establish over time the broad patterns of regional development convergence and divergence within the macro-region. The geographic range of East Asia's development corridor broadly stretches from Japan down through the southern Korean peninsula, along coastal China, taking in Taiwan, and eventually reaching across from Bangkok to Jakarta at the bottom of the corridor zone (see Figure 2.12). The patterns of East Asia's regional infrastructure network development, as well as typical examples of international production network activity mapped in Figures 2.3 to 2.8b, are in broad terms spatially consistent with the pan-regional development corridor zone illustrated in Figure 2.12, and most of East Asia's 'world cities' are also located within this zone (Figure 2.5). Furthermore, East Asia's main development corridor has emerged out of the deep historic processes of regionalisation noted earlier in the chapter. It is no coincidence that this pan-regional zone takes in many of the region's ancient trading posts located in Japan, coastal China and Southeast Asia.

2.6 Conclusion

2.6.1 Summary overview

This chapter has examined the evolutionary development of East Asia's regionalisation in an economic geography context. As stated in Chapter 1,

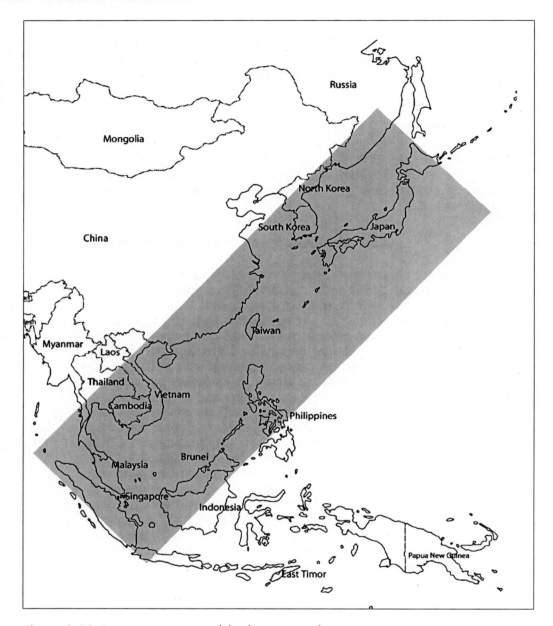

Figure 2.12 East Asia's pan-regional development corridor

regionalisation is concerned with regional concentrations of inter-connecting private or civil sector activities arising at the micro-level. We began with an historic overview of the development of East Asia's regional trade systems, and then looked at more recent developments in its intra-regional trade trends. It was observed that regional economic interdependence in East Asia has moved increasingly beyond deepening intra-regional trade to a situation where micro-level economic relations in the region have become more *functionally integrative*. This related to the expanding development of regional business systems and operations primarily through the growth of IPNs in East Asia. We studied the nature and different types of IPNs, the reasons why IPN activity in East Asia has intensified, and the facilitative role played by regional infrastructure network development. Although the extent of IPN activity may be confined to a relatively small number of industries (e.g. electronics, automobiles, industrial machinery, information and communication technology products, textiles) these account for a large majority share of East Asia's intra-regional trade. This trade is hence organised in an increasingly integrated manner through both deepening and ever more sophisticated IPN developments.

We also explored how growing networked linkages between trade, production and investment should be understood in relation to certain zonal dimensions of East Asia's regionalisation. We saw how nodes of IPN activity tend to be situated in the region's main industrial districts and urban-industrial zones, where much of East Asia's most advanced economic activity is concentrated. In addition to examining the contribution that industrial districts and major city zones make to East Asia's regionalisation, we also examined the emergence of sub-regional 'growth polygons'. Finally, it was noted that a pan-regional 'development corridor' zone could be observed on the broadest geo-spatial scale, this being the prime axis of East Asia's regional economic development. In sum, we have seen how the East Asian regional economy is not 'bloc-like' but rather based on a patchwork of developed economic zones that are inter-linked through IPNs and other forms of networking.

2.6.2 International Political Economy (IPE) theoretical analysis

In one sense, the study of regionalisation would seem to challenge the core assumption of *neo-realist* theory that nation-states are the primary unit of analysis in IPE. The spread of international production networks across East Asia reflects how business in the region is being increasingly conducted on a transnational scale, cutting across country borders and therefore integrating different elements of East Asia's national economies more closely together. Furthermore, the emergence of growth polygons and other forms of sub-regional economic zones compels us to think further about East Asia's economy and economic development in spatial terms other than that of the region simply comprising a series of national economic 'boxes'. And yet the nation-state or the state remains relevant in the analysis of regionalisation for a number of reasons. First, there is the counterpoint that East

Asia's regionalisation has only advanced so far to date. National economic coherence remains strong in East Asia, as reflected in the still high number of studies on 'national economies' (e.g. the Chinese economy, the South Korean economy, etc). Second, IPN development remains constricted by the various regulations and barriers imposed by national governments on international trade and foreign investment. For example, rules of origin regimes and high tariffs levied on certain imported component products are intended to compel the foreign investor firms to source locally within the host nation-state. Third, the neo-realist axiom that nation-states are competitive power maximisers is relevant with regard to how East Asian countries are actively competing with each other to attract IPN investments by foreign firms. For example, Case Study 3.2 in Chapter 3 (see p. 99) details how the Thai and Philippine governments have recently been using tax policy measures to induce higher levels of assembly production investment in the automobile sector. Most East Asian governments have also implemented 'industrial cluster' policies in order to attract foreign IPN-related investments into the country's industrial district zones. Further evidence of the state's active role in East Asia's regionalisation can be seen in its involvement in developing certain growth polygon projects and also nurturing the nation's major cities as logistical 'hubs' in which firms can base their regional operations.

The *neo-liberal* theoretical perspective on East Asia's regionalisation would, however, stress the primacy of private organisations (i.e. firms, business) rather than states regarding the subjects covered in this chapter. It is firms that trade with each other rather than nation-states as such. The rise of IPNs in particular – which is closely connected with the growing power of MNEs in the region – is indicative of the wider trend of how non-state actors have become increasingly important in East Asia's regional political economy. Furthermore, IPN activities and growth polygon developments are constituent to the broader complex interdependence trend in East Asia, forging closer transnationalised linkages amongst different actor groups and agencies within the region. According also to the neo-liberal view, where governments are actually reducing trade and investment barriers to attract IPN investments, this is leading to a retreat of state power and influence in economic management, and hence a further shift from states to markets. At the same time, *neo-liberal institutionalists* would argue that deepening economic interdependence caused by East Asia's regionalisation has led to closer international or inter-state co-operation on matters of regional trade, production and investment, as demonstrated in the various projects initiated by East Asia-related regional organisations. The chapters that follow explore the evidence of this in some detail.

The relevance of *social constructivism* to the subject matter of this chapter mainly concerns how regionalisation is helping to forge a stronger sense of regional community and regional identity-formation in East Asia. In addition to other transnationalised linkages that are studied in Chapter 7 (e.g. international migration), the development of regionalised business systems (e.g. through IPNs) and new transborder economic spaces (e.g. through growth polygons) have created new associative connections amongst agency groups within the region. For example, personnel working in an IPN-related firm form part not just of that firm's workforce but also that of the whole international production network. They hence may consider themselves as being part of a region-wide organisation or association, depending on their knowledge level of the firm's operations and their predilection to think in such terms. Likewise, growth polygons may help create a sense of sub-regional community amongst the protagonist actors and agencies involved, be they from the public or private sector. This, for instance, has been an objective of the Great Mekong Sub-region project, in which the sponsoring Asian Development Bank and involved government authorities have promoted the idea of a Mekong basin community. Moreover, we could even say that certain growth polygon zones are socially constructed themselves, the most obvious of these being the socio-cultural ties that underpin the South China Sea Growth Triangle that encompasses Taiwan and various coastal China cities and provinces.

Finally, *Marxist* and *structuralist* viewpoints would highlight how our study of East Asian regionalisation simply reveals the growing prominence of transnational capitalism in the world system generally. According to this view, IPNs are simply exercises in the so called new international division of labour, whereby MNEs are exploiting their positions of market power in their bargaining with governments and workforces to extract as much surplus value from labour as possible. The still well defined hierarchy of core–semi-periphery–periphery divisions within the East Asian regional economy provides great scope for this exploitation, as it allows MNEs to extensively fragment their international production networks and play off workforces against each other in order to secure the best deal for the firm in terms of minimised labour costs and maximised profits. Industrial districts and urban-industrial zones generally also play their role as key nodes in East Asia's regional circuits of capital presided over by commanding multinational enterprises. Thus, *Marxism-structuralism* asserts that East Asia's regionalisation may be essentially understood as the prevailing regional structures of production, technology, finance and other forms of economic activity that are primarily determined by transnational capital. In the next chapter, we examine the development of regionalism in Southeast Asia and its principal regional organisation, the Association of Southeast Asian Nations.

Chapter Study Questions

1. To what extent are there deep historic origins to contemporary patterns of regionalisation in East Asia?
2. Account for the rise of international production networks (IPNs) in East Asia. How are they contributing to East Asia's regional integration?
3. How may we analyse East Asia's regionalisation from perspectives of network development and expansion?

4. 'East Asia's regionalisation is essentially a city-based phenomenon.' Discuss
5. Why might we think of growth polygons as being good examples of zonal regionalisation in East Asia?

Notes

1   By 1900, Japan's trade with East Asia accounted for around half the country's total trade.
2   Harmonised System of Tariffs.
3   Japan's foreign aid programme towards East Asia certainly augmented the country's growing commercial ties with East Asian countries to a significant degree. The programme was initially based on war reparation payments from the 1950s onwards but these were of a 'tied' aid nature, thus ultimately aimed to benefit Japanese commerce. As Miyashita (1999: 699) contended, the reparation payments were 'designed primarily to help rebuild Japan's industrial capacity and re-establish economic ties with its wartime "co-prosperity sphere" in Asia', while Katada (2002a: 335) noted on the subject that an important objective of Japan's aid was to 'solidify the hierarchy of the regional production network'.
4   This was later relocated to Chachoengsao in 1997.
5   On a country bilateral or ASEAN group-level (see Chapter 6).
6   *Bangkok Post*, 20.12.2006.
7   *Business Week*, 16.05.2005.
8   Another science-based industrial park was developed at Tainan during the late 1990s, and a third was later developed at Taichung by the mid-2000s. These parks were established by two Taiwan government agencies, the National Science Council and the Industrial Technology Research Institute (ITRI).
9   Taiwan Semiconductor Manufacturing Company.
10   United Microelectronics Corporation.
11   *Business Week*, 16.05.2005.
12   This is actually managed by the Taiwanese-owned Subic Bay Development and Management Corporation, which set up the industrial park in collaboration with Philippines government authorities in 1994. A number of large Taiwanese firms, such as Wistron, are based here.
13   The member countries of TAR Network are Armenia, Azerbaijan, Bangladesh, Cambodia, China, Democratic People's Republic of Korea, Georgia, India, Indonesia, Islamic Republic of Iran, Kazakhstan, Kyrgyzstan, Lao People's Democratic Republic, Malaysia, Mongolia, Myanmar, Nepal, Pakistan, Republic of Korea, Russian Federation, Singapore, Sri Lanka, Tajikistan, Thailand, Turkey, Turkmenistan, Uzbekistan, and Vietnam.
14   Research interview with Telegeography representative, March 2007.
15   *Bernama News*, 04.11.2006.

Chapter 3

ASEAN
and Southeast Asia

3.1 Southeast Asia: an introduction

Southeast Asia is a highly diverse region. It is host to some of the world's poorest countries (e.g. Myanmar, Laos), one of its richest (Singapore) and also a spate of other newly industrialising economies such as Thailand, Malaysia and the Philippines. A broad spectrum of government systems and regimes define Southeast Asia's political landscape, comprising young democracies, socialist-communist states, military juntas and an absolute monarchy. A broad mix of Confucian, Buddhist, Muslim and Christian socio-religious or socio-cultural traditions also span the region (see Table 1.1, Chapter 1). The region consists of 11 nations, namely Brunei, Cambodia, East Timor, Indonesia, Laos, Malaysia, Myanmar, Philippines, Singapore, Thailand and Vietnam, all of which, except East Timor, are members of ASEAN, East Asia's longest established regional organisation.

There are some notable differences between Southeast Asia and its Northeast Asian counterpart region. First, whereas Northeast Asia comprises some of the world's most ancient nations, Southeast Asia is composed of *comparatively young nation-states*. With the exception of Thailand, all of Southeast Asia was at one point colonised by Western powers: Myanmar, Malaysia, Singapore and Brunei by Britain; Vietnam, Laos and Cambodia by France; Indonesia by the Netherlands; the Philippines by Spain and then the United States. Independence came to some by the late 1940s (Indonesia, the Philippines, Myanmar) and to most others by the 1950s (Cambodia, Laos, Malaysia, Singapore) with Brunei finally becoming fully independent in 1984. Being comparatively young nation-states that have emerged from colonial domination, Southeast Asian countries place great value on national sovereignty. As we later discuss in relation to ASEAN, this has implications for the development of regional institutions that function on pooled sovereignty: in other words, managing regional-level policies or making regional-level executive decisions on behalf of all member countries. It should be noted too that much tension surrounded the nation-building process in Southeast Asia during the early post-colonial years (Charrier 2001, Christie 1996). This has arisen on two main accounts, out of Cold War divisions between communist states (i.e. Cambodia, Laos and Vietnam) and US-backed capitalist states (e.g. Thailand, Singapore, Indonesia, the Philippines, Malaysia) on the one hand, and on the other from territorial and sovereignty disputes amongst certain Southeast Asian nations, e.g. the Malaysia/Singapore–Indonesia *Konfrontasi* conflict of 1963–5, and Singapore's separation from the Malaysian Federation in 1965.

Second, Southeast Asia has been generally *historically more open to foreign commerce* than Northeast Asia, especially in the modern historic era. For centuries the peninsula and archipelago territories of Southeast Asia have been an important thoroughfare for traders passing between China and the Indian subcontinent. Today, some 25 per cent of world trade passes through the Malacca Straits, which is situated in western Southeast Asia and links the Indian and Pacific Oceans. As Chapter 2 noted, the colonial powers further developed the region's trading posts and trade networks, making investments in infrastructure to facilitate this. In contrast, Japan, China and Korea had all at some point experienced long periods of self-imposed isolation (lasting into the nineteenth century) in which contacts with foreign commerce were generally limited. Consequently, Southeast Asian nations have been more used to hosting foreign investment and foreign commercial interaction (Doner 1991, Freeman and Bartels 2004, Lim 1995). Many of them have developed a notable capital dependence on inward foreign direct investment (FDI). Singapore actively courted investment from American electronics manufacturers from the late 1960s onwards, and today hosted foreign investor firms account for around 80 per cent of the city-state's exports. Foreign investment accounts for between 30 to 50 per cent of all investment in Singapore, Malaysia, Thailand, the Philippines and Vietnam. China is also in this range but ratios for Japan (2 per cent), South Korea (7 per cent) and Taiwan (10 per cent) are well below it. Much of Southeast Asia's inward FDI and trade are with other East Asian countries, and its openness to foreign commerce has thus helped spur various regionalisation processes.

Third, Southeast Asia has a *much smaller weight than Northeast Asia in the East Asia regional economy*. Southeast Asia's contribution to East Asia's GDP is only around 10 per cent. Whilst GDP criteria has limitations when judging the comparative economic importance of regions, it is to some degree indicative of Southeast Asia's at times often minor position in East Asia's regional political economy. For example, ASEAN countries together make a significantly smaller financial contribution to the Chiang Mai Initiative's regional network of bilateral currency swap agreements. Northeast Asia's substantial financial resources are likely to confer much greater influence accordingly to China, Japan and South Korea in the future development of regional financial governance structures. There are, however, other factors to consider when assessing Southeast Asia's impact upon regionalism in East Asia. To start with, there are many more Southeast Asia nations than Northeast Asian, and this numeric advantage can be exploited in regional meetings where decisions made are supposed to take into account the interests of all represented member countries around the table, no matter how small their economies are. In a similar vein, strong charismatic leaders from almost any country can shape the regional political economy by their advocacy of ideas and initiatives that are subsequently adopted by others. Southeast Asia has produced a number of such leaders, most prominently Lee Kwan Yue from Singapore, Mahathir Mohamad from Malaysia, and Thaksin Shinawatra from Thailand. Notwithstanding the controversies surrounding the issue, both Lee and Mahathir, for instance, helped articulate ideas on 'Asian values' and how these served as important binding forces within the region. Southeast Asia's economic importance to East Asia must also take account of regional integration itself. Without Southeast Asia, Japan could not have so easily undertaken crucial techno-industrial restructuring of its economy through relocating labour-intensive industrial activities in nearby low-cost countries (see Chapter 2). The same also applies to South Korea and to Taiwan to a lesser extent. Furthermore, the economic development of Japan, Korea, China and Taiwan has been critically dependent on imported supplies of materials (e.g. fuels, minerals) from Southeast Asia. The region's own techno-industrial advancement, especially in certain 'core' zones identified in the previous chapter, is having a growing impact on East Asia's regional economic development and regionalisation generally.

3.2 The Association of Southeast Asian Nations (ASEAN)

For some time, ASEAN was East Asia's only regional organisation grouping of nation-states. The APT framework, as its names indicates, essentially stemmed from ASEAN itself and is organisationally bound within an ASEAN summitry process. A similar story applies to the ASEAN Regional Forum in the security field (see Chapter 1). As Chapter 5 discusses, the East Asia Summit (EAS) process group arose more or less by itself from the APT, so ASEAN can claim to be an antecedent of all of East Asia's most prominent regional organisations. ASEAN was founded in August 1967 with five original member nations: Malaysia, Singapore, the Philippines, Indonesia and Thailand. The United States had a conspicuous hand in the project, motivated by its interest of coalescing a group of ideologically compatible regimes in Southeast Asia to act as a bulwark against a further communist advance in the region (Sum 1996, Yahuda 1996). The formation of ASEAN could also be construed as a reconciliation process between Southeast Asian countries that had been embroiled in the aforementioned territorial and sovereignty disputes during the early post-independence period. To assist in normalising and harmonising relations amongst its member states, a proposal was introduced in 1971 through ASEAN to create a Zone of Peace, Freedom and Neutrality (ZOPFAN) that envisaged the creation of a neutralised security zone across Southeast Asia. However, this had little effect on improving relations with then non-ASEAN states, especially at a time when the Vietnam War still raged in Indochina.

ASEAN remained an overtly security-focused regional organisation until the mid-1970s. Apart from helping normalise relations amongst its constituent membership, it had done very little on developing programmatic initiatives to enhance regional community-building in Southeast Asia. The organisation did not hold its first summit until 1976, and this really being prompted only by the need to discuss the ramifications of the communist victory in the Vietnam War the year before. At the summit, held in February at Bali, it was agreed regional economic co-operation should be conferred greater priority on the ASEAN agenda. Regular meetings between economic ministers were to be held, and at the 1977 meeting a proposal for establishing the Preferential Trading Arrangement (PTA) was adopted that would entail a series of tariff reductions on selected product lines. The PTA, though, proved an ineffective mechanism for promoting regionalised trade. Cynical product line inclusions (e.g. snow-ploughs, toothpicks) and exclusions of major industry sectors meant that by the mid-1980s the PTA only affected around 5 to 10 per cent of intra-ASEAN trade (Chng 1985). Parallel initiatives like the ASEAN Industrial Projects (AIP) and ASEAN Industrial Joint Venture (AIJV) schemes, both initiated around the same time, also proved a disappointment.

Security relations continued to dominate the organisation's agenda right up until the late 1980s. At the inaugural 1976 summit, ASEAN member states signed the Treaty of Amity and Co-operation that stipulated signatory countries must not use violence against other signatory members. The second summit held in August 1977 at Kuala Lumpur introduced the ASEAN's 'dialogue partner' framework, which brought together foreign ministers from ASEAN, the European Community, the US, Japan, New Zealand, Australia and South Korea in a forum to discuss Southeast Asian security matters. This was in effect the forerunner of the ASEAN Regional Forum (ARF), and discussions in the 1980s were largely focused on Vietnam's occupation of Cambodia that lasted from 1979 to 1989. ASEAN continued to be a relatively dormant organisation during this period. A third summit was not held until 1987, convened in Manila, the most important outcome being a five-year plan to extend PTA coverage to 90 per cent of intra-ASEAN trade that was never actually realised. The newly independent Brunei had meanwhile joined the organisation in 1984.

However, ASEAN was compelled to reassess its *raison d'etre* in the context of significant geopolitical changes brought about by the end of the Cold War, as well as by the deepening globalisation and regionalism in the international system (Nesadurai 2003). The implementation of market-based reforms in Vietnam from the late 1980s onwards also suggested that the ASEAN's expansion into the Indochina sub-region might be possible. There was a growing consensus within ASEAN's membership that the economic agenda of the organisation should be substantially enhanced. We examine in the following section how this was primarily to better champion Southeast Asia's interests in the new international order. At the fourth summit held at Singapore in January 1992, a proposal was tabled to create an ASEAN Free Trade Area within 15 years. This was a relatively ambitious plan given ASEAN's previous poor record on cultivating regional economic co-operation, and as we discuss below the realisation of AFTA has not been without its problems.

Other developments of note during the 1990s include the creation of the ARF in 1994 with the inclusion of additional 'dialogue partners' of Russia, China, Vietnam, Laos and India (joined in December 1995). At the December 1995 ASEAN Summit held in Bangkok, all member states signed the Treaty on the Southeast Asia Nuclear Weapon-Free Zone (SEANWFZ), which came into force in March 1997. During the latter years of the decade, ASEAN expanded to 10 member states, Vietnam acceding in 1995, Myanmar and Laos 1997 and Cambodia in 1999 (see Figure 3.1).

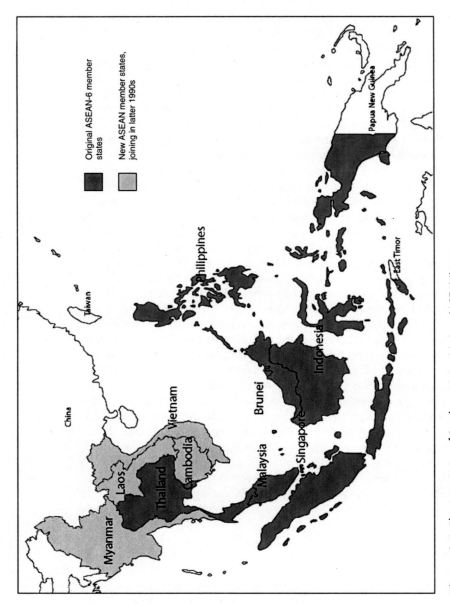

Figure 3.1 The Association of Southeast Asian Nations (ASEAN) group
Note: Vietnam joined ASEAN in 1995, Laos and Myanmar in 1997, and Cambodia in 1999.

In 2001, ASEAN member states signed the Hanoi Declaration on narrowing the development gap for closer regional economic integration in Southeast Asia, which in turn underpinned the Initiative for ASEAN Integration (IAI) examined later in this chapter.

The following year, ASEAN signed a free trade agreement with China to be fully implemented by 2010. Security issues continue to have prominence within ASEAN (Ojendal 2004). The ASEAN Declaration on Joint Action to Counter Terrorism, signed in 2001, was followed in 2002 by an ASEAN–China agreement on the Spratly Islands and an ASEAN–US Joint Declaration for Co-operation to Combat International Terrorism. Ministerial level meetings on how to tackle transnational crime and international terrorism have been held on a regular basis since the late 1990s, and ASEAN has intensified its efforts more generally in tackling new transnational issues such as international migration, and the forest fire 'haze' problem (see Chapter 7).

There has, in addition, been much debate over the extent to which ASEAN is able to deepen regional co-operation and integration in Southeast Asia generally given that the organisation continues to operate on the cardinal principles of 'non-interference' (i.e. of one member state in another member state's affairs) and soft institutionalism (Dosch 2006). This relates back to the earlier point concerning the value Southeast Asia's relatively young nation-states place on safeguarding their national sovereignty. Consequently, ASEAN has avoided the 'EU route' of developing the kind of supranational institutions (e.g. the European Commission) and inter-governmental decision-making mechanisms (e.g. the European Council of Ministers) that are deemed necessary to advance regional integration to higher and more sophisticated levels, such as operating a common trade policy as entailed with a customs union or establishing monetary union managed by a regional central bank.

Yet as was argued by Chapter 1, the 'institutionalised regionalism' approach, as derived from classic regionalism theory, offers an important but not comprehensive analytical framework for assessing the development of regionalism in different parts of the world. However, this chapter does focus on more formalised, state-led aspects of Southeast Asian regionalism that have arisen through ASEAN as an organisation or institution. Other chapters in this book do, though, also analyse wider aspects of regionalism in Southeast Asia, such as Chapter 2 discussions on regionalisation (e.g. sub-regional 'growth polygon' integration) and the analysis of transnational issues in Chapter 7.

3.3 The ASEAN Free Trade Area (AFTA)

The idea for establishing a regional free trade area in Southeast Asia was first formally proposed by Singapore in 1976 at the first ASEAN Summit. However, other member states were opposed to the idea, believing it to be too ambitious at that particular stage of ASEAN's development. Singapore was a free-trading entrepôt economy with very low tariffs while the other less developed member countries maintained relatively high tariffs to protect infant industries, so their liberalisation adjustment costs would be proportionately much higher. The aforementioned PTA scheme was instead proposed as a compromise, being a partial scope trade liberalisation agreement rather than a full FTA. A number of discussions were held on creating a regional FTA from the mid-1980s onwards. At the 18th ASEAN Economic Ministerial Meeting (AEMM) held in August 1986, the hosting Philippines government proposed both the enhancement of PTA liberalisation, as well as the application of a selected common external tariff that set a basic foundation for eventually establishing an ASEAN customs union.

These proposals were, however, rejected by other member states (Bowles 1997). In 1990 at the 22nd AEMM held in Bali, it was agreed that a new Common Effective Preferential Tariff (CEPT) scheme be introduced on selected industrial items, such as fertiliser, pulp and cement. This led the following year to further discussions on creating a regional FTA at the 1991 ASEAN Senior Official Meeting at Kuala Lumpur, with Singapore and Thailand being the most ardent supporters of the idea. This followed through to the Fourth 1992 ASEAN Summit, where the host, Singapore, was also the official proposing member state of the ASEAN Free Trade Area, and this time all member states unanimously supported the proposal.

As already suggested, the AFTA project was the principal basis on which ASEAN would develop its new economic rationale in the post-Cold War era (Bowles and Maclean 1996). It can also be understood as a response to particular events and developments in the international economic system occurring at the time. These can be categorised as follows:

- *As a response to external pressures*: the GATT's Uruguay Round negotiations had well overshot the initial 1990 deadline for concluding a new global trade agreement. In addition to this, intensified regionalist activity in both the developed and developing world during the early 1990s presented a future possible scenario of entrenched protectionism and regional trade bloc proliferation. Furthermore, many of ASEAN's economic rivals (i.e. newly industrialising or intermediate industrialising countries) could anticipate preferential access to important regional markets, most importantly Mexico to NAFTA and East European countries such as Poland, Hungary and the Czech Republic to the EU's Single European Market (Means 1995).[1]
- *To improve ASEAN's collective bargaining position in international economic negotiations*: if the international system was to become ever more defined by regional blocs and groupings, then consolidating Southeast Asia's regional market of around 500 million people would strengthen ASEAN's position within that system, for example, in international trade negotiations.

- *To counteract China's economic rise in the region*: by the late 1980s, it became increasingly clear that China's economic reforms would attract increasing levels of inward foreign investment, investment that would perhaps otherwise have been destined for Southeast Asia. China was also posing a significant competitive challenge in key export sectors for ASEAN countries such as electronics and textiles. AFTA was thus intended to appeal to foreign investors by offering a more integrated and liberalised regional market, and also to improve the export competitiveness of Southeast Asian based producers in an attempt to counteract the 'rising China' effect.

- *Further internationalising ASEAN's business community*: AFTA would reduce trade barriers in the regional market in a far more comprehensive manner than previously achieved under the PTA scheme. By learning to first compete with local regional rivals, ASEAN based companies could thereafter progress to compete more effectively in global markets. This was seen as an important conditioning process for Southeast Asian firms as they prepared to meet the challenges of globalisation. The region's business community, and in particular the ASEAN Chambers of Commerce and Industry, had long supported the idea of AFTA (Bowles 1997). Those firms involved in the operation of Southeast Asia's international production networks (see Chapter 2) had a special interest in the regional market liberalisation and integration that AFTA would bring (Tongzon 2002).

The main trade liberalisation mechanism of AFTA is the Common Effective Preferential Tariff scheme, this being subdivided into four main product categories. *Inclusion List* products largely comprise those items that already had comparatively low tariff rates (e.g. electronics) and hence would easily achieve so-called 'fast track' liberalisation. Under these terms, products with tariff rates of 20 per cent or below would be reduced to the 0–5 per cent range by January 2000, while products with 20 per cent plus tariff rates were to be reduced to within this range by January 2003 for the core ASEAN-6 member states (i.e. Brunei, Indonesia, Malaysia, Philippines, Singapore and Thailand). New ASEAN members (Cambodia, Laos, Myanmar and Vietnam, or CLMV group) were given longer to comply: Vietnam was granted a 2006 deadline, Laos and Myanmar to 2008, and Cambodia to 2010. By 2000, the Inclusion List covered 53,229 items, this being about 83 per cent of all CEPT product lines (see Table 3.1). By 2006, the ASEAN-6 had reduced 99.5 per cent of Inclusion List product tariffs to the 0–5 per cent level, and for the ASEAN group as a whole this was 90 per cent.

Temporary Exclusion List products meanwhile were those to be protected for a short period and then gradually transferred into the Inclusion List. By 2000, 15 per cent of CEPT product lines fell into this category. *Sensitive List* products were on the other hand granted longer tariff liberalisation phase-in schedules, mainly because tariff rates on these products were comparatively high and the gradual reduction of these rates would take longer. This category represented only a small proportion of the total. *General Exception List* products (around 700 in total by 2005) are excluded from AFTA liberalisation for reasons of national security, environmentalism and cultural-sensitivity. The overall CEPT product range covers manufactured and processed agricultural products but not unprocessed agricultural products and service sector products.

By 2000, the average CEPT tariff rate for the ASEAN-6 was 4.4 per cent compared to 12.8 per cent in 1993. By 2003 this had fallen to 2.9 per cent and by 2005 to 1.5 per cent (see Table 3.2). In addition, the ASEAN-6 countries were obliged under AFTA to remove quantitative restrictions and non-tariff barriers by 2010, while extended deadlines applied here to the newer member states: 2013 for Vietnam, 2015 for Laos and Myanmar, and 2017 for Cambodia. The supplementary ASEAN Framework Agreement on Services (AFAS) was agreed upon at the 1995 ASEAN Summit with the goal of establishing free trade in services by 2020. Although a number of key sectors were identified for negotiation (e.g. banking, tourism, telecoms,

Table 3.1 AFTA's Common Effective Preferential Tariff product list for the year 2000

Country	Inclusion list	Temporary exclusion list	General exclusion list	Sensitive list	Total
Brunei	6,276	-	202	14	6,492
Indonesia	7,158	21	69	4	7,252
Malaysia	9,092	-	63	73	9,228
Philippines	5,571	35	27	62	5,695
Singapore	5,739	-	120	-	5,859
Thailand	9,103	-	-	7	9,110
Cambodia	3,114	3,523	134	50	6,821
Laos	1,247	2,126	90	88	3,551
Myanmar	2,356	2,987	108	21	5,472
Vietnam	3,573	984	219	51	4,827
ASEAN Total	**53,229**	**9,676**	**1,032**	**370**	**64,307**

Source: ASEAN Secretariat official website (accessed 2003) at: http://www.aseansec.org/13100.htm

Table 3.2 Average CEPT rates for the ASEAN group, 1998–2003

	1998	1999	2000	2001	2002	2003
Brunei	1.35	1.29	1.0	0.97	0.94	0.87
Indonesia	7.04	5.85	4.97	4.63	4.20	3.71
Laos	5.0	5.0	5.0	5.0	5.0	5.0
Malaysia	3.58	3.17	2.73	2.54	2.38	2.06
Myanmar	4.47	4.45	4.38	3..32	3.31	3.19
Philippines	7.96	7.0	5.59	5.07	4.80	3.75
Singapore	0.0	0.0	0.0	0.0	0.0	0.0
Thailand	10.56	9.75	7.40	7.36	6.07	4.64
Vietnam	6.06	3.78	3.30	2.90	2.89	2.02
ASEAN	**5.37**	**4.77**	**3.87**	**3.65**	**3.25**	**2.68**

Source: ASEAN Secretariat official website (accessed 2003) at: http://www.aseansec.org/13100.htm

shipping) no actual programme or schedule was put in place for achieving services liberalisation. The AIA scheme was also introduced at the 1995 Summit based on the prime aim of inducing more FDI into the region, mainly through active investment promotion measures and easing restrictions on foreign investment (see Case Study 3.1).

Case Study 3.1 The dynamic effects of AFTA integration: the AIA and AICO schemes

There is a widely held view that the principle aim of AFTA was not to enhance intra-regional trade flows within Southeast Asia as such but rather to make the region more attractive to foreign direct investors (Narine 1999, Nischalke 2002). Bowles and MacLean (1996) have argued, for example, that AFTA is aimed more at outward looking investment creation than inward looking trade creation. As we know from Chapter 2, much of Southeast Asia's inward FDI is international production network (IPN) related, foreign investing firms using the region as an export–production platform for various multi-component products, such as electronics. As AFTA in effect helps reduce the transaction costs of conducting IPN trade, it may be perceived as a collective export-oriented industrialisation strategy, or simply a method for enhancing other more informal but perhaps more significant forms of regional economic integration taking place in Southeast Asia. Tariff liberalisation should also foster the development of the region's 'growth polygons' and other forms of transborder networked trade.

This connects with the issue of AFTA dynamic integration effects as opposed to the static or one-off effects of trade creation and diversion (see Case Study 1, Chapter 1, p. 13). In relation to this, the *ASEAN Investment Area* is an associated scheme of AFTA that aims to establish liberalised foreign investment conditions within the region by 2010. Together, the intra-regional trade and investment linkages cultivated by AFTA and AIA are intended to bind the market access interests of ASEAN member states into deeper interdependent alignment, thus contributing to the wider regional community-building process in Southeast Asia.

The Framework Agreement on the AIA was signed at the AEMM of October 1998. New measures to improve the investment climate of the crisis-torn region were later approved at the 1998 ASEAN Summit as part of the AIA framework, and in correspondence with the broader aims of the Hanoi Plan of Action (HPA). Full national treatment and market access privileges to ASEAN investors were supposed to be granted in manufacturing sectors by 2003 for the ASEAN-6 and by 2010 for the CLMV group. All member countries were allowed to maintain exemptions in primary sector (e.g. agriculture, mining) and service sector industries until 2010.[2] However, many sectors across the board were placed in the Sensitive List category, and hence were completely exempt from liberalisation without much recourse to future review.

Member countries were also supposed to implement co-ordinated ASEAN investment co-operation and facilitation programmes, actively involve the private sector in the AIA development process, and introduce greater transparency in their investment policies, rules and procedures generally. Yet these were guiding principles rather than contractual commitments. With the limitations of the AIA in mind, the scheme could be thought of not so much as a substantive policy framework but more as a marketing device for attracting more foreign investment into ASEAN. It is difficult to measure what impact the AIA scheme has had on inward FDI flows but by the mid-2000s these had yet to return to pre-crisis levels of investment. In 1997, Southeast Asia attracted US$34.1 billion worth of FDI, this level falling year-on-year to US$13.8 billion in 2002. Foreign investment levels began to rise again in 2003 to US$18.4 billion, but the 2004 figure of US$25.7 billion was still well below the 1997 peak.

Another AFTA associated initiative designed to promote greater economic integration and co-operation within the region is the *ASEAN Industrial Co-operation (AICO)* scheme. This became operative in 1996 and is specifically intended to foster industrial and technological co-operation and investment links between ASEAN firms. It was primarily designed to replace the predecessor ASEAN Industrial Joint Venture and Brand-to-Brand Complementation schemes, which had largely failed to deliver results. These earlier schemes had been beset with disputes amongst member states over the allocation of projects, production facility incompatibility problems between joint partner countries, divergent investment interests, and bureaucratic obstacles at both the national and regional levels that hindered the realisation of projects (Pangestu et al. 1992, Rao 1996, Suriyamongkol 1988). Overcoming such problems posed the main challenges for the new AICO scheme. Its main objective was to promote joint production ventures amongst firms from different ASEAN countries, thus cultivating further regionalisation linkages within Southeast Asia. Products from AICO projects enjoyed CEPT tariff rates of no higher than 5 per cent when exported within ASEAN. The scheme stipulated a 30 per cent national equity requirement upon companies wishing to qualify for AICO treatment. In addition, involved parties were obliged to share resources with each other to enhance their complementary production activities.

Under AICO, firms from a minimum of two member countries only were required whereas under the AIJV the minimum was four countries. While AICO was also supposed to be more bureaucratically streamlined than previous schemes, only 14 applications were approved in the first two years of its operation, and this was not for lack of private sector interest (Nesadurai 2003). Furthermore, the 30 per cent national equity requirement restricted foreign (i.e. non-ASEAN) firm involvement to some extent, which was proving counter-productive in certain key sectors (e.g. electronics, autos) where domestic and foreign capital worked closely together. In the wake of the 1997/8 financial crisis AICO rules were relaxed to allow more flex-ibility in participation. By 2002, the number of AICO approved proj-ects was approaching the 100 mark, and by April 2005 the number had risen to 129, the overwhelming majority of which concerned joint ven-tures in the autos sector. In 2004, a new protocol amendment to the AICO agreement brought in lower preferential tariff rates, six ASEAN member states committing to a zero per cent duty application on AICO product imports. Both the AIA and AICO schemes are thus designed to promote the further regionalisation of economic activity within Southeast Asia.

Study Questions

1. In what ways are the AIA and AICO schemes intended to help realise the objectives of AFTA trade liberalisation?
2. Could the problems encountered by these schemes be mostly over-come with substantially greater funding?

Notwithstanding the substantial progress made by the AFTA project, a number of significant problem issues remain. The first concerns *asymmet-ric tariff rates within ASEAN*, these being within the ASEAN-6 group com-paratively high in Thailand, Indonesia, the Philippines and Malaysia but notably low in Brunei and virtually non-existent in Singapore. There has, therefore, been much debate about the relative distribution of AFTA's ben-efits within the group. For example, Singapore stands to gain to a propor-tionately high degree not just because of its comparatively liberal tariff regime but also owing to its highly internationalised production interests in Southeast Asia. Another problem issue concerns *non-tariffs barriers (NTBs)*, such as complex customs procedures, quarantine rules, health and safety regulations, biased domestic policies towards local products, etc. These have long been seen by many as more important barriers to free trade in Southeast Asia than import tariffs and other conventional trade barriers, e.g. quotas. Thus, even after AFTA tariff liberalisation significant barriers to intra-ASEAN trade could persist, even though as previously noted member states are committed to eradicate NTBs too. The main problem is that disagreements often arise in trade negotiations over what qualifies as an NTB and what does not.

Southeast Asia's relatively low *intra-regional trade ratio* at around 22 per cent in 2005 poses another challenge for AFTA. This figure drops quite dramatically if Singapore's ASEAN trade is left out of the equation: nearly half of all the region's trade passes through or derives from the entrepôt city-state. With AFTA only currently covering a fifth of Southeast Asia's trade, many have questioned the potential contribution it can make to advancing economic regionalism. As Schwarz and Villinger (2004) further observed, ASEAN's intra-regional trade ratio actually fell over the initial AFTA implementation period, from around 21 per cent in 1993 to 19 per cent in 2001. This compared to NAFTA's 17 per cent increase in its first seven years of operation, and Mercosur's 67 per cent rise in intra-group trade achieved after just nine years.

We should, though, take into account the significant downward effects on regional trade caused by the 1997/8 financial crisis, and also that the core of AFTA was not implemented until 2003. Substantive and meaningful ex-post studies of AFTA's impact on Southeast Asia's intra-regional trade, and therefore on fostering regionalisation, had yet to be made at time of writing. Moreover, AFTA is now seen as a foundation on which deeper regional economic co-operation and integration will be built, as plans in progress for establishing an ASEAN Economic Community indicate. Efforts have also been made to make AFTA's rules of origin regime (which stipulates a 40 per cent minimum ASEAN content on eligible products) more flexible and transparent in order to assist firms to take more advantage of the freer trade conditions that AFTA offers them.[3]

In one respect, however, AFTA's *relative simplicity as a free trade agreement* itself represents another problem. It may be considered a 'narrow band' FTA that is primarily concerned with trade in goods liberalisation. As previously mentioned, the agreement does not directly cover services trade, or various important areas of commercial regulation such as government procurement, intellectual property rights (IPR) or competition policy rules. With the gradual reduction of tariffs and other conventional trade barriers worldwide over recent years, regulatory issues have grown in importance in international trade negotiations, as the WTO's own agenda testifies. The main explanation for the relative weakness of AFTA's regulatory dimension – which is a source of frustration for many Southeast Asia based firms – is that most ASEAN members lack the development capacity to operationalise sophisticated regulatory regimes. This weak regulatory dimension also limits AFTA's scope for creating an integrated regional market by not addressing differentiation in national regulatory regimes, but this task seems likely to be taken on to some extent by the ASEAN Economic Community project discussed at length later in the chapter.

Another problem area for AFTA has been the *political and economic fallout from the region's 1997/8 financial crisis*. In general, the crisis averted the attention of certain ASEAN member states from fulfilling their AFTA obligations (Kraft 2000, Ruland 2000, Stubbs 2000). As previously stated, ASEAN has been implementing AFTA since the early 1990s, but the crisis severely tested member states' commitment to the process as they became increasingly preoccupied with domestic economic problems.

This especially applied to Indonesia and the Philippines, two of the largest ASEAN economies, whose crisis-induced economic and political turmoil was particularly pronounced. Singapore's proposal in 1998 to accelerate the pace of AFTA trade liberalisation – as embodied in the Hanoi Plan of Action and Statement of Bold Measures – was opposed by the Indonesian government. The general chairman of Indonesia's Chamber of Commerce and Industry, Aburizal Bakrie, even called for the implementation of AFTA between core ASEAN states to be postponed from 2003 to 2005 or 2006.

Meanwhile, the Philippines government expressed concern over how the AFTA-induced loss of tariff revenue would significantly compromise its fiscal position.[4] Both Indonesia and the Philippines unilaterally delayed AFTA liberalisation of their respective petrochemical trade regimes. In addition, tensions arose between Malaysia and Thailand over the former's decision to delay the phase out of its tariffs on automotive product imports in the AFTA schedule by three years (see Case Study 3.2). Not only did the 1997/8 financial crisis lead many ASEAN states to drag their feet on AFTA trade liberalisation, but it also made AFTA itself a relatively less attractive proposition given the subsequent decline of the sub-region's overall market value. This partly explains why, from a comparatively early stage, Singapore and Thailand initiated their respective bilateral FTA policies, in some way compensating for AFTA downward-revised market potential (see Chapter 6).

Finally, there is the issue of *AFTA's relationship with other regional trade agreements* to consider. First, there is the still maintained plan within the APEC forum to achieve its 'Bogor Goals' of trade and investment liberalisation across the Asia-Pacific by 2010 for APEC's developed country members and 2020 for developing country members. If this is achieved, AFTA may simply be subsumed into this arrangement, although a target has been set of 2015 for evolving AFTA into the AEC, and thereby an integrational step ahead of APEC's Bogor Goals. The same applies to any future plans to create an East Asia Free Trade Area (EAFTA) that emerges through the APT or EAS process (see Chapter 5). To maintain ASEAN's relevance in the regional political economy, the AEC project is seen by many as a vital extension of AFTA. In the meantime, AFTA must to some extent compete with the growing number of bilateral FTA projects that many Southeast Asian countries have entered into with trade partners outside the region. Chapter 6 discusses more generally how reconciling this trade bilateralism with Southeast and East Asian regionalism has become a somewhat problematic issue.

Case Study 3.2 AFTA and automobile sector trade in Southeast Asia

The automobile sector is one of Southeast Asia's most important industries. A number of foreign auto manufacturers have production plants and operate international production networks across the region (see Chapter 2). Malaysia has also developed its own home-grown producers, the state-owned Proton and Perodua enterprises. These two firms have been nurtured within an import substitution industrialisation programme that has entailed a combination of state investment and growth within a highly protected domestic market. Thus, Proton and Perodua cars have gradually substituted imported foreign cars in the Malaysian market that by 2002 had reached a combined share of 75 per cent. At this time, Malaysia's import tariffs on autos sector products ranged from between 42 per cent and 300 per cent, and this lower rate had been reduced from 120 per cent in 2001.

The automobile sector was one of the most highly protected industries in Southeast Asia in the 1990s. All ASEAN-6 countries group maintained high tariff rates on imported cars during the 1990s, and autos trade had been placed in the CEPT's Temporary Exclusion List by all ASEAN governments. Under AFTA's tariff liberalisation schedules, duties on autos were supposed to be reduced to a 20 per cent maximum rate by 2000, and then reduced further to the 0–5 per cent range by the end of 2002. However, the Malaysian Government had announced beforehand in 1999 that it would seek a delay in automobile sector liberalisation, arguing that this was to provide some respite to Proton and Perodua after their sales were badly hit by the 1997/8 financial crisis (Nesadurai 2003).

Malaysia then later confirmed in 2001 that it intended to delay its CEPT liberalisation in the automobile sector by three years. The decision was widely criticised by other Southeast Asian countries, especially Thailand – the region's largest producer of automobiles – that was host to a large number of foreign car manufacturers and auto component makers (see Case Study 2.1, Chapter 2, p. 52). The situation was further aggravated by the introduction by the Malaysian Government of a new regulation in 2003 that stipulated imported cars now had to pay excise duty, whereas beforehand this had only applied to locally made cars. There were wider political economic motives behind Malaysia's delayed liberalisation. Proton and Perodua were high profile national economic development projects that were closely associated with the country's long-standing Prime Minister Mahathir Mohamad, who was reluctant to allow Malaysian car producers to succumb to highly competitive rival producers (e.g. Nissan, Toyota, Honda, BMW) based in Thailand.

After Mahathir left office, the new Badawi Government decided to curtail the delayed liberalisation by a year. However, a minimum 20 per cent tariff still applied to imported cars from 1 January 2005. Duties on automobiles imported from elsewhere in ASEAN countries were cut the most (reductions from 70 to 190 per cent), whereas import duties on cars from outside ASEAN were only reduced by 50 per cent, leaving them still facing tariff rates of between 80 and 200 per cent.

Duties on automobile components from other ASEAN countries brought in for assembly in Malaysia were reduced to zero from 25 per cent, whereas those originating from outside Southeast Asia were reduced to 10 per cent from 35 per cent. On the one hand, other ASEAN member states were pleased that Malaysia had brought forward the delay deadline, and also continued to confer on them preferential treatment over other countries. On the other hand, they were disappointed by Malaysia's simultaneous introduction of new excise duties (raised to a range of 90 to 250 per cent, up from 60 to 100 per cent), the result of which was that Malaysia's domestic market prices for cars would not change that significantly overall.[5]

The Malaysian Government defended its simultaneous excise duty hike on the grounds that it helped compensate for the tax revenue loss caused by AFTA tariff liberalisation. The main text has already noted how other ASEAN member states had used the same argument for similar changes made to their tax structures. Import tariffs can be a very important source of tax revenue for developing countries, and so to maintain fiscal stability during a period of programmatic trade liberalisation the government must look to develop new sources of tax revenue. In October 2004, for example, the Philippines Government even contemplated introducing a 3 per cent surcharge on almost all products imported from other Southeast Asian countries.[6]

The Proton/Perodua case also showed how import and excise duties can be used to gain a price competitive advantage over foreign rival producers. Another automobile sector related case of this arose between the Philippines and Thailand around the time of AFTA implementation. In 2004, the Philippines protested against Thailand's decision to impose an excise tax on imported off-road purpose vehicles. This affected Ford's exports of sports utility vehicles (SUVs) from its production plants based in the Philippines. The new tax was perceived by some observers as not only bestowing a price competitive advantage on Thai-based producers but also as an attempt by the Thai Government to persuade Ford to relocate their SUV production from the Philippines to Thailand. By doing so, Ford would avoid being subject to an increased excise tax of between 35 and 40 per cent for their SUV models. The official reason for this move given by the Thai Government was that these tax changes were in line with the international trend of applying higher excise duties on fuel-hungry SUVs for environmental reasons.[7] Whatever the true balance of motives was in this case, it provides further illustration of AFTA's limitations in creating a 'free' regional market in Southeast Asia. At the same time, these two automobile sector case studies were indicative of certain tensions that arose amongst ASEAN countries as they adjusted to the intensified competitive conditions brought on by AFTA.

Study Questions

1. What were the main motives behind Malaysia's decision to delay the liberalisation of its automotive trade regime?
2. How does this case study reveal the difficulties that can arise in trying to reconcile the pursuit of economic nationalism with the objectives of regional community-building? Is it just developing country regional groups that face this problem?

3.4 The Initiative for ASEAN Integration (IAI)

We have already seen how AFTA has been accompanied by a number of parallel supporting schemes, such as AIA and AICO, the main purpose of these being to further extend the reach of liberalisation and integration into various areas of the regional economy. The AIA has been devised to achieve this in investment liberalisation, and the AICO scheme in promoting international joint ventures between ASEAN-based firms. The IAI is similarly designed to help realise the wider integrational objectives of AFTA but in a somewhat different way to other parallel schemes. Trade integration projects such as AFTA tend to primarily benefit more developed economic zones within the trade area that are best able to exploit the new trade, investment and other commercial opportunities presented by these projects. For example, firms operating in Singapore or the Bangkok Metropolitan Region in Thailand or the Kuala Lumpur district in Malaysia have the infrastructural facilities, state technocratic support and the commercial experience and networks to make much more of the new market openings arising from the AFTA.

Such 'core' zones of development within Southeast Asia were always more likely to benefit when compared to the region's less developed 'periphery' zones, and from an ASEAN macro-perspective this especially concerns the CLMV group. The IAI, first proposed in November 2000, was at least partly conceived as counteracting core-periphery divergence arising from AFTA commercial liberalisation. It drew in principle upon the European integration experience whereby a periphery-serving regional policy (e.g. through the Structural Fund process) was to ensure that weaker regions were better empowered to take advantage of region-wide market liberalisation.

The IAI's primary objective was to bridge the development gap among ASEAN members and is specifically focused on fostering intra-regional economic development and co-operation through capacity-building and other measures. Significant levels of development asymmetry exist within Southeast Asia. Average annual GDP per capita levels in 2004 ranged from Singapore's US$24,840 and Brunei's US$18,690 down to Cambodia's US$338 and Myanmar's US$160 (see Table 1.1, Chapter 1). The United

Nations Development Programme's (UNDP) 2004 Human Development Report recorded a poverty incidence of below 2 per cent in both Malaysia and Thailand, and 34 per cent for Cambodia, while the UNDP's Human Development Index ranked Singapore at 25th and Laos at 135th in the same year.

After the IAI's official launch in November 2000, ASEAN member states signed the Hanoi Declaration on Narrowing Development Gap for Closer ASEAN Integration[8] in July 2001, this being followed by the introduction of the IAI Work Plan at the November 2002 summit convened at Phnom Penh. Acknowledging that, 'widening of the development gap between the older ASEAN-6 members and the CLMV countries could undermine regional solidarity', this six-year programme (2003–8) primarily focused on the CLMV countries but also on the poorer sub-regions in the ASEAN-6 countries. By September 2006, the IAI Work Plan had initiated 132 projects at various stages of implementation,[9] which comprised 19 infrastructure projects (11 transport and 8 energy projects), 48 human resource development (HRD) projects, 22 ICT projects, 32 projects specifically for fostering regional economic integration, one tourism project and eight other miscellaneous 'general coverage' projects.

Of the US$45.1 million funding secured for the IAI Work Plan, the ASEAN-6 countries contributed almost US$28.2 million (63 per cent of the total) while 11 dialogue partner countries and development agencies contributed the remaining US$16.9 million, the top five donors being South Korea, Japan, India, Norway and the EU.[10] Table 3.3 shows that amongst the ASEAN-6, Singapore was by far the biggest contributor with US$21.5 million committed to the IAI, and Malaysia the second with just over US$4.1 million.[11] In addition, Table 3.4 illustrates that on a bilateral basis the ASEAN-6 countries had contributed US$159.5 million by this time to the CLMV countries to implement various development projects, with Thailand making the largest contribution to the tune of around US$100.4 million and Singapore second with US$52.3 million.

Table 3.3 ASEAN-6 contribution to IAI Work Plan (funding secured, by September 2006)

Country	Projects/programmes	Funding Secured (US$)	%
Brunei Darussalam	8	1,500,000	5.3%
Indonesia	6	599,000	2.1%
Malaysia	47	4,080,590	14.4%
Philippines	2	30,932	0.1%
Singapore	11	21,554,456	76.3%
Thailand	13	480,902	1.7%
TOTAL	**87**	**28,245,880**	**100.0%**

Table 3.4 ASEAN-6 bilateral contributions to the CLMV group (at September 2006)

Country	Number of projects	Cost of project (US$)	Date of implementation
Brunei Darussalam	4	358,605	15 Sep – 15 Dec 2002
Indonesia	18	135,054	30 Jul 2000 – 23 Mar 2003
Malaysia	62	5,874,249	1992 – 2005
Philippines	31	261,833[1]	1995 – 7 Feb 2003
Singapore	9	52,495,275	2001 – 2008
Thailand	97	100,358,255[2]	1996 – 2004
TOTAL	**221**	**159,483,271**	**1992 – 2008**

Source: Data provided by ASEAN Member Countries to the IAI Unit of the ASEAN Secretariat
Notes: [1] Only the amount of 7 projects out of the 31 projects is available
[2] Does not include assistance of any kind

While these may look impressive figures in a relative sense within the group, the development divide within Southeast Asia is such that these amounts are unlikely to make a substantial difference. However, the IAI's work on closing development gaps within Southeast Asia is being augmented by the aid diplomacy of Japan, China and European countries in particular, and also by the ADB. As part of the Japan–ASEAN Comprehensive Economic Partnership (JACEP), Japan has dedicated a fund of around US$4 billion to help narrow economic gaps among ASEAN states, enhancing the competitiveness of ASEAN countries and strengthening co-operation between Japan and ASEAN on issues such as institutional and human capacity. China is also trying to extend its influence over Indochina through its aid diplomacy.[12] The ADB's involvement with funding initiatives such as the GMS project is also contributing to this process (see Chapter 2).

3.5 Towards an ASEAN Economic Community (AEC)?

The idea for creating an ASEAN Economic Community has its roots in the 1998 HPA. Forged in the aftermath of the region's 1997/8 financial crisis, the HPA stated ASEAN's intentions to promote further economic and financial co-operation amongst its member states as well as accelerate AFTA progress towards implementation (Kraft 2000, Ruland 2000). In addition, the HPA formally extended ASEAN regional economic and financial co-operation to the wider APT group (Mahani 2002). As the key implementation deadlines for AFTA approached, the group looked towards the next stage of regional economic integration. The AEC proposal originally came from Singapore at the November 2002 ASEAN Summit, and was later co-sponsored by Thailand from January 2003.

The AEC plan was formally proposed at the 9th ASEAN Summit held at Bali, Indonesia in October 2003. This was later formulated into the Vientiane Action Programme, another six-year plan that superseded the HPA and focused the AEC on achieving the twin aims of narrowing the development divide within Southeast Asia – thus intersecting with the IAI – and further deepening regional economic integration (Ferguson 2004, Soesastro 2003). The latter objective envisaged the establishment of a single or common market to promote the free flow of goods, services, people and capital within Southeast Asia. This was with a view to creating 'a stable, prosperous and highly competitive ASEAN economic region' based on the aims of achieving 'equitable economic development, and reduced poverty and socio-economic disparities' in Southeast Asia (ASEAN Secretariat 2003). Furthermore, the AEC was intended to establish the ASEAN economy as a single 'production base', and making the region 'a more dynamic and stronger segment of the global supply chain', thus acknowledging the important micro-level regionalisation processes that were examined in Chapter 2 (ASEAN Secretariat 2003). An initial deadline of realising the AEC by 2020 was set but a decision was taken at the 2006 ASEAN Economic Ministers Meeting to shorten the deadline to 2015.

The AEC was also intended to strengthen the ongoing implementation of AFTA (goods trade liberalisation), AFAS (services liberalisation) and the AIA (investment liberalisation) by introducing new measures and mechanisms in their respective areas of coverage. More generally, the AEC provided a more holistic regional integration agenda that at least potentially could encompass various different initiatives into a more unified framework. Furthermore, the AEC formed just the 'economic pillar' of a broader ASEAN Community that was proposed at the 2003 Bali Summit: an ASEAN Security Community (ASC) and ASEAN Socio-Cultural Community (ASCC) would also be created by 2020. Thus, the AEC was embedded in a wider regional community-building project. As new regionalism theorists would particularly argue, economic regionalism does not advance in a political, social or cultural vacuum.

Chapter 1 discussed how deeper regional economic integration cannot easily progress in an unstable political or security environment, or when socio-cultural bonds within the regional community are weak. There was hence a purposeful complementarity of running these three regional community-building processes alongside each other, especially when it came to addressing important transnational challenges facing ASEAN member countries. For example, tackling the problems of transborder pollution, drug trafficking, health epidemics and migration all have security, economic and socio-cultural dimensions to them, and therefore are best tackled in a holistic manner. Developing a balanced and multi-dimensional regional community-building process was thus essential.

Although some parallels could be drawn with the EU's Single European Market project, the AEC does not aspire to the same level of integrational ambition. For example, there would be no common external tariff (and hence no customs union) established between ASEAN member states. The diversity of development levels and trade policies (significant tariff level variance) makes such a goal difficult. However, under the AEC eleven priority sectors are selected for fast-track liberalisation, namely agro-based products, air transport, automotive, e-commerce, electronics, fisheries, healthcare products, rubber-based products, textiles and apparels, tourism and wood-based products. These cover about 4,000 tariff lines or around 40 per cent of total tariff lines in ASEAN trade.

Furthermore, early preparatory targets were set on a wide range of cross-sectional co-operative and integrative measures.[13] It was also originally agreed that a so-called 'ASEAN minus x' approach be adopted in realising AEC objectives, whereby all member states were set a specific target to realise an objective but some members would be permitted to implement at a slower pace to accommodate development asymmetry within the group (Cuyvers et al. 2005). However, as the case study on the Singapore–Thailand Enhanced Economic Relationship (STEER) details, these two member states were pushing for a different integrational formula ('2 plus x') to be adopted.

Case Study 3.3 The Singapore–Thailand Enhanced Economic Relationship (STEER) framework and multi-speed regional integration

Singapore has long been ASEAN's most ardent proponent of deepening regional integration in Southeast Asia. The city-state's backing behind the AFTA and AEC projects, from inception to implementation, are testament of this. Singapore's motives for advocating deeper integration lie in its functional position within the regional economy, this being Southeast Asia's premier entrepôt hub economy through which a high proportion of ASEAN's trade passes and which also hosts normally around half the region's total inward FDI, a high proportion of this being of a very high-tech nature (Dent 2001a). The Singaporean economy may be considered a key node in various global circuits of capital. No other ASEAN economy is so integrated into the regional and global economy as Singapore, and this has accordingly defined its interests in ASEAN's economic agenda. Thailand has also in more recent years (especially during the premiership of Thaksin Shinawatra, 2001–6) joined Singapore as a fellow advocate of Southeast Asia's accelerated economic integration. This has perhaps been more for political reasons, being part of Prime Minister Thaksin's strategy of positioning Thailand as ASEAN's emergent leading nation.

As noted in the main text, both countries have been frustrated by the troubled progress of AFTA and other parallel integrative elements of the programme, such as the AIA. Singapore and Thailand's approach to trade and economic integration policy was also converging around the pursuit of bilateral FTAs with non-ASEAN countries (see Chapter 6). These factors helped forge common positions on, and a similar vision for, future ASEAN economic integration. Out of this growing coincidence of interests came the STEER framework, first announced in February 2002 and formally established by an inaugural summit convened in August 2003.[14] Here, Singapore and Thailand stated their intention to create a bilateral foundation for greater economic integration within ASEAN based on a *'one economy, two countries'* approach. Both sides would accordingly strengthen bilateral economic co-operation, liberalisation and integration across various fields, including the automotive industry, electronics, agro-based products, air transport, trade and investment promotion, healthcare, tourism, transport logistics, financial services, information and communication technology, small business formation, and mutual recognition agreements.

The STEER framework was a unique bilateral economic agreement between two ASEAN member states. It has been a vehicle for advocating a more ambitious integrational agenda to be adopted by ASEAN as a whole. It was Singapore and Thailand that together had proposed the AEC initiative, and for its original deadline of 2020 to be brought forward to 2012 or 2015. Furthermore, the above mentioned sectors targeted for closer bilateral Singapore–Thailand integration and liberalisation formed a core basis of the AEC's own eleven priority sectors selected for fast-track liberalisation (see main text). The bilateral framework was also intended to have demonstration effects for other ASEAN member states generally through its so-called 'pathfinding' approach to economic integration. This particularly concerned the '2 plus x' principle championed by Singapore and Thailand in relation to ASEAN integration, whereby two member states would be allowed to pioneer integration on a bilateral basis initially with other member states open to join at a later date when ready. At the October 2003 ASEAN Summit, Singapore's then Minister for Trade and Industry, George Yeo, articulated the '2 plus x' approach in the following terms: 'it is better to catch up with those who are faster than to be dragged back by those who are slower'.

Singapore and Thailand thus essentially wanted STEER to be both the fundamental test-bed and a prime agenda-setter of future ASEAN economic integration. Furthermore, STEER's '2 plus x' approach was a challenge to the 'ASEAN minus x' approach noted previously in the chapter that had been consensually agreed as the process by which the AEC would be realised. This latter approach worked more on the principles of group consent and accommodating weaker members in the integrational process, whereas the '2 plus x' formula allowed stronger pairs or sub-sets of members to surge ahead of others in the group. In defence of the '2 plus x' approach, Singapore and Thailand argued that ASEAN integration should not be constrained by the 'convoy problem' of having to proceed at the lowest common denominator pace of slower member states. Yet, as other member states counter-argued, STEER's

'2 plus x' approach could be ultimately divisive by creating further tiers within the group that is already stratified along ASEAN-6 and CLMV sub-group layers.[15]

In the end, other ASEAN member states remained cool to the '2 plus x' approach as championed by STEER. Furthermore, cracks in the Singapore–Thailand alliance on ASEAN's integrational affairs and other matters began to emerge in 2005 and 2006. To begin with, nothing of much substance appeared from STEER related initiatives themselves, leading some even within government circles to refer to it as simply a political marketing exercise.[16] The second STEER summit was delayed and not held until November 2005, from which little was added to the original framework. A total of nine deals were signed at the meeting but none of the agreements marked a notable policy change for either country, or involved new substantial investment projects.[17] Furthermore, STEER was believed by many to essentially rest on the close links that existed between the political leaderships of both countries. This relationship was first placed under extreme duress as a consequence of the Shin Corporation affair. Shin Corporation, Thailand's largest telecommunications firm, was founded and 49.6 per cent owned by Thai Prime Minister Thaksin Shinawatra and his family. In January 2006, it transpired that Shin Corporation was being sold in a tax-free deal estimated at US$1.9 billion to Temasek Holdings, the Singapore government's state investment arm that happened to be run by Singapore PM Lee Hsien Loong's wife, Ho Ching.

The public outcry in Thailand against both Singapore and the Thaksin Government concerning the sale of an asset of such national strategic importance placed considerable pressures upon the countries' bilateral relationship. Moreover, it was a contributing factor to events that led to the September 2006 military coup in Thailand that ousted Thaksin Shinawatra from power. Their bilateral relations took a further turn for the worse when the new Thai leadership, under General Surayud Chulanont, accused the Singapore authorities of eavesdropping on Thai government meetings through its ownership of Shin Corporation. Around this time, Singapore–Thailand economic relations were also becoming increasingly competitive, adding further tensions to the relationship overall. For example, Thailand's new Bangkok airport project is seen as challenging Singapore's Changi Airport as Southeast Asia's main regional air transportation hub. In addition, Thailand's Kra Isthmus canal project, which would cut through the Malaysian peninsula and thus bypass the Straits of Malacca, could, if built, undermine the strategic importance of Singapore's port complex and as a entrepôt trade centre generally.[18]

The STEER issue raises the more general point of how pressures can often arise within regional groups for adopting a multi-speed approach to integration. This tends to occur when significant development asymmetry exists amongst member countries, as is the case for ASEAN. We have seen how the group's less developed member states – the CLMV countries – have been conferred longer adjustment periods concerning AFTA and the AIA that take into account the various notable capacity constraints (e.g. industrial, technocratic and institutional) they face. The main issue with STEER is, though, whether multi-speed integration arrangements should apply to the ASEAN-6 group. While this may yield certain economic benefits and efficiencies, it may not be politico-economically expedient to create an 'elite' advanced tier of integrating member states because of its potential to undermine regional community-building solidarity within the group.

Study Questions

1. What was the main basis of the Singapore–Thailand alliance within the ASEAN group, and why has it floundered lately?
2. Assess whether multi-tiered membership within a regional organisation or framework generally helps or hinders regional community-building.

3.6 ASEAN and East Asian regionalism

Over recent years, Southeast Asian regionalism has become increasingly embedded within the broader development of East Asian regionalism. As already noted, the ARF had from the mid-1990s onwards extended Southeast Asia's regional dialogue mechanisms to include Northeast Asian states and other partners outside the region. In the meantime, Southeast Asia's economic and social network linkages with Northeast Asia continued to strengthen, cultivating deeper regional interdependences within East Asia as a whole. Indeed, the contagion effects of the region's 1997/8 financial crisis exposed just how economically interdependent East Asia had become by this time. In the common pursuit of East Asian states to avert another such crisis, a proliferation of new international agreements followed with the aim of better managing their regional economic interdependence. With the launch of the Hanoi Plan of Action and Statement of Bold Measures in December 1998, ASEAN more formally acknowledged that its economic destiny was closely tied to that of its Northeast Asian partner countries within the then emerging APT framework. As Chapter 5 discusses, ASEAN's own regional economic integration has become increasingly subsumed into wider East Asian regionalism processes.

A second key development concerns the growing number of FTAs that ASEAN countries have signed with Northeast Asian states, as well as with other countries in the Asia-Pacific (Dent 2005b, 2006a, 2006b). Figures 6.1 to 6.4 in Chapter 6 (see pp. 187–90) show the extent to which Southeast Asia has become entwined in the expanding web of Asia-Pacific FTAs. By June 2007, Japan had signed full bilateral agreements with Singapore, Malaysia, the Philippines and Thailand. Meanwhile, South Korea's bilateral FTA negotiated with Singapore in 2004 was a precursor to negotiating a broader ASEAN–Korea agreement. The most significant of all these agreements, the ASEAN–China FTA, was signed in November 2002, to be fully implemented by 2010. This formed part of a wider 'Framework Agreement' that aimed to promote closer relations between China and the ASEAN group generally.

Japan and South Korea had in the meantime initiated bilateral FTA talks in December 2003, although these had became deadlocked by March 2005. In 2006, China and South Korea initiated feasibility studies into a bilateral FTA project of their own. Certain ASEAN countries (Singapore, Malaysia and Thailand) have also entered into bilateral FTA projects with the South Asian countries of India, Pakistan and Sri Lanka. Whether this spate of bilateral FTAs will lead to the creation of a unified East Asian regional trade agreement is a debateable matter, as extensively discussed in Chapter 6. What is apparent, however, is that ASEAN is becoming more enmeshed in an East Asian regionalism process through the combination of FTAs, the APT framework, and the EAS process that has as its ultimate goal the creation of an East Asian Community.

3.7 Conclusion

3.7.1 Summary overview

Southeast Asia is a diverse region comprising a number of relatively young nation-states. Its long history of being open to the outside world has made it a highly internationalised region, and hence one used to dealing with foreign powers. Over recent years and decades, Southeast Asian countries have had to learn to interact more harmoniously with each other, which has not always been an easy task. The formation of the Association of Southeast Asian Nations in 1967 – East Asia's longest standing regional organisation – was an important development in this respect, providing the means by which the regional affairs of Southeast Asia could be better organised and managed. As geopolitical circumstances changed, so did ASEAN's role and agenda, moving from its overt focus on politico-security matters to one embracing a more comprehensive range of regional issues. The introduction of the ASEAN Free Trade Area project in the early 1990s in particular signalled the new priority afforded to promoting regional economic co-operation and integration in Southeast Asia.

Through the 1990s and into the 2000s, other regional-scale projects were launched to complement AFTA, most notably the ASEAN Investment Area, ASEAN Industrial Co-operation, ASEAN Framework Agreement on

Services, and Initiative for ASEAN Integration schemes. Together, these provide a platform for implementing the next planned stage of Southeast Asia's regional economic integration, this being the common market arrangement embodied within the ASEAN Economic Community project. The AEC forms the economic element of a broader ASEAN Community concept that in addition embraces security (ASC) and socio-cultural (ASCC) relations in Southeast Asia. As this chapter has stressed, advances in economic regionalism are set within wider endeavours and objectives of regional community-building. However, the chapter also noted the significant past, present and future difficulties confronting ASEAN countries in their attempts to realise such goals, the region's development asymmetry being particularly highlighted as a problem in both the main text and case study material. Notwithstanding the substantial obstacles that lie in the path of achieving greater regional coherence in Southeast Asia, the region has an important part to play in helping advance East Asian regionalism more generally. This was discussed towards the end of the chapter, and is further discussed elsewhere in the book, especially in Chapter 5.

3.7.2 International Political Economy (IPE) theoretical analysis

Neo-realists would especially note how competing national interests have often undermined ASEAN's regional community-building endeavours, for example with regard to how Malaysia, Indonesia and the Philippines all protected certain domestic industry sectors from AFTA trade liberalisation during the 1997/8 financial crisis period. Indeed, *neo-realists* would further point to the large number of bilateral tensions that usually exist amongst ASEAN member states, including:

- Disputes over natural resource supplies, e.g. the terms of Malaysia's freshwater supply to Singapore, Indonesia's export ban of sand to Singapore
- Thailand–Singapore's relations over Shin Corp and Temasek Holdings (see Case Study 3.3)
- Malaysia–Indonesia relations over illegal immigration
- Indonesia's forest fire haze pollution and relations with Malaysia, Singapore and other ASEAN member states (see Chapter 7)
- Philippines, Malaysia, Vietnam and Brunei claims over ownership of the Spratly Islands in the South China Sea

Neo-realist thought would also argue that the formation of bilateral coalitions, such as the Singapore–Thailand Enhanced Economic Relationship, was ultimately motivated by competitive power objectives. These were primarily to further consolidate these two countries' already advanced competitive positions within the ASEAN regional economy, as well as force the pace of regional integration in accordance with their own national interests. As noted in Chapter 1, neo-realism asserts that inter-state coalitions arise only when there is a coincidence of national or political interests between partner states. The STEER bilateral coalition soon fell apart once this coincidence of interest unravelled. Similarly, AFTA was formulated partly to help Southeast Asian states better compete with rival industrial states (e.g. in East Europe and Latin America) in the international market, improve ASEAN's collective bargaining position in international economic negotiations, and counteract the competitive economic threat posed by an ascendant China. More generally, the primacy of the nation-state in South Asia's relations is perhaps best revealed by ASEAN's cardinal principle of 'non-interference' regarding the internal affairs of member states, which hinders the degree to which deeper regional co-operation and integration can be achieved. Our study on ASEAN has shown also some of the inherent difficulties arising from the enlargement of regional organisations in that a wider range of national interests have to be consequently reconciled across the group. At the same time, the English School strand of neo-realist theory concerning ideas of international or regional societies of nation-states would contend that the ASEAN group aspires to form a closer regional community of nations (i.e. through the planned AEC, ASC and ASCC projects) whilst retaining the inviolability of national sovereign rights (Narine 2006).

Neo-liberal thinkers, on the other hand, place greater emphasis on both the achievements of ASEAN regional co-operation and the development of a more pluralistic regional agenda that extends well beyond the neo-realist preoccupation with politico-security matters. Neo-liberal institutionalists in particular have argued that Southeast Asian countries have come to better appreciate the deepening interdependence that has developed between them over time, and hence the ever greater imperative to co-operate more closely together (Dosch 2006). Furthermore, Southeast Asia's interdependence has been increasingly viewed on a wider regional scale, and consequently ASEAN has worked more closely with its 'Plus Three' neighbours (Japan, China, South Korea) and other external partners, such as India, Pakistan, Australia, New Zealand, the United States and the European Union. The broadening of the ASEAN agenda, especially since the early 1990s, is indicative of the stronger role now played by non-state actors in Southeast Asian affairs. For example, the region's business associations and larger firms have been influential advocates of ASEAN's regional economic integration and co-operation projects such as AFTA (Nesadurai 2003). Non-government organisations also have become more actively engaged and influential in ASEAN affairs, especially when there are matters of transnational interdependence at stake, e.g. 'haze' pollution and international migration (see Chapter 7). In such situations, non-state actors have an important role to play in formulating regional co-operative solutions. Neo-liberals also note how Southeast Asia has become an even more open and porous region as a result of various ASEAN programmes (e.g. AFTA, AFAS) and other arrangements (e.g. bilateral FTAs with external trade partners), and has subsequently become more closely integrated into the wider East Asia regional economy and global economy.

For their part, *social constructivists* would contend that the gradual broadening of ASEAN's regional agenda of co-operation over the years has similarly widened the scope for socialisation amongst different stakeholder groups, helping foster a deeper sense of regional community and identity. This follows on from the point made above under neo-liberalism about the widening of stakeholder interest in Southeast Asia's regional affairs beyond state-centred interests and those determined by security policy-making elites. Ba (2006) refers to this broadened stakeholder socialisation within ASEAN as a 'complex engagement' process, which in turn has fostered a stronger identification and formation of shared ideas, values and beliefs across Southeast Asia's different communities. At the same time, though, there may arise clashes of ideas and beliefs between these communities regarding how regional community-building in Southeast Asia should proceed. For example, the region's business associations and civil society organisations (e.g. environmental NGOs) may have quite different views on this matter. More generally, the idea of constructing an ASEAN 'community' is a powerful one, and has been a focal point of discussions within ASEAN over recent years. Notwithstanding its aforementioned limits placed on deepening integration, the so called 'ASEAN way' of non-interference has also been a longer-standing guiding idea on how Southeast Asia's intra-regional relations should be conducted (Eaton and Stubbs 2006). We noted too that Southeast Asia has produced a number of 'thinker' leaders (e.g. Lee Kwan Yue from Singapore, Mahathir Mohamad from Malaysia) who have professed highly publicised ideas on Asian values, identity, distinctiveness and regional community. Yet as we know, difficulties exist in cultivating a sense of regional cohesion amongst the peoples of Southeast Asia because of the complex diversity that prevails in the region.

Finally, theoretical perspectives from *Marxism-structuralism* schools of IPE thought would perhaps first highlight, from an historic perspective, that Southeast Asia's regional economy remains critically rooted in old imperial systems of commerce. While the foreign colonial administrations have long departed, the power and influence of foreign businesses originating outside the region have not. Many Southeast Asian countries depend very heavily on foreign MNEs for investment, technology transfer and other value-adding activities. Transnational capital exerts a powerful politico-economic influence on these countries and also ASEAN as a group, playing, as discussed earlier, a strong advocatory role in promoting deeper regional economic integration. The historic legacy of imperial commerce is also revealed in the key hub position of Singapore – established in the early nineteenth century as a British colonial trading centre – in the early twenty-first century regional economy of Southeast Asia. In this chapter it was noted how half of ASEAN's trade passes at some point through the city-state. Most foreign MNEs locate their Southeast Asia regional headquarters there, and its government purposely fosters a close relationship with transnational capital, a relationship that at times has led Singapore to promote key and often controversial initiatives on regional integration. In addition, structuralists would also stress the pronounced 'development divide' that still persists in Southeast Asia, and how core–periphery dependency relationships that extend beyond the region continue to be a significant obstacle to advancing regional community-building. Certainly, addressing the considerable structural differences in terms of development and prosperity that exist amongst Southeast Asian countries is one of the most important future challenges facing the ASEAN group. In the next chapter, we look at the development of the Asia-Pacific Economic Co-operation forum and how this has engaged East Asia in certain forms of trans-regionalism across the Asia-Pacific.

Chapter Study Questions

1. To what extent may we consider Southeast Asia as being more 'regionalised' than Northeast Asia?
2. Outline the main factors behind the creation and early development of ASEAN as a regional organisation.
3. Why was ASEAN compelled to find a new rationale and purpose in the early 1990s?
4. How successful have ASEAN's regional economic integration and co-operation schemes been in fostering closer relations amongst Southeast Asian countries?
5. 'ASEAN may not have much of a future in light of deepening regionalism at the wider East Asian level'. Discuss.

Notes

1   Means (1995) cites a study conducted by Michigan State University that estimated NAFTA would have a trade diversion effect of around US$484 million, and roughly affect about 4 per cent of ASEAN exports to North America. More specifically, the trade diversion effect was estimated to be between 8 to 12 per cent for Southeast Asian exports in food, chemicals, textiles, metals, and electronics sectors.
2   Previous to 2001, a 2020 deadline applied to foreign (i.e. non-ASEAN) investors.
3   For example, these revised rules include: (a) a standardised method of calculating local/ASEAN content; (b) a set of principles for determining the cost of ASEAN origin and the guidelines for costing methodologies; (c) treatment of locally-procured materials; and (d) improved verification process, including on-site verification. These came into effect in 2004.
4   *The Economist*, 06.11.2002.
5   *International Herald Tribune*, 27.12.2004.

6   This was a contingency measure in case the Philippines Congress did not pass the government's eight priority tax measures, including increased excise duties on demerit goods (e.g. alcohol) and petroleum products, as well as a rationalisation of tax incentives. *Manila Times*, 21.10.2004.

7   *Philstar News*, 23.08.2004.

8   This committed ASEAN to 'promote, through concerted efforts, effective co-operation and mutual assistance to narrow the development gap among ASEAN member countries and between ASEAN and the rest of the world for the sake of dynamic and sustained growth of our region and prosperity of all our peoples'.

9   By this time, funding had been secured for 118 projects (89.5 per cent of the total), of which 87 projects had been completed, 22 projects were being implemented, and 9 projects were in the planning stage.

10 These five accounted for around US$14.4 million, or 85 per cent of funding by development partners. It is interesting to note that the US was not in this top five.

11 A proposal to establish an ASEAN Development Fund (ADF) to help further facilitate IAI objectives emerged at the 2004 APT Summit. A formal agreement on creating the ADF was signed at Vientiane in July 2005 with each member state agreeing to contribute US$1 million initially.

12 Research interview at the Singapore Institute for International Affairs, December 2004.

13 These included standardising custom costs and procedures, and harmonising technical regulations across the region by the end of 2004; the elimination of identified NTBs from 2005; capital controls must be progressively removed and intellectual property rights regimes strengthened, including co-operation in exchange of copyright information to take effect in 2004; visa-free travel for ASEAN nationals within the region by 2005; standardised requirements for professional services to enable free movement of professional and skilled labour within ASEAN; accelerating the implementation of mutual recognition arrangements for five priority sectors, these being electrical and electronic equipment, cosmetics, pharmaceuticals, telecommunications equipment and processed foods.

14 The STEER framework arose out of the Singapore–Thailand Enhanced Partnership (STEP), launched in 1997 with the aim of establishing 'a broad vision for a long-term strategic partnership between both countries' (from Singapore Ministry of Foreign Affairs website, http://www.mfa.gov.sg/sections/fp/sea_thailand.htm). The STEP framework provides for the expansion of sectoral co-operation across four pillars, namely: (1) enhanced economic co-operation; (2) defence relations; (3) people-to-people co-operation; (4) the Civil Service Exchange Programme (CSEP). Hence, STEER arose from the first of these.

15 This view had been particularly expressed by Malaysia, Indonesia and Brunei. Research interviews in Jakarta, Indonesia and Bangkok, Thailand, July 2005.

16 Research interview with Thai Ministry of Affairs official, July 2005.

17 *Thai Day News*, 24.11.2005.

18 This project is, however, technologically very difficult for geological reasons (e.g. tides, shallow waters, ground height differentials), but as an alternative Thailand is looking to construct an oil pipeline across the narrowest point of the Isthmus to shorten the oil supply line from the Middle East to East Asia.

Chapter 4

APEC and Asia-Pacific trans-regionalism

4.1 East Asia and trans-regionalism in the Asia-Pacific

In Chapter 1, we discussed how East Asia's regionalism both overlapped with, and was embedded in other integrative processes arising within the international economic system. As we also know from Chapter 1, East Asia may be considered one of three macro-regions (the other two being Pacific America and Oceania) that make up the Asia-Pacific 'trans-region'. Trans-regions are essentially hemispheric or inter-continental entities, other examples being Eurasia (Europe and Asia) and the Americas (North, Central and South America), which are often used as referents when discussing the establishment of common 'spaces' or intensifying linkages (economic, political, socio-cultural) between and across macro-regions. The formation of trans-regions is thus closely connected to discourses on the development of international society and globalisation because of the large geographic scale of integrational or associative processes that are involved.

This chapter examines the emergence and development of the Asia-Pacific Economic Co-operation forum, the most prominent trans-regional organisation in the Asia-Pacific. It is also the most important exercise of trans-regionalism in which East Asian countries participate. The organisation was established in 1989 with 12 original members from East Asia (Japan, South Korea, Brunei, Indonesia, Malaysia, the Philippines, Singapore, Thailand), Oceania (Australia and New Zealand) and Pacific America (Canada and the United States). Others joined in the 1990s (China, Taiwan and Hong Kong 1991; Mexico and Papua New Guinea 1993; Chile 1994; Russia, Peru and Vietnam 1998), expanding APEC to its current membership of 21 economies (Figure 4.1).

As we shall see, APEC has evolved in the context of long-standing endeavours to substantiate a Pacific (economic) community. Furthermore, many scholars were suggesting at the time of APEC's creation that it marked a further consolidation in the shift in the global economic centre of gravity to the Asia-Pacific (away from the historic transatlantic centre) as well as augmenting deepening transpacific alliances between the United States and certain East Asian countries. This was of particular concern to Europe, which faced potential geo-economic marginalisation in a then anticipated 'Pacific Century' (Dent 2001b, 2001c). The founding aim of APEC was to advance regional economic co-operation in the Asia-Pacific but this was significantly enhanced in 1994 when member-states agreed to realise the so called Bogor Goals of establishing trade and investment liberalisation across the Asia-Pacific by 2020. This was to be achieved by the process of 'open regionalism', whereby APEC member-states would unilaterally (i.e. on their own without direct negotiations) eliminate their international trade and investment barriers not just with other APEC countries but all trade partners globally. Hence, this was not an attempt to create a regional free trade agreement in the conventional sense.

By the late 1990s, however, the Bogor Goals project had more or less stalled. Around this time, serious disagreements had emerged amongst

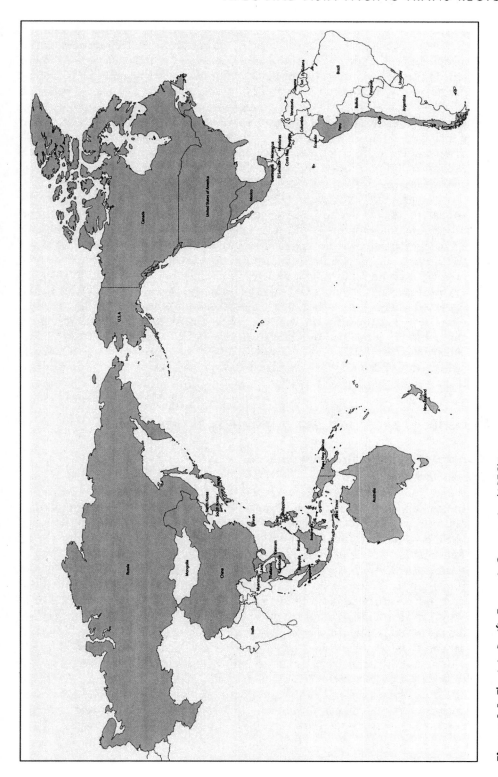

Figure 4.1 The Asia-Pacific Economic Co-operation (APEC) group

Note: APEC member states are shaded in grey

APEC member states over which paths of trade liberalisation should be followed. Most East Asian members have never really supported the organisation's trade liberalisation objectives, preferring instead to promote APEC's trade facilitation (e.g. regional infrastructure development, e-commerce) and economic and technical co-operation (ecotech) initiatives. By the early 2000s, even the most ardent supporters of the Bogor Goals project (e.g. the United States, Australia and Singapore) had turned instead to the alternative trade liberalisation route of bilateral FTAs. More generally, we discuss both in this chapter and in Chapter 6 how APEC's relationship with the intensifying bilateral FTA trend in the Asia-Pacific is one of the most critical with regard to the organisation's future.

On the one hand we may view the trans-region's new FTA trend as subverting APEC's founding principles and organisational purpose. On the other hand, an evolving APEC may harness the Asia-Pacific's proliferating FTA activity to serve the organisation's regional community-building objectives. Here, though, it is more likely that APEC will be adapting to the bilateral FTA trend than vice versa. In this chapter, we shall also broadly examine how APEC has come under increasing pressure to adapt and evolve in recent years. This particularly relates to addressing economics-security nexus issues in the aftermath of the 11 September 2001 terrorist attacks on the United States (see Case Study 4.2). In addition, since the 1997/8 financial crisis, East Asian countries have become more preoccupied with developing the APT and EAS regionalist frameworks than advancing the trans-regional projects of APEC.

4.2 The emergence and early development of APEC

4.2.1 Constructing a Pacific economic community: early ideas and initiatives

In one sense, APEC is the culmination of many decades of preceding ideas and initiatives on Pacific regional community-building. Three Asia-Pacific nations – Australia, Japan and the US – have played an especially important role in this historic process. The earliest endeavours at developing Pacific community initiatives originated from the United States in the form of the Pan-Pacific Union (established in 1907) and the Institute of Pacific Relations (established in 1925). Both these initiatives created epistemic communities of policy-makers, other public figures and academics in which ideas on how to forge closer relations across the Pacific were discussed and proposed. However, both also made a limited impact in this regard. The US did make other institutional contributions to fostering transpacific relations (e.g. the United Nations Economic and Social Commission for Asia and the Pacific, or UNESCAP) but during the Cold War period its economic and security relations strategy in the Pacific was primarily based on 'hub-and-spoke' bilateral alliances.

By the 1960s, Japan had begun to show an interest in developing ideas pertaining specifically to Asia-Pacific *economic* regionalism. In 1965, the government-sponsored Japan Economic Research Centre (JERC) proposed that a Pacific Free Trade Area (PAFTA) be created between the region's five advanced economies (Japan, the US, Canada, Australia and New Zealand) with developing countries in the region conferred associative membership (JERC 1966). Japan also proposed the creation of the Pacific Basin Economic Council (PBEC) based on an existing Japan–Australia private sector forum that was extended to include representations from the US, New Zealand and Canada. Running in parallel with the inaugural meeting of PBEC in 1968 was the first Pacific Trade and Development (PAFTAD) conference – a forum of economists from academia, government and international organisations – and organised by Japan's Ministry of Foreign Affairs and the JERC. Subsequent PAFTAD conferences provided an important framework for early technical discussions on enhancing regional economic co-operation, including how PAFTA could be realised.

Although support for establishing PAFTA waned during the 1970s, Japan and Australia continued to push new initiatives, including the Pacific Economic Co-operation Conference (PECC) that comprised representatives from academia, business and government. Certain commonalities of interest bound Japan and Australia together in such joint endeavours. Both feared the effects of deepening regionalism elsewhere in the international system and the effects this would have on their exports, especially with respect to any ensuing protectionism that accompanied deeper European Community integration (Korhonen 1994). For Japan, rising US protectionism against its exports during the 1970s was also a growing concern. Both Japan and Australia furthermore felt outsiders in their own regional backyards, and thus promoting ideas and initiatives on Pacific regional community-building were intended to foster their closer identification with the region in a general sense (Terada 1998).

4.2.2 The emergence of APEC

The PAFTAD/PBEC/PECC framework made some progress through the 1980s, keeping alive various levels of trans-regional dialogue on strengthening economic and business ties within the Asia-Pacific. The idea of establishing an Organisation for Pacific Trade and Development (OPTAD) was particularly discussed. This was modelled on the OECD (Organisation for Economic Co-operation and Development) and thus charged with facilitating mutual policy-learning that could in some cases lead to setting norms of economic policy practice amongst participating countries. Japan and Australia continued to be the principal advocates of OPTAD and other such initiatives, yet other Asia-Pacific countries remained rather unenthusiastic. Although the US was showing more interest in Pacific community-building ventures by the late 1970s and early 1980s, it still eschewed regionalism in strategic diplomacy terms, preferring instead multilateralism on the trade liberalisation front through GATT negotiations in tandem with maintaining strong bilateral alliance relationships with key economic and security partners in the trans-region (Morrison 1981, Ravenhill 2001).

Elsewhere, Southeast Asian countries were more interested at the time in upgrading their own regional organisation, ASEAN, than engaging in a wider Asia-Pacific regional project. The persistence of Cold War divisions during the 1980s meant that China and other communist–socialist countries in East Asia (e.g. Vietnam) were excluded from any Pacific regional community-building process led by the trans-region's capitalist states. Meanwhile, South Korea and Taiwan were still only emergent newly industrialising economies in the close economic and security embrace of the United States. Many East Asian nations were also highly circumspect of any Japan-led regional initiative given lingering memories of the country's aggressive imperialism that it exercised in the early twentieth century.

Both Japan and the US also had the problem of many other states fearing these two economic giants would dominate any transpacific regional organisation that emerged. With this in mind, it became politically more expedient for Australia to take a higher profile lead in new Pacific diplomacy initiatives relative to Japan. It was therefore Australia that officially proposed the creation of APEC in 1989, the inaugural ministerial meeting being held at Canberra in November of that year with significant financial and technocratic support provided from Japan. By the late 1980s, various events and developments were conspiring to make other Asia-Pacific nations more interested in joining a Pacific regional organisation. Ravenhill (2001:88) neatly summarises these as being,

> a significant surge in US unilateralism, the agricultural trade war between Washington and Brussels, the conclusion of negotiations between the United States and Canada to establish a free trade area, the move towards a single internal market in the European Community, and deadlock in the Uruguay Round of GATT talks.

We should also remember that the launch of APEC – the most substantial inter-governmental arrangement proposed by this time – was the culmination of three decades of discussions on how to better promote and organise closer regional economic relations in the Pacific (Garnaut 2000, Ravenhill 2002a).

At the inaugural Canberra Ministerial Meeting, the Australian Government's proposal that APEC be modelled on (like the earlier proposed OPTAD) an OECD-style organisation was coolly received by East Asian member countries, most of which preferred a looser, less institutionalised, consensus-building arrangement (Drysdale 1991, Garnaut 2000, Kahler 1995). It was this latter approach that prevailed in the organisational construction of APEC, and hence European style, treaty-driven regional integration was also to be avoided. Rather, APEC would foster closer economic

relations on a trans-regional scale through inter-governmental consultations and other non-binding mechanisms. East Asia's developing economy
members in particular had an obvious interest in APEC's work on economic
and technical co-operation, or 'ecotech' programmes. Japan too wanted the
organisation to have a substantive regional economic co-operation agenda,
which it believed would complement the country's own development
aid strategy at work in East Asia. Some ASEAN countries were nevertheless
concerned over APEC's impact on Southeast Asian regionalist initiatives,
especially the AFTA project (see Chapter 3). Subsequently, they agreed
to participate subject to 'three no's', these being that APEC would have
no legal binding authority, no negotiating right and pursue no regional
agreements beyond those permitted under GATT/WTO trade rules.

There were 12 original member countries in attendance at the 1989
Canberra Ministerial Meeting, these being Japan, South Korea, Brunei,
Indonesia, Malaysia, the Philippines, Singapore, Thailand, the United
States, Canada, Australia and New Zealand. It was Japan rather than
Australia that insisted on the US being invited to the inaugural Canberra
meeting. Japan's motives lay in the desire to contain American unilateralism on trade affairs by incorporating the US in multilateral fora like APEC
(Hayashi 2006, Krauss 2000). It was also a means of keeping the US engaged
in the region as the Cold War appeared to be drawing at that time to a close.
At Canberra, attending foreign and economic ministers agreed that APEC's
basic objectives should be to promote regional economic growth and development, to uphold an open multilateral trading system, and thus there was
to be no recourse to building a Pacific trade bloc but rather to foster a con-
structive economic interdependence between members. Ministerial meetings were also to be held annually, while regular and intermediate Senior
Officials Meetings would oversee and co-ordinate, with ministerial
approval, APEC's work in progress between Ministers Meetings. Key developments in the following three APEC Ministerial Meetings were as follows:

- *Second APEC Ministerial Meeting (Singapore, July 1990)*: seven
  Working Groups were created to enhance co-operation in trade promo-
  tion, technology transfer, human resource development, energy,
  telecommunications, marine resources, and the collection of regional
  economic data. Later on, three more Working Groups (transportation,
  tourism and fisheries) were added to the framework.
- *Third APEC Ministerial Meeting (Seoul, November 1991)*: China, Hong
  Kong and Taiwan were admitted as new member economies, with
  Taiwan being referred to as 'Chinese Taipei' at Beijing's insistence.
  APEC's scope of activities and general objectives were further defined,
  these being the: exchange of information and consultation on policies
  relevant to common efforts to sustain growth, promote adjustment and
  reduce economic disparities; development of strategies to reduce impediments to trade and investment; promotion of objectives specifically set
  within APEC's Working Groups.

- *Fourth APEC Ministerial Meeting (Bangkok, September 1992)*: agreement to establish a permanent APEC Secretariat, later implemented by January 1993 and based in Singapore. It was also decided to create an Eminent Persons Group (EPG) that would produce 'future vision' reports on how APEC should progress, especially on advancing regional trade liberalisation.

Most observers agree that APEC made a reasonably solid start in its first four Ministerial Meetings (Garnaut 2000, Okamoto 2004, Ravenhill 2001, Ruland et al. 2002). The profile of APEC was to be raised further still as a result of higher level ambitions set during the 1993/4 period of the organisation's development.

4.2.3 APEC raises its ambitions

A number of critical factors converged to make the Fifth APEC Ministerial Meeting, convened at Seattle in November 1993, a landmark event. To start with, it was accompanied by the inaugural APEC Economic Leaders Meeting, held nearby at Blake Island, which was the first of subsequent annually held APEC summits to run parallel to the Ministerial Meeting process. Virtually all the member premiers attended the first summit, helping raise APEC to a new level of politico-diplomatic significance. At both APEC meetings, the EPG's first report entitled *'A Vision for APEC – Towards An Asia-Pacific Economic Community'* was tabled for discussion. In the report, the EPG recommended that a programme of trade and investment liberalisation measures be collectively implemented by member economies (APEC 1993). This was a prelude for the more defined and ambitious EPG second report tabled at the following year's meetings, as discussed below. The first EPG report was accepted but with reservations from many East Asian states who saw this as a departure from APEC's original aims of promoting informal economic co-operation. However, the newly inaugurated Clinton Administration wanted the US to become more actively engaged in APEC, and to enhance the organisation's trade agenda in particular.

There were strategic advantages at this time for doing so, especially in relation to what was happening in the Uruguay Round of GATT talks during the latter half of 1993. Negotiations between the US and the European Union were at an impasse over agriculture. Some observers believe that the US's strong backing of the EPG recommendations sent a signal to the EU, pressuring them to make further concessions in the Uruguay Round of talks as the benefits from a secured WTO accord would help offset the costs of being excluded from a prospective Asia-Pacific free trade zone (Bergsten 1996). At the 1993 APEC meetings, Mexico and Papua New Guinea were also admitted into membership. In addition, a Committee on Trade and Investment was established,[1] as well as the Pacific Business Forum in which business representatives were to examine how the private sector could positively contribute to APEC's work on various policy-related matters.

The new momentum created by the 1993 meetings was carried forward into the following year's APEC Ministerial Meeting held in Jakarta and the APEC Summit convened nearby at Bogor in November 1994. Asia-Pacific premiers endorsed the proposals outlined in the EPG's second report for creating a *free and open trade and investment zone* within APEC by the two-stage deadlines of 2010 and 2020 (APEC 1994). Developed member economies were to realise this objective by the former date, while the developing members were to meet the latter. These became known as the 'Bogor Goals', and these were to be achieved in accordance with the principle of 'open regionalism'. This implied that APEC members were to open up their economies in a unilateral and non-discriminatory manner not just to each other but also to non-members (see Case Study 4.1), thus complying with the 'most favoured nation' (MFN) principles on which WTO liberalisation was based. Although the EPG Chair, Fred Bergsten of the Washington-based Institute for International Economics, had allegedly pushed for a conventional regional FTA to be recommended, most other EPG members insisted upon the adoption of the 'open regionalism' approach, especially those members from Japan and Australia with prior deep involvement in the PAFTAD and PECC processes.[2]

The majority EPG view was that the Asia-Pacific's economic dynamism was ultimately dependent upon an open and flourishing multilateral trading system, and that the expansion of exclusive regional trade blocs could easily undermine that system. Under the Bogor Goals plan, which became APEC's centrepiece project from 1994 onwards, all members were to initiate their unilateral trade liberalisation programmes no later than the year 2000. Tariff-free trade was to be achieved by the 2010 and 2020 deadlines, and national treatment conditions were to apply on all foreign investment by these dates also, in compliance with an Asia-Pacific Investment Code. Various trade and investment facilitation programmes were set in motion to complement the commercial liberalisation process. The Bogor Goals project would involve creating a free trade and investment zone covering almost half of world trade between economies that accounted for just over half of world GDP.

4.3 East Asia and APEC's economic liberalisation agenda during the 1990s

4.3.1 East Asia and the EPG reports

There was a general unease amongst East Asian countries from the start concerning APEC's aspirations on regional trade and investment liberalisation. Many were disappointed that ecotech issues were poorly prioritised in EPG reports, only being afforded a few pages in each. It was this area of APEC's work that was the primary interest of East Asia's developing country members, most of which moreover wished to maintain some kind of trade protection in strategic or infant industries for developmental purposes. This was a view shared to some extent by the strong neo-mercantilist and economic nationalist lobbies in the more developed economies of Japan, South Korea and Taiwan.

Differences of opinion soon arose between East Asian countries on the one side and Anglo-Pacific countries on the other regarding APEC's *modus operandi* of implementing the Bogor Goals project. As Case Study 4.1 discusses, considerable ambiguity existed over the exact meaning of open regionalism. After the dissolution of the EPG he chaired, Fred Bergsten (1996) argued that the non-discriminatory free trade was neither practical nor desirable because it conferred APEC with no leverage in global trade negotiations. Bergsten (1994) had even earlier argued that pursuing a 'temporary conditional MFN' approach, whereby APEC applies pressure to secure reciprocal tariff concessions from non-APEC trading partners, would serve as a solution to this problem. The specific reciprocity terms and modalities that Bergsten was advocating would also require APEC members to agree to more definitive commitments on implementing trade and investment liberalisation.

Ravenhill (2001) notes that East Asian countries were already arguing the counter-case for greater flexibility to apply, both in terms of what was implied by trade and investment liberalisation and the means by which it was to be realised. For example, many ASEAN member states believed that AFTA's targets of reducing tariff rates to the 0–5 per cent range should be the benchmark for meeting their Bogor Goal objectives. At the ASEAN Economic Minister's Meeting held in Chiang Mai in September 1994, the general consensus was that the EPG's second report recommendations on trade liberalisation were too specific. In 1995, Malaysia announced that the Bogor Goals were largely indicative, and therefore it was not bound to abolish its tariffs by the deadlines set. Government officials from other East Asian countries expressed similar views about how APEC should adopt a 'flexible' approach on liberalisation.

4.3.2 The Individual Action Plan (IAP) and Manila Action Plan (MAPA) frameworks

In the lead up to the 1995 Osaka APEC Summit, most East Asian members had become increasingly wary of the EPG's advocacy of commercial liberalisation becoming the core of APEC's agenda. Many of the recommendations made in the EPG's third and final report (APEC 1995a), such as on antidumping policies, were rejected largely due to opposition expressed by East Asian members. Nevertheless, it was agreed that trade and investment liberalisation was to progress by each APEC member state preparing their own IAPs on meeting Bogor Goal objectives. This was the core basis of the Osaka Action Plan (APEC 1995b). First draft IAPs were to be submitted at the following year's summit at Manila and implemented from the beginning of 1997.

Each IAP was to cover trade and investment facilitation measures (e.g. on customs procedures) but the main emphasis was on commercial liberalisation. Although there were agreed guidelines on the formulation of IAPs these were very general, and it was left up to each member state to determine the programmatic content of their Plans. In the first drafts, for example, China committed to reducing simple average tariffs to around 15 per cent by 2000, Japan to expand its Tariff Elimination Initiative on pharmaceuticals, South Korea to start eliminating its tariffs on ships from 1997, and Taiwan to lower most of its average tariff rates to 5 per cent or under by 2010.

The IAPs were to run in parallel with a series of Collective Action Plans on commercial liberalisation that together formed the basis of the overarching MAPA, which consisted of six main areas of work: 1) greater market access in goods; 2) enhanced market access in services; 3) an open investment regime; 4) reduced business costs; 5) an open and efficient infrastructure sector; 6) strengthened economic and technical co-operation. Many East Asian states were unhappy with the fact that ecotech appeared to be bolted on at the end of this list. The MAPA process was carried forward to APEC's 1997 summit convened at Vancouver that November. Each member state had submitted the IAPs and many had in theory committed to unilaterally extend beyond their WTO Uruguay Round obligations on removing trade barriers.

The IAP process was APEC's first *modus operandi* on trade liberalisation, often referred to as 'concerted unilateral liberalisation'. However, in practice many East Asian member states had in particular dragged their feet on either initiating their IAP commitments or incorporating substantive liberalisation measures and targets in their Plans (Soesastro 1999). Furthermore, Petri (1997:1) observed that the IAPs were generally speaking 'vague on overall goals and short on specifics'. Meanwhile, East Asian countries were pressing for higher priority afforded to APEC's ecotech agenda. Some success was achieved here. The number of ecotech initiatives was growing, and at the Osaka Summit it was agreed that ecotech should be conferred equal status with trade and investment liberalisation. However, the actual substance of ecotech initiatives remained thin and in reality commercial liberalisation continued to dominate the APEC agenda (Ravenhill 2001).

4.3.3 *The Early Voluntary Sectoral Liberalisation (EVSL) debacle*

With slow progress being made on the IAP front, APEC's most ardent pro-liberalising member states supported a new initiative tabled by the United States at the 1997 APEC Summit held in Vancouver. This was the EVSL scheme in which 15 specific industry sectors were targeted for accelerated or 'fast track' liberalisation that would, it was hoped, catalyse a broader trade liberalisation process. Member governments were asked beforehand at the May 1997 APEC Trade Ministers Meeting to nominate sectors they wished to be included in the scheme, which was also to comprise various facilitation and ecotech measures. In some sectors (e.g. telecoms and automotive) emphasis was placed on the mutual recognition of standards rather than eliminating tariffs.

Of the 15 chosen sectors, nine were conferred high priority and placed in the first tier (chemicals, rubbers and plastics; energy; environmental goods and services; forestry products; fisheries; gems and jewellery; medical equipment and instruments; telecoms; toys) and the other seven (automotive; civil aircraft; fertilisers; food; natural and synthetic rubber; oilseeds and oilseed products) in the second tier. Essentially first tier sectors were to liberalise at a more accelerated pace than second tier sectors. Ravenhill (2001) notes that the EVSL initiative was to some extent riding the momentum of the Information Technology Agreement, a sectoral liberalisation initiative that had originated in Quad Group (US, Japan, EU, Canada) discussions and then passed through APEC for approval before being forwarded to the WTO where it eventually became a plurilateral trade accord signed by around 40 countries.

However, the EVSL was beset with disagreements arising over the perceived nature of the scheme and how it was to be operationalised. This especially related to interpretations of its 'voluntary' aspect. For Anglo-Pacific member governments in particular, this implied that APEC members had voluntarily nominated sectors and had voluntarily decided to support the scheme as a whole. Some member governments, and especially those from East Asia, were of the understanding that the 'V' in EVSL implied there was scope for concentrating on certain sectors or sector-specific elements (e.g. ecotech over liberalisation) rather than others, or in how and when the scheme's targets were to be realised. Confusion arose over other matters, such as whether developing member economies should be given longer phase-in schedules to maintain consistency with the differentiated liberalisation deadlines of the overarching Bogor Goals. The exact product coverage within each selected sector was also a contentious issue, as was the actual level of tariff reduction supposed to be achieved in the scheme.

It was already clear at the June 1998 APEC Trade Ministers Meeting hosted by Malaysia in Kuching that the planned official launch of the EVSL at the Kuala Lumpur Summit later that year was going to be problematic. The Japanese Government in particular was refusing to accept the EVSL as a complete package, and insisted upon an opt-out from liberalising its fisheries and forestry sector. Agriculture was an extremely sensitive area in Japan's domestic political economy, and the country's trade negotiators enjoyed strong public and lobby group support back home on this matter. Japan came under considerable pressure from the US and other pro-liberalisation member governments but Tokyo refused to yield. Other East Asian member states – most notably China, South Korea and Taiwan – tacitly supported Japan's veto, as agricultural trade liberalisation was a politically sensitive issue for them also (Krauss 2004, Rapkin 2001, Ravenhill 2001). Food security was a key problem. The agricultural sectors of Japan, South Korea and Taiwan were all based on relatively uncompetitive small-scale farms. Consequently, all three economies imported the majority of consumed foodstuffs (e.g. Japan had a 60 per cent food import ratio and South Korea a 70 per cent ratio).

At the 1998 APEC Summit in Kuala Lumpur, Indonesia, Malaysia and Thailand also chose not to support the EVSL scheme. Unable to broker a resolution within APEC, the matter was referred to the WTO for possible inclusion in the then named 'New Millennium Round' agenda for global trade talks, due to be launched at the WTO's Seattle Ministerial in December 1999. As a result, then, of largely East Asian opposition, this second APEC strategy on advancing towards the Bogor Goals had failed too. Furthermore, there was mounting frustration amongst East Asian countries concerning APEC's failure as an organisation generally to address the fallout from the region's 1997/8 financial crisis that was raging at this time (Okamoto 2004, Ruland et al. 2002). This issue is discussed towards the end of the chapter.

Case Study 4.1 The 'open regionalism' debate

There has been a great deal of discussion on the definitional meaning of 'open regionalism'. To many, it essentially concerns how a regional group of countries commit themselves to a WTO-consistent, MFN-based liberalisation process (Drysdale 1991, Drysdale and Elek 1996). They thus do not discriminate between trade barrier reductions made in relation to regional group members and non-members, i.e. those lying outside the region. In one way, such groups may be considered regional branches of the WTO, and indeed back in the mid-1990s this was what some thought APEC could be considered as being (Dieter 1997). The idea of open regionalism is then to make regionalism compatible with multilateralism and avert the risk of the international economic system being fragmented into competing, adversarial regional trade blocs.

Ravenhill (2001) notes that the first articulation of 'open regionalism' came from a PBEC/PECC related study group report commissioned by the Japanese Government and published in 1981, which proposed that: 'a regionalism that is open to the world, not one that is exclusive or closed, is the characteristic of our concept. We are fully aware that a regional community without a perspective for a global community, a regionalism that excludes Globalism, has no possibility of development or prosperity' (Pacific Basin Co-operation Study

Group 1981: 184). The first mention of 'open regionalism' in official APEC documentation came in the Joint Statement of the Fifth Ministerial Meeting held at Seattle in November 1993, in which member states expressed their commitment to attain regional trade and investment liberalisation 'through consultation in a manner consistent with the principles of GATT and open regionalism' (APEC 1993, paragraph 6). Ravenhill (2001) argues, however, that there has never been any firm consensus within APEC as to how open regionalism should be specifically defined.

Yet at the same time he notes there has been a general understanding amongst officials and analysts working in PAFTAD and PECC circles about what open regionalism implies, this being 'a continuation of the process of unilateral liberalisation that has characterised the economic policies of countries in the region for several decades, a market-driven process rather than one directed by government officials to construct formal free trade areas' (Ravenhill 2001: 141).

However, to many, putting open regionalism into practice was problematic on various levels. First, and most fundamentally, as a concept it was somewhat oxymoronic – a contradiction in terms. Organisational expressions of regionalism are by their very nature exclusivist as they distinguish a regional group or club of countries from others in the international system. As social constructivists would especially note, summits and other meetings of regional officials help create a sense of regionness and defined regional community through various socialisation processes. Moreover, while APEC's Bogor Goals did not originally aspire to establish an Asia-Pacific regional FTA, its potential for imposing indirect exclusivist effects on non-APEC economies remains considerable.

This is particularly relevant to the convergent regulatory environments that APEC members are endeavouring to establish between themselves (Dent 1999). Recognising this dilemma for the European Union back in the mid-1990s, the European Commission stated in one of its official documents that 'if the countries of East Asia were, as a result of regulatory co-operation within APEC, to align their regulatory systems practices to those of the United States, this would place the EU at a competitive disadvantage, at least to the extent that a large and dynamic part of the world economy developed as result of a system which diverged significantly from that of the Union' (Commission of the European Communities, 1995: 7).

Another predicament of open regionalism is the free-rider problem: countries outside APEC may not reciprocate in kind after APEC member states have unilaterally liberalised their trade and investment regimes. Bergsten's (1994) suggestion of adopting a 'temporary conditional MFN' approach, noted in the main text, was an early indication of how APEC could be pressuring outside trading powers like the EU into making reciprocal liberalisation concessions. This more accurately related to specific reciprocity, entailing concessions between involved parties simultaneously agreed on a specific and direct *quid pro quo* basis (Ruggie 1993).

As Chapter 6 examines in more detail, FTAs are negotiated on a specific reciprocity basis. Trade liberalisation through APEC open regionalism was, however, like WTO multilateralism to be negotiated on a diffuse reciprocity basis, whereby involved parties profit over time from the aggregated benefits derived from the collective actions of the group (Keohane 1990). In this respect, no one party is supposed to confer a specific preference or advantage to another. Any drift towards either FTA activity in the Asia-Pacific or using APEC as a bargaining tool to secure its member states with direct reciprocated gains from outside trade partners would thus mark a shift in reciprocity choice, from the diffuse reciprocity of open regionalism to specific reciprocity.

The US has particularly demonstrated an interest in this switch in reciprocity choice, and thus undermining APEC open regionalism. The preference of the EPG's American Chair, Fred Bergsten, for a Pacific regional FTA has been previously mentioned, and Bergsten has continued to advocate this idea into the 2000s. Even when the Bogor Goals project was being launched in 1994, US President Bill Clinton was of the view that, 'any market opening granted by one country would have to be met with equivalent concessions in other APEC countries.'[3] After the breakdown of the EVSL scheme in 1998, the US proposed that APEC trade liberalisation should not proceed unless matched by similar concessions made by outside trade partners (Rapkin 2001). We later note in the chapter how the US was also the primary advocate of the Free Trade Area of the Asia-Pacific (FTAAP) proposal that was tabled at both the 2004 and 2006 APEC summits. This plan essentially subverted the open regionalism principle by its aspirations to create an exclusivist Pacific regional FTA rather than realise the Bogor Goals by 'concerted unilateral' measures, as originally embodied in the IAP scheme.

Study Questions

1. To what extent can 'open regionalism' be considered an oxymoronic concept?
2. Is APEC still operating on the basis and principles of open regionalism?

4.3.4 *Continued inertia on APEC trade liberalisation*

After the EVSL debacle, APEC struggled to make substantive progress on advancing its trade liberalisation agenda. At the September 1999 APEC Summit in Auckland, the hosting New Zealand Government tried in vain to salvage something from the EVSL package. By this time, a number of APEC members (mostly East Asian) had begun to initiate bilateral FTA projects with each other for the first time. The first wave of bilateral projects (South Korea–Chile, Japan–South Korea, Thailand–South Korea) had been formally launched in November 1998, either at or around the same time of the previous year's Kuala Lumpur Summit (Dent 2006a). A further four bilaterals were officially proposed at the Auckland 1999 Summit itself (Singapore–New Zealand, Mexico–Singapore, Japan–Singapore, Japan–Mexico) and two other projects (South Korea–New Zealand, Japan–Chile) were initiated at other times that year. As Chapter 6 examines, this was the start of a rapid expansion of bilateral FTA activity in the Asia-Pacific. This development made an increasingly significant impact upon APEC over time, and indeed threatened to make the organisation look irrelevant. As we discuss, FTAs appeared to be gradually supplanting APEC as a mechanism for both advancing region-wide commercial liberalisation and fostering closer relations amongst Asia-Pacific states generally.

During the years 2000 to 2003, no new trade liberalisation initiative was introduced at APEC summits. In the meantime, the IAP scheme continued to operate in the same ineffective manner. While a proposal was endorsed at the 2001 Shanghai Summit to strengthen the IAP peer review process, which included the establishment of new IAP Peer Review Teams, progress made down this path remained very limited. As always, APEC members played a wait-and-see game on IAPs, proving reluctant to voluntarily jump first on unilateral trade liberalisation to any significant extent. Member governments were content in this period simply to make generally vague pledges in APEC summit declarations 'to continue and accelerate' movement towards the Bogor Goals, as specifically stated in the 2002 APEC Los Cabos Summit declaration. New initiatives on other fronts did little to provide APEC with new impetus.

At the 2001 summit, the Shanghai Goal on Trade Facilitation was launched with its aim of reducing trade transaction costs by 5 per cent by 2006 (APEC 2002). This was followed in 2004 by a similar trade-facilitating programme, the Santiago Initiative for Expanded Trade whereby APEC member states committed themselves to further reduce business transaction costs 'by cutting red tape, embracing automation, harmonizing standards and eliminating unnecessary barriers to trade'.[4] The very generalised objectives of this programme were typical of the non-specific, lowest common denominator approach that by this time had become the APEC norm on its new trans-regional initiatives.

Countries such as the US and Australia, which had been amongst the most proactive member states in APEC during the 1990s, were gradually downgrading the organisation's importance during the early 2000s (Beeson 2006a, Dent 2006a). The US's new preoccupation with the 'war on terror' after the 11 September 2001 terrorist attacks switched its geopolitical attention to the Middle East and Central Asia. East Asian member states were meanwhile busy constructing new regional frameworks of co-operation through the APT arrangement. Like other APEC members, East Asian member states were further developing their FTA policies in this period. It was at the 2002 APEC Summit held in Los Cabos, Mexico that Asia-Pacific leaders first officially acknowledged how APEC needed to better address the bilateral FTA trend issue, including whether bilaterals could be incorporated into the Bogor Goals project. The 2002 Leader's Declaration also hinted of concern over the variance of trade rules generated by bilateral FTA proliferation in the region, and the need to establish some consistency between the growing number of agreements. More specifically, the 2002 Leader's Declaration called for 'an exchange of views in APEC on regional and bilateral trade agreements, noting that these agreements need to be consistent with WTO rules and disciplines and APEC's goals and principles'.[5]

The following year, PECC's Trade Forum section was commissioned to propose a code for FTA 'best practice', their recommendations (PECC 2003) being then forwarded to the 2004 APEC Ministerial Meeting where they were duly endorsed (APEC 2004). However, there were notable inconsistencies between most key areas of 'best FTA practice' being proposed on the one hand and what kind of FTAs had been or were being negotiated on the other. For example, many FTAs concluded within the Asia-Pacific did not have *comprehensive sectoral coverage* as a number exempted various agricultural and industrial sectors from the agreement. Many agreements also did not have *simple rules of origin*, rather complex sets of product-specific rules of origin that often took up hundreds of pages in the FTA text.[6] A number of other agreements omitted *accession clauses* that would allow third parties to sign the agreement at some later date. Many also did not incorporate *co-operation provisions* (e.g. the US's FTAs) in the text.

Furthermore, the 'best practice' guidelines did not clarify exactly how FTAs were to achieve the overarching objective of being *consistent with APEC principles and goals*, meaning *inter alia* the realisation of the Bogor Goals and therefore the construction of open regionalism in the Asia-Pacific. Taking one technical policy example to illustrate the point, many FTAs that have been signed amongst APEC member economies carried very long tariff liberalisation phase-in schedules that actually extended beyond the Bogor Goals' 2010/2020 deadlines. For instance, the Australia–US FTA, signed in 2004, had many tariff liberalisation schedules (some lasting up to 18 years in the agricultural sector) that ran some way past the 2010 target date set for developed member states, into which category Australia and the United States both fall. The Thailand–Australia FTA meanwhile has tariff liberalisation schedules on certain agricultural products that run up to 2025, thus beyond the 2020 deadline for developing country liberalisation.

By the end of 2004, the time by which APEC had endorsed these 'best practice' guidelines, the number of negotiated FTAs within the trans-region had risen to 30. Retrospective application of the guidelines was not, though, being explicitly recommended.

4.4 The Free Trade Area of the Asia-Pacific (FTAAP) initiative

At the same time the best FTA practice guidelines were being considered at the 2004 APEC Summit held in Santiago, a proposal originating from the APEC Business Advisory Council (ABAC) was tabled to create an FTAAP. This was essentially a revival of the old PAFTA idea, and hence could be conceived as bringing the whole Pacific regional community-building project to its original starting point. The FTAAP proposal was supported by a number of member economies, namely Chile, Canada, Australia, New Zealand, the US and also two from East Asia, Singapore and Taiwan. As we know from Chapter 3, Singapore has long been a strong advocate of trade liberalisation generally owing to the core entrepôt function of its economy. Taiwan's motives for supporting the FTAAP were more geopolitical as the transregional FTA would help circumvent the significant politico-diplomatic difficulties Taiwan faced in developing its bilateral FTA policy because of its contested sovereignty predicament (Dent 2005a).

As it transpired, opposition from mostly East Asian countries (especially from China, Japan, Malaysia and Indonesia) scuppered the FTAAP proposal at the 2004 APEC Summit, with them again noting their preference for APEC to confer greater priority to its ecotech agenda. At the following 2005 APEC Summit convened in Busan, a mid-term review on progress towards the Bogor Goals was considered. However, the review proposed no new substantive measures to realise the 2010/2020 commercial liberalisation objectives. Following on from the previous year's discussions establishing FTA best practice guidelines, the 2005 APEC Leaders Declaration did, though, call for 'the development of model measures for as many commonly accepted FTA chapters as possible by 2008'.[7]

The idea of creating an FTAAP re-emerged at the 2006 APEC Summit at Hanoi, this time being advocated by the US. Prior to the summit, US State Department officials approached their counterparts in Japan's foreign and trade ministries to discuss the idea. President George W. Bush also used a preliminary visit to Singapore to try to build coalitional support for the new FTAAP initiative. A number of motives were at play here. First, the US was concerned that East Asia was looking to develop its own regional FTA, as had been just earlier proposed by Japan in both April and August that year (see Chapter 6, Case Study 6.2, p. 219), and how this could according to one interviewed government source 'draw a line down the middle of the Pacific'.[8] As we noted in Chapter 1, the US has an obvious strategic interest in promoting Asia-Pacific rather than East Asian regionalism.

The FTAAP plan was thus intended to counteract the regional FTA initiatives of East Asian countries.

Fred Bergsten, who strongly supported the FTAAP initiative, was of the opinion that an East Asia regional FTA would 'create a new Asian bloc that, along with the European Union and the North American Free Trade Agreement, would produce a tripolar world with all its inherent instabilities,' and that,

> By contrast, an FTAAP would embed these Asia-only arrangements in a broader Asia-Pacific framework. It would prevent the creation of a new division across the Pacific...The US and China would be the natural leaders of an FTAAP process and could simultaneously improve the prospects for resolving their bilateral trade tensions through such a regional framework.[9]

The argument that a relatively smaller East Asia trade bloc would cause greater geopolitical instability than a much larger Asia-Pacific trade bloc is somewhat questionable. Moreover, a key issue concerning the FTAAP was on which FTA model was this regional agreement to be based? The big powers of APEC – the US, Japan and China – had all developed their own quite distinct approaches to constructing free trade agreements by this time in terms of technical policy content and ideational foundation (see Chapter 6). This could lead to conflicts between them in the formation of any prospective FTAAP arrangement as each power seeks to champion particular aspects of their own FTA model.

A second motive for the US's promotion of the FTAAP was linked to the then stalled Doha Round of WTO negotiations. On the one hand, it was thought that plans to create a Pacific regional FTA would jolt the EU, India, Brazil and others into making the necessary concessions that would revitalise the inert Doha Round talks. Parallels with the 1993 situation between APEC and the Uruguay Round were made by those making this argument, which included Fred Bergsten and Australian Foreign Minister Alexander Downer.[10] But this case for 'competitive liberalisation' in which relatively lower level FTAs help catalyse free trade movement at the multilateral level is not based on firm empirical evidence (Dent 2006a). In addition, there was stronger linkage between the FTAAP and the Doha Round in the US's calculus of motives, namely that the former was a fall back plan if the latter failed to materialise.

Other pro-liberalising member states of APEC also held this view, as did many ABAC representatives.[11] A third more general motive for the US was its desire to keep commercial liberalisation at the heart of APEC's agenda. No new substantive trade liberalisation initiative had been proposed since the EVSL back in the late 1990s. The FTAAP initiative thus sought to revive APEC's commercial liberalisation programme, especially keeping in mind that the Bogor Goals' 2010 developed country deadline was only a few years away.

Singapore, Brunei, Canada, New Zealand and Chile supported the US's new FTAAP initiative. The ABAC also backed the plan, their main motive being to rationalise the trans-region's 'complete chaos' of bilateral and sub-regional FTAs into one harmonised Asia-Pacific agreement.[12] However, as in 2004 when the FTAAP was first proposed, a number of East Asian countries were opposed to the idea, most notably China, Japan, Thailand, Indonesia, Malaysia and the Philippines. Japan stated its preference for focusing on an East Asian regional agreement based on EAS membership (i.e. also including India, New Zealand and Australia) while China was generally unreceptive to the FTAAP initiative. Malaysia meanwhile stated that its main priorities in APEC concerned 'trade facilitation, human and institutional capacity building, and economic and technical co-operation to promote sustainable growth and equitable development for shared prosperity in the Asia-Pacific region'.[13]

Meanwhile, Malaysian Prime Minister Abdullah Ahmad Badawi called for APEC to be made more relevant to the needs and aspirations of all member economies instead of just a few. The implicit target of this criticism was the US and other developed APEC members, particularly with regard to how both the FTAAP initiative and the US's push of security-related issues onto the APEC agenda (see Case Study 4.2) played more to the interests of certain member states than others. In support of Japan's preference for an East Asia regional FTA and the APT/EAS regional frameworks generally, Badawi commented in relation to APEC that, 'It is critical that we preserve the integrity of the respective [regional] processes. We must not allow the pursuit of narrow national interests to subvert the integrity of one process against the other process'.[14]

Thailand's Director-General of the Trade Negotiations, Chutima Bunyapraphasara, was of the view that the FTAAP was both 'unnecessary and impractical' owing to the diversity that existed amongst APEC member economies, and moreover that the initiative 'was against APEC's original objective of voluntary economic co-operation'.[15] Thai Commerce Minister Krirk-krai Jirapaet expressed a similar opinion, furthermore stating that the FTAAP should be no more than a 'very, very, long-term goal'.[16] Krirk-krai also drew parallels with the Free Trade Area of the Americas (FTAA), another trans-regional project led by the US in which progress had become almost impossible due to the problems of reconciling so many diverse national interests in trade negotiations. It is worth noting that the breakdown in FTAA negotiations owed much to the friction arising between the US and Brazil, each championing their own particular FTA model, i.e. NAFTA and Mercosur, respectively. At the 2006 APEC Summit, the Philippines Trade Secretary Peter Favila expressed his government's view that, 'An FTAAP at this point will only distract us from the more important goal of restarting and concluding the [Doha Development Round] negotiations'.[17]

In the end, APEC leaders at the Hanoi 2006 Summit acknowledged that there were 'practical difficulties' in realising the FTAAP and proposed that ministerial officials should study the idea as a long-term prospect and report back at the 2007 Sydney Summit (APEC Leader Declaration 2006). In the meantime, APEC leaders agreed to give 'top priority' to re-initiate Doha Round negotiations, although no details emerged from the summit regarding any movement from APEC members beyond their current Doha Round positions. Other issues discussed at Hanoi included technical co-operation and capacity building; intellectual property rights; anti-corruption and transparency; counter terrorism and secure trade; avian flu and other health security matters; disaster preparedness; and energy security and high oil prices. In addition, it was agreed to establish six 'model measures' or chapters on FTA practice by 2008 on issues including government procurement, trade in commodities and technical barriers to trade. These would presumably dovetail into feasibility studies conducted on a possible FTAAP arrangement although this was not clarified in the 2006 Leaders Declaration.

A number of East Asian countries particularly insisted the Declaration stated that, 'We also reiterated the non-binding and voluntary nature of the model measures, bearing in mind that they will not prejudice the positions of APEC members in their existing and future RTAs/FTAs negotiations.' As a senior Thai official, Virachai Plasai, commented at the time, 'APEC is not a negotiating forum. It is designed for co-operation that is non-binding.'[18] Certainly the earlier IAP and EVSL episodes had demonstrated APEC's limitations in brokering new trade deals. According to PECC's international chairman, Charles Morrison, 'Even before [FTAAP] negotiations could begin, they would require major and controversial changes in APEC's social contract'.[19] There were, though, plans for the 2007 Summit at Sydney to reassess APEC's organisational capacities and operational principles, including the possible enhancing of its Singapore-based secretariat. However, many East Asian countries remain opposed, as they did at the start in 1989, to conferring too much independence or any executive policy-making powers to APEC as an organisational entity.

In addition to the above mentioned difficulties involved with operationalising any future FTAAP plan, APEC has increasingly faced a credibility problem. Most of its summits have produced a special plan or programme ascribed to the summit-hosting city but the lack of progress made by APEC on its centerpiece Bogor Goals project since the mid-1990s has created some confusion regarding how certain plans and programmes relate to others. For example, proposals on feasibility studying the FTAAP and establishing the six model measures of FTA practice are embodied within the 2006 Hanoi Action Plan, which is not to be confused with ASEAN's Hanoi Plan of Action on regional economic integration (see Chapter 3). Does the Hanoi Action Plan make redundant the preceding 1995 Osaka Action Agenda and 1996 Manila Action Plan on achieving the Bogor Goals? This has not been clarified. Furthermore, the official name of the 2006 'plan' is the 'Hanoi Action Plan to Implement the Busan Road Map to achieve the Bogor Goals', which appears to be a clumsy attempt to establish some kind of bureaucratic consistency between three 'plans' spanning over a decade. One could argue that subsequent plans upgrade and augment the proposals embodied by preceding plans, for instance 2006 Hanoi in relation to 2005 Busan, yet the impact of the Busan Road Map has nevertheless been somewhat diminished by this cannibalisation process. The Hanoi Plan – that has not really added much additional substance to the Busan Plan – may suffer a similar fate at the hands of any forthcoming Sydney Plan that emerges at the 2007 summit.

Each hosting country of course wishes to leave its mark on the development of APEC, but the organisation's propensity to produce monumental-sounding plans of thin and easily recyclable substance only serves to undermine the organisation's credibility and relevance. Indeed, at the 2006 summit, leaders from Australia, China, Malaysia, New Zealand and Singapore told their audience that APEC was in danger of becoming increasingly irrelevant in Asia-Pacific affairs.[20] This was supported by evidence from a recent PECC survey conducted amongst 370 regional opinion leaders in which only 42 per cent agreed with the statement 'APEC is as important today as it was in 1989' (PECC 2006). The majority of those surveyed believed that APEC's biggest problem was the low commitment shown by its member states to advance its main projects, and its lack of focus on new emerging issues such as energy security, water pollution and financial market instability. Deepening regional integration in East Asia was also highlighted as another key challenge facing APEC.

Case Study 4.2 APEC's economics–security nexus

When APEC was created in 1989, it was conceived first and foremost as an economic-focused organisation dealing with economic policy issues. It had no remit to cover conventional security matters or any other political affairs in the international relations of APEC member states. However, like many other regional organisations, including ASEAN and the APT framework, APEC has had to address issues arising within emerging 'new security' sectors, e.g. energy security, environmental security (Buzan 1998, Katzenstein 1996). Many issues associated with these sectors intersected with aspects of economic development and diplomacy, and therefore a case could be made for APEC's engagement with these issues. APEC has a Working Group on Energy, has introduced 'sustainable cities' and 'cleaner production' initiatives, and in 2001 launched its Energy Security Initiative (see Chapter 7). At the 2006 Hanoi Summit, a new Biofuels Task Force was created, while much emphasis was placed on enhancing 'human security' in that year's Leaders Declaration.

Since the 11 September 2001 terrorist attacks on New York and Washington, the US has sought to make APEC more security-focused but primarily in the context of the 'war on terror', and hence in a politico-military security sense. The US has subsequently tried to lead the organisation down a new path where economics and security have become increasingly conflated (Dent 2003, Ravenhill 2006). The first proposals with these ends in mind were made at the 2001 APEC Summit held at Shanghai, where in initial solidarity with the US the group's leaders proclaimed in their joint statement that terrorism was 'a direct challenge to APEC's vision of free, open and prosperous economies, and to the fundamental values that APEC members hold'. In addition, they specifically pledged to 'adopt financial measures to prevent the flow of funds to terrorists, to adhere to international requirements on air and maritime security, and to have their transportation chiefs discuss additional measures to enhance airport, aircraft and port security' (APEC 2001 Leader's Declaration).

At the following 2002 Brunei Summit, APEC's leaders, under the banner of 'Counter-Terrorism and Economic Growth', agreed to launch the Secure Trade in the APEC Region (STAR) Initiative that aimed to improve transportation security, customs and immigration co-operation amongst member states, while a new Action Plan on Combating the Financing of Terrorism was devised to halt the flow of financing to terrorists. Furthermore, APEC's new Cyber-security Strategy was intended to debilitate the communication capabilities of terrorist groups operating in the Asia-Pacific, whilst maintaining the free flow of information that permitted markets to operate effectively. The 2002 APEC Leaders Joint Statement stated 'the importance to achieving the twin goals of enhanced security against terrorist threats and continued protection of economic growth' (APEC 2002 Leaders Declaration). A Counter-Terrorism Task Force has also been created, further consolidating the new economic–security nexus in APEC diplomacy.

Essentially, these were economic policy measures with an anti-terrorist security purpose, and other member-states were happy to support these initiatives if economics remained APEC's primary focus. However, with many APEC member states condemning the US-led invasion of Iraq in 2003 it was more difficult for the Bush Administration to push new 'war on terror' related initiatives onto the organisation's agenda. Reassurances that APEC member states would take measures to 'combat terrorism' continue to be included in annual Leader Declarations, and ongoing work in improving transportation security is being conducted in various APEC programmes. Yet by the mid-2000s, many East Asian member states in particular had become increasingly wary of US security-related proposals and statements made in relation to its APEC diplomacy.

At the 2006 Hanoi Summit, the US delegation led by President George Bush tried to advance a position of agreement with other member delegations and within APEC generally on the issue of North Korea and Iran's nuclear weapon programmes but with no real success. Vietnam's President Nguyen Minh Triet, the hosting chair of the Leaders Meeting, did state in his final address to the summit that North Korea's missile and nuclear tests were 'a clear threat to our shared interest in peace and security' but the Leaders Declaration document made no reference to North Korea's nuclear weapons programme.

Malaysian Prime Minister Abdullah Ahmad Badawi was the most vocal East Asian critic of the US's strategy on this matter, commenting with regard to APEC that, 'Its assumption of some security role following the September 11 attacks in the United States has compromised its original purpose and blurred its focus'.[21] Badawi further argued that discussions on 'political security subjects' were taking up too much time at APEC meetings generally leaving less time to debate trade promotion issues, and moreover that the ASEAN Regional Forum, Six Party Talks framework and United Nation's Security Council were more appropriate fora for discussing such regional security matters. China and many other East Asian countries also proved reluctant to support the US's position on North Korea and Iran security-related issues. Accommodating politico-military related security issues on the APEC agenda remains problematic even if the Asia-Pacific continues to have no pan-regional security organisation or arrangement.

Study Questions

1. Why have economic and security-related matters become increasingly bound together in today's international system?
2. Why have so many East Asian countries opposed the idea of APEC adopting a more security-related agenda?

4.5 East Asia, APEC and regional economic community-building

We have seen how East Asian countries have become increasingly frustrated with APEC over recent years, especially relating to the following areas:

1) the prioritisation of commercial liberalisation over ecotech and trade and investment facilitation;
2) APEC inadequate response to the 1997/8 East Asian financial crisis; and
3) the gradual drift towards discussions on certain security-related issues.

East Asian countries have represented an important core of APEC membership from the start, and each has a vested interest in the organisation's endeavours at regional economic community-building in the Asia-Pacific. Most of East Asia's main trade and investment partners are still located within the trans-region, and the maintenance of open markets and freer flows of foreign investment have been critical factors behind the outward-oriented development of East Asia countries.

However, for these countries it has been the special emphasis afforded to commercial liberalisation as the prime modality of regional economic integration that has been the problem. East Asian member states have especially highlighted the limitations of this approach. Progress made towards the Bogor Goals will reduce trade and investment barriers between national economies in the Asia-Pacific, and thereby help cultivate integrative linkages. This may be referred to as a 'passive integration' approach, in that all governments are simply removing impediments to integration rather than developing new integrational linkages themselves through economic and technical co-operation, policy co-ordination and harmonisation, and other such measures that may be viewed in contrast as a 'proactive integration' approach (see Chapter 8 for a broader discussion on these two approaches in relation to regionalism more generally). APEC's ecotech and trade/investment facilitation programmes – the preferred choice of its East Asia member states – thus fall into the proactive integration category.

To most East Asian countries, APEC has remained too preoccupied with the passive integration of commercial liberalisation initiatives like the EVSL and the proposed FTAAP than the 'proactive integration' embodied by ecotech. The relatively strong East Asian support for APEC's ecotech programmes lay in its emphasis on development capacity and development co-operation matters. Many have argued that given the development diversity within APEC's membership, far more action was required to assist less developed countries with their capacity-building efforts, as best served by ecotech measures. Moreover, richer member states doing more to directly foster the development of weaker member states would better enhance the sense of regional solidarity within APEC than commercial liberalisation. East Asian countries have also pushed for greater integration between APEC's ecotech and commercial liberalisation programmes, arguing that it would take more account of developing members' need for stronger institutional infrastructure and regulatory capacities to better equip them when meeting the competitive challenges posed by liberalisation (Elek and Soesastro 2000). The US, though, has generally insisted on keeping these two programmatic strands of APEC separate. Nesadurai (2006) remarks how this typified the differences of approach that existed within APEC's membership concerning the state-market relationship, and therefore how economies should be governed. East Asian members were generally more interested in APEC's 'developmental' programmes while Anglo-Pacific members used the organisation as a vehicle for market-liberal advocacy.

The lower priority afforded by the US and other developed Anglo-Pacific countries to ecotech was also partly motivated by their concern over

APEC evolving into an aid and development assistance forum rather than one principally designed to advance market liberal reforms within the trans-region (Berger and Beeson 2005). As has been previously noted, the US has especially championed the market liberal position of integration primarily through liberalisation. Although a large number of ecotech projects have been initiated – covering areas such as human capital, infrastructure development, new technology development, sustainable development, and SME growth – the whole ecotech framework has suffered from 'a general lack of co-ordination and setting of priorities' (Ravenhill 2001: 193) leading to an ineffective impact overall. Many projects were not goal-oriented with explicit objectives or performance criteria to be matched, or subject to rigorous external assessment of their outcomes. Ecotech programmes have also suffered from underfunding. Up to the year 2000 the total annual budget for these programmes never exceeded US$2 million, and this situation has improved little.[22]

At the 1997 and 1998 APEC Summits, East Asian countries proposed a number of new initiatives to address the crisis. The first and also most important of these was Japan's proposal, initially made in September 1997 at a G7 meeting, to create an Asian Monetary Fund (AMF) based on US$100 billion of standby funds to assist countries in a currency crisis (see Chapter 5). However, the US was particularly hostile to the idea, stating that it could potentially undermine the IMF's position in dealing with international financial crises. The AMF proposal was consequently rejected at the 1997 Vancouver Summit by the US and other supporting member states. Other East Asian states, such as Malaysia, made proposals for measures that would help regulate speculative capital flows, which were generally viewed in East Asia as having triggered the initial currency crisis in July and August 1997. Ideas on how to strengthen the Asia-Pacific's regional financial architecture were also put forward. However, these too were rejected.

Instead, the APEC response was to call for renewed commitments to trade liberalisation and to improve transparency in member states' financial systems (Ravenhill 2002a). A meeting held at Manila in November 1997 brought together APEC's senior finance officials to discuss the crisis but the main outcome of the agreed 'Manila Framework' was the endorsement of the IMF programmes for the region. There was some reference to enhancing regional surveillance, intensifying economic and technical co-operation to improve domestic financial regulatory capacities, yet no concrete new measures proposed as to how this was to be achieved. At the May 1998 APEC financial ministers meeting, the chair's statement emphasised the domestic causes of the crisis and said nothing of external systemic factors concerning the crisis. Garnaut (2000) argues this was a lost opportunity for APEC in demonstrating its value and worth to its East Asian constituents as a regional organisation. More significantly, APEC's failure to address the concerns of East Asian countries galvanised them into establishing their own regional institutional framework, ASEAN Plus Three, the core subject of the next chapter.

4.6 Conclusion

4.6.1 Summary overview

East Asia may be considered one of three macro-regions (the others being Oceania and Pacific America) that constitute the Asia-Pacific trans-region. East Asian countries have developed particularly close economic, political, security and socio-cultural ties with other Asia-Pacific nations, especially the United States. The Asia-Pacific Economic Co-operation forum has emerged as the most important regional organisation within the trans-region. It was established in 1989 after many years of diplomatic efforts, made notably by Japan and Australia, at fostering closer 'Pacific community' relations from the 1960s onwards. East Asian countries form much of APEC's core membership, and hence APEC-led developments on trans-regional community-building may have notable impacts on East Asian regionalism. Broadly speaking, it may on the one hand have a positive reinforcing effect by further cultivating closer co-operative and integrative links amongst the organisation's East Asian member states. On the other hand, APEC may dilute East Asian regionalism by blending the regional community-building endeavours of East Asian states within the larger Asia-Pacific trans-regional mix. As indicated in this chapter, many East Asian countries have become increasingly wary of the latter, especially after APEC demonstrably failed to address the fallout from the 1997/8 financial crisis.

It was also during and after the 1997/8 financial crisis that the differences between East Asian and Anglo-Pacific member states concerning the main purpose and objectives of APEC became more starkly revealed. Whereas commercial liberalisation has been prioritised and promoted by the Anglo-Pacific countries (Australia, Canada, New Zealand and the US), most of their East Asian counterparts have instead championed APEC's economic and technical co-operation (ecotech) agenda. In a way this marked a clash of economic cultures within the Asia-Pacific, between Anglo-Pacific market liberalism and East Asian developmentalism. The failure of APEC to make substantial progress with its trade and investment liberalisation initiatives, such as the IAP, EVSL and FTAAP, owes much to these economic cultural differences. The US's preoccupation with closer linking APEC's core economic agenda with 'war on terror' related security objectives has further complicated APEC politics. Moreover, East Asian states have diverted increasing attention to developing their own more exclusive regional frameworks of co-operation and integration – the ASEAN Plus Three and East Asia Summit – with the inevitable de-prioritisation of APEC this has generally entailed. As was also discussed, many Asia-Pacific countries were being drawn into a proliferating trend of bilateral free trade agreements (FTA) from the late 1990s onwards, and this too has undermined APEC.

4.6.2 International Political Economy (IPE) theoretical analysis

A *neo-realist* assessment of APEC would highlight how competing and often seemingly irreconcilable national interests have significantly impeded the organisation's progress, as well as that of Asia-Pacific trans-regionalism generally. This chapter noted various contests between certain APEC member states over the nature and future direction of the organisation's agenda. For example, Japan was willing to jeopardise the EVSL scheme because it wished to safeguard certain national interests, i.e. politically sensitive agricultural sectors. Neo-realists may in addition argue that sub-group coalitions of nation-states (e.g. for and against the FTAAP proposal) are the best instances of member state solidarity that APEC has thus far achieved. Moreover, it is the wide diversity of nation-states encompassed within APEC's membership that has ultimately been the organisation's undoing – there are simply too many divergent national interests to reconcile. Hence to some, APEC may be considered too large and unwieldy a regional organisation. Furthermore, neo-realists may contend that APEC contains too many 'great power' nations (China, Japan, Russia, the United States), each competing with the other for hegemonic position and influence in the Asia-Pacific trans-region, and subsequently raising the prospect of anarchic or adversarial relations between APEC member states. On whose FTA model, for example, is any future FTAAP arrangement to be based? Both China and Japan would strongly resist any attempt by the US to promote its own model as the FTAAP template, and vice versa. More generally, there is a view held by many East Asians that the US has used APEC as a tool to advance American geopolitical and geo-economic interests in the Asia-Pacific. This particularly relates to how the US's promotion of Asia-Pacific regionalism narrows the chance of an exclusive East Asia regional organisation or framework forming, one that could potentially marginalise American strategic interests.

A *neo-liberal institutionalist* evaluation of APEC would in contrast stress how the regional organisation, like others of its type, is essentially a tool for managing interdependent links and interests that have developed amongst a regional group of states. In addition, APEC provides mechanisms for these states to co-operate at the trans-regional level rather than just compete in an anarchic fashion, and also to provide the basis for cultivating an Asia-Pacific community. Deepening interdependence requires APEC member states to work more closely together rather than engage in zero-sum competition, as the national interests of member states are increasingly interwoven in a regionalising and globalising world. The United States used such reasoning when advocating that APEC should adopt more security-related measures after the 11 September 2001 terrorist attacks on US soil as the 'war on terror' in some way impacted on, and hence involved all APEC member states according to Washington. From another neo-liberal perspective, APEC's centrepiece Bogor Goal project on commercial liberalisation has to some extent helped advance economic liberalism in East Asia and elsewhere in the Asia-Pacific. It may be going too far, though, to assert that APEC has become a club of liberal economies. As frequently discussed in this chapter, East Asian developmental interests have often been divergent to those of Anglo-Pacific market-liberalism. Whereas the latter have naturally championed APEC's market-liberal integration schemes (e.g. EVSL, FTAAP), the former have backed APEC's developmental integration agenda, especially its ecotech programme. Neo-liberals would also note the important role played by non-state actors in the creation of APEC and its antecedent organisations, namely the Pacific Basin Economic Council, the Pacific Trade and Development conference, and the Pacific Economic Co-operation Conference forum. In all three cases, business representatives, academics and research analysts were vital members, working alongside government officials in seeking how to best manage deepening economic interdependence in the Asia-Pacific. The crucial role of non-state actors has continued: for example, it was the APEC Business Advisory Council that first tabled a proposal in 2004 to initiate an FTAAP project.

Turning now to the *social constructivist* perspective of IPE, this chapter noted that ideas on forging a 'Pacific community' have been around for some time, dating back to the early twentieth century. These ideas were the seeds from which material actions on Pacific community-building have grown. The construction of a stronger and more coherent Pacific regional identity would prove an important unifying force in the further development of Asia-Pacific trans-regionalism. However, our discussions have highlighted the many difficulties involved in achieving this. The Asia-Pacific is an immensely diverse trans-region. Finding sufficient economic, political, ideational and socio-cultural commonalties amongst APEC's member states on which common policies, schemes, declarations and so on can be formulated has been a significant challenge to the organisation throughout its existence. Certain East Asian states have found it easier than others to assume some kind of Asia-Pacific identity, especially Japan because of its close links with the US and its island seafaring history, and Singapore owing to its long-established trade hub position in the regional and global economy. Most East Asian nations, though, consider themselves fundamentally far more Asian than Asia-Pacific in identity because they lack the same kinds of bonds across the Pacific. Thus, APEC can only be expected to achieve so much in fostering a sense of Asia-Pacific regional community amongst its East Asian member states. Furthermore, this chapter has shown the clash of various ideas and values that have arisen over APEC's agenda and organising principles. For instance, in relation to ideas over trade and development this has concerned contested notions of free trade, sustainable and equitable development, what kind of trans-regional community APEC should be building, etc. We discussed how the idea of 'open regionalism' was supposed to represent APEC's core principles and *modus operandi*, thus as an inclusive, globalisation-oriented approach to promoting Asia-Pacific trans-regional relations. Yet, the precise meaning of open regionalism was never properly clarified. There is bound to be significant discord amongst the membership of any organisation whose core principles and founding ideas remain ambiguous and contested.

Finally, *Marxist-structuralist* IPE perspectives on APEC would generally frame the organisation's main purpose as being to advance the development and interests of transnational capital within the trans-region. According to this view, the whole APEC project is managed and organised by the transnational capital class elite, namely political leaders, academics and MNE executives who all have a vested interest in removing obstacles (e.g. trade and investment barriers) that have hitherto impeded the trans-regional operations of MNEs in the Asia-Pacific. APEC's centrepiece Bogor Goals project is thus essentially a transnational capital class led scheme that further enables the progress of neo-liberal globalisation. Furthermore, it has been devised more with the needs of 'core' advanced industrial economies in mind whilst those of the Asia-Pacific's developing country 'periphery' are neglected. Thus, just as in other regions and trans-regions, this basic core–periphery hierarchy of relations amongst APEC member economies is determined by the patterns of production and exchange between them. The power and influence of the transnational business lobby (e.g. the ABAC) in APEC affairs was previously noted. As with other regional organisations and frameworks studied in this book (e.g. ASEAN, APT/EAS), the persistence of a significant core-periphery 'development divide' hinders the progress of regional community-building *per se*. It is difficult to build a regional economic community when such inequitable levels of development exist within a regional organisation unless more advanced and powerful member states are willing to more effectively subordinate their interests to those of their less developed counterparts, for instance by operationalising and funding substantive schemes of economic and technical assistance that better empower periphery economies to more effectively participate in the world economic system. The following chapter examines the development of the ASEAN Plus Three and East Asia Summit regional frameworks.

Chapter Study Questions

1. To what extent could the creation of APEC be considered as a Japan–Australia diplomatic joint venture?
2. Discuss the view that APEC could have achieved significantly more if it had not expanded to include so many member economies.
3. How were APEC's trade and liberalisation schemes supposed to enhance regional integration in the Asia-Pacific?
4. 'APEC's main problem is that there exists a fundamental clash of politico-economic cultures amongst its core member economies'. Discuss.
5. On balance, has APEC worked for or against the development of East Asian regionalism?

Notes

1   Upgrading the former Informal Group on Regional Trade Liberalisation.
2   Author's research interviews, Canberra, August 2003.
3   *Bangkok Post*, 14.11.1994.
4   Leader's Declaration of the 2004 APEC Economic Leaders Summit.
5   Leader's Declaration of the 2002 APEC Economic Leaders Summit.
6   Japan and the US particularly insisted on product-specific rules of origin in their FTAs as a means to protect certain industries from foreign competition.
7   APEC 2005 Leaders Declaration, or Busan Declaration, 18–19 November, p. 2.
8   *Associated Press*, 05.11.2006.
9   *Financial Times*, 15.11.2006.
10 Bergsten believed that the FTAAP would serve as a 'credible political jolt' to the European Union, India and Brazil into making new offers in the Doha Round (*Agence France-Presse*, 11.11.2006). Similarly, Downer commented that the FTAAP would be 'a way of reminding the Europeans that there is greater virtue in a successful conclusion to the Doha round' (*Bloomberg News*, 19.11.2006).
11 For example, Australia's ABAC representative Peter Charlton stated that, 'Although the best position is to have a successful outcome to the WTO negotiations, the primary position is that if everything else fails and the WTO fails on the Doha Round, then the FTAAP is the secondary choice' (*Business Times*, 14.11.2006).
12 *Washington Post*, 20.11.2006.
13 Malaysia Minister of International Trade and Industry press release, 11.11.2006.
14 *Malaysian Star*, 18.11.2006.
15 *Bangkok Post*, November 10, 2006.
16 *The Nation*, 18.11.2006.
17 *Washington Post*, 20.11.2006.
18 *Associated Press*, November 14, 2006.
19 *Agence France-Presse*, 11.11.2006.
20 *New Straits Times*, 20.11.2006.
21 *Malaysian Star*, 18.11.2006.
22 Although the Japanese government continues to provide some generic funding for APEC's trade and investment facilitation projects, ecotech programmes are usually funded by individual member states that have a strong interest in supporting particular projects.

Chapter 5

ASEAN Plus Three and East Asia Summit

Financial regionalism and beyond?

5.1 Introduction

This chapter examines the emergence of two inter-related regional frameworks, APT and EAS. The use of the term 'frameworks' denotes that these are not organisations or even institutions but rather a system of mostly inter-governmental meetings for fostering regional co-operation and integration. Neither APT nor EAS has a secretariat or any other permanent co-ordinating agency, yet this does not appear to have hindered the quite significant progress made by APT-led co-operation in particular. The APT framework was established in December 1997 at an inaugural summit convened in Kuala Lumpur. Its membership comprises the ten ASEAN member states plus the three Northeast Asian states of China, Japan and South Korea. The inaugural APT summit was of some historic importance as it was the first time the leaders of most East Asian countries had met together as an exclusive regional grouping.

The meeting was planned before the outbreak of the region's 1997/8 financial crisis but it was the collective response to the crisis that shaped the initial APT agenda, this being to develop new mechanisms of regional financial governance in East Asia. This remains the main focus of APT-led co-operation, and its advance of East Asia's 'financial regionalism' has centred on three main projects, namely the Chiang Mai Initiative (CMI), the Asian Bond Market Initiative (ABMI) and the Asian Currency Unit (ACU) initiative. In addition, the APT framework has gradually broadened its agenda to other areas of regional co-operation, for example, on tackling avian flu, addressing food security issues and cultivating a stronger sense of East Asian regional identity.

It was from the APT framework that the idea to establish a regular East Asian Summit process arose. At first it was thought that the EAS would supersede the APT and mark a step up in East Asia's regional integration ambitions. However, most of the debate and diplomacy over the EAS's inauguration centred on its membership. As we shall see, the inclusion of Australia, New Zealand and India into the grouping was controversial and connected with important geopolitical issues concerning East Asian regionalism. This chapter examines pre-APT initiatives on forming an East Asia regional grouping before then looking at the development of the APT and EAS frameworks themselves. We also consider the importance of the Japan–China relationship in advancing East Asian regionalism. The main objectives of this chapter are to assess achievements made on developing financial co-operation and integration since the 1997/8 crisis, and discuss to what extent APT and EAS can provide the organisational foundations on which East Asian regionalism may progress generally.

5.2 Forming an East Asia regional grouping: precursory developments

We know from previous chapters how East Asian countries had participated in a number of regional fora and organisations before the introduction of the APT framework. However, these were not exclusively East Asian arrangements. Examples include the Asia-Pacific Economic Co-operation (APEC) forum (see Chapter 4), ASEAN Regional Forum (ARF), Council for Security Co-operation in the Asia-Pacific (CSCAP), and United Nations Economic and Social Commission for Asia and the Pacific (UNESCAP). Chapter 4 examined how regional co-operation and integration among East Asian states was bound up in wider trans-regional processes, or Asia-Pacific trans-regionalism through APEC. From 1997 onwards, though, the APT framework has sought to establish a more distinctive East Asian regional grouping.

This was not the first time that such a grouping had been officially proposed. In the early 1990s, Malaysian Prime Minister Mahathir Mohamad advocated the idea of an East Asian Economic Grouping (EAEG), to rival or run parallel to APEC. Mahathir argued that this would bring geopolitical and integrational balance to an emerging post-Cold War world in which Europe was implementing its Single Market and the United States and its closest regional partners the North American Free Trade Agreement (NAFTA). Moreover, Mahathir suggested the EAEG would be a vehicle for championing East Asia interests generally on the global stage. The original EAEG blueprint was launched in December 1990, containing plans to form a preferential trading arrangement between East Asian countries.

The US was vehemently opposed to the proposal and applied heavy diplomatic pressure on its closest East Asian allies to reject it. Japan and South Korea complied with Washington's demands, while Indonesia and Thailand also argued against the EAEG proposal, stating it could undermine the then recently launched APEC forum. Some years later, Mahathir (2006:13) remarked that,

> for reasons we could not understand, the US objected strongly to the EAEG. James Baker, who was then the US Secretary of State, visited South Korea and Japan and told them to have nothing to do with the proposal. Certain ASEAN countries were also advised not to support EAEG. It would seem in the US view that while European countries could get together, and Canada, the US and Mexico could form NAFTA, East Asian countries were not even allowed to talk to each other.

In response, Malaysia consequently modified their EAEG proposal, suggesting instead a more informal East Asian Economic Caucus (EAEC) arrangement. This was put forward in October 1991 at that year's ASEAN Economic Ministers Meeting, and was conceived as a dialogue mechanism for discussing international economic matters affecting the East Asian region. However, the US was concerned that the EAEC would undermine APEC-led endeavours at fostering closer transpacific ties, and also be a platform for East Asian countries exerting their collective interests in multilateral fora, for example the GATT Uruguay Round negotiations. The US Secretary of State, James Baker, visited Japan and South Korea in November 1991 to lobby against Malaysia's EAEC initiative. When South Korean Foreign Minister Lee Sang Ok suggested that his government might support it, Baker reminded him that, 'it was Americans, not Malaysians, who had shed their blood for Korea forty years before', and that 'all countries are not equal' (Baker 1995:611).

In spite of this continued opposition, Malaysia tabled its revised EAEC proposal at the 1992 ASEAN summit in Singapore and at the 1993 APEC Ministerial Meeting at Seattle. At both meetings, the Malaysian Government had to argue that the EAEC would augment both ASEAN and APEC unity rather than undermine it. As it transpired, the EAEC proposal failed to gain sufficient support, although it was nevertheless discussed amongst other matters at the inaugural foreign ministers meeting between ASEAN, China, Japan and South Korea held in July 1994. References to the EAEC continued to be made in Malaysian Government and ASEAN Secretariat documents for some time afterwards, and Malaysia has remained a standard-bearer for advancing the idea of an East Asian Community. More recently, Malaysia proposed the creation of an APT Secretariat in 2002, although this too failed to receive enough support amongst other group members. In August 2003, Malaysia also organised the First East Asia Congress, bringing together delegates from APT countries. Playing host, Prime Minister Mahathir's opening address was entitled 'Building The East Asian Community: The Way Forward', and pointed out that the idea of East Asian regional co-operation and community-building was no longer viewed with the same degree of disdain as before.

Another important precursory development in relation to the APT grouping concerns preparations made by the East Asian member countries of the Asia-Europe Meeting (ASEM) framework leading up to its inaugural summit held in March 1996 at Bangkok. Economic ministers from the region's 10 representing states assembled for an informal lunch meeting in November 1995 to discuss preparations for the first ASEM summit. A Foreign Ministers' meeting and another Economic Ministers' meeting followed in February 1996. Social constructivists have particularly argued that the ASEM process played a vital role in East Asian regional identity-formation, and hence East Asian regionalism *per se* (Gilson 2002). As Japan's Finance Minister Kiichi Miyazawa was to later comment, 'these talks with Europe are helping us build up our own Asian identity'.[1]

The ASEM framework involves the engagement of two distinct and relatively distant regional groups, Asia and Europe, and is therefore an inter-regional arrangement and not a trans-regional arrangement like APEC. In APEC, East Asia's regional identity is bound up to some degree in a wider constituent Asia-Pacific trans-regional identity. This is not the case in ASEM, which from the very beginning helped to define East Asia as a separate regional group – '*we* East Asians are meeting with *you* Europeans' – and consequently some regional interest formation and regional identity formation arose from this process. As the inter-regional ASEM framework took off, Japan, China and South Korea all expressed their interest in establishing regularised summits with the ASEAN group. Southeast Asian states' positive response to this interest led to the first APT summit in December 1997, as detailed in the following section.

5.3 The ASEAN Plus Three (APT) framework

5.3.1 Introduction

Despite the failure of Malaysia's EAEG and EAEC proposals, they nevertheless raised the idea of forming some kind of distinct East Asian regional grouping in the consciousness of the region's policy-makers and other elite groups. The discourse on an EAEG/EAEC type arrangement was also spurred by growing academic interest in the idea (Higgott and Stubbs 1995, Rudner 1995). In December 1995 at the Fifth ASEAN Summit held in Bangkok, Singapore Prime Minister Goh Chok Tong proposed that ASEAN should invite their three Northeast Asian neighbours – Japan, China and South Korea – to its first informal summit meeting planned for a year later, in which prospective new ASEAN member countries (Cambodia, Laos and Myanmar) were invited. This proposal found particular support from Malaysia, which was still endeavouring to keep alive its EAEC concept (Terada 2003). However, no agreement or progress was made until Japanese Prime Minister Ryutaro Hashimoto proposed in January 1997 that a Japan–ASEAN summit be held in conjunction with the ASEAN informal summit later that year (Tanaka 2007). In response, ASEAN countries suggested the framework be broadened to include China and South Korea as well, not wishing to discriminate against them. It was therefore agreed that ASEAN would hold an informal leaders meeting involving all three countries, and then separate summits with each of the three Northeast Asian countries in December 1997 at Kuala Lumpur. This formed the basic structure of the APT framework.

However, it was not until after the first meeting of deputy finance ministers and deputy governors of central banks of the APT countries held in March 1999 that the term 'ASEAN Plus Three' came into widely used parlance. It was also only by the Third Informal Summit held in November 1999 at Manila that the thirteen heads of government together issued their first 'Joint Statement on East Asia Co-operation'. At the 1999 summit, it was agreed that the scope of APT co-operation would be comprehensive, covering the following areas: economic co-operation, financial and monetary co-operation, social and human resource development, scientific and technical development, cultural and information areas, development co-operation, political–security areas, and transnational issues (Stubbs 2002, Tay 2001, Webber 2001).

5.3.2 Pre-APT developments in East Asian regional financial co-operation

As Hamilton-Hart (2004) notes, much of East Asia's earliest work on regional financial co-operation centred on Southeast Asia. She identifies that the first initiative taken in this area was SEANZA (Southeast Asia,

New Zealand, Australia), a central bank group established in 1957. Japan and South Korea later joined the arrangement in the 1960s, and its primary function was to provide training and advisory services for Southeast Asian central banks. This role was later taken over by the SEACEN (Southeast Asian Central Banks) organisation, created in 1966. Later in 1972, ASEAN undertook its first foray into regional financial co-operation with the establishment of the Central Banks and Monetary Authorities Committee. In 1977, a small-scale ASEAN Swap Agreement (ASA) facility was created in which member states could draw upon some form of currency swap assistance from other members in time of financial crisis. However the ASA has never been used, even during the 1997/8 financial crisis, as the sums committed to the scheme (just US$200 million at that time) were so small. Also in 1977, the first meeting of the ASEAN Committee on Banking and Finance was held, and meanwhile public and private sector representatives discussed matters of financial policy in the ASEAN Banking Council, set up in 1976. From the Council's work sprang the ASEAN Finance Corporation, which became incorporated in 1981 and whose main purpose was to be a guarantor of bond issues and to serve as a channel for equity and loans from outside Southeast Asia.

As the long-standing primary financial power in East Asia, much of Japan's role in advancing regional financial co-operation was played through its overseas development assistance policy in the region. The most important example of this was the creation of the Asian Development Bank in 1966, which was the product of low profile but substantial Japanese efforts (Hamilton-Hart 2004, Yasutomo 1983). The ADB, with its headquarters in Manila, essentially performs similar functions to the World Bank but at the region-specific level, providing financial and technical assistance to Asia's developing countries with the principal objective of alleviating poverty in the region. Its membership extends across the entire Asian continent (48 countries, 19 partner countries outside the region) and, as we later discuss, the ADB has become an increasingly prominent actor in East Asian regional financial governance, especially under the leadership of Haruhiko Kuroda, a former Japanese Vice-Minister for Finance. Kuroda was a principal architect of many of the regional financial governance schemes developed during the early APT period, including the New Miyazawa Initiative (NMI) and Chiang Mai Initiative.

Returning to Japan's pre-APT contributions to regional financial co-operation, the Japan–ASEAN Investment Company was established in 1981 and aimed to attract development-oriented funds into Southeast Asia in conjunction with the ASEAN–Japan Development Fund set up in 1987 as part of Japan's capital export programme (Hamilton-Hart 2004). A few years later in 1991, a Japanese Government proposal led to the creation of the Executives' Meeting of East Asian Central Banks (EMEAP) that has more recently played a key role in developing the Asian Bond Market Initiative, discussed later. Finally, there was much discussion in the early 1990s concerning how a more widely internationalised yen could provide the basis for strengthening regional financial co-operation in East Asia (Frankel 1993, Ito 1993, Kwan 1994). However, interest in this subject gradually waned with the prolongation of Japan's economic malaise through the decade. While there appears to have been many pre-APT initiatives and dialogues on regional financial co-operation, overall very few substantial developments had actually occurred, the most important being the creation of the ADB. It was not until 1997 that ASEAN established regular meetings of finance ministers.

5.3.3 Early developments within the APT framework

The 1997/8 East Asian financial crisis presented the APT group with a clear set of imperative challenges from the very start. The crisis broke in early July 1997, triggered by Thailand's de-pegging of its currency, the baht, to the US dollar. The mass selling of the baht by currency speculators precipitated a general loss of confidence in other Southeast Asian currencies in the money markets. The currency crisis thereafter spread across the wider East Asia region, and deepened into a full-blown financial crisis as stock markets, real estate markets and banking systems crashed in many East Asian economies. Japan made a number of early attempts at constructing financial crisis recovery packages for the region, its first being the Asian Monetary Fund (AMF). Proposed in September 1997, the AMF was conceived as a standby fund of US$100 billion to provide emergency financial assistance to East Asian countries whose currencies were subject to disruptive speculative pressures. The plan was based on pooling together the foreign exchange reserves mostly from Japan, China, Hong Kong, South Korea, Singapore and Taiwan, although Japan proposed to make the majority contribution. There were various motives at play here. Japan felt partly culpable for the crisis as many of its banks had made substantial levels of bad loans, which had contributed to the region's financial market problems. As the region's pre-eminent financial power, Japan also felt the onus of perceived or actual expectation from other East Asian countries to provide some kind of solution to the crisis. Japan's push behind the AMF proposal could also be construed as a test of its regional leadership. At the time, it was the most important regional economic initiative that Japan had ever made.

Like the EAEC and EAEG proposals, US opposition primarily obstructed the AMF's progress. Washington was concerned the AMF would undermine the multilateral competence of the IMF, and hence indirectly lead to a loss of American structural power and influence over the international financial system (Higgott 1998, Rapkin 2001). As a result, the proposal failed to gain sufficient support and was dropped. However, in the months that followed Japan worked on alternative options in which to strengthen financial relations and co-operation within the region. The most important of these was the New Miyazawa Initiative (named after Japan's then finance minister) that was launched in October 1998, whereby US$30 billion of extended liquidity provision was being offered to East Asian economies if they again found themselves in financial crisis. One half of this fund was dedicated to guaranteeing any government bonds issued by crisis-afflicted countries, and the other half gave provision for operationalising bilateral currency swap arrangements with any interested APT member states.

A currency swap is an agreement to exchange one currency for another and to reverse the transaction at some later date. Under the NMI, Japan would swap its foreign exchange reserves (mainly held in US dollars) for under pressure local currencies in an attempt to avert a run on the swap partner's currency. Malaysia and South Korea subsequently signed US$2.5 billion and US$5 billion swap agreements with Japan, respectively, that were later upgraded to larger amounts under the Chiang Mai Initiative as later noted. Also under the NMI, a US$3 billion Asian Currency Crisis Support Facility was introduced that was to be administered through the ADB and would help APT countries raise funds through guarantees, interest subsidies and other means.[2]

The NMI was generally welcomed by other APT countries, especially because of the then perceived failures and inadequacies of the IMF in dealing with the crisis. Moreover, the NMI laid an important foundation for subsequent developments in East Asian financial co-operation (Hayashi 2006, Hughes 2000, Katada 2002b). At the Second APT Summit held in December 1998, Japan also introduced the launch of its new US$5 billion Special Yen Loan Facility that would offer low interest, long-term loans for infrastructure development projects in crisis-afflicted economies. In addition, East Asia's leaders agreed under the ASEAN-based Hanoi Plan of Action to develop new methods for improving regional financial stability (see Chapter 3). China's proposal for regularised APT finance meetings at the vice-ministerial level was accepted and operationalised in March 1999. This was upgraded to full ministerial level the following year at Chiang Mai, Thailand.

5.3.4 The Chiang Mai Initiative (CMI)

By the time the first APT Finance Ministers Meeting was held in May 2000 at Chiang Mai there was growing support to create a region-wide mechanism on financial governance in East Asia (Bird and Rajan 2002, Rana 2002). At the Chiang Mai meeting, it was agreed to establish a system of bilateral currency swap agreements (BCSAs) among APT member states. This was essentially an extension of Japan's NMI framework and was referred to as the Chiang Mai Initiative. The previously mentioned small-scale ASA facility, based on a US$200 million fund, was boosted to US$1 billion as part of the CMI scheme. This was joined by a number of new BCSAs in addition to the already operational Japan–South Korea and Japan–Malaysia agreements. By May 2003, a total of 14 bilateral arrangements had been either signed or concluded. Together with the ASA, these currency deals then amounted to US$36 billion. The system continued to expand over subsequent years. At the Eighth APT Finance Ministers Meeting held in May 2005, it was agreed to double the total funds committed to the CMI, then standing at US$39.5 billion, as well as improving the integration of the scheme's surveillance mechanisms, and adopting a collective decision-making process on CMI operations (Hamilton-Hart 2007). The month before the ASA fund had been increased to US$2 billion. By September 2005, the CMIs operated on a US$54.5 billion total, and by May 2007 this had risen to US$82.5 billion based on 16 bilateral agreements (Figure 5.1).

Some of these CMI agreements evolved from one-way 'donor–recipient' arrangements into two-way arrangements whereby each BCSA partner is offering to assist the other. Examples include the revised Japan–South Korea agreement (Japan to swap up to US$13 billion for South Korean won while South Korea to swap up to US$8 billion for Japanese yen in the event of a crisis), and the Japan–Singapore agreement in which Japan offers up to US$3 billion of assistance and Singapore US$1 billion. Aside from the BCSA network, the CMI system also includes the following aspects:

1) an information exchange mechanism on short-term capital movements in East Asia, including the establishment of an early warning system to monitor signs of emergent financial crises;
2) a dialogue framework for APT group discussions on reforming the international financial architecture;
3) regularised meetings between deputy or vice-ministers of finance to review all CMI-related developments.

An important step forward in the CMI's development occurred in May 2007 when APT Finance Ministers endorsed a plan to multilateralise the scheme. This entailed the conversion of the funds under its 16 bilateral agreements into a common funding pool of foreign exchange reserves from which CMI members could draw upon in times of crisis.[3] For a while there had been discussions on multilateralising the CMI into what would essentially be an AMF-style arrangement. However, very few details emerged from the APT Finance Ministers meeting regarding the technical features of the new regional-multilateral scheme, for example what contributions would be made by each country, how the scheme would be managed, when it would start operating, the nature of its various mechanisms (e.g. on surveillance, reserve eligibility, borrowing quotas, activation of funds), and its functional relationship with the IMF.[4] These matters would be discussed over forthcoming months with a progress report on the new scheme presented in 2009. Depending on how substantially the new multilateralised CMI is developed, it could play a key role in establishing a regional exchange rate system, another idea that has been raised in APT meetings and studied by some East Asian governments (especially Japan) and is discussed later with respect to the Asian Currency Unit scheme.

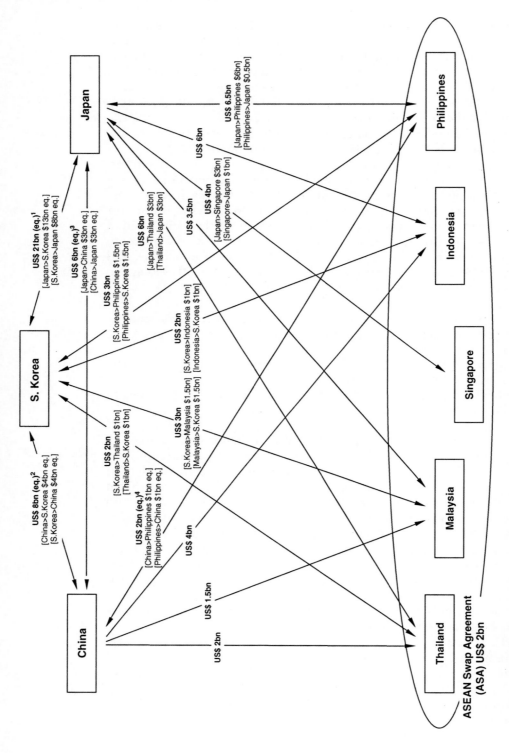

Figure 5.1 Bilateral currency swap agreements under the Chiang Mai Initiative (by May 2007)

Source: Japan's Ministry of Finance and author's own research.

Notes: All swaps denominated in US dollars except for: 1. Japanese yen – Korean won currency swap. 2. Chinese yuan – Korean won currency swap. 3. Japanese yen – Chinese yuan currency swap. 4. Chinese yuan – Philippine peso currency swap. These four agreements denoted in US dollar equivalent (eq.) sums. Total sum of CMI agreements by this time was US$82.5 billion.

The amounts of foreign exchange reserves committed to the CMI remain key to the scheme's future. Even though these have more than doubled since the CMI inception, they still represent a mere fraction of the combined foreign exchange reserves at the disposal of East Asian states. Table 5.1 shows that by the end of 2006 these stood at over US$2.9 trillion (up from US$0.7 trillion in 1997), or around 75 per cent of the global total. At this time, China possessed US$1,068 billion worth of foreign exchange reserves, Japan US$880 billion, Taiwan US$266 billion, South Korea US$239 billion, Singapore US$136 billion, Hong Kong US$133 billion, Malaysia US$82 billion and Thailand US$65 billion, all thus higher than the United States' figure of US$55 billion (see Table 5.1). Foreign exchange reserves are essentially the foreign currency deposits held by central banks and other monetary authorities, the main reserve currencies being US dollars, euro and yen. Governments may use these reserves to help stabilise the country's exchange rate by intervening in the currency markets, for example buying their own currency with foreign reserves to counter downward pressures caused by mass selling of the local currency by speculators. Table 5.1 indicates a rapid accumulation of these reserves over recent years within East Asia, which has been primarily fuelled by persistent and substantial current account (i.e. trade) surpluses.

The experience of the 1997/8 financial crisis has motivated East Asian governments to stockpile foreign exchange reserves as a defence mechanism against future speculative attacks on their currency (Aizenman and Marion 2003). Even though the amounts committed to the CMI have more than doubled since the introduction of the system, they may as they currently stand prove insufficient to stave off a major speculative attack on an unstable currency (Bird and Rajan 2002, Chalongphob 2002, Kohlscheen and Taylor 2006). For example, there was an estimated US$150 billion capital outflow in the three months following the Thai baht devaluation in July 1997.[5] The then US$200 million ASA was not even activated during the 1997/8 financial crisis because it was simply too small to have any noticeable effect on the currency markets. Furthermore, up until May 2007 only 20 per cent of the initial swap arrangements could be released unconditionally without IMF approval.[6] Thereafter, beneficiaries were obliged to reach agreement with the IMF on a programme of economic reforms before further assistance was approved. This situation may, though, be reviewed and changed under the new plans to multilateralise the CMI scheme.

There are a number of reasons why the funds committed to the CMI have been somewhat limited. First, there are various competing demands on East Asia's foreign exchange reserves, a substantial proportion of them being tied up in various assets, especially US Treasury Bills. Second, the CMI is still a relatively young arrangement involving nation-states with little prior experience of managing financial co-operation of this kind at either the bilateral or regional level. In this respect, the CMI has been an important confidence-building exercise in East Asia's first venture at regional financial governance. Hence, it has been politically expedient

Table 5.1 East Asia's foreign exchange reserves, 1980–2006 (US$ millions)

	East Asia												Other Selected			
	China	Japan	Taiwan	Korea	Singapore	Hong Kong	Malaysia	Thailand	Indonesia	Philippines	Vietnam	East Asia (total)	US	Germany	France	UK
2006	1,068,490	879,682	266,148	238,882	136,260	133,168	82,133	65,291	40,934	20,025	13,384	2,944,397	54,854	41,687	42,652	40,698
2005	821,514	834,275	253,290	210,317	115,794	124,244	70,172	50,691	32,989	15,926	9,051	2,538,263	54,084	45,140	27,753	43,531
2004	614,500	833,891	241,738	198,997	112,232	123,540	66,384	48,664	34,953	13,116	7,041	2,295,056	75,890	48,823	35,314	45,343
2003	408,151	663,289	206,632	155,284	95,746	118,360	44,515	41,077	34,962	13,655	6,224	1,787,895	74,894	50,694	30,187	41,850
2002	291,128	461,186	161,656	121,345	82,021	111,896	34,222	38,046	30,969	13,329	4,121	1,349,919	67,962	51,171	28,365	39,360
2001	215,605	395,155	122,211	102,753	75,375	111,155	30,474	32,355	27,246	13,476	3,675	1,129,480	57,634	51,404	31,749	37,284
2000	168,278	354,902	106,742	96,131	80,132	107,542	29,523	32,016	28,502	13,090	3,417	1,020,275	56,600	56,891	37,039	43,891
1999	157,728	286,916	106,200	73,987	76,843	96,236	30,588	34,063	26,445	13,230	3,326	905,562	60,500	61,039	39,702	35,870
1998	149,188	215,471	90,341	51,975	74,928	89,650	25,559	28,825	22,713	9,226	2,002	759,878	70,715	74,024	44,312	32,212
1997	142,762	219,648	83,502	20,368	71,289	92,804	20,788	26,180	16,587	7,266	1,986	703,180	58,907	77,587	30,928	32,317
1996	107,039	216,648	88,038	34,037	76,847	63,808	27,009	37,731	18,251	10,030	1,736	681,174	64,041	83,178	26,796	39,896
1995	75,377	183,250	90,310	32,678	68,695	55,398	23,774	35,982	13,708	6,372	1,324	586,868	74,782	85,005	26,853	42,016
1990	29,586	78,501	72,441	14,793	27,748	24,568	9,754	13,305	7,459	924	–	279,079	72,258	67,902	36,778	35,854
1985	12,728	26,719	22,556	2,869	12,847	–	4,912	2,190	4,974	615	–	90,410	32,096	44,380	26,589	12,859
1980	2,545	24,637	2,205	2,925	6,567	–	4,387	1,560	5,392	2,846	–	53,064	15,596	48,592	27,340	20,652

Source: IMF International Financial Statistics (IFS); Financial Statistics of the Central Bank of China, Taiwan (http://investintaiwan.nat.gov.tw/en/env/stats/foreign_exchange.html).

to begin with relatively small sums at the outset and then build from there. It is, though, conceivable that in the event of further financial turbulence, or warning signs of another full-blown crisis, the CMI system will be significantly bolstered at short notice to deal with unfolding events. Third, the APT group are no doubt wary of the CMI being perceived as a challenge to the IMF's multilateral competence, hence their agreement to IMF conditionality on operationalising their BCSAs under relatively strict conditions (Henning 2002, Ravenhill 2002b).

Further increases to the CMI's funding may be expected if APT member governments with especially large and fast expanding foreign exchange reserves (e.g. China and Japan) wish to diversify the purposes of holding them. There are, however, opportunity costs to consider of holding a growing mass of reserves that are tied up in relatively low yield US government bonds and other such assets when they could be invested in high-yield domestic projects and assets (Rajan and Siregar 2002). As we later discuss, these reserves may be increasingly used to help develop East Asia's nascent government bond markets. Many East Asian governments are developing special investment corporations to more purposely manage foreign exchange reserve investments generally. Singapore's Government Investment Corporation is an early established example of this, providing the model for the Korean Investment Corporation that was created in June 2005, as well as China's Central Huijin Investment Company set up in 2003.

5.3.5 The Asian Bond Markets Initiative (ABMI)

The Asian Bond Markets Initiative was the second main new structure of regional financial co-operation to emerge from the APT framework. Like the CMI, the ABMI provides East Asia with the opportunity to utilise the region's huge financial resources for promoting its own regional financial stability and economic development, rather than investing in, or diverting these resources to other regions or countries. East Asia not only has huge foreign exchange reserves but also very high levels of domestic savings, at around 30 to 40 per cent of GDP. A large proportion of the region's financial resources have over time been invested in bonds and other securities originating outside the region, especially in advanced industrial countries like the United States. East Asia's own capital markets have generally been slow to develop, with only higher income countries like Japan and South Korea having established credible markets for bonds. Moreover, Asian currency-denominated bonds were not internationalised. For example, by 2004 only 4 per cent of Japanese government bonds were held outside the country.[7]

A bond is usually a fixed-interest, long-term security that can be issued by governments, firms, banks and other institutions. The ABMI is designed to foster domestic and regional bond market development in East Asia with a general view to better utilise the region's substantial financial resources towards meeting the region's investment needs over the early twenty-first century. In contrast to the CMI, which provides a mechanism for *short-term* counteractions to financial market instability, the ABMI forms a basis for gradually strengthening East Asia's *long-term* financial market development. In this sense, the ABMI may be considered more *strategic* in conception than the CMI, as it moves East Asia beyond measures simply aimed at crisis-aversion towards building more substantive financial market integration in the region. In further contrast, the ABMI is more a *regional co-ordination* project involving several countries initiating their own new local currency bond issues with the assistance of the ADB and other agencies, leading to a particular form of *financial market regionalisation* in which the private sector plays a key role. The CMI, on the other hand, arguably involves greater levels of *region-wide co-operation* amongst East Asian states as the scheme's currency swaps are international agreements in which at least one partner is obligated to assist the other in times of financial difficulty. It is therefore more likely that the CMI will develop into a regional inter-governmental governance mechanism (i.e. *financial regionalism*) than the ABMI (Grimes and Kimura 2005).

Like the CMI, the ABMI too has been conceived in crisis-aversion terms. A key cause of the 1997/8 financial crisis was the over reliance on short-term borrowing in foreign currencies by East Asian firms, banks and other institutions. After East Asia's huge accumulation of savings had been initially deposited in local banks, much of this was then funnelled to international financial centres and a significant amount in turn invested back into the region but mostly in the form of short-term loans. Pempel (2000:67) usefully summarises the situation:

> Foreign capital was readily available at low interest rates. Meanwhile, rates on local debt were about double that for foreign debt. Consequently, local banks found it highly profitable to borrow overseas and lend locally: most domestic loans were short-term, with multiple roll-overs expected to complete long-term projects.

This made the region prone to the maturity and currency 'double mismatch' problem after sharp currency depreciations had significantly inflated the short-term foreign loan payments East Asian firms were obliged to make to overseas banks. Many of these firms did not have sufficient investment returns or other funds on stream to help meet these payments, leading to mass bankruptcies and a banking crisis. This was a key trigger of a wider financial crisis in the region. In addition, the region's local banking systems had developed an over-reliance on equity markets to fund the investment demands of East Asian companies, which were over dependent on banks generally in raising finance. Investing in long-term, local currency bonds issued by governments and companies themselves would help avoid the above predicaments, and make East Asia financially more self-sustainable as a region generally in the longer run (Plummer and Click 2005). Developing an Asian regional bond market would also enable wider currency diversification to take place, leading to East Asian countries becoming less dependent on US dollar-dominated assets in particular.

Although the ABMI has mainly developed through APT processes, these have worked in tandem with certain other related institutions and organisations. Discussions on the ABMI were first made at the APT Deputy Ministers Meeting held in Chiang Mai in December 2002. The scheme was further considered a few months later in June 2003 at an EMEAP group meeting, its eleven member state representatives agreeing to establish an Asian Bond Fund with initial capital of US$1 billion.[8] The ABMI plan was then formally endorsed at the APT Finance Ministers Meeting held in August 2003, and in the following month the ADB gave grants to Indonesia, Malaysia, Philippines, and Thailand to help them develop domestic bond markets as part of the APT's new Guarantee Mechanism for the ABMI.[9] In April 2004 the EMEAP group gave its approval to launching a much larger Second Asian Bond Fund worth around US$11 billion.[10] As with the first Fund, this was to be managed on behalf of the central banks by the Bank for International Settlements based in Hong Kong, but unlike the first Fund, these new bonds were denominated in Asian currencies rather than in US dollars. This time also, foreign exchange reserves could be used for the first time to purchase these new Asian-currency bonds.

The Second Asian Bond Fund was implemented from May 2005 onwards with the ADB playing an instrumental part in issuing the bonds in domestic markets. The ADB's role in developing the ABMI is indicative of the organisation's growing involvement in promoting East Asian economic regionalism generally. It had helped Japan open up its first domestic bond market in the early 1970s, and in other East Asian economies up to the 1997/8 financial crisis, including in Hong Kong, South Korea, Singapore and Taiwan. Since the ABMI's launch, the ADB has provided new bond issue assistance to a wider range of East Asian countries, including China, Malaysia, Philippines, Thailand and Vietnam from 2003 onwards. By the end of 2004, East Asian local currency bond markets had tripled in size since the 1997/8 financial crisis. The ADB's first Asia Bond Monitor also reported at this time, however, that the region issued only 3 per cent of local currency bonds outstanding worldwide.[11] By November 2006, the ADB reported that the volume of outstanding local currency bonds had expanded from US$2 trillion to US$2.4 trillion over the first half of 2006.[12] Yet this was still some way behind the US$16.8 trillion US dollar bond market, of which about 30 per cent are government issues.[13] While, then, it was noted that the ABMI had made an important contribution to bond market growth in the region, the ADB also stated that there remained huge scope for further expansion. Surveys had long indicated the significant potential demand for Asian currency-issued bonds. For example, the ADB itself estimated that between 2005 and 2010, East Asia would require US$180 billion (approximately 6 to 7 per cent of the region's annual GDP), in new physical infrastructure investments.[14] According to a Citigroup report, Asia's investment needs generally would be around US$20 trillion over 2005 to 2015, and moreover that the long-term and stable financing provided by bond markets was ideal for facilitating the region's strategic investments.[15]

Six Working Groups have been established under the ABMI to support the development of the region's bond markets. These comprise:

1) New Securitized Debt Instruments (WG1);
2) Credit Guarantee and Investment Mechanisms (WG2);
3) Foreign Exchange Transactions and Settlement Issues (WG3);
4) Issuance of Bonds Denominated in Local Currencies by multilateral development banks (e.g. the ADB), foreign government agencies, and Asian multinational corporations (WG4);
5) Rating Systems and Information Dissemination on Asian Bond Markets (WG5);
6) Technical Assistance Co-ordination (WG6).

Taking the fifth of these as an illustrative example of this support, the development of a robust rating system for new bond issues bestows on them an important level of credibility amongst investors, which is essential if the bonds are to be purchased in the finance markets, especially when they are competing with more established and trusted assets.

5.3.6 The Asian Currency Unit (ACU)

The introduction of a basic form of Asian Currency Unit represents the APT's third main scheme for advancing regional financial integration in East Asia. At the 1999 APT summit, hosting Philippines President Joseph Estrada recommended that the APT group should have the long-term objective of creating an East Asian common currency. Establishing some form of ACU system would provide the first step towards this goal but it was not until 2006 that introducing an ACU scheme was first formally proposed. The idea for an ACU draws upon the European experience of regional economic and financial integration in which the European Currency Unit was used to achieve exchange rate stability and convergence as a precursor to economic and monetary union. Here again, the ADB has worked in unison with the APT framework on this particular project. In the ADB's original proposal, the ACU was conceived as a unit of exchange based on a 'basket' (or weighted average) of APT currencies that would be used to monitor moves in the values of these currencies in the formulation of exchange rate policy. These moves could be judged relative to each other, and also collectively against major external currencies, such as the US dollar and the euro. Furthermore, the ACU would function as a unit of account for invoicing regional trade and financial transactions.

The ACU system is thus designed to help APT governments co-operate with each other to achieve greater exchange rate stability or predictability as individual currencies can be judged to be either diverging or converging with the weighted ACU rate. At a more fundamental level, by lowering uncertainty and commercial transaction costs the ACU scheme will further enhance regional trade and financial integration in East Asia. In connection with the ABMI, it was also hoped that the ACU would facilitate the development of an Asian multi-currency bond market, as well as the deepening of East Asia's capital markets. It was at the same time recognised that this was only a very preliminary step towards monetary union. At the launch of the ACU proposal in March 2006, ADB President Haruhiko Kuroda noted that this would only be achieved after the region had evolved into a highly integrated common market, and this could take decades to realise. Further steps along the way were thus required including strengthening the CMI system, further developing Asia's regional bond markets, greater trade co-operation through free trade agreements, and convergence on monetary policy between APT governments.

There is also the wider debate concerning East Asia's potential as an 'optimum currency area', this essentially relating to its long-term viability for regional monetary integration (Ahn et al. 2006, Ito 2004, Kawai and Takagi 2005, Kim et al. 2005, Zhang et al. 2004). We are some way yet from serious discussions on this matter given that the different aspects of regional financial co-operation studied in this chapter are all at a relatively young stage of development. In the meantime, the ACU proposal's launch was marred by disagreements over ACU membership and how the ACU system should be weighted. The ADB argued that the scheme should only include APT countries owing to reasons of regional economic and financial coherence, and that India, Australia and New Zealand – the remaining EAS countries – should not be allowed to join at least in the first instance.[16] Intense discussions also followed on why the Hong Kong dollar and Taiwan dollar were to be excluded, whereas the currencies of much weaker economies (e.g. Cambodia and Laos) were to be included. Differences of opinion also arose over the calculations of ACU weightings, with some like China arguing that they should be based on each country's respective share of GDP measured at purchasing power parity while others like Japan argued for a wider range of criteria to be used, such as trade volume, financial transaction flows and currency convertibility.[17] It was the stand-off between China and Japan over these issues that halted somewhat the ACU scheme's progress into 2007.

5.3.7 Other aspects of APT regional co-operation

While improving regional financial governance remains a core task of the APT, its agenda has also expanded to embrace various other issues. By 2006, the regional framework comprised 49 consultative bodies working in 17 different fields. Its aim has been to advance regional economic co-operation generally across a wide range of areas, including small business development, environmental technologies, infrastructure logistics, food and health security issues, human resource development, e-commerce, energy resource management, pollution abatement, international migration, maritime piracy, ICT co-operation, customs information exchange, agricultural technology, and management training programmes.

At the apex of APT's organisational structure are annual summit meetings held towards the end of the year, as well as annual meetings of Economic, Financial and Foreign Ministers. Meetings for Labour, Health, Energy, Agriculture, and Tourism Ministers are held on a more irregular basis. The East Asia Vision Group (EAVG) and East Asia Study Group (EASG) have meanwhile provided ideas on where and how to advance regional co-operation in East Asia (EAVG 2001, EASG 2002). Examples of the 26 specific recommendations made by the EASG report, published for adoption at the 2002 summit, include:

- *Short-term measures*: East Asia human resource development programme, Network of East Asia Think Tanks (NEAT), East Asia Forum, East Asia Business Council, poverty alleviation programmes, regional identity-building exercises.
- *Medium to long-term measures*: high-level conference on investment and SMEs; feasibility study on an East Asia Free Trade Area convening of an East Asia Summit; create a regional financing facility; expand the ASEAN Investment Area to an East Asia Investment Area arrangement; establish a framework for energy policies, strategies and action plans.

Plans to initiate or further study a good majority of the above have been drawn. Every regional organisation or framework has to start from somewhere, and the strategising functions performed by bodies such as the EAVG and EASG can play an important part in advancing the regional co-operative agenda, just as the Eminent Persons Group did for APEC in the early 1990s. One interesting EASG recommended initiative that has been taken forward concerns the APT Workshops on Promoting East Asian Identity and Consciousness. The second of these was convened in November 2006 at Brunei, and is seen as an essential part of the East Asia community-building process.[18] In the same month, APT diplomacy led to Japan, China and South Korea joining ASEAN's emergency rice reserve programme, first set up in 1979, to create a new and much extended East Asia Emergency Rice Reserve (EAERR) system, boosting the original ASEAN system reserve from 87,000 tons to 500,000 tons.[19] The EAERR would essentially serve the ASEAN countries, consisting of rice stocks held in each member state and earmarked for emergency distribution within Southeast Asia should the need arise. This was set within the context of APT endeavours to improve regional food security and safeguard rural livelihoods in the region, as well as putting in place systems for meeting humanitarian needs during periods of emergencies or natural disasters.

Although conventional security issues, such as North Korea's nuclear programme, have been discussed at APT meetings, they have not become codified into the APT agenda or works programme. The APT group have also only just begun to explore the geopolitical advantages of acting in some kind of collective sense in global affairs. Probably the best example of this to date concerns the IMF voting rights issue. With the APT group holding around 75 per cent of the world's foreign exchange reserves and yet holding less than 13 per cent of the quotas in the IMF – to which voting shares are closely tied – APT members called for a review of the quota allocation system, which was first established back in the 1940s. This was being considered by other IMF member states in 2007.

Case Study 5.1 Taiwan's marginalisation in East Asian regionalism?

Taiwan is East Asia's fourth largest economy, after Japan, China and South Korea. It also has one of the region's most dynamic and innovative business communities. As we know from Chapter 2, Taiwanese firms are at the cutting edge of East Asia's ICT sector. They had also invested around US$80 billion in various industries across mainland China by 2005. The Taiwanese economy also weathered the storm of the 1997/8 financial crisis better than any other, recording 6 per cent economic growth in 1998 while most East Asian economies experienced a fall in their gross domestic product. Taiwan has a well educated, enterprising and prospering people, and is plugged into many important regionalisation processes in East Asia, such as ICT and electronics sector international production networks (see Chapter 2).

Yet Taiwan has an ambiguous position in East Asia's regional community owing to the Peoples Republic of China's insistence that Taiwan is a Chinese province and not a sovereign nation-state, a view formally accepted by the large majority of foreign governments. Consequently, Beijing has strongly objected to any attempts made by the Taiwanese Government to join international organisations or become signatories to any international agreement that in any way acknowledges Taiwan as an independent nation-state. Taiwan's contested sovereignty has meant it is unable to become a member of either the APT or EAS framework. Its FTA options are limited for the same reasons. In June 2002, China's Minister of Foreign Trade and Economic Co-operation, Shi Guangsheng, stated Beijing's opposition to any of China's diplomatic partners signing FTAs with Taiwan, stating that there would be significant economic and political consequences for their relations with China if they did (Dent 2005a). This effectively applied to all Taiwan's major trade partners, and Taipei has been limited to doing FTA deals amongst the group of 24 small developing countries, mostly from Latin American and Africa, with which it still maintains formal diplomatic relations (see Chapter 6).

Taiwan's contested sovereignty in relation to developments in East Asian regionalism was not so much a problem as it is now. Back in the first half of the 1990s, there were no FTAs between East Asian countries and the APT framework had not been formed. Furthermore, Taiwan had succeeded in acceding to APEC in 1991 as the organisation's membership was based on 'economy' rather than 'nation-state' qualification, as with the WTO.[20] However, things have since changed with FTAs in East Asia proliferating and the APT framework advancing whilst APEC has lost much of its initial momentum. Taiwan's subsequent marginalisation in new integrative and co-operative processes in East Asia has become a notable concern for Taipei. Although the APT and EAS have only just begun to develop new structures of regional co-operation and integration, it is more a question of what these frameworks could become and achieve over the next decade and beyond. This most crucially relates to how the APT or EAS provide the basis on which an East Asian regional community could be more substantively built. Taiwan's non-participation in this process may lead to potentially very damaging geopolitical and economic marginalisation.

There are in the meantime more immediate potential costs and risks facing Taiwan. For example, in the advent of another regional financial crisis, Taipei cannot turn to the CMI scheme for assistance, or indeed the IMF because its members must be nation-states. Fortunately, Taiwan has at its disposal the world's third highest stock of foreign exchange reserves (see Table 5.1) to help defend its currency, the NT dollar, if it ever came under downward speculative pressure in the money markets. On the FTA front, although ACFTA and other agreements signed by China may actually help Taiwanese firms producing mainland 'local content' products being exported to important foreign markets, Taiwan based firms are adversely affected through trade diversion effects (see Case Study 1.1, Chapter 1, p. 13). As Taipei Mayor, Ma Ying-jeou, commented in October 2003 regarding the effects of ACFTA, 'Although it will take place seven years from now, still you can see that goods ... in the ASEAN countries can enter the Chinese mainland without tariffs ... Taiwan will still have to pay tariffs, which will put Taiwanese businesses at a competitive disadvantage'.[21] He further stated, 'We do not want to be left in the cold when regional integration is taking place'.[22] More recently, there was some concern over the trade diversion effects caused by the US–South Korea FTA (USKFTA) signed in June 2007, South Korea being a close trade competitor to Taiwan. According to a study made by Taiwan's Ministry of Economic Affairs, the USKFTA could reduce Taiwan's trade with the United States by up to US$2 billion a year (around 5 per cent of Taiwan's total exports) and trigger the loss of 20,000 jobs at home. The same report stated USKFTA could lead to a significant redirection of US investment away from Taiwan to South Korea.[23]

Overall, unless the nature of its relations with mainland China change dramatically, Taiwan must face the challenge of being marginalised from important new agreements and frameworks arising within East Asia's regional political economy. As well as being disadvantageous to Taiwan, this marginalisation is also in many ways a loss to the rest of East Asia. Taiwan could make a significant contribution, for example, to the work of the ASEAN Plus Three (or 'Asia Minus Taiwan' as some Taiwanese quip) framework, especially on regional financial governance, as it has considerable financial resources and technocratic expertise to offer. Taiwan is also the world's twentieth largest economy and its fifteenth largest trader, and could therefore add further notable geo-economic weight to an East Asian regional grouping.

Study Questions

1. Why is the distinction between micro-level regionalisation and state-led regionalism so important for Taiwan?
2. What are the costs and risks of Taiwan remaining outside the APT and EAS regional frameworks?

5.4 The East Asia Summit (EAS) framework

In one sense, the East Asia Summit framework maybe considered a spin-off of the APT framework. The idea for establishing an EAS was first raised at the 2000 APT Summit in Singapore, and thereafter the East Asia Study Group was charged with examining the proposal and reporting back with its recommendations. These essentially focused on the desirability of transforming the APT into a more coherent and developed regional framework in which any APT member could host a summit, not just an ASEAN country. The EAS also embodied a more holistic regional concept and not just an appendage arrangement to ASEAN, as many view APT. A further perceived advantage of the EAS over APT was that it would potentially confer on China, Japan and South Korea a greater sense of ownership over the East Asia regional community-building process.

It was initially believed that the APT would simply evolve into the EAS, subsuming all its work programmes and adopting its framework structure. This was the general understanding that prevailed right up until the November 2004 APT Summit.[24] However, what transpired was the EAS becoming neither a substitute for the APT nor a distinctly separate mechanism in its own right during the mid-to-late 2000s period. The main underlying reason for this is that EAS membership not only comprises the APT group but also – at primarily Japan and Indonesia's insistence – India, Australia and New Zealand (see Figure 5.2). The first East Asia Summit was held in December 2005, hosted by Malaysia at Kuala Lumpur, and much of the discussion at the meeting revolved around membership issues and

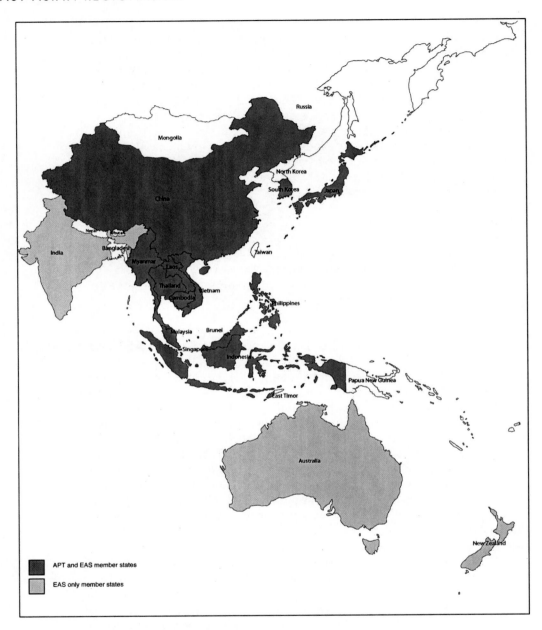

Figure 5.2 APT and EAS group members

what value the EAS framework could add to the regional community-building process beyond what was already being achieved by the APT.

To help consolidate this new regional grouping, Japan pushed the idea of an EAS-based free trade area or agreement, and made formal proposals on this in April and August 2006 (see Chapter 6, Case Study 6.2, p. 219). As the chapter's case study on Sino-Japanese relations notes it is a generally held view that Japan's strategic interest in broadening the membership of the EAS was to add greater counterweight to an ascendant China in any emerging East Asian regional organisation or framework. Japan's predilection for a broad East Asian grouping pre-dates the EAS issue (Hund 2003). Back in the mid-1990s, Tokyo had advocated the inclusion of Australia and New Zealand in the ASEM framework. Chapter 4 also charts the close links that formed between Japan and Australia from the 1960s on developing ideas on Pacific regional community-building. China, Malaysia and others on occasion, though, have argued for a more conventional East Asian grouping.[25] At the inaugural East Asia Summit, hosting Malaysian Prime Minister Abdullah Badawi commented in relation to the grouping that, 'You are talking about a community of East Asians. I don't know how the Australians could regard themselves as East Asians, or the New Zealanders for that matter', and inferred that the main architects of the EAS process should be the 'core' APT member states.[26] His predecessor, Mahathir Mohamed, also questioned why Australia and New Zealand should be permitted to join the EAS because they are essentially Oceanic countries with limited socio-cultural linkages with East Asia (Mahathir 2006).

China's stated opposition to a broad 'extra-regional' EAS membership centred on how the regional body could become too unwieldy and incoherent if the interests of many disparate nations were to be accommodated. Moreover, Beijing argued the greater the number of countries involved, the less integrated and coherent a future East Asian community will be.[27] It was previously noted how the ADB adopted a similar position to China's with respect to the proposed Asian Currency Unit scheme. However, Japan lobbied other East Asian nations hard on the EAS membership issue and managed to secure enough support for its own position. It was agreed, though, at a May 2006 meeting of ASEAN senior officials that EAS membership would be frozen for at least two years. This was in response to various countries expressing their interest in joining the group, namely Russia (observer status gained at the First East Asia Summit, full membership supported by China), Pakistan and Mongolia (supported by Malaysia), and Papua New Guinea (supported by Australia). The EU had in addition noted its wish to gain observer status, and the United States to be involved somehow although this had not been clarified. The EAS framework has to consolidate around its existing membership first before enlargements could be considered.

Over forthcoming years, the EAS framework has a number of important operational issues to address, not least because there remains a lack of clarity concerning the division of labour and co-ordination of tasks between the APT and the EAS frameworks. What may transpire is that the APT countries will constitute the core in most EAS-led regional community-building projects, with India, Australia and New Zealand becoming in effect associate-style members. It would naturally depend on the issue addressed at the EAS level. In many transnational issues, such as drugs trafficking and cross-border pollution, there may be a strong consensus for a comprehensive EAS membership approach. However, getting China and Japan to agree to such an approach on higher-order integrational issues, for example participation in the ACU scheme or a regional free trade area, will be far more problematic. Indeed, when Japan did unveil its proposal for an EAS-based regional free trade area – officially known as the Comprehensive Economic Partnership in East Asia (CEPEA) – it received a lukewarm response from China and many other East Asian countries, including South Korea (see Chapter 6, Case Study 6.2, p. 219).[28] At the Second East Asia Summit held in January 2007 at Cebu,[29] it was agreed only to study the idea but not necessarily proceed to negotiations. However, at the Cebu Summit all EAS member countries did agree to sign the Declaration on East Asian Energy Security (see Chapter 7).

In sum, the APT framework could remain the main vehicle for advancing regional economic co-operation and integration in East Asia while the EAS framework offers a broader and more outward-looking dialogue forum for discussing a wide range of political, economic and other foreign policy-related issues. Whether such a division of labour of tasks is viable is a matter of some debate, and it may take a few years yet to determine an appropriate functional relationship between these two regional frameworks.

Case Study 5.2 Japan and China – hegemonic rivals or regional co-leadership?

In Chapter 1 there was some discussion on how the China–Japan relationship is of critical importance to the future of East Asian regionalism. They are the region's two great powers, and together they account for almost 80 per cent of East Asia's GDP. Without either one of these countries, East Asia's impact on the international system would be considerably diminished. But how have Sino-Japanese relations developed over recent years? On the one hand, their destinies have become increasingly interlinked through growing economic interdependence and the deepening integration of the East Asia region generally. There is also an expectation from other East Asian countries for both China and Japan to take a lead on regional-level affairs (Rose 2004). Both have done so but invariably without compliance of, or co-ordination with the other. Sino-Japanese relations remain problematic owing to a combination of unresolved historic issues and the potential for regional hegemonic rivalry between the two countries. Japan, once East Asia's supreme ascendant economic power, experienced a long period of economic malaise from the early 1990s into the 2000s, and moreover has had to come to terms during this time with a fast rising China.

If China manages to sustain its economic momentum then it will enjoy certain strategic advantages over Japan. This is because it will offer dynamism (e.g. fast expanding commercial opportunities) with an economy many predict will be bigger than Japan's in the not too distant future. China is also able to play a more comprehensively proactive role in international affairs, especially in conventional security matters as Japan is encumbered by certain constitutional constraints in this area. For example, China is a permanent member of the United Nations Security Council, and it is Beijing not Tokyo that hosts the Six Party Talks on North Korea's nuclear programme. China has also been busy fostering closer security ties with a number of Asian countries and, arguably, has played a more proactive role in multilateral institutions over recent years. Yet Japan has an essential role in the region's future, and the advancement of East Asia's regionalism is to a large extent dependent on an effectively working Sino-Japanese partnership.

Taking first recent developments in Japan–China economic relations, both have become vitally important trade partners to each other. By 2005, their bilateral trade was approaching US$200 billion per annum. Japan has become a crucial source of foreign capital and technology for China, and China a critically important production base for many of Japan's multinational enterprises (see Chapter 2). By 2004, Japanese companies had invested around US$56 billion in China covering almost 28,000 projects. Japan is also China's largest source of overseas development assistance (ODA) and accounts for around half the loans it received from foreign governments.[30] However, the amount of Japanese ODA given to China has been steadily falling and a growing number of trade disputes have arisen between the two countries, e.g. over certain agricultural and textile products.

At the same time, new forms of dialogue and co-operation established at the Northeast Asian sub-regional level have helped China and Japan resolve such disputes and moreover place their economic relations on a more positive footing (Aggarwal and Koo 2005). China–Japan–South Korea trilateral summits have been held since 2000. Corresponding trilateral meetings of Economic and Foreign Ministers have followed, as well as new dialogue frameworks at a lower government level and various 'track II' initiatives, such as studying the feasibility of creating a Northeast Asia Free Trade Area.[31] At the 2003 Northeast Asia Summit, the three countries agreed to substantially expand their co-operation across a range of fields, including on security, trade, investment, technology, environment, human resource development and energy security issues.[32] At the Seventh Trilateral Summit held in January 2007, plans were announced to start negotiations on a trilateral investment treaty later that year, and also establish a mechanism of regular consultations among senior foreign affairs officials of the three countries.[33] Japan, China and South Korea furthermore agreed to further extend the scope of their trilateral co-operation, naming a number of new priority areas including finance, public health, tourism, logistics and distribution, youth and teenager communications. The three countries also agreed to hold annual trilateral Environment Ministers meetings in the future.

In addition to APT, EAS and APEC, these new forms and structures of co-operative economic diplomacy are helping establish a firmer foundation on which a Sino-Japanese partnership can be developed, and therein the basis of their co-leadership in East Asian regional affairs. Yet Japan has found it particularly hard to gain the trust of other East Asian nations with regard to adopting a regional leadership role. The past horrors of Japanese imperialism remain in the memories of many of East Asia's older generations. Continued visits made by the country's top political leaders, most notably Prime Minister Junichiro Koizumi, to the Yasukuni Shrine – amongst its honoured war dead of around 2.5 million Japanese (over the 1853–1945 period) are over 1,000 Second World War criminals, including 14 convicted Class-A criminals – has angered many Chinese and other East Asian peoples. The issue of Japan's school history textbooks has further compounded the problem. According to its critics, the textbooks present a distorted view of Japanese military practices in East Asia during the Second World War. A renewed sovereignty dispute arising in 2005 between Japan and South Korea over the Dokdo/Takeshima Islands has also made other East Asian countries somewhat wary of rising nationalist sentiments in Japan. However, the same countries are concerned too about the growing sense of nationalism within China's society. Moreover, as noted elsewhere in this book, reconciling nationalism with regional community-building is a fundamental challenge that is relevant to many parts of East Asia.

While these disputes and acrimonious issues have simmered, Japan has demonstrated an interest in acting as a benefactor to the region as a whole, thereby attempting to build trust with other East Asian countries. Japan's ODA programme has made an important contribution to the economic development of the region's poorer nations since the 1960s (Yoshimatsu 2003). As we have seen with the 1997/8 financial crisis and APT diplomacy, Japan has been willing to dedicate considerable financial and technocratic resources to improving East Asia's regional financial governance structures. Japanese diplomacy concerning the 2004 Asian Tsunami disaster was also revealing. Tokyo reacted quickly to the crisis, offering US$30 million of humanitarian aid just a few days after the disaster struck, which was double the initial US offer of financial assistance. After the US raised its offer to US$350 million, and China announced its own contribution of US$63 million, Japan then quickly upped its offer to US$500 million (representing a quarter of the world's total pledge), keen to show that it was a dependable and generous partner on matters of great regional importance. Many though interpreted this counter-move as being motivated more by diplomatic rivalry rather than humanitarian concern, for example Japan offering an aid package that could not easily be matched by China at such short notice. Japan's financial diplomacy has proved a key instrument when the country has sought to practise regional leadership, as this chapter has shown, and China has at times been somewhat wary of this. For example, China was concerned that the proposed Asian Currency Unit scheme would be dominated by the Japanese yen if the weighting criteria advocated by Japan were to be used.

At the January 2005 conference of major tsunami aid donors and relief organisations held in Jakarta, Japanese Prime Minister Junichiro Koizumi and Chinese Premier Wen Jiabao reportedly could barely manage a few pleasantries when they walked past each other on the conference main stage.[34] A similar scene played out at the inaugural East Asia Summit held later that year, and the difference in opinion between Tokyo and Beijing over the EAS membership issue was noted in the main text. Relations between the leaderships of both countries had been strained around this time owing to aforementioned reasons, e.g. Yasukuni Shrine visits by Prime Minister Koizumi. In addition to this, China was refusing to back Japan's application to become a permanent member of the UN Security Council, and Japan likewise opposed China's bid to accede to full membership of the G8 group. High-level Sino-Japanese relations began to thaw somewhat, however, when in October 2006 newly elected Japanese Prime Minister Shinzo Abe made the first visit to Beijing by a Japanese premier in many years.[35]

A new positive trend in Sino-Japanese relations continued into 2007, with Chinese Premier Wen Jiabao making a return visit to Tokyo in April that year. In his speech addressing the Japanese Diet – the first ever given by a Chinese premier – Wen recognised Japan's apologies for its aggression in Asia and called on both countries to reconcile their differences. He furthermore highlighted China and Japan's deepening economic interdependent relationship and how closer co-operation was in the long-term interests of both countries.[36] Notwithstanding these positive developments, there remain a number of long-standing and relatively new issues that need to be addressed in Sino-Japanese relations if East Asian regionalism is to advance substantially over forthcoming years and decades. One of the most important of these concerns the different views and interests each country has regarding the constituent membership of any emergent East Asia Community, as APT and EAS diplomacy has thus far demonstrated. Another relates to Japan and China finding mutually compatible energy security strategies in a world of diminishing fossil fuel supplies, the subject of one of Chapter 7's debates on key regional issues in East Asia.

Study Questions

1. Why is the future of East Asian regionalism so dependent on positive developments in Sino-Japanese relations?
2. For what reasons do China and Japan have different views on the nature and membership of the EAS group?

5.5 Conclusion

5.5.1 Summary overview

The establishment of the APT and EAS regional frameworks have been historic events, marking especially in the APT's case the first exclusive and formalised grouping of East Asian nations. The chapter began by analysing precursory developments in East Asian regional grouping, such as Malaysia's proposed East Asian Economic Caucus, as well as the participation of East Asian states in other region-based organisations and frameworks, e.g. APEC, ARF, CSCAP and ASEM. Although East Asian states had planned to hold their first APT summit prior to the outbreak of the region's 1997/8 financial crisis, the crisis provided vital impetus to the subsequent development of the new regional framework. Through the APT, new forms of regional financial governance have been constructed, with Japan in particular playing an early instrumental role. For example, the NMI was the forerunner to the CMI network of bilateral currency swap agreements. Other core elements of the APT framework have included the ABMI and ACU scheme. Together, these have constituted important steps forward in the evolution of East Asia's new 'financial regionalism'.

The APT framework has helped advance other aspects of regional co-operation in East Asia, including on business, environment, social, energy, technology, health, human resource and security related matters. Progress at the APT level in these areas has, though, only just begun. The even newer EAS regional framework may itself be considered a by-product of APT diplomacy. It was also argued in this chapter that the EAS embodies a more holistic regional concept in comparison to APT as it confers non-ASEAN member states a greater sense of ownership over the East Asia regional community-building process. However, the decision to include the hitherto usually perceived non-East Asian countries (India, Australia and New Zealand) into the EAS grouping has been contentious. Japan was the primary advocate of incorporating these countries while China was initially opposed for reasons explored earlier. The strategically important relationship between Japan and China in relation to East Asian regionalism generally was furthermore discussed in Case Study 5.2. Meanwhile, some of the implications of Taiwan's omission from both the APT and EAS frameworks, as well as East Asia's FTA trend, were considered in Case Study 5.1.

5.5.2 *International Political Economy (IPE) theoretical analysis*

In its assessment of East Asian regionalism generally, *neo-realist* analysis would contend that its future development is largely contingent upon the establishment of a workable relationship between the region's two dominant nation-states, China and Japan. Neo-realists would further argue that past experience indicates that there is little hope of this occurring. This is mainly because of long-standing and unresolved antagonisms between both nations, as well as intense competition that exists between them regarding international commerce, energy resources, economic and financial power generally, and influence in the East Asia region and in multilateral fora (see Case Study 5.2). If anarchic competition does indeed prevail between Japan and China then it is difficult to see an easy path ahead for East Asian regionalism. In employing the neo-realist 'absolute versus relative gains' approach, Japan or China would be willing to suffer absolute losses in power, influence or welfare if it meant relative advantages over the other were safeguarded. Thus, according to this view, either country would try to sabotage the other's attempts of leading regional co-operation ventures in East Asia even though both would benefit in absolute terms from this co-operation. On the other hand, the international society approach of the English School may contend that China and Japan's anarchic competitive behaviour could be eased by the norms and values of East Asia's emerging regional society of nation-states, as embodied by the APT and EAS. China and Japan have really only just started, though, to engage with each other within the APT and EAS frameworks and concerning regional affairs more generally so perhaps it is too early to fully test the above theoretical perspectives.

In addition, we have the United States to consider. Staunch American resistance to the formation of Malaysia's proposed EAEG/EAEC grouping relates closely to Chapter 4's analysis on Asia-Pacific geopolitics. Neo-realists especially assert that it is not in the US's strategic national interest to allow an exclusive East Asian regional grouping to form because it would marginalise America's position and influence in East Asia regional affairs overall. This partly explains why the US has tried to embrace East Asia within a broader Asia-Pacific regionalism, primarily through APEC. However, APEC's failure to offer any substantive solution or assistance to East Asia's crisis-afflicted countries was an instrumental factor behind why those same countries looked to the APT framework as an alternative path of regional co-operation. Lastly, this chapter noted the contention over the nation-state membership of the EAS framework, and how some observers believed Japan's insistence on including India, Australia and New Zealand as founding members was a geopolitical balancing manoeuvre to counteract China's ascendant power within the East Asia region.

A *neo-liberal institutionalist* assessment would amongst other things focus on the role played by international institutions and institutionalised arrangements concerning new developments in East Asian regional co-operation studied in this chapter. Both APT and EAS may themselves be considered as regional frameworks of institutionalised co-operation between East Asian countries. The governments of each have all agreed to forge closer co-operative links amongst themselves for the greater benefit of the region as a whole. While this has not entailed any significant loss of national sovereignty, the new forms of regional financial governance introduced through the APT especially have signalled a more substantive intent by East Asian countries to realise regional economic objectives as well as national economic ones. From another institutional perspective, this chapter has highlighted the more proactive contributions made by the Asian Development Bank (ADB) in promoting East Asian regional economic co-operation and integration, and how this has been welcomed by East Asian countries. In contrast, the IMF's interactions with the region during the 1997/8 financial crisis is viewed in generally negative terms. At the same time, the IMF's own institutional failings helped spur East Asian nations to formulate their own regional institutionalised arrangements to avert a future crisis occurring.

In a further neo-liberal line of thought, we saw that influential individuals, such as ADB President Haruhiko Kuroda and Malaysia's Prime Minister Mahathir Mohamad, can have catalytic effects on the development of East Asian regionalism. The region's financial crisis also revealed the growing primacy of market power over state power in certain respects. Furthermore, the crisis revealed the depth and extent of East Asia's deepening regional economic interdependence more clearly than anything beforehand and arguably since, presenting East Asian countries with a strong imperative to significantly enhance their level of regional co-operation. For similar reasons, neo-liberal institutionalists are more optimistic than neo-realists regarding the prospects of Japan and China working positively together on East Asian regional affairs. This is based on a mutual understanding that their destinies are increasingly entwined by growing interdependent linkages. Lastly, APT diplomacy has not so much led to the opening up or liberalising of East Asian economies but rather to improving various forms of regulatory, technocratic and development capacity, especially in the financial sector.

From a *social constructivist* perspective, this chapter discussed how both APT and EAS frameworks aspire to create an East Asian Community, yet the very idea of an East Asian Community is contingent on more general ideas about the nature of the East Asia region itself. As noted elsewhere in this book, there are contesting notions of how the East Asia region should be perceived and what are its demarcations if these indeed can be defined in a meaningful way. However conceived, East Asia is a diverse region as first discussed in Chapter 1 (see Table 1.1, p. 4), and many would argue there is a limited range of core political, economic and socio-cultural values shared amongst the region's peoples. This infers that an EAS-type expansion of the East Asia region into hitherto conceived neighbouring regions (i.e. India in South Asia; Australia and New Zealand in Oceania) may not be that problematic as it simply makes an already very diverse region somewhat more diverse. Yet it is essentially a question of degree, and as we discuss in more detail in Chapter 8 the EAS is arguably a much less coherent regional grouping than the APT.

For example, the market-liberal underpinnings of Australia and New Zealand's political economy may not sit well alongside the developmental statist traditions of many East Asian countries. Chapter 4 has already discussed how different value-based perceptions have arisen within APEC between East Asian and Anglo-Pacific countries concerning the methods and objectives of regional community-building. It is therefore more likely that the APT's noted efforts to promote a stronger East Asian regional identity amongst its member states will prove more effective than any similar attempts made at the EAS level.

Marxist-structuralist thinking on the APT framework would stress how it was essentially created in reaction to the power of global financial capital. According to this view, this power was forcefully demonstrated in the events leading up to and during the 1997/8 East Asian financial crisis. Inter-governmental co-operation embodied in the APT framework represents the collective effort of the region's states to address the volatility of unfettered global financial market forces, of which they had become victims. Notwithstanding the debate on the prime causal blame for the 1997/8 crisis, the Chiang Mai Initiative in particular may be conceived as a regional mechanism for countering certain risks posed by financial globalisation. Its system of currency swaps is purposely designed to redress speculative disturbances in East Asia's currency markets. Meanwhile, the Asian Currency Unit scheme, if implemented, will begin to construct new ways of managing financial market volatility through closer co-operation on exchange rate policy in the region. The Asian Bond Market Initiative on the other hand has been devised to more positively harness the power of financial globalisation by helping channel investment funds from both inside and outside East Asia into the region. The notably higher wariness amongst East Asians since the 1997/8 financial crisis regarding international financiers, foreign banks and financial globalisation generally has been a key political factor in the development of these new regional financial governance initiatives. In the next chapter, we examine the new FTA trend and its impacts on East Asian regionalism.

Chapter Study Questions

1. What were the past main obstacles that lay in the path of forming an exclusive regional grouping of East Asian countries?
2. Assess the impact of the 1997/8 financial crisis on the development of the ASEAN Plus Three (APT) framework.
3. To what extent have APT schemes of co-operation like the Chiang Mai Initiative brought greater organisational coherence to East Asian regionalism?
4. 'The controversies over the formation of the East Asia Summit group show just how contested the concept of an East Asia region is in reality'. Discuss.
5. What are the key challenges facing both the APT or EAS regional frameworks on the way to establishing an East Asian Community?

Notes

1   *Financial Times*, 16.01.2001.
2   In addition, the NMI framework included a US$1.1 billion Trade Insurance Facility (offered to Malaysia and Thailand), and US$1.2 billion of trade credit guarantees offered by the Export-Import Bank of Japan to the Philippines and Malaysia.
3   This new plan was first officially proposed at an APT senior finance and central bank officials meeting held in April 2007, and then forwarded to the aforementioned APT Finance Ministers meeting convened a month later. In the words of their joint communiqué, the APT Finance Ministers unanimously agreed at this time to establish 'a self-managed reserve-pooling arrangement governed by a single contractual agreement'.
4   *Daily Yomiuri*, 05.05.2007; *South China Morning Post*, 07.05.2007.
5   United Nations Economic and Social Commission for Asia and the Pacific (UNESCAP), 'Regional Financial Co-operation in East Asia: The Chiang Mai Initiative and Beyond', *Bulletin on Asia-Pacific Perspectives 2002/2003*, 1 March 2002, p. 89.
6   A 10 per cent threshold applied before it was doubled to 20 per cent at the Eighth APT Finance Ministers meeting held in May 2005.
7   *Business Times Singapore*, 24.05.2004.
8   The EMEAP group was first established in 1991 at the initiative of the Bank of Japan. Its membership comprises the central banks from Australia, China, Hong Kong, Indonesia, Japan, South Korea, Malaysia, New Zealand, the Philippines, Singapore, and Thailand.
9   *INQ7 News (Philippines)*, 31.10.2003.
10   This Fund consists of two parts, including a pan-Asian bond index fund and a fund of bond funds. Both funds will invest in sovereign and quasi-sovereign issuers but not corporate bonds and are open to all investors. The index fund is a single bond fund investing in EMEAP countries, excluding the more developed markets in Japan, New Zealand and Australia. The fund of funds will have a two-tiered structure with a parent fund investing in eight country sub-funds. *Financial Times*, 16.04.2004.
11   *China View*, 23.11.2004.
12   *ADB Press Release*, 15.11.2006.
13   Ibid.
14   *ADB Press Release*, 05.08.2004.
15   *Business Times*, 24.05.2004.
16   *Financial Times*, 26.03.2006.
17   Some currencies like the Chinese yuan were not fully convertible into foreign currency because exchange restrictions applied.
18   *Brunei Times*, 09.11.2006.
19   *Bloomberg News*, 22.11.2006.
20   Taiwan became a WTO member in January 2002.
21   *Taipei Times*, 14.10.2003.
22   Ibid.
23   *Taipei Times*, 01.07.2007.
24   *Associated Press*, 29.11.2004.

25 For example, Thailand and the Philippines, along with Malaysia, were more inclined to support China's APT-based regional FTA idea than Japan's EAS-based alternative (see Chapter 6, Case Study 6.2, p. 219).
26 *Japan Times*, 22.12.2005.
27 *Asahi Shimbun*, 04.01.2005; *The Yomiuri Shimbun*, 25.11.2005.
28 *Peoples Daily*, 26.08.2006; *Gulf Times*, 25.08.2006; *Bernama.com*, 24.08.2006.
29 The second East Asia Summit was rescheduled from December 2006.
30 *People's Daily*, 05.01.2004.
31 The Chinese Development Research Centre of the State Council (DRC), the National Institute for Research Advancement (NIRA) of Japan and the Korea Institute for International Economic Policy (KIEP) published a joint scoping study report on the NEAFTA idea in November 2003. (*Asia Times*, 20.11.2003.)
32 *Financial Times*, 07.10.2003.
33 *Associated Press*, 11.01.2007.
34 *China Daily*, 31.01.2005.
35 *Yomiuri Shimbun*, 23.10.2006.
36 *Japan Times*, 13.04.2007.

Chapter 6

Free Trade Agreements and East Asian regionalism

6.1 Introduction

A free trade agreement is an undertaking by signatory parties (e.g. countries) to remove the barriers of trade between them. These agreements can vary significantly in terms of the number of signatory parties involved, their technical policy content, their ideological foundations, the balance of preferences conferred amongst signatory parties, and so on. They have also been a feature of the international economic system for some time. The first period of rapid FTA growth occurred over 1860–1914, which saw a deepening of internationalised business and economic activity generally and is often referred to as the 'proto-globalisation' era. The most recent period of intensified FTA activity occurred from the early 1990s onwards, the end of the Cold War and 'contemporary' globalisation being the main instrumental factors behind this trend. In 1990 there were only 16 fully operative FTAs that had been notified to the WTO's predecessor, the General Agreement on Tariffs and Trade. By 1997 this number had increased to 72, and by 2005 to 153, most of these (around 90 per cent) being bilateral in nature (Table 6.1).

Table 6.1 Global FTAs by region, 1990–2005

FTAs by Region	1990	1997	2003	2005
Intra-Regional	**[12]**	**[58]**	**[103]**	**[98]**
Europe	7	40	65	43*
North Africa and the Middle East	0	1	1	8
Sub-Saharan Africa	1	1	2	2
Western Hemisphere	3	9	20	24
[Pacific America]	[1]	[6]	[8]	[14]
East Asia	0	0	5	8
Oceania	1	1	2	2
Central and South Asia	0	6	8	11
Inter-Regional / Trans-Regional	**[4]**	**[14]**	**[59]**	**[55]**
Europe - North Africa and Middle East	3	8	35	16
Europe - Sub-Saharan Africa	0	0	1	1
Europe - Pacific America	0	0	4	4
Europe - East Asia	0	0	1	2
Europe - Central and South Asia	0	4	6	6
Central and South Asia - North Africa and Middle East	0	0	0	1
Pacific America - North Africa and Middle East	1	2	4	7
Pacific America - Oceania	0	0	0	1
East Asia - Central and South Asia	0	0	1	2
East Asia - North Africa and Middle East	0	0	1	2
East Asia - Oceania	0	0	3	4
East Asia - Pacific America	0	0	3	8
East Asia - Pacific America - Oceania	0	0	0	1
[Asia-Pacific]	[2]	[7]	[21]	[38]
Total	**16**	**72**	**162**	**153**

Notes: End of year figures for FTAs where their negotiations have been concluded. These figures appear generally lower than the WTO official 'notified RTA' figures because they only take into account Article XXIV 'free trade agreements' (on merchandise trade) and not 'service agreements' that, for broader band FTAs that include services liberalisation, have to be notified separately under Article V of the WTO rules and lead to these FTAs being effectively double-counted on the WTO notification list. Partial scope and non-reciprocal agreements, under the WTO's 'Enabling Clause', are also not counted in these figures, but it does include certain full FTAs that have been signed but not yet officially notified to the WTO, as determined by the author's research. It also includes customs unions (e.g. Mercosur) and common markets (e.g. the EU) as they contain de facto FTAs within their frameworks. * After the EU's May 2004 enlargement involving 10 East European states, a number of preceding FTAs were subsumed into the European Economic Area arrangement as a consequence, which explains the drop in the actual number of FTAs in Europe. This peaked at 65 leading up to the May 2004 enlargement. Sources: WTO, various government and media sources.

However, East Asia was by the mid-1990s the only region in the world not to have concluded an FTA of any kind. While the Association of Southeast Asian Nations group was putting in place the ASEAN Free Trade Area, its first phase was not due for implementation until 2003. The situation changed dramatically, though, from the late 1990s onwards. As we shall later examine, FTA activity in East Asia, as well as the wider Asia-Pacific region, has intensified considerably, indeed more than in any other region. Most of East Asia's new FTAs are bilateral in nature, thus being consistent with the global trend. The main focus of this chapter is to examine how this new economic bilateralism impacts upon East Asian regionalism, and furthermore whether bilateral FTAs are having a positive or negative effect on regional community-building in East Asia.

6.2 The growth of FTA activity in East Asia

East Asian countries were at the forefront of an Asia-Pacific trend of intensified FTA activity that took off in the late 1990s. Table 6.2 and Figures 6.1 to 6.4 illustrate how East Asia's various new FTA projects with other East Asian and Asia-Pacific trading partners developed from 1998 onwards. Below is a yearly outline of key events and developments:

In 1998
- In November, three new FTA projects were proposed, between Japan and South Korea, South Korea and Chile, and South Korea and Thailand. These were the first ever bilateral FTA projects initiated involving East Asian countries.

In 1999
- South Korea–New Zealand FTA proposed in July.
- On the sidelines of the September 1999 Auckland APEC Summit, four other bilaterals are proposed: Singapore–New Zealand, Singapore–Mexico, Japan–Mexico and Japan–Singapore.
- A Japan–Chile FTA proposed in November.
- South Korea–Chile negotiations commence in December.

In 2000
- First round of Singapore–New Zealand FTA negotiations held in January, and are concluded by August.
- In November, Singapore initiates bilateral FTA projects with Australia and the United States. An ASEAN–China FTA is also proposed in this month.

In 2001
- The Singapore–New Zealand FTA comes into force in January, the first operational FTA involving an East Asian country.

Table 6.2 East Asian country FTA projects within the Asia-Pacific: time phase development, 1998–2007 (June)

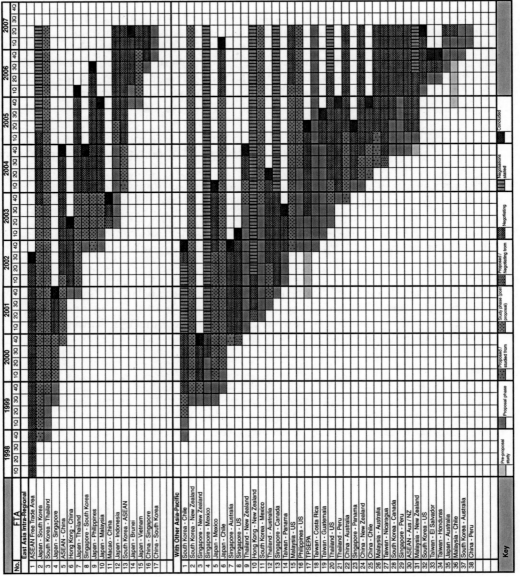

Source: Author's research

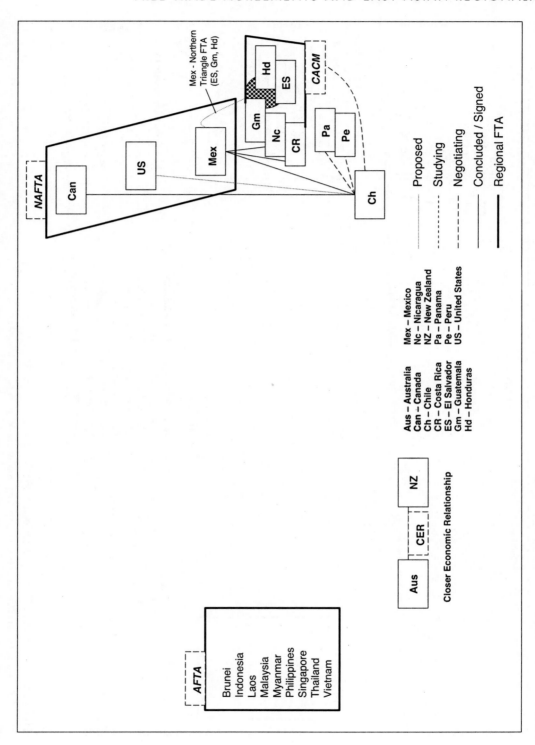

Figure 6.1 Asia-Pacific FTA projects (before 1998)

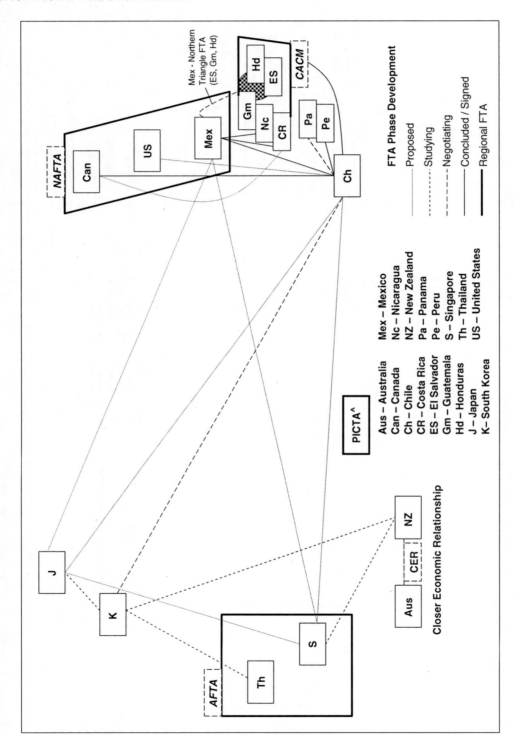

Figure 6.2 Asia-Pacific FTA projects (by end of 1999)

Note: ^ PICTA (Pacific Island Countries Trade Agreement) involves the 14 Pacific Island Countries.

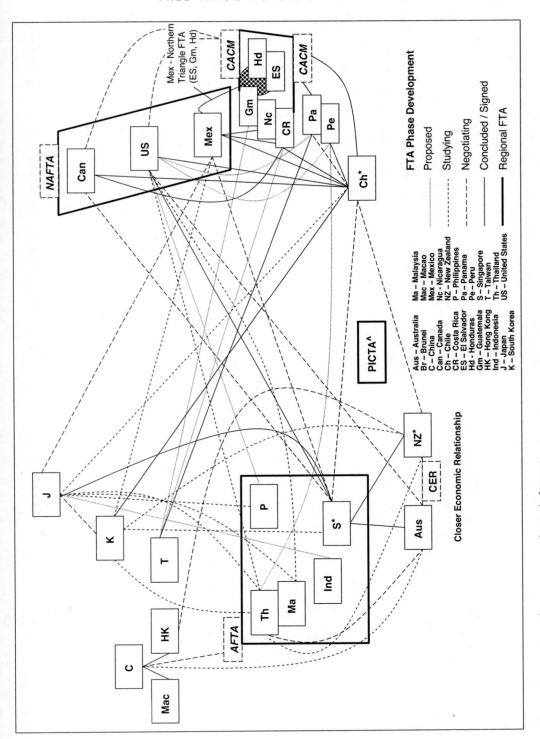

Figure 6.3 Asia-Pacific FTA projects (by end of 2003)

Notes: * Pacific-3 FTA negotiating parties, later expanding to quadrilateral Trans-Pacific Strategic Economic Partnership (TPSEPA) arrangement in 2005. ^ PICTA (Pacific Island Countries Trade Agreement) involves the 14 Pacific Island Countries.

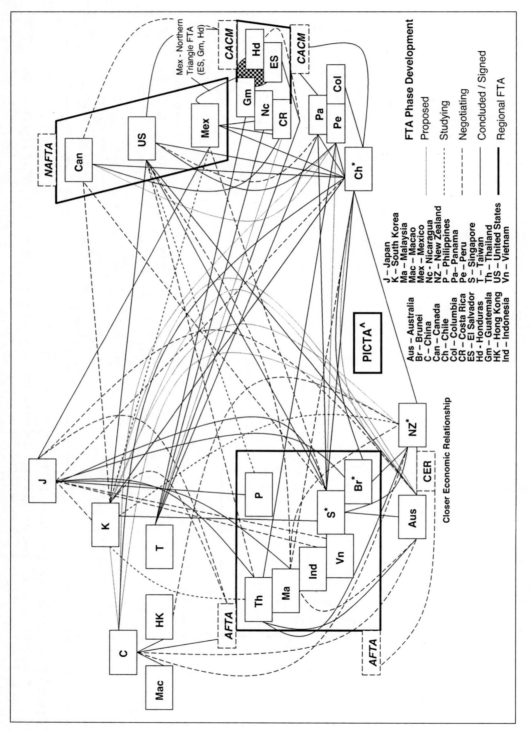

Figure 6.4 Asia-Pacific FTA projects (by June 2007)

Notes: * Pacific-3 FTA expands to quadrilateral Trans-Pacific Strategic Economic Partnership (TPSEPA) project including Brunei as full negotiating partner from April 2005. ^ PICTA (Pacific Island Countries Trade Agreement) involves the 14 Pacific Island Countries.

- Japan–Singapore FTA negotiations commence in February and are concluded by October.
- Singapore starts FTA negotiations with Australia and the US.
- Various other FTA projects proposed: Hong Kong–New Zealand, Hong Kong–China, Japan–Thailand, Thailand–New Zealand, South Korea–Mexico, Thailand–Australia and Singapore–Canada.

In 2002
- First round of ASEAN–China (ACFTA) negotiations held in March.
- Taiwan initiates its FTA policy.
- South Korea concludes negotiations of its very first FTA, with Chile in October.
- Singapore concludes FTA negotiations with Australia in November.
- Singapore–South Korea, Japan–Malaysia and Japan–Philippines FTA projects are proposed.
- Other FTAs involving East Asian states and Asia-Pacific trade partners are initiated (see Table 6.2), including the plurilateral Trans-Pacific Strategic Economic Partnership Agreement (TPSEPA) between at this stage Singapore, New Zealand and Chile.

In 2003
- Singapore concludes FTA talks with the US in January.
- Hong Kong–China FTA negotiations are concluded in June, and China–Macao FTA negotiations in October.
- Japan–Indonesia FTA project proposed in June.
- Taiwan concludes negotiations on its first ever FTA, with Panama in August.
- Japan–South Korea FTA talks commence in December.
- By the year-end, there are 34 FTA projects in the Asia-Pacific involving East Asian states, and 12 amongst East Asian states themselves.

In 2004
- South Korea–ASEAN FTA (KAFTA) project formally proposed.
- ASEAN and China reach an agreement in November on trade in goods liberalisation in ACFTA negotiations. Singapore–South Korea FTA negotiations also concluded this month.
- Thailand concludes its bilateral FTA talks with both New Zealand and Australia.
- Japan signs its second ever FTA, with Mexico in September.
- Eight other FTA projects proposed this year involving East Asian and other Asia-Pacific states, including that between ASEAN and Australia–New Zealand.

In 2005
- Japan–Vietnam and Japan–Brunei FTA projects proposed in December.

- Japan–South Korea talks stall primarily owing to disagreements over agriculture.
- Japan–Malaysia negotiations concluded in May, as are TPSEPA talks with Brunei as an additional negotiating party.
- Taiwan–Guatemala and Thailand–Peru negotiations concluded.
- In this year, there were 20 FTA projects being negotiated in the Asia-Pacific involving East Asian states.

In 2006
- Japan–Thailand FTA negotiations concluded in February, and Japan–Philippines FTA negotiations in September.
- Taiwan concludes its joint FTA talks with El Salvador and Honduras in December.
- China–Singapore, and China–South Korea bilateral FTA projects formally proposed.
- A South Korea–US FTA also proposed and negotiations commence in March.
- Japan and South Korea both initiate bilateral FTA projects with Australia, and Malaysia with Chile.
- By the end of the year 17 FTA projects had been initiated within the East Asia regional group (8 bilaterals concluded) and East Asian states were by this time involved in 37 additional projects (16 concluded) with other Asia-Pacific states.

In 2007, by June
- The idea for studying EAS based regional FTA accepted in January.
- China–Peru FTA proposed in February.
- Japan–Chile FTA signed in March, the Japan–Thailand FTA in April.
- South Korea–US FTA negotiations concluded in April. Seventh round of ASEAN–Japan FTA talks and first round of Japan–Australia FTA talks also held this month.
- KAFTA agreement on goods (Thailand a non-party) comes into effect in June.

East Asian countries have also courted FTA partners from outside the Asia-Pacific. Popular choices have been India (Japan, Singapore, Malaysia, Thailand, ASEAN as a group), Pakistan (Malaysia, China, Japan, Singapore), the Gulf Co-operation Council group (China, Japan, Singapore), and the European Free Trade Association group (Singapore, South Korea, China), and more recently the EU (ASEAN as a group, South Korea). We can also observe that East Asian states are involved in twice as many projects within the Asia-Pacific region relative to those just within the East Asia region (Table 6.2), the US, Australia, New Zealand, Mexico and Chile being the most popular partners.

So why did the new East Asia FTA trend take off so suddenly? There are four main reasons for this. The first concerns what can be referred to as

'*FTA catch-up*' with other parts of the world. It was noted in the chapter's introduction that FTA activity had proliferated globally over the first half of the 1990s but that East Asia still had no operative FTA in place by the time of the 1997/8 financial crisis. The new global trend of FTA activity can be seen as a parallel or connected development to deepening regionalism and globalisation. FTA-induced commercial liberalisation helped facilitate integration at both the regional and global levels. Conversely, states have pursued FTAs as part of their globalisation strategies, especially with regard to securing preferential market access with key trade partners. In Europe and to a lesser extent Latin America's case, FTAs have to be used to consolidate a regional integration process, a comparative analysis of which we shall explore in greater detail. For East Asian states, whose economies were generally outward-oriented and highly trade dependent, it was a case of making up for lost time concerning FTA projects. This point was acknowledged in many East Asian government trade policy documents around the time their FTA policies were initiated (Dent 2006a).

One reason why many East Asian states – most notably Japan and South Korea – had long resisted FTAs was because they had been traditionally committed to the GATT/WTO-led multilateral approach on trade liberalisation. This is because they subscribed strongly to the view that the inherent preferential nature of FTAs only served to undermine the non-discriminatory principles on which GATT/WTO multilateralism was based, and a multilateralism that had succeeded over recent decades to progressively open up international markets to East Asian exports, hence helping facilitate the region's export-driven economic growth. This leads us to the second main factor behind East Asia's new FTA trend, namely *trade institution failure*. Most relevant here were problems arising within the WTO, especially from the December 1999 Seattle Ministerial Meeting onwards.

At the Seattle meeting, the planned launch of the New Millennium Round of global trade talks was aborted due to various disagreements arising broadly between developed and developing countries. The Seattle debacle was a particular cause for alarm for those East Asian countries whose trade liberalisation diplomacy was overtly and almost singularly focused on WTO multilateralism. Subsequent difficulties in WTO diplomacy (e.g. the September 2003 Cancun Ministerial) strengthened the imperative of East Asian countries to shift to a multi-track approach, i.e. bilateral, regional and multilateral trade agreements. Previous chapters have already discussed how other aspects of trade institution failure (Chapter 3 and AFTA, Chapter 4 and APEC) also spurred East Asian countries to pursue FTAs as an alternative to faltering trade liberalisation endeavours at the regional level.

Another key initial catalyst behind the new FTA trend in East Asia, and our third main factor, was *the 1997/8 financial crisis*. The contagion spread of the crisis had exposed the extent to which economic interdependence had deepened in the region and at the same time the lack of co-operative mechanisms amongst East Asian states to cope with such turbulent events. In addition to APT led improvements in regional financial governance structures,

FTAs were conceived among other things as a means of establishing closer and more co-operative trade and economic relations between East Asian countries. From the beginning, most East Asian FTA projects have had a strong co-operative dimension to them: they were not simply preferential market access deals. For example, most of Japan's free trade agreements are officially referred to instead as economic partnership agreements that tend to contain various economic co-operation measures across a number of fields (Table 6.3). A similar approach is apparent in ACFTA, which is embedded within a wider ASEAN–China Framework Agreement that primarily aims to promote closer co-operation between both sides. Furthermore, China's FTAs with Hong Kong and Macao are officially referred to as Closer Economic Partnership Agreements (CEPAs), and the Singapore–South Korea FTA is closely modelled on the negotiating framework of the Japan–South Korea FTA project. The extent to which a discernible East Asian FTA model has emerged is debateable, as is the actual effectiveness of the economic co-operation measures incorporated into these agreements, an issue discussed in some detail later on in the chapter.

The fourth and last factor, *strategic diplomacy motivations*, can be viewed from two inter-related perspectives, these being 'isolation avoidance' and 'competitive bilateralism'. These both became increasingly relevant as the FTA trend in East Asia intensified. Isolation avoidance related to how those countries that had for whatever reason not initiated a bilateral FTA policy found themselves disadvantaged, especially in market access terms, in relation to those countries that had become FTA-active. Malaysia provides a good illustrative example. For some time, it was a vocal critic of Singapore and Thailand's bilateral FTA policies, arguing it undermined AFTA and ASEAN solidarity. Singapore, Thailand and Malaysia are close competitors in key industries such as electronics and information and communication technology products. As Singapore and Thailand secured bilateral FTAs with important trade partners such as the US, Japan (Singapore only) and Australia, so there was pressure upon the Malaysian Government (e.g. from the business sector) to do the same. This relates to the concept of trade diversion first introduced in Chapter 1. There are also politico-diplomatic costs involved in being isolated from the FTA trend as one by-product of these agreements is the strengthening of ties generally between participating countries, e.g. in political and security relations. Once countries have embarked on an FTA policy, they may become embroiled in a competitive bilateralism process, each trying to secure FTAs with key trade partners before others, and moreover achieve better preferential terms. This drives the FTA trend further forward once a critical mass of FTA-active countries has been reached, and what has also been referred to as a 'domino effect' (Baldwin 1999).

Thus, the bilateral FTA project phenomenon has become a new defining feature of East Asia's regional political economy (Aggarwal and Urata 2005, Dent 2005b, 2006a, Okamoto 2003, Ravenhill 2003, Tran and Harvie 2007).

Table 6.3 Thematic content of East Asia FTAs

Thematic content	Japan–Singapore (JSEPA) 2001	Japan–Malaysia (JMEPA) 2005	Japan–Philippines (JPEPA) 2006	Indonesia–Japan (IJEPA) 2006	Japan–Thailand (JPEPA)* 2006	Japan–South Korea (JKEPA)* in neg	South Korea–Singapore (KSFTA) 2004	ASEAN Free Trade Area (AFTA) 2003	ASEAN–China (ACFTA) 2002	Hong Kong–China (HKCCEPA) 2003	Macao–China (MCCEPA) 2003
Miscellaneous Headings											
Accession clause	•									•	•
Disputes settlement mechanism	•	•	•	•	•	•	•		•	•	•
E-commerce	•						•				
Movement of natural persons	•						•				
Paper-less trading	•						•				
Periodic review (whole agreement)	5 yrs	5 yrs	5 yrs	nyk	nyk	nyk	1 yr		2 yr	1 yr	1 yr
Rules of origin (generic only)		•	•		•	nyk	•		•	•	•
Rules of origin (product-specific included)	•					nyk		•			
Sanitary and phytosanitary measures	•	•	•	•	•	•	•		•		
Services trade	•	•	•	•	•	•	•	•	•	•	•
TBTs, safeguards, regulatory conformity	•	•	•	•	•	•	•	•	•	•	•
'Behind the Border' Market Access/Rights											
Competition policy	•	•	•	•	•	•	•				
Financial sector (liberalisation)	•						•				
Government procurement	•		•		•	•	•				
Intellectual property (rights emphasis)	•	•	•	•	•	•	•				
Investment (rights emphasis)	•	•	•	•	•	•	•				
Economic Co-operation											
Agriculture / primary industry		•	•	•	•	•	•		•		
Broadcasting sector	•						•				
Economic co-operation (general chapter)	•	•	•	•	•	•	•		•	•	•
Education / Human Resource Development	•	•	•		•	•	•		•		
Energy sector	•		•		•		•				
Entertainment industry	•						•				
Environment	•						•				
Financial sector	•	•	•	•	•	•	•		•		
Information and Communication Technology	•	•	•	•	•	•	•		•		
Intellectual property (co-operation emphasis)	•	•	•		•	•	•				
Investment (co-operation emphasis)	•	•					•				
Science and Technology	•	•	•	•	•	•	•		•		
Small and Medium-Sized Enterprises	•	•	•	•	•	•	•		•	•	
Telecommunications (co-operation emphasis)	•	•	•	•	•	•	•		•	•	•
Tourism	•	•	•	•		•	•		•		
Transportation		•	•	•	•	•	•		•		

Notes: *HRD* (human resource development), *SME* (small and medium sized enterprises) *TBTs* (technical barriers to trade). Period review row gives details of how often whole agreement reviews are undertaken. * Thematic content details to be confirmed. *Nyk* - not yet known.

Sources: Original FTA texts.

FTAs were the most important and comprehensive international economic agreements signed amongst East Asian states by the mid-2000s. They have changed the calculus of economic relations within the region to a significant extent and could bring notable changes to the flows of intra-regional trade and investment in East Asia. The region's new FTA trend is essentially bilateral in nature, so how exactly will the relationship between this new bilateralism and East Asia's regionalism develop over forthcoming years? This is the key study question of the chapter.

6.3 East Asia's bilateral FTAs and economic integration

6.3.1 The nature of Free Trade Agreements

In classic regionalism theory, a free trade agreement or area is the most basic form of trade or economic integration (see Chapter 1). It is essentially a preferential agreement between countries that commits them to the mutual removal of all tariff, quota and other trade restrictions. An FTA's basic integration effects thus come primarily through liberalisation, allowing participating economies to fuse closer together through freer flows of trade, investment and other forms of business interaction. Chapter 8 further discusses these effects in the context of 'passive integration'.

The degree of FTA-induced integration will of course depend on the nature and scope of the agreement. Free trade agreements are heterogeneous: they can vary enormously in terms of their technical policy content and ideational approach. Each agreement is a bespoke product, crafted in accordance with the particular politico-economic interactions between the countries in negotiation. They can differ significantly in terms of their *scope of liberalisation*. This can relate to liberalisation exemptions (typically in agriculture) or multi-level trade liberalisation phase-in schedules for certain 'sensitive' industrial sectors and sub-sectors, such as textiles. The inclusion of service trade sectors (e.g. financial services, telecoms) can also vary to a wide degree. Second, there can be many differences in the *thematic content* of FTAs. Less developed economies tend to opt for relatively simple agreements, such as AFTA and ACFTA, where the thematic content range on commercial liberalisation and regulatory matters (e.g. intellectual property rights) is relatively narrow. In contrast, the negotiating frameworks of the Japan–South Korea FTA and the Singapore–South Korea FTA covered a wide range of areas for liberalisation, this being consistent with the more sophisticated commercial regulatory nature of the economies involved.

Differences in *ideational approach* also shape an agreement's thematic content. As noted earlier, East Asian countries have a preference for including economic co-operation measures into their agreements, partly stemming from their developmentalist economic tradition and practices. This differs from the more overt market-liberal approach of Anglo-Pacific countries like the US and Australia, which view FTAs primarily as market access deals. East Asia's 'economic partnership' approach to free trade agreements is, at least in theory, more likely to have wider integrational effects, especially when they combine measures on economic co-operation with regulatory conformity (e.g. on investment rules, government procurement). These effects are more broadly discussed in the context of 'proactive integration' in Chapter 8.

The variance in technical policy content found in FTAs can, however, create a multitude of different rules and regulations governing international trade. This is often referred to as the 'spaghetti bowl' effect. For example, each FTA will have its own *rules of origin regime* that determines the eligibility of products for free trade treatment. This is based on whether products under assessment have sufficient levels of local value-added processing to qualify for tariff-free entry into one FTA party from another. Different value-added thresholds and assessment criteria can apply across FTAs, and further complications arise when product-specific rules of origin are incorporated into the agreement. Furthermore, FTAs can vary in terms of their *implementation schedules, liberalisation modalities and other technical arrangements*. For example, some may apply a negative list on product sector liberalisation (everything to be liberalised now and in the future except for an explicit list of products) and some a positive list approach (only those products listed in the agreement to be liberalised now and in the future), and countries will tend to prefer one method or the other.

6.3.2 FTA integration in East Asia

It is helpful at this point to assess what FTAs have been thus far concluded within East Asia, as well as the progress of other unconcluded FTA projects by mid-2007. A summary of developments is given below:

- *Japan–Singapore*: in force from November 2002.
- *AFTA*: core of the agreement in force by January 2003.
- *ASEAN–China*: partially in force from 2004, to be fully implemented by 2010.
- *China–Hong Kong, China–Macao*: both in force from January 2004.
- *South Korea–Singapore*: in force from February 2006.
- *Japan–Malaysia*: in force from July 2006.
- *Japan–Philippines*: agreement signed, yet to enter into force.
- *Japan–Thailand*: agreement signed, yet to enter into force.
- *Japan–Brunei*: agreement signed, yet to enter into force.
- *Japan–Indonesia*: basic agreement reached, yet to enter into force.
- *Japan–South Korea*: in negotiation, but stalled since early 2005.
- *Japan–Vietnam*: in negotiation.
- *Japan–ASEAN*: in negotiation.
- *South Korea–ASEAN*: partially in force, still in negotiation.

- *China–Singapore*: in negotiation, a more sophisticated FTA than ACFTA.
- *China–South Korea*: proposed 2006.

Figure 6.5 gives a graphic illustration of the above projects in their different levels of development, and the overlapping linkages amongst them. We can see that much overlapping exists, especially with ASEAN at the centre. The ASEAN–China agreement encompasses a substantial part of the East Asian region in its own right in geographic terms, and will create some kind of quasi-regional free trade area. Similar arrangements are set to arise between Japan and ASEAN, and South Korea and ASEAN. In Northeast Asia, we have the long-stalled Japan–South Korea FTA and an only recently proposed China–South Korea FTA. From this macro-perspective it may appear that region-wide FTA integration has developed, or will develop to a significant degree in the future. These agreements should induce a freer flow of trade and investment across the region, as well as foster closer economic co-operative linkages at various levels, thus further spurring East Asia's regionalisation. At the same time we must remember that notable differences exist amongst these FTAs. Table 6.3 provides a comparative overview of the thematic content of each FTA thus far concluded, or in the case of not yet concluded FTA their known negotiating frameworks. We can see that the main apparent differences are between Japan-centred agreements on the one hand and China/ASEAN-centred agreements on the other. This can be broadly explained by the fact that Japan's economy has more sophisticated commercial and regulatory interests that impinge upon the negotiation of FTAs in comparison to China and most ASEAN countries.

In Japan-centred agreements there is far wider incorporation of commercial regulatory measures with a liberalisation or rights emphasis, for example on investment, intellectual property and competition policy. Japanese companies are used to operating in a sophisticated regulatory environment at home, where their 'rights' are legally upheld (e.g. protecting their intellectual property, such as patented technologies), and any FTA signed by Japan should try to extend elements of this regulatory environment, where possible, into FTA partner economies. This at least is what Japanese companies lobby the government to achieve in FTA negotiations. Japan's preference for product-specific rules of origin (RoO) also takes Japanese business interests closely into account, especially those operating in industries that face significant foreign competition. Product-specific RoO are a mechanism for protecting firms in these industries through setting FTA partner exporting firms higher thresholds (these can range up to 60 per cent or higher) for local content in the manufacture of certain exported products (e.g. textiles), thus denying them scope for using cheaper imported inputs in the production process. The price competitive position of Japan-based firms is hence improved because FTA partner firms now have to use relatively

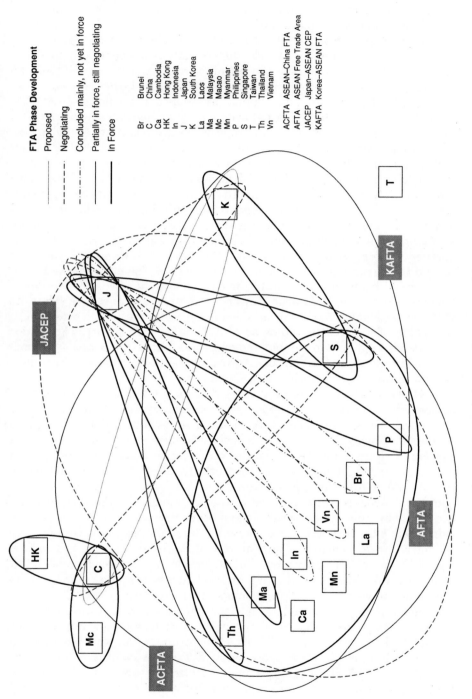

FTA Phase Development

Proposed

Negotiating

Concluded mainly, not yet in force

Partially in force, still negotiating

In Force

Br	Brunei
C	China
Ca	Cambodia
HK	Hong Kong
In	Indonesia
J	Japan
K	South Korea
La	Laos
Ma	Malaysia
Mc	Macao
Mn	Myanmar
P	Philippines
S	Singapore
T	Taiwan
Th	Thailand
Vn	Vietnam

ACFTA ASEAN–China FTA
AFTA   ASEAN Free Trade Area
JACEP Japan–ASEAN CEP
KAFTA Korea–ASEAN FTA

Figure 6.5 FTA linkages within East Asia (by June 2007)

more expensive inputs from domestic sources in order to qualify for FTA treatment when exporting to Japan.

In contrast, China and ASEAN-centred FTAs use just a generic RoO regime where one percentage threshold (typically 40 per cent) is applied universally to all products. Furthermore, China and ASEAN-centred FTAs tend to cover only a few areas of commercial regulation, and where they do a 'co-operation' rather than a 'rights' emphasis is applied. For example, in ACFTA both China and the ASEAN states have committed themselves to work closer together generally on intellectual property issues (e.g. new technology co-operation projects) rather than simply the mutual enforcement of IPR rules and regulations, although this is also briefly mentioned in the agreement.

Table 6.3 also shows that all East Asian FTAs thus far signed have economic co-operation elements incorporated into them, but that again differences are apparent. As with commercial regulation, the wider breadth of Japan-centred FTAs here can be primarily explained by the relatively more sophisticated nature of the Japanese economy. Japan has more to offer FTA partners in terms of economic co-operation because of its economy's broad techno-industrial and infrastructural foundations. There is also a conflation here with Japan's well-established and comprehensive overseas development assistance (ODA) policy towards other parts of East Asia. Thus, its FTAs or 'economic partnership agreements' are in some way an extension of that policy of co-operative diplomacy. China and ASEAN-centred FTAs also place much emphasis on economic co-operation, and ACFTA itself is embedded within a broader 'Framework Agreement on Comprehensive Economic Co-operation between ASEAN and China'.

However, as Table 6.3 indicates there are fewer areas of economic co-operation covered relative to Japan-centred agreements owing mainly to capacity constraint factors. It should also be noted that although no economic co-operation measures are directly incorporated into the AFTA agreement, it is augmented by various complementary regional integration and co-operation schemes such as the Initiative for ASEAN Integration (see Chapter 3). While there are commitments to develop the economic co-operation measures incorporated into both 'models' of East Asian FTAs through joint committee processes and other means, there is often rather thin detail in the text of the agreements on the actual co-operative objectives set and concrete measures to be achieved. At this early stage of the new East Asia FTA trend, with only a handful of agreements in force for only a few years, it is difficult to tell what impact they will make on enhancing economic co-operative relations amongst East Asian countries.

Reconciling the differences between Japan and China/ASEAN-centred FTAs on economic co-operation is not really an issue, but the same cannot be said for other areas of technical policy. As was discussed in Chapter 4 in relation to the proposed Free Trade Area of the Asia-Pacific (FTAAP), significant problems may be anticipated when attempting to unify several bilateral or sub-regional FTAs into one harmonised regional agreement. The following section will discuss this in further detail.

6.4 Towards an East Asia regional Free Trade Area or Agreement (EAFTA)?

6.4.1 Introduction

In both APT and EAS processes there has been talk of one day creating an East Asia Free Trade Area or Agreement, albeit as a long-term objective. Aside from forging closer regional economic linkages through commercial liberalisation, regulatory conformity, economic co-operation and other integrational effects, an EAFTA would also lay an important foundation for regional community-building generally. The emergence of new and more coherent regional economic space will strengthen economic-related associative ties generally within the region through the expansion of various activities spurred by EAFTA's development, for example with regards to transnational business linkages, NGO networking, international labour migration, and inter-governmental dialogue mechanisms. We may thus expect certain region-wide socialisation processes to deepen in response to this integrational development, as would be predicted by new regionalism theory. According to classic regionalism theory, a regional FTA is the conventional precursor to deeper forms of economic integration and community-building, such as a common market and monetary union. However, given FTA developments thus far in East Asia or involving East Asian states, what are the prospects for establishing an EAFTA? In answering this we must consider whether an increasingly dense pattern of FTA bilateralism is making the realisation of a regional FTA in East Asia more easy or difficult. There is, moreover, the broader question of what impact FTA bilateralism is having upon regional community-building in East Asia generally.

To frame this discussion on the bilateralism–regionalism relationship, we shall draw upon a previously developed analytical framework, namely the 'lattice regionalism' hypothesis (Dent 2006a). The essence of this hypothesis is whether or not deepening economic bilateralism enhances the prospects for the development of economic regionalism, and its analytical framework has two converse elements or counter-perspectives. 'Region-convergent' bilateralism looks at how intensifying economic bilateralism within a region can make positive contributions to the development of regionalism, and this hence supports the lattice regionalism hypothesis. 'Region-divergent' bilateralism on the other hand speculates that that intensifying economic bilateralism can undermine the regionalism process, thus rejecting the lattice regionalism hypothesis. Under each counter-perspective there are specified 'points of contention' that in turn will further structure our analysis on this subject.

6.4.2 Bilateral FTAs help foster East Asian Regionalism: region-convergent perspectives

6.4.2.a Sub-structural foundation for regionalism

This first 'region-convergent' point of contention considers the different means by which a dense pattern of bilateral FTAs may lay the politico-diplomatic, technical policy and general economic grounds on which deeper regional integration is founded. In this sense, bilateral FTAs are an important evolutionary or precursory development towards realising a regional trade agreement. This is especially relevant when the initiation of regional FTA negotiations is difficult in the first instance owing to reasons such as economic diversity, political tensions between certain countries in the region, and so on. Bilateral agreements are a path of least resistance at this stage, and a means to gradually build trust and strengthen trade diplomacy linkages and co-operation on a region-wide basis. A bilateral-to-regional evolution process may thus lead to the development of new regionalist forms of co-operation and integration as the pattern of bilateral links matures and becomes increasingly dense. This at least is the theory.

As we see in Case Study 6.1, this approach is somewhat relevant to how Japan has gone about establishing its FTA link with ASEAN through the JACEP framework of negotiating separate bilaterals with individual ASEAN countries in the initial phase. Furthermore, in a 2002 report on free trade agreements, the WTO noted that dense patterns of bilateral FTA activity 'should lead to the consolidation of [FTAs] and rationalisation among participants who may be forced to align themselves with one or other regional grouping', and that, 'harmonisation in the granting of tariff concessions and in the rules of origin can reduce significantly the administrative burden associated with membership in multiple [FTAs]' (WTO 2002: 11). Hence, there are significant incentives for countries within a region to unify their different bilateral agreements into a regional agreement.

We have already noted that achieving harmonisation of the various technical policy aspects of different bilateral FTAs is a real challenge. However, this may be overcome if there is sufficient political will and technocratic resources at hand to bring about such an alignment. For example, rules of origin regime harmonisation can at least be partly achieved through adopting certain 'cumulation' arrangements (e.g. diagonal cumulation) that allow a number of FTA partners to qualify for local value-added contributions to the final products made. The technical policy content of existing bilateral agreements may form the foundational basis of a future negotiated regional FTA. Furthermore, there have been some statements and discussions made by East Asia's political leaders on eventually weaving their bilateral FTAs together into an EAFTA or Asia-Pacific arrangement. This was particularly the case at the start of the new FTA trend, and Singapore – the most FTA-active player in the region – has been the most articulate in this respect (Daquila and Huy 2003, Dent 2006b, Desker 2004). For example, then Singapore Prime Minister Goh Chok Tong stated in January 2001 regarding the Asia-Pacific region that, 'our FTAs actually will pave the way for [the] APEC-wide trade area', and that it was 'Singapore's intention to spin a web of interlocking free trade agreements between APEC members, which could help move the organisation toward achieving free trade in the Asia-Pacific'.[1]

After the FTA trend had deepened still further, Goh stated in October 2003 that, 'after some time, we must sit down to see how we can link up all the FTAs to create a larger, regional or cross-regional agreement'.[2] Government officials from other East Asian states – most notably from Japan, China and South Korea – have expressed similar views and ideas. Soon after the Japan–South Korea FTA project had been initiated, both sides considered that China should one day accede to the agreement making it a trilateral arrangement (Dent and Huang 2002). However, Japan and South Korea subsequently changed their minds when China later expressed its interest in creating a Northeast Asia FTA, first in 2002 and then many times thereafter.[3] Beijing had also previously toyed with the idea of establishing a Greater China FTA that would be based on its CEPAs with Hong Kong and Macao that could in addition incorporate Taiwan at some point.

Around the same time, the APT commissioned East Asia Vision Group report (EAVG 2001) envisaged an EAFTA being achieved by a building block approach of consolidating existing bilateral and sub-regional FTAs in the region, suggesting this objective should be realised well in advance of APEC's 'Bogor Goals' deadlines of 2010 and 2020 (see Chapter 4). This idea was followed up in the subsequent East Asia Study Group report, submitted at the 2002 APT Summit (EASG 2002) and which recommended East Asian countries should pursue an EAFTA project as 'a long-term goal', and should, 'take into account the variety of differences in developmental stages and the varied interests of the countries in the region' (p. 44). However, at the 2003 APT Summit, East Asian states could not then fully agree on the steps towards establishing an EAFTA, stating instead that they planned to 'explore, in a timely manner, the direction of a closer future economic partnership'.[4]

Discussions and diplomatic rhetoric on 'lattice regionalism' outcomes from bilateral FTA activity quietened down, however, during the years that immediately followed. While the deepening bilateral FTA trend continued to constitute some kind of convergence in trade policy practice within the region, by 2005 there was still no accepted formal plan being proposed to create an EAFTA-type arrangement. Another breakthrough came at the January 2007 EAS meeting where member states formally endorsed Japan's proposal to commence feasibility studies into an EAS-based regional FTA, officially termed the Comprehensive Economic Partnership for East Asia, or CEPEA (see Case Study 6.2). It was not clear, though, whether this would be based on harmonising existing bilateral and sub-regional FTAs into a single agreement. We can nevertheless be sure that it would involve complex negotiations over many years if talks were ever initiated, as we later discuss under region-divergent bilateralism.

6.4.2.b Congruent processes and objectives

This point of contention is concerned with the extent to which the processes and objectives of bilateral FTAs are congruent with those of regional organisations, frameworks and regional community-building efforts.

For example, is FTA bilateralism compatible with the aims of AFTA and those of ASEAN more generally? Also, are bilateral FTAs and regionalist projects serving similar ends and perhaps even working in alignment with each other? There is a close link between this second point of contention and the first as there is often an analytical co-determinacy between *structure* and *process* in the study of international political economy. However, this point of contention focuses more on whether bilateral FTAs are harmoniously co-existing with current forms of regionalism rather than providing a basis on which future regionalist structures will develop.

Let us begin by looking at AFTA and ASEAN. The AFTA project was initiated long before the new bilateral FTA trend took off in East Asia, and no bilateral FTA links existed within the ASEAN beforehand. It is therefore a question of whether the various bilateral agreements ASEAN member states have signed, or are due to sign with countries outside the region are at least compatible with AFTA. As Table 6.2 and Figures 6.1 to 6.4 show, Singapore and Thailand have been the most FTA-active members of ASEAN but many others have also become increasingly active. Looking at this relationship from a positive perspective, the engagement of ASEAN states in various other FTAs has improved their learning of free trade agreements generally, for instance in terms of technical policy instruments and commercial regulatory norms and practices. This learning could be used to improve and upgrade AFTA in the future, helping it adapt to changing regional and global economic conditions. Given that there has been some criticism of AFTA's relatively simple and narrow framework (see Chapter 3), this process may be of considerable importance by making the regional trade agreement more effective and relevant to its signatories. Learning from various bilateral FTAs will also have helped develop other AFTA associated projects, such as the ASEAN Framework Agreement on Services (on services liberalisation) and the ASEAN Investment Area (on investment liberalisation).

There are certain limitations we face when assessing congruence and compatibility issues between bilateral FTAs and the APT/EAS regional frameworks. As previously discussed, plans for conducting initial EAFTA feasibility studies (i.e. on the Japan proposed CEPEA) only began in early 2007, hence there is no regional trade agreement in place at this level to make a relational analysis. Furthermore, the more established APT framework has focused more on regional financial integration projects than regional trade integration (see Chapter 5). If anything, the APT framework has helped facilitate the development of bilateral FTAs rather than vice versa. For example, China and ASEAN used APT meetings as a means of developing the ACFTA project. At the 2000 APT Summit, an agreement was struck between both sides on initiating an ACFTA joint feasibility study. The following year at the 2001 APT Summit, both sides came to a general agreement concerning an ACFTA negotiating framework, and at the 2002 APT Summit an ACFTA accord was formally signed. Also at the 2002 APT Summit, Japan and ASEAN launched the JACEP initiative that contained a commitment to at some point negotiating a Japan–ASEAN FTA. South Korea too announced at the same summit its interest in signing an FTA with the ASEAN group (see Case Study 6.1). APT-led discussions through the EASG and EAVG reports on creating an EAFTA as a long-term goal were noted in the previous section.

Lastly, and again from a positive perspective, how have bilateral FTAs been congruent with the processes and objectives of APEC, and in particular its trade liberalisation agenda embodied by the Bogor Goals project? As Chapter 4 details, APEC member states' compliance with the Bogor Goals objectives involve completely liberalising their trade and investment regimes by 2010 for developed member economies, and by 2020 for developing member economies. In light of failed or thus far largely ineffective APEC-led strategies to move towards these objectives (e.g. the Early Voluntary Sectoral Liberalisation and Individual Action Plan schemes), bilateral FTAs have emerged as an alternative method to advance commercial liberalisation within the trans-region. In one sense, the Bogor Goals project may be realised if either all the 21 member economies sign FTAs with each other, or an APEC-based regional FTA (i.e. the recently proposed Free Trade Area of the Asia-Pacific, or FTAAP, project) is established. Both outcomes would appear unlikely at this stage, and as is argued under region-divergent bilateralism (undermining or capturing effects), FTAs are seen by many as subverting APEC's founding principles and organisational purpose, these being centred on the 'open regionalism' concept. Nevertheless, FTAs have at least helped keep trade liberalisation, and hence the Bogor Goals, on the APEC agenda, and have furthermore strengthened bilateral and sub-regional economic relations amongst APEC member states.

6.4.2.c Preliminary conditioning to regional economic liberalisation and integration

This point of contention focuses on how bilateral FTAs help make economic agents (e.g. firms, governments, consumers) more conditioned to international economic liberalisation processes, as well as integrational links with other trade partners. By gradually getting domestic economic agents used to the rigours of foreign competition through bilateral FTAs it may be easier for governments to secure the necessary public support to eventually move ahead with more ambitious regional economic integration projects. Bilateral FTAs may be considered a gradual adjustment mechanism in this respect. Protected firms in particular may strongly resist the sudden opening up of their home markets to all rival competitors within the region. Bilateral FTA liberalisation and integration offer a preliminary or intermediary conditioning process in this respect.

The average import tariff rates of East Asian countries vary significantly. For example, in the mid-2000s Singapore's average rate was virtually zero, Japan's 2.9 per cent (but agricultural goods rate is 12.0 per cent), China's 9.8 per cent, South Korea's 6.5 per cent, Indonesia's 6.4 per cent, Malaysia's

7.3 per cent, Philippines' 4.5 per cent, Thailand's 14.0 per cent, and Taiwan's 4.8 per cent. This is compared to the EU's 1.4 per cent and the US's 3.2 per cent.[5] It is difficult to establish empirically to what extent FTAs already signed and implemented by East Asian states have contributed to the lowering of these average rates. Other factors such as compliance to the Uruguay Round agreement and other WTO accords continue to have some effect. FTAs may only be able to achieve marginal tariff rate reductions in East Asia's key industries such as electronics and ICT products where rates are already very low. There is also the question of how much of East Asian trade has thus far actually been covered by FTAs, in other words what is the scope of their conditioning effects?

Let us take Japan, the region's biggest trader, as an example. By the end of 2006, the share of its total trade covered by concluded or substantially agreed EPAs/FTAs with other East Asian countries accounted for only 12.3 of Japan's total trade (Indonesia 2.7 per cent, Malaysia 2.4 per cent, Philippines 1.5 per cent, Singapore 2.3 per cent and Thailand 3.4 per cent). Concluded FTA/EPA negotiations with South Korea would add another 6.4 per cent, with China and Hong Kong another 20.0 per cent, and with Taiwan 5.5 per cent, the remainder of ASEAN just 1.0 per cent, but with East Asia as a whole 45.2 per cent of Japan's total trade. Thus, just over a quarter of Japan's total East Asian trade was covered by FTAs by this time. It was, however, Japan that proposed at the January 2007 EAS meeting that an official study be conducted into creating an EAFTA arrangement (i.e. the CEPEA), and was supported by other bilateral FTA-active member states of the group.

There is also the view that advances in commercial liberalisation brought about from the new FTA trend in East Asia have helped deepen economic regionalisation (see Chapter 2). Although import tariff rates on component and material products in East Asia are generally low, FTAs have had, or will have some rate reduction effects and thus further reduce the costs of operating international production networks (IPNs) in the region. Other elements of commercial liberalisation (e.g. on services and investment) embodied in these agreements also spur this and other forms of regionalised business activity in East Asia. FTAs may too create a more conducive regulatory environment for transnational business to flourish generally – for example through improved investment and intellectual property rights for foreign investing firms – hence further driving forward East Asia's regionalisation (Zhai 2006). Yet as was noted in Chapter 2, trade regulatory variance (e.g. on rules of origin measures) amongst FTAs within a region may be more of a hindrance than help to IPN trade and other business operations. This is discussed in more detail under region-divergent bilateralism in relation to the so called 'spaghetti bowl' problem.

Case Study 6.1 ASEAN's Free Trade Agreement projects with China, Japan and South Korea

From Figure 6.5 we can see that ASEAN, or ASEAN countries, appear to be at the pivotal centre of East Asia's network of bilateral FTAs.

Aside from having its own regional free trade agreement (AFTA), it had also initiated FTA projects with China, Japan and South Korea. Those with China and South Korea were negotiated on a country-to-group bilateral basis, and in a sense may be considered *quasi-regional* in nature because they incorporate a large number of countries from the East Asia region. Japan, on the other hand, insisted on negotiating separate bilateral FTAs with ASEAN countries with a view to eventually merging these together into an overall Japan–ASEAN arrangement, or Japan–ASEAN Comprehensive Economic Partnership (JACEP) as it is formally known.

The basis of an ASEAN–China Free Trade Agreement (ACFTA) was signed in 2002, and certain elements of a South Korea–ASEAN FTA (KAFTA) were signed in 2005. Negotiations on both agreements are still ongoing by 2007, and Japan had concluded, or substantially concluded bilateral agreements with a number of countries. In the meantime, no agreements between these Northeast Asian countries themselves had been signed: Japan–Korea FTA talks had been long stalled, and a China–South Korea FTA project was only initiated in 2006. Below is an outline of how the ACFTA, KAFTA and JACEP projects have developed, and are scheduled to develop over time, as well as other pertinent issues.

ASEAN–China Free Trade Agreement (ACFTA)

- *November 2000*: Formally proposed at the 2000 APT Summit.
- *November 2001*: Broad negotiating framework of ACFTA agreed.
- *May 2002*: First round of ACFTA negotiations.
- *November 2002*: First phase FTA negotiations concluded. ASEAN and China sign their 'Framework Agreement' at the 2002 APT Summit, committing both sides to liberalise bilateral trade by 2010 with Cambodia, Laos, Myanmar and Vietnam to meet this target by 2015. ASEAN and China also agree to an 'Early Harvest' programme (EHP) of immediate tariff cuts to be implemented within three years mainly on selected agricultural and forestry products but also 130 specific manufactured goods.
- *November 2003*: All ASEAN member states and China sign an EHP protocol agreement at that year's APT summit.
- *January 2004*: EHP protocol agreement enters into force.
- *November 2004*: Second phase FTA negotiations concluded. Both sides reach an agreement on the framework for eliminating tariffs for all products, with sensitive list exemptions and phase-ins. Some inclusion of services trade liberalisation also agreed upon.
- *December 2004*: Tariff levels on EHP products reduced to a 10 per cent maximum.

- *January 2005*: Tariff elimination on non-EHP manufactured products commences.
- *June 2005*: Trade in goods agreement reached that will lead to the elimination of tariffs on 7,445 categories of goods, or a total of 95 per cent of overall goods, by 2010.
- *July 2005*: Both sides start to implement the above agreement.
- *December 2005*: EHP products import tariffs reduced to a 5 per cent maximum.
- *December 2006*: EHP products import tariffs reduced to zero per cent.
- *January 2007*: Trade in services agreement signed as part of ACFTA, providing for liberalisation and national treatment provisions covering a wide range of service sectors.
- *July 2007*: Trade in services agreement enters into force.
- *January 2010*: ACFTA comprehensively in force between China and ASEAN-6 group.
- *January 2015*: ACFTA comprehensively in force between China and the entire ASEAN group.

By 2007, ASEAN and China had, then, concluded and signed all elements of the ACFTA deal and were thereafter continuing to implement its various elements up to the 2010 and 2015 deadlines. In many respects, ACFTA has already achieved considerable success. It has helped boost trade and investment flows between China and Southeast Asia. In 2004, their bilateral trade was US$106 billion, and this had grown by over 50 per cent to US$161 billion by 2006 (their bilateral trade in 1991 was just US$8 billion). In 2005, ASEAN foreign direct investment in China stood at US$3 billion, and China's FDI in Southeast Asia was just US$158 million, but the latter was expected to rise dramatically over forthcoming years to around US$6 billion as a result of ACFTA.[6]

The ACFTA forms part of a broader 'Framework Agreement on Comprehensive Economic Co-operation between ASEAN and China', which has augmented their relations more generally across a number of areas. For example, since signing the Framework Agreement, China has been busy assisting Southeast Asia's less developed countries with loans, infrastructure provision and other forms of aid. In security relations, China and ASEAN have agreed to the establishment of a code of conduct in the South China Sea, and China has also acceded to ASEAN's Treaty of Amity and Co-operation. This has helped reduce ASEAN's threat perception of China, and in October 2006 both sides announced in a joint statement entitled 'Towards An Enhanced China–ASEAN Strategic Partnership' that the creation of an East Asia community should be a long-term goal for the wider region.[7]

South Korea–ASEAN FTA (KAFTA)

- *March 2004*: Formally proposed. Both sides also announce the initiation of a Joint Study Group process.
- *February 2005*: First round of KAFTA negotiations.
- *December 2005*: Trade in goods negotiations substantially concluded.
- *April 2006*: Trade in goods agreement fully reached in which both sides agree, in principle, to eliminate tariffs on 90 per cent of their respective imports by 2010. Tariffs on a further 7 per cent of imports are to be reduced to 0–5 per cent by 2016. Thailand is a non-signatory owing to its objection to South Korea's insistence that rice is omitted from the agreement.
- *June/July 2006*: Negotiations on investment and trade in services commence.
- *August 2006*: Trade in goods agreement officially signed. Around 100 goods produced in North Korea's Kaesong Industrial Complex (co-managed with South Korea) were also included in the agreement.
- *November 2006*: Fifteenth round of negotiations held.
- *June 2007*: KAFTA's trade in goods liberalisation comes into initial effect, Thailand being exempted.
- *January 2010*: KAFTA's trade in goods liberalisation substantially realised.

South Korea and ASEAN had missed their initial December 2006 deadline to conclude negotiations on all KAFTA elements. Talks on services and investment liberalisation continued well into 2007. Meanwhile, Thailand – which had opted out of the trade in goods agreement owing to the above noted rice market dispute – was looking for a compromise with South Korea so that it might later sign the agreement. In 2005, trade between ASEAN and South Korea stood at US$51 billion, registering a 15 per cent increase from the previous year. South Korea's large *chaebol* companies (e.g. Samsung) had made increasingly large investments in Southeast Asia since the early 2000s – around US$600 million in 2005 – and KAFTA was expected to increase this level still further.

Japan–ASEAN Comprehensive Economic Partnership (JACEP)

- *January 2002*: On a visit to Singapore, Japanese Prime Minister Junichiro Koizumi outlines his vision for a Japan–ASEAN Comprehensive Economic Partnership (JACEP), though this does not at this stage include a firm commitment to negotiate a Japan–ASEAN free trade agreement.

- *March 2002*: ASEAN Economic Ministers group and Japan's Ministry of Economy, Trade and Industry discuss JACEP terms of reference and agenda items. A JACEP Expert Group is established to undertake a scoping study.
- *October 2002*: In their report, the JACEP Expert Group recommends that the JACEP should 'include elements of a possible FTA'.
- *November 2002*: JACEP signed at the 2002 APT Summit. It includes wide-ranging measures on economic co-operation and a commitment to negotiate a Japan–ASEAN FTA, to be implemented within 10 years, i.e. by 2012. JACEP's elements to be initially realised through a series of bilateral agreements (including FTAs) between Japan and ASEAN member states within 5 years, i.e. by 2007.
- *October 2003*: The Framework for Comprehensive Economic Partnership between Japan and ASEAN is signed that contains commitments on realising the above.
- *April 2005*: First round of JACEP negotiations, running in parallel with various bilateral FTA negotiations between Japan and individual ASEAN member states, by this time Thailand, Malaysia and the Philippines, and from July 2006 with Indonesia.
- *March 2007*: Deadline missed for concluding JACEP negotiations owing to a number of unresolved issues.
- *May 2007*: Both sides announce they hope to conclude the 'trade in goods' element of JACEP by November that year.
- *December 2007*: Initial target date for signing Japan's bilateral FTAs with individual ASEAN member states. Thereafter, negotiations to commence on unifying these into a Japan–ASEAN free trade agreement (JAFTA).
- *December 2012*: Target date for realising JACEP, including its JAFTA element.

The JACEP negotiations, which started in 2005, have included discussions on FTA-related issues (e.g. IPR, rules of origin, agricultural trade liberalisation) but very little details on the outcomes of these talks (seven rounds held by May 2007) have been published, most likely because of the limited progress that had been achieved by this time. It is also not exactly clear how the JACEP–bilateral FTA harmonisation process will be achieved given the significant technical policy differences that exist across already negotiated Japan–ASEAN country bilateral FTAs.

If all these three projects are realised, then a substantial share of East Asia's regional trade will be conducted on FTA terms by 2012. Yet as we have discussed at some length in this chapter, these terms may be significantly heterogeneous. Not only are there notable differences between ACFTA, KAFTA and the Japan–ASEAN country bilaterals regarding thematic content (see Table 6.3) but also in relation to the scope, schedules and modalities of trade liberalisation. Furthermore, Japan and ASEAN have yet to comprehensively negotiate their 'harmonising' JAFTA arrangement. Will there be any point in initiating these talks if negotiations on Japan's proposed EAS-based regional free trade agreement commence around the same time?

And what role is ASEAN able to play in bringing regional convergence to the ACFTA, KAFTA and JACEP projects? Sheng Li Jun from the Institute of Southeast Asian Studies offered some interesting and useful comments on this matter: 'China, Japan and South Korea need ASEAN as a platform to discuss regional integration; they can't deal directly, bilaterally, because of border rivalries or historical mistrust. ASEAN is in the driver's seat of Asian economic integration, and it can stay there, if only as a taxi driver.'[8] Playing on this 'taxi driver' analogy we can make the following relevant points. First, the FTA links that China, Japan and South Korea all have with ASEAN allow them to be taken in generally the same direction in terms of trade integration and diplomacy within the region. Second, all have agreed to end up in roughly the same destination at roughly the same time. Third, ASEAN, which has limited capacity itself to act as a regional hub power (see Chapter 3) is not in command as such of the FTA 'vehicle' but has provided this vehicle so that near region-wide trade integration may advance.

We should finally note that in addition to its FTA projects with China, Japan and South Korea, ASEAN has also initiated those with India, Australia–New Zealand, and the EU. There has also been talk of a similar project with the US. All but the EU of this trade partner group had previously either concluded or initiated country-to-country bilaterals with certain ASEAN member states.

Study Questions

1. Compare and contrast the different approaches taken by China, Japan and South Korea to negotiating their FTAs with the ASEAN group.
2. Critically assess the view that ASEAN may be considered the 'taxi driver' of region-wide free trade integration in East Asia.

6.4.3 Bilateral FTAs destabilise East Asian regionalism: region-divergent perspectives

6.4.3.a Undermining or capturing effects

This first point essentially offers a counter-view to that of *congruent processes and objectives* under region-convergent bilateralism. Instead, we consider here how intensifying FTA bilateralism may undermine the integrity or capture key aspects of regional organisations and frameworks. There are two main aspects to this. First, the objectives and very nature of bilateral FTAs may be inconsistent with the principles and aims of a regional organisation to which both parties belong. Second, certain bilateral FTA partnerships may exert certain influences upon a regional organisation or framework that are not in the interests of its wider membership.

There are a number of issues that relate to AFTA and ASEAN here. In the early years of East Asia's new FTA trend, Malaysia especially took the view that bilateral FTA projects, developed with non-Asian trade partners in particular, were a distraction to Southeast Asia's regional community-building projects, AFTA being especially relevant here. Singapore was the main focus of Malaysia's criticism, the city-state being quick to initiate bilateral FTA projects with Japan, New Zealand, the US, Australia, Mexico and Canada by 2001. It had also by this time approached the EU and China for bilateral deals but was turned down. At first, Malaysia argued these trade agreements would compromise the integrity of AFTA by allowing extra-regional trade partners to gain 'back door' access to the regional free trade area. Singapore counter-argued that the rules of origin measures in these FTAs ensured this would not happen as they would classify imports from non-ASEAN free trade partners as being such, and therefore not qualify for AFTA treatment, thus negating the *trade deflection* problem (see Case Study 1.1, Chapter 1, p. 13).

Malaysia in addition claimed, however, from a more politico-economic perspective, that a preoccupation with signing various bilateral agreements with extra-regional partners was indicative of a relative loss of interest in the home region. As Chapter 3 noted, both Singapore and Thailand's early pursuit of bilateral FTAs could be at least partly understood as compensating for the (financial) crisis-affected AFTA market. Former Malaysian Government minister, Ramon Navaratnam, contended that, 'Even if Singapore's Free Trade Agreements are consistent with AFTA and WTO, the real issue is whether Singapore's unholy haste is consistent with the ASEAN spirit of optimising co-operation, consultation and fraternal goodwill, in the longer term'.[9] Negotiating multiple FTAs simultaneously also required a great deal of economic diplomacy effort, thus potentially diverting technocratic resources away from regional community-building endeavours.

It is difficult to establish the extent to which this may have occurred, and as we know from Chapter 3, Singapore had long taken a lead in ASEAN's new regional integration projects such as the AEC. The new FTA trend has also enabled ASEAN to be linked as a group to other East Asia trade partners, as discussed in Case Study 6.1. Finally, Malaysia and other ASEAN states such as Indonesia and the Philippines were also somewhat concerned over how Singapore and Thailand's common ardent pursuit of FTAs was further strengthening an emerging and dominant bilateral Singapore–Thailand relationship within the ASEAN group. Case Study 3.3 in Chapter 3 (see p. 106) discusses the contentious issues surrounding this bilateral alliance with regard to Southeast Asia regional community-building processes, especially concerning how Singapore and Thailand together sought to shape ASEAN's future regional integration agenda.

With the proliferation of heterogeneous bilateral FTAs within a region comes the proliferation of different rules and regulations governing trade in that region. We have already examined the significant differences that exist amongst the free trade agreements thus far signed in East Asia. This so called 'spaghetti bowl' effect (Bhagwati 1993) poses a considerable technical policy and diplomatic challenge when attempting to unify these agreements into a single regional agreement. To recap, FTA heterogeneity can arise in terms of scope and implementation schedules of liberalisation, rules of origin regime, regulatory conformity measures, liberalisation modalities, customs procedures, and so on. In an era of historically low tariff rates, rules and regulations have an ever more important impact on trade flows. The convoluted pattern of trade rules caused by bilateral FTAs is especially a problem for firms exporting to multiple markets, imposing additional managerial and transaction costs upon firms through first having to identify which specific rules apply to what flow of trade (depending on the FTA partner market), and thereafter having to take differentiated actions (e.g. in production, distribution, customs compliance, etc.) in accordance with those rules.

Rules of origin are often cited as a key element of the spaghetti bowl problem, and are particularly important to East Asia because of how they can affect international production networks. As noted earlier, FTA trade liberalisation can help reduce the transaction costs of operating IPNs but compliance to the RoO regimes of one or many FTAs may require the firm to make substantial and costly changes to IPN sourcing and production logistics (see Chapter 2). Many firms may thus decide not to seek qualification for FTA 'free trade', and hence the regionalisation effects of FTAs can be lower when they contain more restrictive RoO regimes, e.g. those with high 'local content' requirement thresholds (Estevadeordal and Suominen 2005). Indeed, an APEC report stated that, 'RoO can be at least as important as tariff elimination in determining the degree of market access conferred by an FTA' (2005:1).

There are politico-economic dimensions to this issue also. Countries may prove reluctant to enter into a regional FTA when it means foregoing many hard-won preferential benefits secured in bilateral FTA negotiations with especially important trade partners as these benefits will be multilateralised in a regional arrangement. There may be other reasons why certain countries find it difficult to progress to a regional FTA because of existing bilateral agreements. Free trade agreements are forged by the interplay of the different national interests of the countries involved. These become more discernible in bilateral FTAs as there are just two countries' interests to consider. As previously discussed, more dominant countries, such as Japan and China, are able to develop a particular FTA model applied to many if not all agreements these countries sign with others. The more embedded this model becomes, as advanced through bilateral FTAs, the more reluctant dominant countries will be to deviate from this model, with all its specific technical policy and ideational features. This development may further undermine the prospects of establishing a regional free trade agreement, at least one based on a commonly agreed model.

Chapter 4 details how there have been attempts made within APEC to establish some form of common or best FTA practice in order to address the spaghetti bowl problem in the Asia-Pacific. These attempts have, however, achieved very limited success mainly because the region's FTA trend had already developed significantly by the time such 'best practice' measures were being discussed, and also because APEC lacks the institutional mechanisms required to ensure its member economies comply with these measures. More importantly, and as noted earlier, bilateral FTAs have undermined the original founding principles and organisational purpose on which APEC is based, namely 'open regionalism' (see Case Study 4.1, Chapter 4, p. 129). Essentially, it relates to how APEC was conceived as a vehicle to advance closer and non-discriminatory economic relations within the Asia-Pacific through processes that would also not discriminate against non-APEC members, hence 'open' regional integration was the objective. The debate in the Chapter 4 case study largely focused on how proposals to establish a regional FTA (the FTAAP) could be seen as a subversion of APEC's open regionalism principles.

This same argument applies perhaps more so to the growth of bilateral FTA activity within the Asia-Pacific as it has fostered preferential and discriminatory trade relations in both intra-regional and extra-regional respects. Whereas any trade liberalisation in accordance with APEC open regionalism, as with WTO multilateralism, was supposed to occur on a *diffuse reciprocity* basis (i.e. a 'most favoured nation', non-discriminatory approach on which APEC's Individual Action Plan scheme is supposed to be based), FTAs are negotiated on a *specific reciprocity* basis in which negotiating parties agree to offer preferential concessions to the other in a *quid pro quo* manner. Bilateral FTAs thus structure preferentialism into a regional or other trade system. In APEC's case, it could be said they have undermined the organisation's founding 'open regionalism' principles, as well as captured the regional organisation's objectives on trade liberalisation, as encoded in the Bogor Goals. This can be seen in the preference of member states to pursue bilateral FTAs rather than APEC-led commercial liberalisation schemes.

6.4.3.b Intensifying bilateralism and inter-state rivalry

Our next point of contention considers how deepening bilateralism can intensify international rivalries within a region. With respect to our subject matter, this arises when certain states initiate bilateral FTA projects as reactive counter-balancing manoeuvres in relation to projects already initiated by other states. If left unchecked, such 'competitive bilateralism' may make the realisation of regional community-building objectives difficult to achieve, owing primarily to the defensive or adversarial economic diplomacy environment that intensifying bilateral FTA activity can create.

How relevant then is this point to East Asia? Much of the attention here has focused on China and Japan, and in particular their respective FTA projects with the ASEAN group. Japan was caught somewhat wrong-footed by the ASEAN–China FTA proposal when it was first made in November 2000, leading to Tokyo hastily putting together its own plan for a proposed FTA link with Southeast Asia. The ACFTA proposal was seen by some in Japan as a move by China to help build its position as a future regional hegemon in East Asia, thus challenging similar aspirations Japan had either now or in the future (Kagami 2003). Like ASEAN, South Korea is an important intermediary in the China–Japan relationship. Whilst Japan–South Korea FTA negotiations were stalled, China and South Korea were busy planning their own bilateral FTA project and also conducting feasibility studies on a Northeast Asia FTA. Although these kinds of developments do not marginalise Japan as such, they certainly apply pressure upon her to match China's actions to some extent.

More generally, bilateral FTAs offer a means by which such Sino–Japanese rivalry may be played out, each country seeking to develop their own competing network of diplomatic alliances to gain advantage and influence within the region. In addition, there is the aforementioned competing FTA models (i.e. Japan-centred and China-centred) to take into account. There may be some truth in this neo-realist view on the subject, and Case Study 5.2 in Chapter 5 (see p. 172) explores some of the challenges facing Japan–China relations, and their implications for East Asian regionalism more generally. Here, though, we make the point that Sino–Japan economic interdependence requires both countries to work closer together, on FTAs and other trade-related matters in their bilateral relationship, as well as at the regional level.

Competitive FTA bilateralism has also been evident within Southeast Asia, and particularly concerning ASEAN member state bilaterals with Japan. As Case Study 6.1 examines, while China and South Korea took the option of generally negotiating with ASEAN as a group, Japan chose to broker separate deals with ASEAN countries with the view of thereafter stitching these together into a Japan–ASEAN agreement. Table 6.3 shows that there is some similarity in thematic content between Japan's bilateral FTAs with ASEAN countries but that differences also exist. Moreover, Japan has conferred certain market access and preferences to certain ASEAN member states but not to others. There has been very little co-ordination or even information sharing amongst ASEAN countries with the aim of compelling Japan to multilateralise specific benefits conferred to individual member states to all others. This has meant ASEAN member states have competed with each other to secure the best deal possible with Japan, or secure deals ahead of others. For instance, according to one Thai newspaper article published in May 2005, Malaysia's securing of a bilateral FTA with Japan ahead of Thailand – when negotiations on both started around the same time – was a 'slap in the face' for Thailand.[10]

Differentiated market access deals on specific sectors in Japan–ASEAN member state FTAs may not be a problem as such as these deals are negotiated with respect to the particular national economic interests of each member state. Thus, other ASEAN countries are unlikely to be upset over the Philippines being conferred the right to send 1,000 care workers per year to Japan's labour market if the care worker industry is not a key sector for other ASEAN countries (see Chapter 7). Problems arise, however, when certain member states are granted concessions in common important industries such as autos, or common areas of regulatory interest such as investment rights. On these two accounts, for example, Malaysia was allowed to retain higher levels of protectionist controls than other ASEAN countries in their FTA deals with Japan. Furthermore, Japan's predilection for multiple tariff liberalisation phase-in schedules for product and sub-product categories, as well as for product-specific RoO, means that the scope for granting variegated concessions to different ASEAN member states on a bilateral basis is enormous, and is indeed evident in the texts of those bilateral FTAs Japan has already signed with ASEAN countries. The extent to which this has aggravated relations both amongst ASEAN member states, and between ASEAN countries and Japan is difficult to assess. However, competitive FTA bilateralism has reportedly been the cause of some tension and acrimony within the APT group of states,[11] which can only serve to hamper regional community-building efforts. This contrasts somewhat with the experience of ACFTA where negotiations were conducted on a ASEAN group level and concessions granted on a universal basis.

6.4.3.c Reinforced power asymmetries

This point of contention considers how power asymmetries within a region can become further exaggerated or reinforced when bilateral linkages and alliances become a predominant feature of that region's international relations, which may in turn make regional community-building objectives more difficult to achieve. According to this argument, bilateral agreements allow the dominant country to bring its relational power advantages to secure a deal that is more aligned to its own interests rather than those of the relatively weaker partner country. The basis of this relational power advantage may reveal itself in various ways in bilateral negotiations, for example, in the dominant country's wider range of 'bargaining chips' (e.g. being able to offer a larger market, and higher levels of technology transfer, foreign investment and other assets), better negotiating resources at its disposal (e.g. more and better trained technocrats), and its greater influence over international affairs generally. Whereas, then, bilateralism can allow dominant countries to further entrench their advantageous positions of power, this power is more likely to be circumscribed in regional and multilateral agreements. This is because of counter-balancing effects provided by the collective membership of other states in regional or multilateral fora.

Deepening bilateralism can lead to a 'hub-and-spoke' pattern of international relations within a region centred on dominant 'hub' powers. This has occurred to some extent with FTA bilateralism in East Asia with Japan and China as the two hub powers in question, both championing their own quite distinct FTA models. As previously discussed, Japan's country-to-country bilateral approach to negotiating FTAs with ASEAN member states allows Japan to deploy its relational power advantages more easily in comparison to China's country-to-group bilateral approach in ACFTA negotiations. While there was a comparatively stronger alignment of interests between China and ASEAN in their FTA negotiations because of economic structural similarities, the adopted country-to-group approach allowed ASEAN to more effectively incorporate the interests of its member states into the negotiating process (Tongzon 2005, Wong and Chan 2003). It is therefore no coincidence that ACFTA is partly based on AFTA, for example in its RoO measures. Moreover, in ACFTA negotiations, the ASEAN Secretariat acted as a co-ordinating agent between rounds of talks, sending off mutually endorsed papers from ASEAN for China to examine. This was the general framework of talks but there were also specific sectors that were dealt with more on a bilateral or sub-group basis.[12]

It was noted earlier, and shown in Table 6.3 that Japan's FTAs with ASEAN states include higher standards on regulatory compliance that are more aligned with Japan's business interests than those currently of Southeast Asian countries. Tokyo had argued that separate bilateral negotiations would allow for the more flexible approach required to negotiate on more complex regulatory matters, as well as take into account the development asymmetry of the ASEAN group.[13] ASEAN member states acquiesced to Japan's demand even though most had wanted to proceed on a group basis.[14] Although it is too strong to say that Japan acted in an exploitative manner in its FTA diplomacy with ASEAN – especially when it is also offering economic co-operation assistance through its 'economic partnership' FTAs – many Southeast Asian countries were reportedly unhappy with Japan's conduct, particularly with how Tokyo had at times sought to play off ASEAN member states against each other, offering better market access terms to those member states more compliant with Japan's negotiating demands.

This links back to the issue that was raised in the previous section concerning the 'competitive bilateralism' problem and the lack of co-ordination and co-operation amongst ASEAN member states in their respective FTA talks with Japan.[15] Many ASEAN countries also expressed their dissatisfaction with Japan for insisting that AFTA's 40 per cent value-added rule of origin apply to Japanese exports to Southeast Asia whereas ASEAN exporters had to comply with a complex range of product-specific rules when exporting to the Japanese market (Dent 2007b). Overall, there is a quite widely held view that the relative power asymmetries between Japan and individual ASEAN countries were exploited in FTA negotiations, and thereafter reinforced by FTA deal outcomes, and that this has had divisive effects with the East Asian regional community. Learning lessons from this,

ASEAN convinced South Korea of the merits of negotiating their FTA project on a country-to-group basis.

6.4.3.d Exacerbating the development divide

Our last point of contention posits that economic bilateralism may exacerbate the existing development divide within a region. Regarding bilateral FTAs, this particularly arises in relation to development capacity issues: developing countries often lack sufficient levels of technocratic, institutional and industrial capacity to engage in the bilateral FTA trend in the first place. In East Asia's case this particularly relates to Cambodia, Laos, Myanmar and Mongolia. These nations have, for example, very scarce trade diplomacy resources with very few trade diplomats and other technocrats able to negotiate more sophisticated bilateral FTAs (e.g. with developed countries like Japan). Their weak institutional, legal and regulatory frameworks are another hindrance, as is the fact that their highly protected industries would not be able to easily withstand the immediate onslaught of foreign competitive pressure released by bilateral FTAs.

Unlike AFTA's regional trade liberalisation arrangements where ASEAN's less developed countries are given longer phase-in liberalisation adjustments generally (see Chapter 3), bilateral FTAs are based on the principle of immediate liberalisation of most sectors. Thus, Cambodia, Laos, Myanmar and Mongolia may have no desire to initiate bilateral FTA policies anyway, and moreover they are beneficiaries of many developed country trade partners' Generalised System of Preferences (GSP) schemes whereby they are able to export many or most of their products to these trade partners under tariff-free conditions without having to reciprocate in kind.[16]

However, the main problem is one of marginalisation. While these less developed countries remain outside the bilateral FTA trend, other developing countries in their region with stronger capacity functions (e.g. Philippines, Malaysia, Indonesia, Thailand, Vietnam) are able to develop further at a quicker pace through bilateral FTA advantages. This mainly takes the form of preferential access to FTA partner markets that spur the export-led growth rate of these stronger developing countries, which are also likely to attract even more inward FDI and enhance bilateral economic co-operation as a result of their bilateral agreements. Differentials may also arise amongst stronger developed countries where more FTA-active states such as Singapore and Thailand are able to run ahead faster than the remainder of this group. Consequently, income levels between the region's states may diverge over time, making the development divide in the region more pronounced.

Although bilateral FTAs may be deemed pragmatic given extant development asymmetry within East Asia, they also risk making that asymmetry even more pronounced, thus making regional community-building more complex and more difficult to achieve. Ideally, East Asian countries should have from the start agreed to negotiate a regional FTA (i.e. EAFTA), with multi-speed liberalisation and integration provisions to allow less developed countries free market access to stronger capacity countries whilst permitting them to have longer phase-in adjustment schedules, e.g. on tariff elimination. The ASEAN group chose this path with AFTA but of course there was no comparable East Asia wide regional organisation or framework in place to see through a similar project before the bilateral FTA trend took off. As Case Study 6.2 examines, the APT/EAS framework only endorsed official studies to be undertaken into an EAFTA-type project in January 2007.

Case Study 6.2 An APT-based or EAS-based regional FTA for East Asia?

Interest in creating an East Asia Free Trade Agreement has existed for some time. The question is, what kind of regional FTA is likely to emerge and how will its membership be comprised? As noted in the main text, the formation of an EAFTA was one of the key recommended long-term objectives made in the APT sponsored East Asia Study Group report (EASG 2002). However, it was not until 2006 that such a proposal was formally made within the region. This originated from Japan and was announced in April of that year, being conceived as an EAS-based FTA and officially known as the Comprehensive Economic Partnership for East Asia (CEPEA).[17] When launching the initiative, Japan's then Economic Minister, Toshihiro Nikai outlined a plan to commence CEPEA negotiations in 2008 and conclude them by 2010. The plan met with general scepticism, especially with respect to the relatively short time scales involved. In response, Nikai announced a revised CEPEA plan in August 2006 that included funding to help start the negotiation process and to create an East Asia Economic Research Institute for ASEAN and East Asia in an ASEAN country that would undertake facilitating research in support of the regional FTA project.

Some support for the initiative slowly mounted. India, New Zealand and Australia showed immediate and positive interest, while ASEAN's Secretary-General, Ong Keng Yong commented that it could be achieved within 10 years.[18] ASEAN member states, on the other hand, were still generally pessimistic as to the feasibility of the idea by November.[19] China and South Korea were also sceptical, especially China, which thought Japan's EAS-based proposal may have been primarily motivated as a means to outflank China's long-term influence within the East Asia regional community. In a similar vein, the US's push for a FTAAP in the lead up to the November 2006 APEC Summit was viewed as largely in reaction to Japan's CEPEA proposal. As Chapter 4 discusses, an exclusive East Asia FTA could potentially marginalise

American commercial interests in the region. To allay US anxieties on the matter, Japan suggested that the CEPEA would be a building block for a larger Asia-Pacific agreement.[20]

As the Second East Asia Summit approached, Tokyo intensified its diplomatic efforts to build coalitional support for its CEPEA proposal. A number of ASEAN member states (e.g. Singapore, Indonesia, Vietnam) came on Japan's side, and South Korea also became more positively inclined towards the idea. At the regional meeting, held in Cebu, Philippines in January 2007, Japan secured enough support for an agreement to undertake feasibilities studies into the CEPEA, these commencing in March that year and the report from which would be submitted at the next East Asia Summit. If realised, a CEPEA would create a free trade area encompassing a population of 3.1 billion people and a combined GDP of around US$10 trillion.

While Japan has championed an EAS-based regional FTA, China is more in favour of an APT-based alternative, i.e. not including India, Australia or New Zealand. These contrasting views first came to light at the inaugural East Asia Summit meeting held in December 2005. Malaysia, Thailand and the Philippines were more inclined to support China's views on this than Japan's but neither was able to build enough support then to prevail over the other. Even though Japan's CEPEA idea seemed to achieve this at the Second EAS meeting, there was no consensus then on whether the group should necessarily proceed to negotiations. A decision on this may be deferred to a future EAS meeting.

China's case for an APT-based FTA is founded on the argument that the ASEAN Plus Three group is more economically, socio-culturally and to some extent politically coherent than its EAS counterpart. Whilst India, Australia and New Zealand (hereafter referred to as the EAS-3) have developed closer economic ties with APT countries over recent years – including through the signing of bilateral FTAs – they have remained largely peripheral to East Asia's regional economic dynamic, for example, in terms of international production network development (see Chapter 2). In Chapter 5 we saw how the Asian Development Bank made a similar argument regarding APT-based rather than EAS-based financial regionalism. Moreover, EAS-3 approaches to economic governance (e.g. Australia and New Zealand's market-liberal capitalism) are in some contrast to the developmental statist approach still followed by many East Asian countries. This is relevant to the ideational differences between Anglo-Pacific countries and East Asian countries on FTA formation noted earlier in the main text, where the latter have a predilection for incorporating economic co-operative measures in their agreements and the former do not.

Furthermore, no doubt one reason why Japan wanted the two developed countries of Australia and New Zealand included in their CEPEA proposal was to broaden a base of support to include more commercial regulatory measures (e.g. IPR, competition policy) into any future regional agreement. China and many ASEAN countries will resist too much priority being conferred to this area. These could be real problem issues in any future CEPEA negotiations. Yet as the bilateral FTA experience has shown, the biggest challenge for any future EAFTA talks – whether APT or EAS group based – is likely to be agriculture. Many East Asian countries retain highly protected agricultural sectors whilst for many other countries farm products still account for a substantial share of their exports. Reconciling differences on this highly sensitive political issue will be key to establishing a regional free trade agreement in East Asia.

Study Questions

1. In what ways would an EAFTA mark an important advance in East Asian regionalism?
2. What obstacles lie in the path of realising Japan's proposed CEPEA?

6.5 Conclusion

6.5.1 Summary overview

This chapter has charted the development of East Asia's new free trade agreement trend. The FTAs in question have been essentially bilateral in nature, and hence a core theme of discussion has been how this new dense pattern of economic bilateralism has impacted on the current and future prospects of East Asian regionalism. It was noted that FTAs are heterogeneous and that countries have preferences for certain types or models of agreements. The possibility of a particular East Asian model of FTA was discussed, as was whether the proliferation of bilateral agreements would naturally lead in an evolutionary way to the formation of a regional East Asia Free Trade Area or Agreement. This question was addressed in relation to the lattice regionalism hypothesis, which essentially considers whether or not deepening economic bilateralism enhances the prospects for the development of economic regionalism. This analytical framework has two converse elements or counter-perspectives. First, *region-convergent bilateralism* speculates that intensifying economic bilateralism within a region positively contributes to the regionalism's development. Conversely, *region-divergent bilateralism* contends that intensifying economic bilateralism such as through bilateral FTAs can undermine the regionalism process.

The core of this chapter's analysis examined East Asia's new FTA trend from these two counter-perspectives, this being further structured by specific 'points of contention' under each of the two perspectives. On the whole the chapter concluded that there appeared to be stronger evidence and arguments to support expectations for region-divergent outcomes as bilateral FTAs pose more of a risk of fragmenting East Asia's regional economic relations rather than unifying them. The prospects of forming a single region-wide East Asia FTA in the near future are hence slim. The chapter discussed new FTA project developments in East Asia in the context of a broader Asia-Pacific trend of free trade agreements. Case studies were also presented on ASEAN's Free Trade Agreement Projects with China, Japan and South Korea, as well as a discussion on whether any prospective East Asia regional FTA will be based on APT or EAS group membership.

6.5.2 International Political Economy (IPE) theoretical analysis

Various *neo-realist* themes and perspectives were covered in this chapter. There was discussion on how FTAs were both a function of, and vehicle for, inter-state rivalry in East Asia. The new FTA trend has led to a number of East Asia and the Asia-Pacific nation-states becoming engaged in a competitive bilateralism process, which according to neo-realists is further illustration of anarchic inter-state competition in the region. Neo-realist theory posits that bilateral FTAs are essentially driven by the pursuit of national interest as each nation-state seeks to improve their strategic position in economic, political and security related terms with respect to other nation-states. Similarly, those nations that experience a worsening of their market access or general strategic position from the FTA activity of rival states will themselves seek to redress the balance. Japan's reactionary matching of China's move to initiate an FTA project with the ASEAN group was an example of such 'isolation avoidance' manoeuvring. Bilateral FTAs are easier to broker than regional FTAs, and also it is easier to imprint a country's national interests into the negotiated agreement than it is on a regional equivalent. As we would expect and as was discussed, stronger nation-states are particularly able to achieve the latter, and bilateral FTAs confer on them the opportunity to exercise their relative power advantages over weaker nation-states. This was noted, for example, with regard to Japan's dealings with individual ASEAN countries regarding how bilateral FTAs can reinforce power asymmetries amongst a regional group of states generally. There was also discussion on how the Asia-Pacific's main economic powers – Japan, China and the US – were championing their own particular FTA model as a means of extending their commercial regulatory and diplomatic influence in the region.

This chapter also discussed East Asia's new FTA trend from a number of *neo-liberal* IPE perspectives. Taking first a neo-liberal institutionalist view, we noted a strong correlation between proliferating FTA activity in the international system and the faltering of the WTO and multilateral trade order. As was argued, the free-for-all spate of bilateral trade deals has added greater complexity to trade relations in East Asia and elsewhere, presenting a case for some form of institutionalised co-ordination of FTAs at the regional APT or EAS level. However, APEC's largely ineffective attempt to achieve just this in the Asia-Pacific arena does not bode well for its East Asia equivalent. Free trade agreements also present an interesting predicament for neo-liberals more generally. On the one hand, neo-liberals are the natural advocates of FTAs because they entail various forms of commercial liberalisation, hence requiring East Asian countries to relinquish barriers impeding the free flow of international trade and investment amongst themselves. Those agreements signed by East Asian states have in their own way helped advance neo-liberal reform and change across the region. On the other hand, many neo-liberals view the proliferation of bilateral FTAs in East Asia and elsewhere with some alarm because they introduce more complex preferentialism into the international trade system rather than 'free trade' *per se*. Neo-liberal critics of FTAs thus contend that they are a politically distorted and narrow form of free trade (or economic liberalism) that is being established, and which is moreover undermining the basis of the multilateral trade order and its ultimate goal of establishing global free trade on a non-discriminatory basis. In making one last point from the neo-liberal institutionalist perspective, this chapter argued that the growth of FTAs in East Asia was partly motivated by a need to better manage regional economic interdependence after the 1997/8 financial crisis. A regional FTA was not possible then, nor has it been since by this time of writing, but bilateral agreements were and have been possible.

From a *social constructivist* perspective, FTAs are synonymous with the norms and ideas of economic liberalism. Yet as seen just above, even neo-liberals themselves disagree over the idea of whether FTA's represent 'free' trade or 'preferential' trade. Much of the debate and contention over free trade agreements relates to their embodiment of certain economic ideas and values more generally. Those actively supporting or opposing FTAs in East Asia are ultimately acting in accordance with certain ideological or ideational determinants of behaviour, so social constructivists would especially argue. Many East Asian civil society organisations are, for instance, opposed to FTAs as part of their general resistance to the advance of global economic liberalisation, or their wish to safeguard aspects of local or national culture, values and general localised distinctiveness in relation to the homogenising processes of regionalisation and globalisation. It was also discussed how the ideational foundations of FTAs themselves can vary. This was illustrated with regard to East Asia's developmental 'economic partnership' approach that is in some contrast to the 'market access only' approach of Anglo-Pacific countries like the US and Australia. Yet differences were noted too between Japan's FTA model and that of China and ASEAN, although arguably these were more concerned with matters of technical policy omissions or inclusions. Similarly, social constructivists would emphasise that FTAs are not just technical and legalistic constructs but are essentially forged by the interaction of the political economy values and traditions of the trade partners concerned. East Asia's new 'FTA culture' may in addition be contrived as a new norm of common trade policy behaviour in the region that may provide an important basis for developing a future regional FTA project.

Finally, *Marxist-structuralist* perspectives on FTAs in East Asia would generally focus on how they may be considered as essentially transnational capital class projects devised to further the interests of global capitalism. Whereas as previously stated neo-realists tend to emphasise the geopolitical and security related motivations of national governments behind these agreements, Marxist-structuralists instead stress that the motivations are driven more by capitalist desires for increased market shares, profits and economic resources. Of course, both sets of motivational factors are not mutually exclusive: for instance, improved access to foreign markets can confer geopolitical advantage and vice versa. In the meantime according to Marxist-structuralists, the interests of labour and other social groups are not taken much into account in the formation and negotiation of FTAs. As was further discussed at some length in this chapter, the dense pattern of bilateral FTAs now prevalent in East Asia risks exacerbating core-periphery type divisions in the region as stronger capacity countries are able to participate in the new FTA trend, and therein procure certain economic gains from this, whilst weaker capacity developing countries are left marginalised. For reasons discussed earlier, this will most likely have a negative bearing on the prospects for regional community-building in East Asia. In the following chapter, we examine three key transnational issues affecting the East Asia region – namely transboundary 'haze' pollution, international migration and energy security – and how these issues provide different ways of examining the dynamics of East Asian regionalism.

Chapter Study Questions

1. Why do free trade agreements (FTAs) vary so much from each other?
2. Account for the proliferation of FTA activity in East Asia from the late 1990s onwards.
3. Do those FTAs East Asian countries sign with trade partners outside the region help or hinder the prospects of East Asian regionalism?
4. What different impacts may East Asia's FTAs have on the wider international trade system?
5. 'East Asia's now dense pattern of bilateral FTAs provides the basis for one day forming a unified regional free trade agreement'. Discuss.

Notes

1   *Straits Times*, 26.01.2001.
2   *Reuters*, 19.10.2003.
3   For example, in August 2005 China called upon Japan and South Korea to join together to undertake a feasibility study on a trilateral Northeast Asia FTA. *Daily Yomiuri*, 05.08.2005.
4   *Financial Times*, 07.10.2003.
5   These figures are based on 2003 and 2004 rates and were prepared by Japan's Ministry of Economy, Trade and Industry (METI) on their website, www.meti.go.jp
6   *Bernama News*, 08.11.2006.
7   *People's Daily*, 30.10.2006.
8   *Bloomberg News*, 15.01.2007.
9   *New Straits Times*, 16.07.2001.
10   *E-Sinchew-i.com News*, 27.05.2005.
11   Author's research fieldwork conducted in Southeast Asia from December 2004 to July 2005.
12   Research interviews with ASEAN Secretariat representatives, Jakarta, July 2005.
13   Research interview with Thai government officials, July 2005.
14   Research interviews with Thai, Malaysian and Indonesian government officials, December 2004 and July 2005 in respective country capitals.
15   There was reportedly some exchange of information amongst ASEAN member states but, government officials conceded, not a great deal. For instance, the Philippines and Malaysia did share some details with other members about their bilateral talks with Japan, mainly on concessions made on agriculture and automotive sector products. Research interviews with government officials in Kuala Lumpur (December 2004) and Jakarta (July 2005).
16   Stronger developing countries such as Indonesia and the Philippines are, however, also often beneficiaries of the same GSP schemes.
17   The CEPEA proposal was contained within a report published in April 2006 by Japan's Ministry of Economy, Trade and Industry entitled 'Japan's Global Economic Strategy' (METI 2006).
18   *All Headline News*, 08.08.2006.
19   *Kuna News*, 02.11.2006.
20   *Vietnam News*, 14.11.2006.

Chapter 7

Key transnational issues in East Asia

7.1 Introduction

This chapter examines three of the most important transnational issues to have arisen in East Asia over recent years. Transnational issues are those that cut across national boundaries and affect a number of countries. The challenges and problems they present require those countries to work more closely together to address them. The three key issues in question cover the broad themes of environment, labour/human security and energy. Our first transnational issue is transboundary 'haze' pollution, the second is international migration, and the third is energy security in East Asia. The three transnational issues we examine reveal different kinds of linkages that are developing amongst East Asian countries and peoples to those studied in previous chapters, and therefore further perspectives on East Asian regionalism and regionalisation.

7.2 Haze in Southeast Asia: transboundary pollution in focus

7.2.1 What is 'haze'?

Transboundary pollution is a significant issue in East Asia. It is symptomatic of the broader environmental problems that have accompanied the region's rapid industrialisation and economic development more generally. According to studies conducted by the Asian Development Bank and the World Health Organisation, pollution generally across the region could be causing the premature deaths of around half a million people a year.[1] There are many causes of transboundary pollution in East Asia, such as acid rain in the Yellow Sea zone and the South China Sea zone, but arguably the most important is Southeast Asia's forest fire 'haze' problem. Haze is essentially an atmospheric phenomenon where smoke, dust and other pollutant particles accumulate in relatively dry air to form low-hanging blanket cloud that can cover large geographic areas. Haze clouds can severely reduce visibility and raise temperature levels in affected areas, as well as create an 'inversion layer' that traps normal air pollution. The prime cause of Southeast Asia's haze problem is the regular mass of forest fires lit across the Indonesian provinces of Sumatra and Kalimantan.[2] These normally occur during the dry season when farmers and plantation workers have used 'slash and burn' techniques to clear forested areas for new crops (Glover and Jessup 1999). The main countries affected by haze aside from Indonesia are Malaysia, Singapore and Brunei, and to a lesser extent Thailand and the Philippines (see Figure 7.1).

Forest fires have been a regular occurrence in Southeast Asia for some time, either as a result of natural phenomena (e.g. lightning strikes) or human activity, and cases of transboundary haze in the region arise on a regular, almost yearly, basis to varying degrees of intensity.

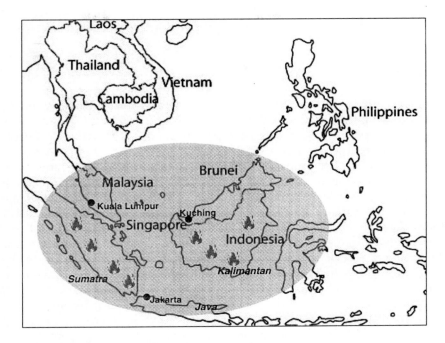

Figure 7.1 Forest fire haze pollution in Southeast Asia

Significant reported cases occurred in 1982/3, 1987, 1991 and 1994, but it was the particularly severe episode of 1997/8 in which the problem reached a whole new critical level. During this episode, around 45,600 square kilometres of forest burned in Sumatra and Kalimantan, but fires lit in other areas of Indonesia also contributed to the ensuing haze. In total, forest fires were burning across around 2.5 to 3 per cent of Indonesia's landmass at this time (Levine 1999). The haze cloud caused by these fires spread to an area of approximately 5 million square kilometres that covered the region for a seven-month period. Around 70 million people were thought to be affected in the 1997/8 episode, and around 40,000 people hospitalised (Jones 2006). In Kuching in Sarawak, Malaysia, its inhabitants could hardly see more than a few metres in front of them at noonday. Most economic and social activities in the city came to a halt and the authorities were at one point on the verge of calling a mass evacuation (Cotton 1999).

Since 1997/8, Southeast Asia's haze problem has shown no signs of abating. In 2000, more than 500 fires raged out of control in parts of Indonesia. Haze has reoccurred on a yearly basis since then. In the 2003 (September to November) episode, Singapore's National Environment Agency (NEA) air quality index registered the air as 'unhealthy' (i.e. hitting above 100) three times in the city-state. This compared to the 12 'unhealthy' days recorded in 1997. In 2005 and 2006 bouts of haze, Malaysia called a state of emergency. Hundreds of schools across the country were closed, and

Kuala Lumpur airport and Port Kelang closed down operations on the worst days of this episode.

7.2.2 Causes and costs

In general terms, Southeast Asia's haze pollution has been primarily caused by increased human activity. This derives partly from recent demographic changes as forested areas have been settled by increasing numbers of people from the cities. For example, the Indonesian Government's introduction of a Transmigration Programme in 1995 encouraged its citizens to move from the country's densely populated urban-industrial areas (especially from Java) and settle in largely unpopulated areas in Sumatra, Kalimantan and Irian Jaya to start up small-scale farming operations (Jones 2006, Sastry 2002). At the same time, large commercial forestry and plantation firms have moved into the forested areas of Indonesia, setting up operations for the production of paper, industrial pulpwood, rubber and palm oil. In the past, the forest's indigenous peoples and small-scale farmers have used burning in a generally sustainable manner. Wood ash increases the pH level of the soil and thus helps kill weed seed banks, as well as generate a quick release of nitrogen for crop growth. However, the scale of forest fire burning in Southeast Asia has reached huge proportions, as previously noted.

For farmers and large forestry and plantation firms alike, the 'slash and burn' technique is the cheapest and fastest way to convert forested areas into alternative land use. It is widely acknowledged that the principal culprits are the large commercial forestry and plantation firms operating in the area (Jones 2006, Quah 2002, Sastry 2002, Siddiqui and Quah 2004, Weatherbee 2005). The Indonesian Government has given extensive concessions in the past to palm oil plantations in particular, especially during the Suharto regime (1967–98). Both farmers and logging companies have used burning as a weapon against the other in their bid for territorial advantage in forested areas. Farmers have burned the new tree plantations of big forestry companies, and in turn these companies have burned land to drive out small farm landowners (Sastry 2002). The ineffectiveness of the Indonesian Government authorities to deal with the forest fire issue is discussed later on, but Indonesia is not the only source of haze pollution. Other albeit considerably smaller sources include Myanmar, parts of the Thai-Cambodian border zone, and the Malaysian provinces of Sabah and Sarawak on the island of Borneo.

Climatological factors have also played their part in the haze problem. This particularly relates to the recurring climatological disturbance known as the El Niño-Southern Oscillation (ENSO), which has brought extraordinarily dry weather to parts of the Southeast Asia region, prolonging drought periods and thus made forested areas increasingly susceptible to fire risk. There remains much debate as to the extent to which the ENSO has been itself a product of human activity, related to the larger debate on global warming. In addition, the mass-scale draining of peat swamps for farming in

Kalimantan in particular has brought about ecological and hydrological changes to substantial areas of land that have rendered them more susceptible to burning.

Haze can have profound environmental, economic and social impacts, and the costs incurred are similarly multi-dimensional. In the 1997/8 episode, the total economic losses measured in terms of agriculture production, destruction of forest lands, health, transportation, tourism, and other economic endeavours were estimated at US$9.3 billion (see Table 7.1). An *Agence France Presse* report released in December 2006 noted that Jakarta is currently estimated to lose US$400 million per year in lost productivity and medical costs.[3] Both Malaysia and Singapore's tourist boards have cited haze as the most significant cause of lost revenue in the industry. Thick haze often leads to shutdowns in airport operations across the affected area, adding to transportation costs and further losses for the tourism industry. However, there are much wider social, environmental, and psychological costs and long-term health effects of Southeast Asia's regional haze pollution. The human costs can also be high. In September 1997, an Indonesian airliner with 234 passengers and crew crashed owing to poor visibility in a haze affected area. It has been estimated that many thousands of people have died as a direct result of haze pollution in the region.

Table 7.1 Total estimated economic losses caused by the 1997/8 regional haze episode

Sector	Estimated Economic Losses (US$ million)		
	Minimum	Maximum	Mean
Agriculture			
Farm Crops	2,431	2,431	2,431
Plantation Crops	319	319	319
Forestry			
Timber from Natural Forest (logged and un-logged)	1,461	2,165	1,813
Lost Growth in Natural Forest	256	377	316
Timber from Plantations	94	94	94
Non-wood Forest Products	586	586	586
Flood Protection	404	404	404
Erosion and Siltation	1,586	1,586	1,586
Carbon Sink	1,446	1,446	1,446
Health	145	145	145
Transmigration, Buildings, and Property	1	1	1
Transportation	18	49	33
Tourism	111	111	111
Fire-fighting Costs	12	11	12
Total	**8,870**	**9,726**	**9,298**

Source: Final Report, ADTA INO 2999: Planning for FirePrevention and Drought Management (BAPPENAS 1999) at http://www.haze-online.or.id/help/history.php

7.2.3 ASEAN environmental co-operation and the haze issue

Environmental co-operation within ASEAN dates back to the 1970s, being formally initiated in 1977 by the 'ASEAN Environmental Programme I'. In 1989, the first ASEAN Senior Officials on Environment (ASOEN) meeting was held, and a year later the ASEAN Ministers on the Environment endorsed the 'Kuala Lumpur Accord on the Environment and Development', which, according to Cotton (1999), was still 'pro-development' in conception. However, the 1994 Strategic Plan of Action on the Environment marked a switch to a more balanced approach in which environmental objectives were afforded greater priority on the ASEAN agenda. Forest fire haze was emerging as a key environmental issue at the time, and since the early 1990s there have been several ASEAN level initiatives that have sought to address the problem, as detailed below:

- *Bandung Conference (Indonesia) of 1992*: the first ASEAN level meeting to discuss the transboundary haze issue. A number of regional workshops and meetings on haze pollution subsequently followed, held in Indonesia and Malaysia during the period of 1992–5.
- *ASEAN Co-operation Plan on Transboundary Pollution of 1995*: the first ASEAN level plan to address the region's haze problem.
- *ASEAN Haze Technical Task Force (HTTF):* proposed in 1995 at the Sixth Meeting of the ASOEN in September 1995 to operationalise and implement the measures of the ASEAN Co-operation Plan on Transboundary Pollution. The HTTF became operational in 1996.
- *Regional Haze Action Plan (RHAP) of 1997*: formulated by the HTTF and endorsed at the *First ASEAN Ministerial Meeting on Haze (AMMH)[4]* held in Singapore in December 1997. The primary objectives of the RHAP are based on three components to: 1) prevent land and forest fires through better management policies and enforcement; 2) establish operational mechanisms to monitor land and forest fires; 3) strengthen regional land and forest fire-fighting capability with other mitigation measures. There is, moreover, a division of labour amongst ASEAN member states in relation to the Plan's three major components (i.e. prevention, mitigation, and monitoring): Malaysia has taken the lead in prevention, Indonesia on mitigation, and Singapore in monitoring of fires and haze. In addition, member states have committed to undertake national-level actions with regard to the three RHAP components.
- *ASEAN Agreement on Transboundary Haze Pollution signed in 2002*: following on from the RHAP, this agreement strengthened provisions

on monitoring, assessment, prevention, technical and scientific co-operation, mechanisms for co-ordination, and so on. It came into force in November 2003 after being ratified by six ASEAN member states. The agreement also called for the establishment of the ASEAN Co-ordinating Centre for Transboundary Haze Pollution Control. This is the first environmental agreement within ASEAN to be legally binding for signatory countries. However, by 2007 Indonesia, Cambodia and the Philippines had yet to ratify the agreement. Moreover, the use of imprecise and somewhat vague language in the agreement (e.g. 'as appropriate', 'as may be necessary') means that the obligations and commitments embodied in the agreement are open to wide interpretation.

- *Anti-Haze Fund established in March 2007*: launched at the 12th AMMH with an initial sum of US$500,000. Indonesia, Brunei, Singapore, Malaysia and Thailand were the main contributors to the fund, the prime purpose of which was to help fully implement the ASEAN Agreement on Transboundary Haze Pollution.

The ASEAN group has also received help in addressing the haze issue from various sources of outside help. In 1997, Germany donated US$5.5 million for purchasing fire-fighting equipment, Australia provided around US$350,000 to help fund fire-fighting operations, and the US gave US$4 million for relevant project finance and another US$2 million to Indonesia to prevent the fires. Canada has also helped develop a Fire Danger Rating System, a monitoring and warning system for forest fires. In April 1998, the Global Environment Facility allocated US$6.75 million to assist Indonesia's fire-fighting efforts. Around the same time, the United Nations Environment Programme tried to raise US$10 million to support regional fire-fighting, although international donors proved generally unresponsive and a much smaller amount was raised. In addition, the ADB has provided support to both Indonesia's national initiative (around US$1 million) for addressing the country's forest fire problem, and also to ASEAN through a regional technical assistance scheme for tackling transboundary atmos-pheric pollution. However, these have been mostly short-term assistance measures (Quadri 2001).

At the Third AMMH held in 1998, ASEAN member states agreed to the principle of Sub-Regional Fire-Fighting Arrangements. In the group division of labour, Singapore agreed to commit financial and technical aid to help abate haze pollution in the nearby Indonesian province of Jambi, Sumatra. Malaysia meanwhile has agreed to provide similar help, especially in the adja-cent Riau province. Both countries were also advising Indonesian farmers on alternatives to 'slash and burn' techniques. Malaysia's Meteorological Service and the ASEAN Specialised Meteorological Centre based in Singapore have also been used to monitor occurrencs of haze pollution.

7.2.4 *Future challenges of governance, capacity-building and regional co-operation*

Despite the various efforts made at the national and regional level, transboundary haze pollution remains as big a problem as ever in Southeast Asia. There are two main challenges that face the region in more effectively addressing this problem, the first being issues of governance and capacity-building in Indonesia, and the second being strengthening environmental co-operation within ASEAN generally. Let us take each of these in turn. Other ASEAN member states have obviously been frustrated with Indonesia's seeming ineptitude to deal with the causes of haze pollution. They believe that Jakarta should be affording greater priority to the issue, and there have been calls for some kind of regional legal framework to be established that would apply greater pressure upon Indonesia to take more effective action on haze abatement. There is also, of course, mounting pressure from within the country to deal with the issue. During the 2002 episode of haze, a journalist writing for the *Jakarta Post* commented, 'What is astonishing, however, is the absolutely inconsistent attitude of the government. Here is a national emergency, if ever there was one, and yet the powers-that-be sit in Nero-like complacency fiddling while major assets burn.'[5]

However, the Indonesian Government lacks the capacity to deal with the problem alone. Quah (2002) argues that it will take years for Indonesia to put in place a robust enough regulatory or institutional framework to effectively address the haze pollution issue. The country already has various environment and land-use statutes in its legislature: a ban on mass forest fires was passed in 1995, and over 20 laws and decrees have been passed since 1985 to deal with forest protection (Jones 2006). The main problem lies in the application and enforcement of the laws concerned, and strengthening existing systems of governance. Before 1998, the Indonesian Government did not have a national strategy for dealing with forest fires. The decentralisation of political authority from the centre to provisional governments has also led to policy co-ordination problems generally (Weatherbee 2005). Enforcement capacity is what Indonesia needs most help with. The country had only 10,000 forest rangers to cover around 100 million hectares of forested land (i.e. 1,000 hectares or 10 square kilometres per ranger). In addition, many of these lack adequate training in fire-related management, and also the local judiciary has often lacked understanding of the relevant laws and regulations leading to a deficient application of them in practice (Jones 2006).

Indonesia's ministries of agriculture and forestry have also been accused of being captured to some extent by corporate interests on the haze pollution issue, obstructing progress on clamping down on the malpractices of large forestry and plantation firms (Tan 1999). What also complicates matters is that many of these firms are foreign multinational enterprises (MNEs). Studies conducted by Glover and Jessup (1999) and Byron and Shepherd (1998) estimated that around two-thirds of the forest fires from the 1997/8 episode could be attributed to MNEs with headquarters outside Indonesia, including those based in Malaysia and Singapore. One reason why the Indonesian Government has refused to sign the 2002 ASEAN Agreement on Transboundary Haze Pollution is because it contends that Singapore and Malaysia have not done enough to control the operations of their own forestry and plantation firms in Indonesia. Jakarta has alleged that Malaysian state holding companies are also culpable. For example, the Malaysian government holds a 70 per cent share in Guthrie, which is engaged in 2,180 square kilometres of plantation development in Indonesia.

On the other hand, Indonesia can learn much from the successes of Malaysia's forestry management policies exercised through its Federal Land Development Authority (FELDA), which for some time has obliged land development companies to use (more expensive) land clearance alternatives to 'slash and burn' techniques. This is an area of technology transfer that ASEAN could be doing more to encourage and facilitate. Furthermore, FELDA operate a strict fire permit system whereby only those with a permit can engage in burning. The Indonesian Government has, though, sought to some extent to learn from the experience of others. Around the time of the 12th AMMH held in February 2007, Indonesia's Environment Minister, Rachmat Witoelar, announced that new funds would be available for educating farmers on non-burn techniques for land clearance, providing them with equipment to both cut down trees and convert agricultural and forestry waste into natural fertilizer. He also announced plans for re-vitalising 13,000 square kilometres of peat land in Kalimantan, for the greater use of satellites to monitor forest fire occurrence, and establishing more air quality monitoring stations to help put in place an early warning system that would alert Indonesia's neighbours in the event of severe haze pollution.[6] However, any newly announced measures on haze abatement by the Indonesian Government have long been treated with scepticism, mainly because of its poor track record on effectively operationalising the measures, or because they have ultimately lacked substance.

Dealing with significant transboundary problems such as haze can thus present complex challenges that involve various stakeholders. To date, ASEAN has proved largely ineffective at tackling the issue at the regional level, despite the previously noted numerous initiatives and frameworks that have been created on haze pollution abatement. The main constraint is ASEAN's cardinal principle of non-interference – member states are not permitted to interfere directly or through regional level mechanisms (i.e. ASEAN) in the domestic affairs of other member states (see Chapter 3). Hence, even the use of satellite monitoring assistance from Malaysia and Singapore on haze pollution may be construed by Indonesia as interference, and ensuring that Indonesia enforces both its national and international agreements on haze abatement is similarly problematic. While ASEAN adheres strictly to its cardinal principle of non-interference, it is unlikely that an effective regional-level solution to haze pollution will be found.

There has been talk within ASEAN of creating a 'transboundary environmental law enforcement network', as suggested by the Philippines Minister for the Environment, Angelo Reyes, in September 2006[7] but the chances of Indonesia agreeing to such a scheme are very limited.

While ASEAN has been incrementally building a firmer regional framework of co-operation and assistance to deal with haze pollution and other environmental problems, it still has a long way to go. Furthermore, considerably more resources are required, both financial and technical, to deal with the haze issue. Ideally, ASEAN needs to bring in more assistance from other richer countries as well as from other regional and international agencies. One method of inducing greater outside help from others is that of the Coasian bargain. This has much to do with how we view the externalities involved in the haze issue. On the one hand, haze pollution is obviously a negative externality that affects third parties but on the other hand Indonesia's rainforests provide various positive global-level externalities to others, such as producing oxygen and acting as carbon dioxide sinks. From this latter perspective, third parties should be entering a Coasian bargain with Indonesia based on providing the country with the necessary assistance to maintain these environmental public goods. The key problem here, though, is how to ensure Indonesia uses this assistance effectively, so again we come back to the fundamental issues of capacity-building and governance.

Chang and Rajan (2001) also identify three additional challenges. First, some parties may decide to free-ride on the efforts made by others to provide the public goods of environmental protection. Providers of 'public goods' – by the very nature of these goods – are not able to exclude free-riders from benefiting from their efforts to address the environmental problem. Second, there is the issue of asymmetric costs and benefits regarding a problem like transboundary haze pollution. Should those affected most in cost terms pay the most to solve the problem, even if they are not the direct cause of the problem? This has implications for any Coasian bargain struck on the matter. Third, ASEAN member states may have different preferences and priorities regarding environmental problems. Less developed states with more immediate and pressing socio-economic objectives to pursue (e.g. poverty alleviation) may attach a lower priority to 'clean environment' objectives. This to some extent applies to Indonesia, who may be ranked as a middle-income economy in the ASEAN scale of development.

Finally, there is the matter of whether regional environmental problems such as haze pollution in some way engender a deeper sense of unity, shared purpose and identity within a region, derived from the region's peoples having to face and deal with a common transboundary (i.e. regional or sub-regional) problem. Haze pollution has affected a large number of Southeast Asians, and has made them realise that they are linked by this issue. As Elliott (2003:47) argues, 'Environmental change and resource scarcity in Southeast Asia provide very real, physical evidence of shared-problems affecting the whole region, and an interconnectedness in which environmental causes and consequences cross borders'. This forms one aspect of what we refer to in Chapter 8 as the 'associative coherence' of East Asian regionalism. Coming primarily at this from a social constructivist perspective, Elliott concludes that, 'Environmental degradation is... slowly and unevenly unsettling the political terrain of Southeast Asian regionalism' (p. 49). This may well be the case, especially if transboundary problems such as haze pollution continue to worsen over time.

7.3 International migration in East Asia

7.3.1 The growth of international migration within the region

Since the early 1990s, there has been a significant rise in international migration levels across East Asia. At the beginning of the decade, there were an estimated one million international migrants within the region but by the mid-2000s this had risen to somewhere between 7 to 10 million (METI 2005). This is against a backdrop of rising international migration levels globally. The World Bank (2006) has estimated that the number of migrants has doubled or even tripled in most net labour-importing countries from the early 1980s to late 1990s. Historically, international migration has been at times a significant factor in shaping the economic, social and cultural structures of the East Asia region, particularly Southeast Asia where waves of migrants from China, India and the Middle East settled in the sub-region over many centuries (see Chapter 2). During the nineteenth century and early twentieth century, the colonial powers also operated extensive 'contract coolie' systems in East Asia involving a substantial movement of workers from one part of the region to another. Huge refugee movements caused by various political and social upheavals during the first few decades after World War Two became the main defining feature of international migration in East Asia during this period, with many refugees and other migrant types seeking shelter outside the region in North America, Europe, Australia and New Zealand.[8] From the 1970s to the mid-1980s, the main outflow of East Asian labour migrants was to the Middle East, where they were employed in 'oil boom' related industries, such as construction.[9]

From the late 1980s and early 1990s, though, two general new trends in East Asian international migration began to emerge. The first concerns the increasing rise of international *labour* migration (ILM) as the predominant migration type, and the second the growth of intra-regional migration flows. According to Athukorala (2006: 19), ILM includes 'persons who migrate for work and long-term settlement and contract labour migrants recruited for specific periods', and within this migrant category contract labour migrants represented well over 90 per cent of ILM flows in East Asia. He further notes that inflows of workers to Singapore and Hong Kong largely accounted for East Asia's intra-regional ILM flows from 1945 to the 1980s.[10] However, since the late 1980s, Japan, South Korea, Taiwan, Malaysia and Thailand have absorbed increasing levels of foreign workers from the region's surplus-labour countries. Migrant workers currently make up over 20 per cent of Singapore's workforce, 12 per cent in Malaysia, 10 per cent in Hong Kong, and around 6 per cent in Thailand.

As we later discuss, a key cause of increasing ILM levels in East Asia has been significant divergences in living standards and wage levels that began to emerge within the region from the 1980s, as faster growing newly industrialising economies (South Korea, Taiwan, Singapore, Hong Kong, Malaysia, Thailand) began to pull away from the region's less dynamic developing countries (Indonesia, Philippines, Cambodia, Myanmar). The comparative data on East Asian economies shown in Table 7.2 gives some idea of the development diversity within the region, and the incentives for those from lower income economies to migrate to higher income ones. Thus, on the one hand, growth in the region's ILM flows has arisen out of fundamental economic structural changes occurring across the East Asian regional economy, and on the other hand has brought about quite profound economic, social, political and cultural changes within the region as ILM flows in East Asia have dramatically expanded. As Manning (2002: 382) comments, 'increased international labour migration was an important dimension of structural change and globalisation in East Asia from the mid-1980s'.

Many differences in the patterns of East Asia's ILM movements can be generally observed over time. In accordance to relative structural economic changes, countries go through transitions of status in terms of being net labour-importers, net labour-exporters, or a balance of the two. For example, South Korea and Taiwan were once both net labour-exporters in the early period of their industrialisation (i.e. 1950s to late 1970s) but then became net labour-importers. The current ILM status of East Asian economies are listed below:

- *Mainly labour-exporters (net outflow)*: Cambodia, China, Indonesia, Laos, Myanmar, Philippines, Vietnam
- *Mainly labour-importers (net inflow)*: Brunei, Hong Kong, Japan, Singapore, South Korea, Taiwan
- Labour-exporting/importing (net balance): Malaysia, Thailand

A second key trend has been the growth in skilled and professional migrant workers over recent years in East Asia, as employers have looked to fill job shortages in professional and technical labour market sectors from overseas sources (Iredale 2000). As we later discuss, there is also a link between foreign investment flows and this particular aspect of international migration. For example, a large percentage of emigrant workers from Japan, South Korea and Taiwan are highly educated technical or professional personnel working in the overseas investment projects of the MNEs that employ them. Yet the overwhelming main bulk of international migrant workers are still employed in low skilled, poorly paid jobs that are shunned by local citizens, the most common employment sectors being construction, labour-intensive manufacturing, agriculture, social/personal service sectors (Athukorala 2006, Hugo 2006a, Manning 2002).

Table 7.2 Comparisons of international migration related data in East Asia, 2004

	Population millions	Per capita GNP (US$)	Unemployment rate (%)	City	Wage levels index (Tokyo = 100 as base)	Gross hourly pay (US$)	Gross annual income of contruction workers (US$)	Gross annual income of female factory workers (US$)
Japan	127.8	36,170	4.7	Tokyo	100.0	13.60	34,300	26,100
Singapore	4.3	24,840	3.4	Singapore	39.2	5.40	6,700	10,300
Hong Kong	7.1	22,960	6.8	Hong Kong	45.5	7.00	11,700	9,600
South Korea	48.0	14,160	3.5	Seoul	44.8	5.90	8,200	6,700
Taiwan	22.7	13,450	4.4	Taipei	47.3	6.90	10,000	12,200
Malaysia	24.9	4,750	3.5	Kuala Lumpur	21.2	3.10	4,200	3,900
Thailand	63.5	2,550	2.1	Bangkok	10.1	1.70	1,500	1,500
China	1313.3	1,470	1.1	Shanghai	18.7	2.40	3,000	3,000
Philippines	81.4	1,040	11.8	Manila	7.9	1.20	1,700	1,600
Indonesia	222.6	1,160	9.9	Jakarta	9.5	1.50	1,200	1,000
Vietnam	82.5	550	5.6					
Laos	5.8	431	n/a					
Cambodia	14.5	338	n/a					
Myanmar	50.1	160	n/a					

Source: Economist Intelligence Unit, Chia (2006)

Another important trend has been the increased feminisation of ILM patterns. Women outnumber men in the emigrant worker category for a number of countries, these being notably high in Indonesia (80 per cent) and the Philippines (70 per cent). The Philippines have long established training institutes that have prepared nurses for the US market, and the Indonesian Government has had a similar arrangement to train women to work as domestic servants in the Middle East region and elsewhere. Overall, the vast majority of East Asia's female migrant workers are employed in low-paid, low skilled jobs, such as house-maids, healthcare providers, factory employment and the entertainment/sex industry. The increased participation of women in East Asia's ILM flows has had an important impact on East Asia's labour markets generally. As Chia (2006: 356) argues,

> The ready availability of foreign female household maids and healthcare workers have helped importing countries improve the quality of life for households and care for the aged as well as relieve domestic women from their traditional roles of household work and care for children and elderly, enabling them to enter the workforce.

A large proportion of East Asia's international migration flows are 'undocumented' or illegal, the extent of which varies from country to country. Estimates for the late 1990s levels of undocumented migrants were around one million for both Malaysia and Thailand, 600,000 for the Philippines and 300,000 for Japan (Hugo 2006a). In some cases, estimates of undocumented migrants can account for near or around the same level of registered migrants. As these are often rough estimates, it makes it difficult to obtain accurate data on East Asia's ILM flows. Indeed, data on international migration is generally quite poor, and therefore establishing the exact scale and composition of the region's migration patterns is difficult. Refugees also still constitute an important element of international migration flows in East Asia, which may be considered as a 'forced' migration flow. One, if not the most significant, case of this in East Asia concerns the Karen and Karenni peoples along the Myanmar–Thailand border. Once independent, the Karen and Karenni have been fighting an insurgency war against Myanmar's military dictatorship for a number of years. To escape persecution, a large number have fled over the Thai border into UNHCR (United Nations High Commissioner for Refugees) monitored camps (Grundy-Warr 2004). By 2006, around 107,000 Karen and 20,000 Karenni peoples were living in these camps, some of whom have slipped out and into Thailand's wider populace further inland.

Students also make up a comparatively small but fast growing share of international migration flows in the region, with an increasing number of East Asians going to study in other East Asian countries. Japan, Singapore, Taiwan, Malaysia, Thailand are the main recipients, but a much larger proportion have continued to go and study in Anglo-Pacific countries such as the United States and Australia. Many overseas students decide to remain in their host country, seeking contracted employment and even citizenship. Of around the 400,000 Chinese nationals that travelled overseas for graduate education in 1979 to the late 1990s, less than a quarter have returned home (Iredale 2000). Finally, while overall international migrants still only make up a relatively small share of the region's labour force, its contribution to labour supply growth has in many East Asian countries been significant. For example, in Malaysia, foreign migrant workers accounted for more than half the growth in the lower-skilled workforce from the mid-1980s to the mid-1990s, and around a third of growth in the same labour market sector for Thailand during 1990–5 (Athukorala and Manning 1999).

Looking generally at the figures on East Asia's international migration, Table 7.3 shows the estimated stock figures of international migrants from and in East Asian countries. The Philippines is by far the largest source of international migrants in the region with 4.75 million in 2004,

Table 7.3 Estimated stocks of international migrants, from/in East Asia

	Estimated Stocks of Migrants from the Source Country		Main Destinations of Migrants
China	1,000,000"	2002	Japan, South Korea, Thailand, Laos, Singapore, Taiwan, Philippines, Cambodia
Hong Kong	330,000*		China
Taiwan	1,000,000^		China
Japan	61,000	2004	Hong Kong, Southeast Asia, China, South Korea
South Korea	632,000⁻	2002	Japan
Indonesia	2,000,000	2004	Malaysia, Thailand, South Korea, Hong Kong, Taiwan
Malaysia	250,000	1995	Japan, Taiwan, Singapore
Philippines	4,750,000	2004	Japan, Taiwan, Malaysia, Hong Kong, Singapore, South Korea
Singapore	n/a		
Thailand	340,000	2002	Taiwan, Malaysia, Singapore, Hong Kong, Japan
Cambodia	n/a		Thailand, Malaysia
Laos	173,000	2004	Thailand
Myanmar	3,000,000	2004	Thailand, Bangladesh, India, China, Malaysia, Singapore, South Korea, Japan
Vietnam	340,000	2004	Cambodia, China, Taiwan, Malaysia, Japan, South Korea, Laos, Thailand

	Estimated Stocks of Foreign Migrants in the Destination Country	
China	299,400	2004
Hong Kong	524,200	2004
Taiwan	600,180	2003
Japan	870,000	2000
South Korea	423,600	2004
Indonesia	91,740	2004
Malaysia	1,850,060	2006
Philippines	9,170	2003
Singapore	580,000	2004
Thailand	1,623,780	2004
Vietnam	30,000	2001

Sources: Based on Hugo (2005) and augmented with data from Asian Migration Centre (www.asian-migrants.org), Department of Statistics, Malaysia (2006) and Rallu (2002).
Notes: " Based on estimates from Rallu (2002). * Estimate of Hong Kong day workers in mainland China referred to in the main text. ^ Higher end of range of very estimate figures for Taiwanese currently working in mainland China referred to in the main text. ⁻ Relates to Japanese-Koreans living in Japan.

followed by Myanmar (3 million, mostly refugees) and Indonesia (2 million). The largest labour-importing countries are Malaysia (1.85 million), Thailand (1.62 million) and Japan (870,000). There have been some dramatic increases in migrant levels for many countries. For example, Singapore has seen the number of hosted foreign migrants increase from 14,000 in 1970 to 580,000 by 2004, Taiwan from 53,700 in 1991 to 600,180 by 2003, South Korea from 41,500 in 1990 to 423,600 by 2004, and Thailand from 200,000 in 1993 to 1,623,780 by 2004. Table 7.4 meanwhile gives an overview of the main flows of international migration between source and destination within East Asia, this being graphically represented in Figure 7.2. The figures are for current migrant levels at any one time, mostly for the 2003–4 period.

As the data indicates, the largest single flows in the region are Indonesia to Malaysia (1.22 million), Taiwan to mainland China (around 1 million), and Myanmar to Thailand (921,490). The Philippines has five migrant outflows with other East Asian countries that range above 100,000. As Figure 7.2 indicates, international migrant activity in East Asia is significantly concentrated in Southeast Asia in comparison to Northeast Asia. In addition, Rallu (2002) highlights the growing importance of China in regional migration flows. According to his estimates, China's outflows of migrants to other East Asian countries totalled 1 million over the 1980–2000 period, these mainly locating in Japan, South Korea, Thailand, Laos, Singapore, Taiwan, the Philippines and Cambodia. It is worth noting that China's *internal* migration flows – mostly people moving from the country's rural areas to its urban-industrial zones – are much greater than international migration flows in East Asia, being measured in tens of millions. As we later discuss, however, there is a complementary linkage between mass internal and international migration.

7.3.2 Causal factors

There are various causal factors behind the growth of international migration in East Asia, and ascribing significance to specific factors can be difficult when these are themselves often closely inter-determinant. Moreover, as Hugo (2006a: 77) comments, 'the complexity of Asian migration is heightened by the region's remarkable cultural, ethnic, religious, and social variation, as well as by large intra-regional differences in rates of economic growth... [and] variations in demographic conditions'. By way of simplifying matters, this section will primarily focus on ILM flows, which can be broadly understood as an economic phenomenon that principally operates on the mechanics of supply and demand, with the inter-mediating effects of government policies and other factors (e.g. socio-cultural ties, geographic proximity) taken into account (Chia 2006). The Lewis (1954) model of migration offers a good starting point for this basic perspective as it sought to explain intra-national labour movements in accordance with both actual and anticipated wage differentials between rural and urban areas.

Table 7.4 International migration flows in East Asia by source and destination (2003–4 most data)

	Destination of Migrants													
	China	Hong Kong	Taiwan	Japan	South Korea	Indonesia	Malaysia	Philippines	Singapore	Thailand	Cambodia	Laos	Myanmar	Vietnam
China		38,200		90,300 444,140	57,700 154,660				60,000	[4] 160,000*	55,000	80,000		
Hong Kong														
Taiwan	1,000,000*													
Japan					22,800									
South Korea				7,300										
Indonesia		105,710 [4]	56,440 [3]	10,700	28,642 [7]		1,215,030 [2]		[6]					
Malaysia		14,280												
Philippines		129,760 197,345	81,360 160,672	96,200 353,250	22,790 47,150		22,080 352,650		136,490					
Singapore														
Thailand		28,550 4,860	104,730	7,100 49,430	18,900 21,370		7,280 9,030		70,000					
Cambodia							6,640 11,000			183,540				
Laos	[5] [2]									179,890				
Myanmar	[1] [7]			10,000	[6]		92,020 [4]		7,000	921,490				
Vietnam	[2] [2]		57,600	6,500 21,050	21,277 15,970		85,840 32,000				150,000	15,000		

Sources: Asian Migration Centre (www.asian-migrants.org), OECD (2006), Hugo (2006b), Department of Statistics, Malaysia (2006).

Notes: Figures are mostly for 2003 and 2004, based on data for current migrant levels. Row figures are for source outflows of migrants to destinations listed by column. Registered or estimated figures on migrant numbers can differ from recording source or destination. Where two figures appear in the same box, the top figure derives from the column listed destination and the bottom figure from the row listed source. Figures positioned in the middle of the box are where source and destination figure comply. Figures in [ ] refer to noted order of importance for outflows/inflows of migrants. For example, China noted Laos as the most fifth important source of migrant inflows [5] into the country while China was noted as the second most important destination of migrant outflows [2] from Laos, although neither offer any firm figure on this flow of Laotian migrants to China. * Higher end of range of very estimate figures for Taiwanese currently working in mainland China. * Estimate from Rallu (2002).

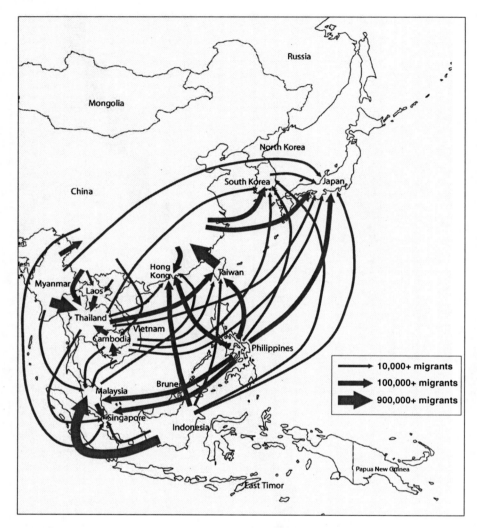

Figure 7.2 Major international migration flows within East Asia

Sources: Asian Migration Centre (www.asian-migrants.org), OECD (2006), Hugo (2006b), Department of Statistics, Malaysia (2006).

Notes: Based on data from Table 7.4

Fei and Ranis (1964) later adapted Lewis's work by taking into account open economy conditions and its implications for ILM flows. In this revised model, fast growing economies led to rising employment and income levels and eventual labour shortages in unskilled, low-wage job sectors. Using South Korea and Singapore as illustrative examples, in both their economies, income and education levels advanced rapidly leaving an ever smaller proportion of their societies wishing to take on menial jobs. Employers in these job sectors thus had to look overseas to fill these positions. Conversely, in less developed countries both wage and employment levels tended to be lower, thus creating pressures for outward migration, often to take on the aforementioned menial jobs (often called 3D jobs – dirty, dangerous and demanding) in more developed economies.

While a prime motivation for individuals seeking to migrate is the expected improvement in their income levels by working in their destination country, certain social, cultural, demographic and geographic factors play an inter-determinant part in shaping ILM flows. For instance, given that Japan, South Korea and Taiwan have a much higher income level than Malaysia, we may expect that this high income group of countries has a much higher level of immigrant labour, yet Malaysia has a foreign labour dependence ratio around five times that of this group (Athukorala 2006). Often, migrants will choose to find work in more geographically and socio-culturally proximate countries to help minimise the economic and social transaction costs involved when finding employment overseas. This makes cross-border movements an important feature of East Asia's international migration patterns overall. Key cases here include, with migrant sources named first, Indonesia–Malaysia, Malaysia–Singapore, Myanmar–Thailand, Taiwan–China, and China–Hong Kong (see Figure 7.2).

The cost of migration can be an issue for poor migrant households, limiting their ability to migrate to countries some distance away, but this is being mitigated by lower transportation costs and remittances sent by family members or other associates already living in the destination country. Furthermore, as East Asia's ILM trend has expanded so it has become more of a *regionalised* phenomenon. This especially relates to workers from Southeast Asia seeking contracted employment or long-term settlement in the distant Northeast Asian destinations of Taiwan, South Korea and Japan.

These and other higher income economies such as Singapore all face the serious 'demographic deficit' challenge of population aging owing to falling fertility rates and rising age longevity rates, and thus the need to attract prosperity-generating, tax revenue-paying migrants to help fund the increasing welfare service needs (e.g. healthcare) of an aging population and address other associated economic and social restructuring imperatives. Japan is already experiencing a decline in its working age population, while South Korea, Taiwan and Singapore are expected to experience this from 2020, Hong Kong from 2025, and China and Thailand from 2030. Japan's total population is currently projected to fall from its 2004 level of 127.8 million to 100.6 million by 2050, South Korea's from 48.0 million to 42.3 million, and Taiwan's from 22.7 million to 19.8 million.[11] Rates of working age population growth are meanwhile expected to rise at least until 2050 for Indonesia, Malaysia, the Philippines and the CLMV countries (Rallu 2002). Structural demographic changes across East Asia will continue to shape the region's patterns of international migration. Countries with aging populations may increasingly compete with each other for migrant labour as demographic pressures intensify over forthcoming decades. This may lead to an ever wider search in the region and beyond for workers across the skills spectrum to fill jobs in critical sectors. However, as we later discuss, the extent to which such a policy can be pursued will be subject to certain social, cultural and political constraints.

Another inter-determinant causal factor behind ILM flows has been the rapid growth in foreign direct investment in East Asia, which has spurred the expansion of international labour movement in particular ways (Tsai and Tsay 2004). Commenting on the FDI–migration relationship, Athukorala (2006: 24) remarks that, 'a peculiarity of this type of migration is that its evolution depends not on the aspiration of the individual to move (as with other forms of migration) but on the development of the organisational infrastructure within which the moves take place'. The relationship can also have a strong socio-cultural dimension. For example, the reason for Taiwanese firms increasingly locating their overseas business operations in mainland China owes much to the close socio-cultural and linguistic ties. There are at any one time around an estimated 500,000 to 1 million Taiwanese working for the 40,000 or so Taiwanese enterprises operating in the coastal provinces of China. Here is a case where FDI and migration have developed closely hand-in-hand. A similar instance of this concerns migrant flows on the Hong Kong–China 'border'. Skeldon (2006) reports that in 2001 around 330,000 Hong Kong residents on average were making daily trips to and from mainland China to work in joint venture enterprises.

East Asian economies with high outward FDI rates have generally been sending increasing numbers of MNE employees to work overseas. For example, according to Okunishi (1995) almost 700,000 Japanese nationals were registered as working overseas in 1994, the large majority of them for Japanese MNEs and mostly in the Asia-Pacific region. An increasing number of Koreans are also being deployed in overseas postings by the large *chaebol* firms such as Samsung and Daewoo. Both Singapore and Hong Kong have a long-standing tradition of hosting relatively large communities of foreign MNE executive and technical professionals, and in Chapter 2 we discussed the importance of East Asia's 'world cities' in the hosting and networking of foreign worker communities across the region generally.

Connected to this issue is the link that exists between internal and international migration (Skeldon 2006). Internal (i.e. intra-national) rural–urban migration has led to significant expansions in the urban populations of East Asia, and the region's major cities have in turn been the main sending centres for migrants seeking employment overseas. These cities have acted as the main centres of information-gathering and network link points for prospective emigrant workers. Skeldon (2006: 19) argues that some patterns of international migration in East Asia could be considered more like internal migration in situations where 'international borders bisect single ethnic groups or traditional trading routes, often where the border was imposed by colonial powers without regard to underlying social and political realities'. Examples of 'transborder' lying minority groups in East Asia include those on the northern Thailand–Myanmar border, between Isan in northwest Thailand and Laos, between southern Vietnam and Cambodia, and between Malaysia and adjacent parts of Indonesia. This restates the earlier made point concerning the importance of social–cultural proximity as a determinant of international migration flows within the region.

Finally, international migration can be a self-reinforcing process, and similarities exist here with the agglomeration effects of industrial district formation that were studied in Chapter 2. Once a critical mass of migrants from a source country has been established in a particular foreign destination, this can act as a 'beachhead' for other migrants from the same source to follow, through the supplying of information and assistance back home to other prospective migrant workers. Migrant networks develop from this process, linking together ever closer both source and destination countries. Naturally, various problems and pressures may weaken these network links over time, and shock events such the 1997/8 financial crisis, which led to significant reductions in foreign migrant worker stocks in some countries such as Malaysia for a few years thereafter (Manning 2002).

7.3.3 Government policies on international migration

As has already been indicated, East Asian governments face many challenges when developing policies on international migration. To generalise, these challenges will depend on whether countries are labour-importing or labour-exporting. The main policy concerns in labour-importing countries from the influx of foreign workers are: 1) the forcing out of locals from the labour market; 2) suppressed wage levels; 3) consequent pressures upon social cohesion, demand for public services and other aspects of the countries' social infrastructure. Trade union opposition to influxes of foreign workers derives from the first two concerns, and public opposition can at times be very strong when these pressures and problems are frequently highlighted in the media. A range of political, social and cultural considerations often shape government policy on foreign workers (Athukorala 2006, Chia 2006). For example, the main reason why Taiwan discourages those coming from mainland China is because resource dependencies that Taipei develops on mainland China carry certain political and security risks. Instead, Taiwan actively seeks manufacturing workers from Thailand, partly to develop an alliance link with a major Southeast Asian country. Meanwhile, Malaysia's foreign worker recruitment policy favours those from Muslim countries, especially from Indonesia and Bangladesh, presumably to ensure foreign workers can more easily assimilate into mainstream Malaysian society.

The main policy concerns of labour-exporting countries are: 1) restrictions imposed on foreign workers by labour-importing countries; 2) migration as a means of alleviating high unemployment levels; 3) reversing the outflow of the country's best educated and skilled workers overseas, i.e. 'brain-drain'; 4) generating foreign exchange earnings from remittances sent back home by the country's emigrant workers and extracting maximum returns from this source of income. This income can be important for developing countries, and especially for the Philippines where foreign exchange earnings from remittances had risen to US$7.6 billion by 2003 (US$4.9 billion in 1995), which equated to a 20.6 per cent equivalent share of the country's export earnings for that year (Hugo 2005, Skeldon 2000).

Many labour-exporting countries in East Asia have long-established government agencies that were set up to specially train their citizens for foreign employment, policies devised to maximise remittances (e.g. tax breaks on foreign earnings), and bilateral agreements with destination countries to supply workers for certain projects (Hugo 2006a). South Korea and Taiwan have both implemented relatively successful 'reverse brain-drain' policies aimed at attracting back home former emigrants (especially those working in the US) who possessed critically important technical, professional and business skills (Iredale 2000). For example, many Taiwanese technopreneurs who were working in Silicon Valley have decided to relocate to Hsinchu Science Park (see Case Study 2.2, Chapter 2, p. 61). Disagreements on foreign worker issues can often arise, and Chia (2006) reports on a number of disputes that have occurred between Southeast Asian countries in recent years, namely:

- Singapore and Philippines in 1998 over the civil rights of Philippine female workers employed in Singapore.
- Concern expressed by Indonesia and the Philippines over Malaysia's mass repatriation of illegal workers during the 1997/8 financial crisis.
- Occasional disputes between Malaysia and Indonesia over illegal labour flows.

Notwithstanding the problems associated with rising levels of international migration, governments have come under increasing pressure from employer groups in labour-importing East Asian countries to adopt a more open and transparent approach on foreign migrant labour (Athukorala 2006). Skills and job shortages can be real issues for economies undergoing dynamic structural adjustment, and this applies to many East Asian countries. Furthermore, Bhagwati (2004) contends that a more liberalised approach to international migration flows can make a significant contribution to redressing income disparities between rich and poor countries. Certainly, in principle, the greater intermingling of East Asian peoples through rising intra-regional migration flows could make a significant contribution to regional community-building through various socialisation effects, as we discuss in Chapter 8. This, of course, assumes certain levels of foreign worker assimilation into the host society and other relevant factors conducive to this process.

7.3.4 *International/regional co-operation and integration*

Labour mobility has grown in prominence as a trade-related issue at various levels of economic diplomacy. However, the international governance of labour mobility remains quite weak. Within the WTO, it is covered only in Article V of the General Agreement on Trade in Services (GATS) that provides for the temporary movement of service suppliers under so called 'Mode 4' labour mobility commitments. This is one of the GATS' four 'modes of supply' for trade in services, relating to individuals travelling to another country to supply services in that country, and is officially known as 'movement of natural persons'. Mode 4 provisions have limited coverage, though, mainly concerning, in practice, temporarily contracted, intra-firm transfers of relatively high-skilled and professional personnel through FDI projects. Moreover, WTO member states with specific preferences for importing labour have proved generally reluctant to enter into MFN-binding agreements with others.

At the regional and FTA level, APEC has a number of measures and programmes that aim to facilitate labour mobility in the Asia-Pacific trans-region. These have sought mainly to simplify short-term entry arrangements for business visitors, streamline processing for skilled persons seeking temporary residence, and develop transparent regulatory arrangements to allow cross-border labour movements. Meanwhile, the ASEAN Plan of Action on Immigration Matters seeks to

> forge and strengthen immigration co-operation with a view to establish an effective network to promote the modernization of immigration facilities, systems and operations; upgrade human resources capabilities and capacities of immigration officials to support the economic aspirations of ASEAN; and support in combating transnational crime.[12]

Despite these lofty sounding objectives, co-operation on international migration in Southeast Asia remains weak on core issues such as protection of migrant worker rights, compensation for loss of skilled workers, facilitating remittance flows, harmonisation of migrant data systems, asylum seekers, and other matters (Chia 2006).

Like GATS, labour mobility provisions in FTAs (similarly referred to as 'movement of natural persons' in the agreement text) generally favour highly skilled and professional workers, and there is a close link between foreign investment and the specialised worker flows that accompany or facilitate it. There are special exceptions to the rule. In the Japan–Philippines Economic Partnership Agreement, Japan agreed to allow 400 nurses and 600 nursing caretakers from the Philippines from April 2007 over two years subject to certain rigorous vocational and language training stipulations. Similarly, in the Japan–Thailand EPA, Japan agreed that Thailand could export quota-limited cooks, healthcare workers, and entertainment industry workers in accordance with relatively strict entry criteria. For both FTAs, immigration was one of the most difficult areas of negotiation, and it remains a politically and socio-culturally sensitive issue in diplomatic relations amongst East Asian countries generally.

Yet the dramatic rise of ILM flows in particular in East Asia will require greater levels of regional co-operation on migration related issues. Rising ILM levels will lead to deepening labour market integration across East Asia. According to Quibria (1997), the long-term drivers behind this process are technological advances, economic and social liberalisation, governments and firms striving, respectively, for national and corporate competitiveness, international economic agreements with provisions for labour mobility, and the continued expansion of transnational business operations. These factors are constituent parts of the broader regionalisation and regionalism processes studied in previous chapters. Even if regional labour market integration progresses at a relatively slow pace, international migration seems set to become an increasingly important regional-level issue in East Asia over forthcoming years and decades.

7.4 Energy security in East Asia

7.4.1 Framing East Asia's energy security predicaments

East Asia's rapid economic growth and development has made energy security and co-operation increasingly important issues for the region. East Asian countries' demand for energy resources has grown substantially over recent years, rising almost five-fold in consumption terms from 1970 to 2005 while world energy consumption had just doubled during this period (IEEJ 2006). Energy, security and the environment have become intimately bound together in East Asian affairs (Hayes and von Hippel 2006). The region's current and projected utilisation of energy resources is both economically and environmentally unsustainable in the long-term (Saha 2003). The environmental consequences of energy use are already severe in many parts of the region, such as acid rain in the Yellow Sea zone and the South China Sea. On a global level, East Asia now accounts for around 30 per cent of all greenhouse gas emissions.

Energy security is primarily concerned with the securing of energy supplies (minimising supply or quantity risk) at stable and affordable prices (minimising price risk), as well as taking into account the environmentally damaging effects of energy consumption (minimising environmental risk), especially from the combustion of fossil fuels (Research and Information System for Developing Countries 2005). Countries and governments still tend to place much greater emphasis on the first two risk elements, and are deemed especially susceptible if they are heavily dependent on foreign sources of energy supply, over which their influence and control may be limited.

East Asia's most developed economies – Japan, South Korea, Taiwan, Singapore and Hong Kong – all face this predicament, having energy import dependency ratios of at least 80 per cent. Moreover, competition for energy assets amongst East Asian countries seems set to intensify as resources world-wide become increasingly depleted and the region's economic development continues apace. As Calder (1997: 1) has remarked, energy is the 'dark side of the explosive economic growth of East Asia, rooted in the region's profound energy insecurities'.

Much of the region's energy security focus is centred on Northeast Asia, primarily because of its extremely high energy import-dependency and energy consumption rates compared to Southeast Asia (Manning 2000). Southeast Asia is currently a net energy exporter but this position will diminish (it is already a net oil importer) over forthcoming years as the energy needs of ASEAN countries increase in the future (Symon 2004). This exacerbates East Asia's energy security predicament overall. The region's main energy security issues are as follows:

- The dependency of Northeast Asian countries on Middle East oil, and attempts to mitigate this by diversifying their energy supply sources.
- Contestations over potential oil and gas fields in certain maritime zones in East Asia (e.g. East China Sea, Spratly Islands).
- Maintaining the security of sea-lane routes by which East Asia's energy supplies pass from sources outside the region.
- Developing alternative sources of energy (e.g. renewables) as well as new energy efficiency methods and technologies to help sustain the region's long-term economic development.
- The security dimension of developing the nuclear power capacities of East Asian states, especially with regards to North Korea.

While East Asian countries are competing with each other to secure future energy supplies there is also a growing imperative for them to co-oper-ate more closely on the above issues. Energy security will certainly become a more prominent agenda issue in East Asian affairs for both these reasons.

7.4.2 Energy resources, production and consumption in East Asia

In general, Southeast Asia and China possess the bulk of East Asia's energy resources while the region's most developed East Asian economies – Japan, South Korea, Taiwan, Singapore and Hong Kong – have large-scale energy processing and refining facilities, e.g. petrochemical products. As Table 7.5 shows, the latter group are heavily dependent on imported energy supplies. China is the region's largest and world's sixth largest crude oil producer (producing 176 million tonnes in 2004) but in 1993 it became a net oil importer. This had various strategic implications for other countries as China has since sought to secure various energy supply deals with other countries, and also is considering exploring new potential oil and gas fields in contested territorial areas within East Asia itself. China is also developing national strategic oil reserve sites at Ningbo, Zhoushan, Qingdao and Dalian, these all lying in the country's east and northeast coastal zone. East Asia's other major oil producers include Indonesia (the region's only member of the Organisation of Petroleum Exporting Countries, or OPEC) with 50 million tonnes produced in 2004, Malaysia with 37 million, Vietnam 21 million, and Brunei and Thailand both with 10 million tonnes (see Table 7.5). However, only Brunei, Malaysia and Vietnam were net exporters of oil that year. In terms of oil refining, Singapore, South Korea and Taiwan are the region's largest net exporters of petrochemical products. Over recent years, Singapore has developed its Jurong district into East Asia's largest petrochemical complex and is the region's largest (and world's fifth largest) exporter of petrochemical products (Table 7.5).

Natural gas is either supplied directly from source by pipeline, or transported in liquefied natural gas (LNG) form usually by sea. LNG is by far the most traded form of natural gas in East Asia. The region has both the world's largest exporters and importers of LNG, making East Asia the world's biggest market for LNG trade (Herberg 2004, Klaassen et al. 2001). Indonesia, Malaysia and Brunei, as well as Australia, are the major suppliers of LNG to Northeast Asia, and Japan, Taiwan and South Korea together account for 75 per cent of the world's total LNG imports (see Figure 7.3). Although as we later examine there are ambitious plans to develop international and regional gas pipeline links, only a few cross-border gas pipeline connections had been constructed in the region by 2007, the first of these being between Malaysia and Singapore, which became operational in 1991 (see Figure 7.4). Southeast Asia has much larger reserves of natural gas than oil because of the region's long history of oil production (dating back to the early 1900s) and subsequent depletion of oil reserves, as well as the geological nature of the region itself (Symon 2004). Most of Southeast Asia's main gas fields are offshore, as indicated in Figure 7.5. Despite the rapid growth in natural gas use by East Asian countries, it still only accounts for around 10 per cent of the region's total energy consumption, which is far below the world average of around 23 per cent (Table 7.5). Furthermore, Southeast Asia's proven natural gas reserves are still considerably lower than those possessed by the Middle East, Russia and Central Asia.

Coal is the most carbon-intense of the fossil fuels and thus it yields the highest proportionate levels of carbon dioxide (CO_2) into the atmosphere when burned. It also has the added disadvantages of emitting sulphur and nitrogen particles, causing acid rain and health hazards. China is by far the region's largest coal producer, its 28,000 coal mines being mostly concentrated in the country's northeast region. China is 71 per cent dependent on coal for electricity generation (see Table 7.5) and has a third of the world's proven coal reserves. It is also twice as coal-dependent for its current energy needs as the next ranked East Asian economy, namely Taiwan with a 36 per cent dependence ratio. Those countries most dependent on coal are confronted with particular severe energy pollution problems. Despite the rhetoric of East Asian governments to reduce CO_2 emission levels, many countries in the region appear to be relying on coal increasingly in their energy mix

Table 7.5 Energy data for East Asia

	Coal (2004) Production	Coal Imports	Coal Exports	Coal Consumption[1]	Oil (2004) Production	Oil Imports	Oil Exports	Oil Consumption[1]	Nat. Gas (2004) Production	Gas Imports	Gas Exports	Gas Consumption[1]	Petroleum Products Imports (2004, Mtoe)	Petroleum Products Exports (2004, Mtoe)	Production/Consumption, Mtoe	Production/Consumption, Mtoe	Imports as a share of Total Energy Consumption	Exports as a share of Total Energy Production	2004 Coal	2004 Oil	2004 Natural Gas	2004 Nuclear	2004 Renewables	2030 est. Coal	2030 Oil	2030 Natural Gas	2030 Nuclear	2030 Renewables	CO2 Emission, 2004 (millions of tonnes)	CO2 Emission, 2030 estimated (millions of tonnes)
China	1,053	10	66	993	176	123	5	290	44	0	2	42	48	16	13	30	13	7	71	22	3	1	3	56	28	7	3	6	1,311	2,445
Japan	0	118	0	118	0.3	200	0	201	3	68	0	71	51	5	74	18	82	1	22	48	13	14	3	19	37	15	24	5	349	303
South Korea	1	50	0	51	0	113	0	114	0	26	0	26	23	32	34	2	80	8	24	47	12	16	1	23	38	17	19	3	128	194
Indonesia	81	0	59	22	50	20	20	50	67	0	33	34	21	9	0	7	32	53	18	51	27	0	4	22	46	28	2	2	96	252
Taiwan	0	40	0	38	0.1	52	0	52	0.7	8	0	9	9	13	10	1	87	8	36	45	8	10	1	48	34	11	5	2	74	129
Malaysia	0.2	6	0	6	37	8	19	25	46	0	26	20	9	9	0	1	45	57	11	50	38	0	1	23	31	45	0	1	41	133
Philippines	1	4	0	5	0.2	10	0	10	2	0	0	2	7	1	0	10	62	14	16	50	6	0	28	23	44	16	0	24	21	63
Thailand	6	4	0	10	10	43	3	52	18	7	0	25	2	5	0	0	59	20	13	56	30	0	1	26	44	29	0	1	63	166
Vietnam	14	0	6	8	21	0	20	1	5	0	0	5	12	0	0	2	64	62	31	45	17	0	7	27	47	16	4	6	22	63
Brunei	0	0	0	0	10	0	9	1	10	0	8	2	0	0	0	0	0	85	0	35	65	0	0	na	na	na	na	na	6	na
Singapore	0	0	0	0	0	45	0	45	0	5	0	5	50	54	0	0	100	100	0	90	10	0	0	na	na	na	na	na	21	na
Myanmar	0.5	0	0.4	0.1	1	0	0	1	7	0	5	2	1	0	0	2	32	46	2	20	42	0	36	na	na	na	na	na	7	na
Hong Kong	0	7	0	7	0	0	0	0	0	2	0	2	17	1	0	0	100	13	76	0	34	0	0	na	na	na	na	na	12	na
EAST ASIA	1,157	239	131	1,258	306	614	76	842	203	116	74	245	250	145	131	73	44	20	48	35	10	4	3	41	34	14	5	5	2,151	4,011
WORLD	2,804	748	741	2,804	3,849	2,235	2,153	3,849	2,369	705	699	2,369	825	892	735	489	na	na	27	38	23	7	5	27	35	26	6	6	7,354	11,390

Sources: International Energy Agency and International Energy Economics Japan databases.
Notes: Production, consumption, import and export figures in millions of tonnes of oil equivalent (Mtoe) on a net calorific value basis. 1. Takes into account stock changes.

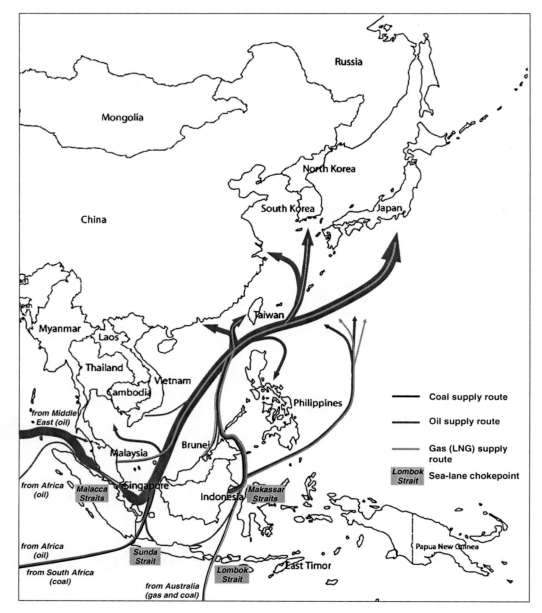

Figure 7.3 Main energy import supply routes in East Asia

Sources: Based on various collected data.

Notes: Flows show main supply routes for different imported energy fuels and arrow ends indicate main areas or countries of destination. For reasons of graphic simplicity, flows of imported coal have been drawn just up to main import stream points.

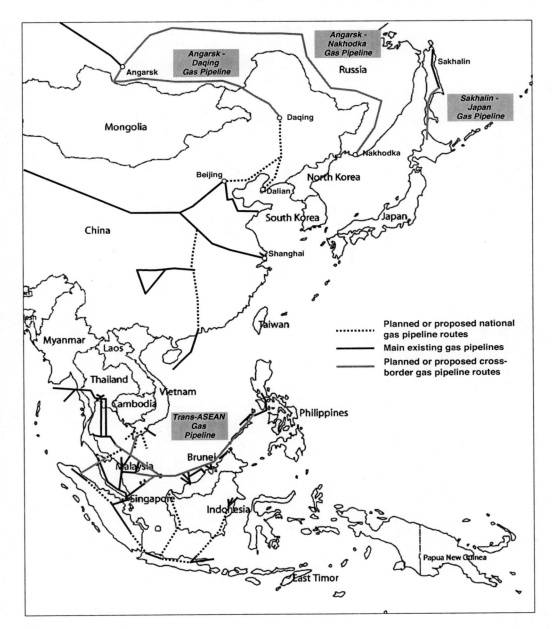

Figure 7.4 Cross-border natural gas pipeline schemes in East Asia
Sources: Amin (2002), IEEJ (2006).

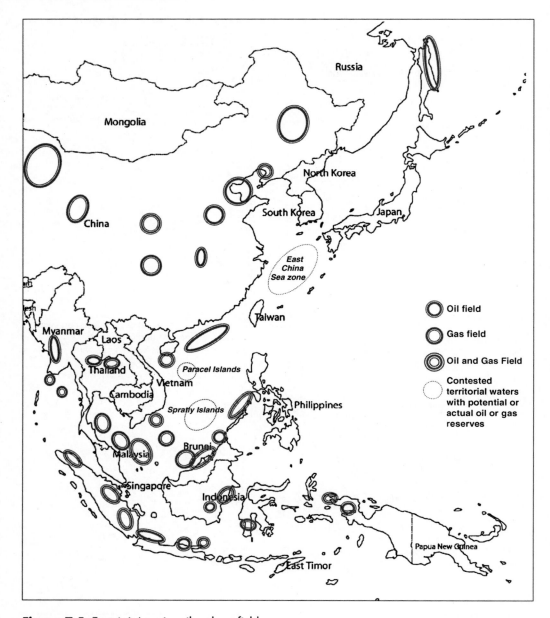

Figure 7.5 East Asia's major oil and gas fields

Sources: Based on graphic data from Petroleum Economist (*www.petroleum-economist.com*), ASCOPE (*www.petronas.com.my/ascope*), IEEJ (2006).

given concerns over high and volatile oil prices, comparatively limited natural gas reserves, persisting fears over using nuclear power and the high cost of developing renewable energy alternatives.[13] This being said, estimates for coal's share in East Asia's total energy consumption are expected to fall over the long term, i.e. by 2030 (Table 7.5). China and Indonesia are the only major exporters of coal in the region. East Asian countries also import coal in significant quantities from Australia and South Africa (Figure 7.3).

Japan, South Korea, Taiwan and China are East Asia's only producers of nuclear energy, this accounting for at least 10 per cent of total energy consumed in the first three listed. As we later discuss, there are security-related complexities concerning North Korea's long held aspirations to also become a nuclear power. Indonesia and Vietnam also have plans to develop nuclear power generation capacities over forthcoming years, and in May 2007 Russia announced it would help Myanmar develop a nuclear research centre based on a 10 MW light water research reactor. Renewable energy sources have meanwhile played an important part in the rural electrification programmes of many ASEAN countries, especially in Indonesia, Laos, Malaysia, the Philippines and Thailand. This has included a diverse energy mix of geothermal, hydro-electric, solar, wind and biomass technologies. The Philippines, which has the region's highest renewable energy ratio at 28 per cent (mostly geothermal) in 2004, is aiming to double its renewable installed capacity over 2003 to 2010, from 4.7GW to 10GW.

China has meanwhile set a goal of producing 16 per cent of its total energy consumption from renewable energy sources by 2020, although this would seem a rather ambitious target. Laos is also attempting to increase its renewables capacity five-fold by 2010, from 620MW to around 3GW and export the surplus to neighbouring countries through the developing ASEAN Power Grid project (Research and Information System for Developing Countries 2005). Cross-border electricity sales currently occur between Thailand and Laos, Thailand and Malaysia, and Malaysia and Singapore. Northeast Asia, too, has a variety of proposed projects on establishing cross-border electricity power grid connections, most of these including the energy resource-rich Russian Far East. These projects face a number of inter-connection technology challenges, including converter stations to deal with different frequencies used by national grids. In addition, the Russian Far East has surplus capacity in the summer but little spare capacity in winter months. There are also technical and political difficulties posed by any plans to route grid connections through North Korea to South Korea and Japan (Hayes and von Hippel 2006).

East Asia's energy consumption growth rate has risen faster than any other region in the world over the last few decades. In 1970, East Asia consumed around 600 million tonnes of oil equivalent (Mtoe) per year, around an eighth of the world total. By 2005 this had risen to around 3 billion Mtoe per year and just under a third of the world total (IEEJ 2006). During the early 2000s, China alone has accounted for 40 per cent of total growth in global demand for oil, and in 2003 it overtook Japan to become the world's second largest oil consumer after the United States. OPEC estimates made in early 2007 indicated that East Asia's demand for oil will nearly double over the following 25 years, and will account for a large majority share of increased global demand for oil over that period.[14] Estimates from the Institute of Energy Economics Japan (2006) predict that East Asia's total primary energy consumption will rise to around 6 billion Mtoe by 2030, approaching 40 per cent of the world total.

7.4.3 *Diversifying sources of energy supply*

Energy supply diversification is a core element of the energy security strategies of most East Asian countries and has both geographic and fuel source aspects, these often being closely inter-connected. The former aspect has primarily concerned reducing a dependency on Middle East oil. Part of this strategy has involved seeking non-oil supply sources from other regions, such as natural gas from Russia and Central Asia. Many East Asian countries have also sought to boost their own domestic renewable energy production capacities, yet in most cases these efforts fall well short of significantly displacing fossil fuel's share of the energy mix. Estimates currently suggest that renewables' share of the region's energy consumption will only rise from 2.7 per cent in 2004 to 4.6 per cent by 2030, compared to the world average of 4.7 per cent and 5.9 per cent, respectively (Table 7.5). Raising the share of renewables further above these rates is a vital twenty-first century challenge at both the regional and global levels.

One of the biggest difficulties facing a number of East Asian countries is their dependence on oil, and that sourced from the Middle East in particular. The Middle East has around 70 per cent of the world's proven oil reserves. Almost 60 per cent of the region's oil exports go to East Asia, and around 70 per cent of East Asia's oil imports come from the Middle East – 90 per cent for Japan, 70 per cent for China, 95 per cent for the Philippines (see Figure 7.3). China and Japan, as well as other East Asian countries, have sought FTAs with Middle East states – including with the Gulf Co-operation Council (GCC) group[15] – as part of their strategy of securing long-term access to the region's oil supplies. Since 2005, Asian and Middle East governments have been discussing energy security issues in Asian Ministerial Energy Roundtable meetings.

While current estimates suggest that East Asia will remain significantly oil-dependent on the Middle East for the foreseeable future (importing 80 per cent of its oil needs from the Middle East by 2010), East Asia's multinational energy firms, such as the semi-privatised China National Offshore Oil Corporation, have been busy purchasing the energy sector assets in other parts of the world as part of their own diversification strategies (Herberg 2007, Jaffe and Lewis 2002). Chinese oil and gas companies have been particularly active, recently acquiring assets in Indonesia, Australia, Nigeria, Kazakhstan, Ecuador, Sudan, Canada and Angola. This is invariably augmented with offers of government-backed aid and finance packages to the host source country to help secure energy deals.

There are geopolitical reasons why East Asian countries have looked to break their dependency on Middle East oil. In the aftermath of the 11 September 2001 terrorist attacks on the United States, confidence in the politico-diplomatic stability of the Middle East region has been undermined. China in particular has targeted African states as new oil supply partners (Salameh 2003), for example, taking 64 per cent of Sudan's oil exports in 2005, while half of China's oil imports from Africa in the same year came from Angola. In addition, China, Japan and South Korea have all sought closer energy supply links with Russia, as well as with certain Central Asian states. As noted in Chapter 1, the Russian Far East has hitherto been largely periph-eral to the East Asia regional economic dynamic but this could change over forthcoming years. Russia has abundant oil and gas reserves, and its geo-graphic proximity has made it a priority partner in the energy diversification strategies of Northeast Asian countries. A number of proposals have been made for exporting oil and gas from Siberia and the Russian Far East to China, Japan and South Korea, ranging from relatively short pipelines (e.g. Sakhalin Island to Japan) to those covering thousands of kilometres (see Figure 7.4). However, most of these proposals involve very long lead times of completion, have estimated costs that run into many billions of US dollars, and Russia's own energy supply infrastructure in the region remains relatively underdevel-oped (Goldstein and Kozyrev 2006, Hayes and von Hippel 2006).

Despite these challenges, Northeast Asian countries have competed with each other to secure new and comparatively large-scale energy supply arrangements with Russia over recent years. At first, it appeared that China would make the first breakthrough, coming to an understanding with Russia in July 2001 to develop the Angarsk–Daqing oil pipeline project at a then estimated cost of around US$3 billion and 2,260 kilometres in length.[16] In the meantime, Japan approached Russia with its own proposal to construct a longer and more expensive pipeline from Angarsk to Nakhodka on the Sea of Japan, from hence oil supplies could be shipped to Japanese seaports close by (see Figure 7.4). In late 2004, Moscow announced it now preferred the Angarsk–Nakhodka pipeline option, which would entail the construction of a special deepwater port facility at Nakhodka from which Russia could export oil to the wider East Asian market. It was a matter of relative commercial advantages: the Angarsk–Daqing pipeline in contrast would only serve one country – China.

However, by early 2007 Russia had still to firmly commit to developing either of the proposed pipeline projects, mainly because of unresolved diplomatic and financing issues. The oil fields around Angarsk may not have sufficient capacity to serve both pipelines, and China has also proposed building an Angarsk–Daqing gas pipeline running parallel to its oil counter-part. China may still have a diplomatic advantage over Japan in Northeast Asia's energy politics. In June 2001, China, Russia, Kazakhstan, Kyrgyzstan, Tajikistan and Uzbekistan formed the Shanghai Co-operation Organisation (SCO) that aims to advance co-operation in economic, security and cultural affairs amongst its member countries. Energy co-operation has emerged as an important element of SCO diplomacy, and high-level discussions on constructing Kazakhstan–China oil and gas pipelines have taken place since 2003.

Meanwhile, South Korea has entered into discussions with Russia over constructing electricity grid interconnections between the two countries. This is based on the broader idea of power stations located in the Russian Far East transmitting their surplus power to Northeast Asian countries during certain periods of the year, especially during the summer months when spare capacity exists (Kanagawa and Nakata 2006, Yun and Zhang 2006). As noted earlier, though, South Korea and Japan both face the technical and political problems of establishing grid interconnections via North Korea. Alternative options of circumventing North Korea through much longer submarine cable links could prove far more expensive than land-laid routes through the Korean peninsula, all other factors remaining equal.

7.4.4 Energy security conflicts: actual and future potential

There have already been conflicts between East Asian states in their competition over energy resources. These, as well as other potential conflicts, may flare up to significant proportions over forthcoming years. The four key cases presented here are the 'chokepoints' predicament, the East China Sea dispute between China and Japan, the Spratly and Paracel Islands in the South China Sea, and North Korea's nuclear programme.

7.4.4.a The 'chokepoints' predicament

Much of East Asia's vital energy supply routes pass through geographic 'chokepoints', these primarily being narrow sea-lane straits. Most critically, most of the region's imports of Middle East oil pass through the Malacca Straits, which is a relatively very shallow stretch of water and only 500 meters wide at its narrowest point but with a sea-lane traffic volume of around 100,000 ships a year (including around half the world's oil-tankers), making it one of the world's busiest shipping routes (see Figure 7.3). Imported energy fuels from Africa and Australia pass through other chokepoints, such as the Sunda Strait (between Java and Sumatra), the Lombok Strait (between Bali and Lombok), and from Australia and Indonesia through the Makassar Straits between Borneo and Sulawesi (Figure 7.3).

These narrow sea-lane passages can be easily blocked and are also highly susceptible to piracy and terrorist attack, thus making them strategically important. It has therefore been in the energy security interest of many East Asian countries to safeguard the security of the region's supply route chokepoints. Regional co-operation on tackling piracy in the Malacca Straits is advancing in particular. In addition, both Malaysia and Thailand have announced proposed projects to build oil pipelines across the Malaysian peninsula and Kra Isthmus, respectively, as shortcut options to passage through the Malacca Straits. Either project, if realised, could significantly undermine Singapore's position as one of the region's major shipping hub and oil-refining centres. China also has plans to build an oil pipeline to link infrastructure in its Yunnan province with a deepwater port in neighbouring Myanmar. This would further reduce oil shipments through Southeast Asia's sea-lane chokepoints.

7.4.4.b The East China Sea dispute

For some years now, Japan and China have been embroiled in a complex legal dispute over seabed jurisdictional rights in the East China Sea, and therein territorial claims over an area thought to hold substantial oil and gas reserves (Harrison 2005). China argues that the entire East China Sea continental shelf, extending eastward almost all the way to the Japanese island of Okinawa, is a "natural prolongation" of the Chinese mainland. Japan meanwhile has claimed the maritime boundary between the two countries should lie along a median line between its undisputed territory and China, thus situated approximately 100 miles west of the Okinawa Trough (Figure 7.5). Until China began to conduct survey operations in the zone in the mid-1990s, it had respected Japan's 'median line' claim for nearly 30 years. However, China became more assertive with its territorial claims after survey results indicated that substantial petroleum fuel reserves could lie in the disputed area. Moreover, these results indicated that the richest deposits could lie more on the Japanese side of its median line. From January 1998 to August 2000, 16 Chinese ships were recorded as intruding across Japan's median line boundary on 12 different occasions.

China raised the stakes further in August 2003 by setting up a production platform at Chun Xiao, just one mile from Japan's median line. In response, Japan sent in surveying teams to assess whether China's operations there were encroaching on the Japanese side by lateral drilling. During 2004, Tokyo called upon Beijing to suspend its Chun Xiao operations and engage in a more co-operative approach to exploration. However, China's next move was to intensify its naval operations in the area during late 2004/early 2005, and refused to share its geological data on the zone's seabed with Japan. Soon afterwards, Japan announced it would give three of its oil companies the go ahead to commence exploration operations opposite Chun Xiao just within the Japanese side of the median line. Although the Japanese Government has already demarcated petroleum development concessions in seabed areas on its side of the median line, production had not started by 2007. China and Japan discussed the East China Sea dispute at 2006 and 2007 bilateral summit meetings but no agreement on territorial rights or co-operation concerning the issue was reached.

7.4.4.c The South China Sea: Spratly Islands and Paracel Islands

The South China Sea is host to two small archipelagos – the Spratly Islands and Paracel Islands – that are thought to hold substantial oil and gas reserves. However, the sovereignty of both sets of these islands is hotly contested by a number of East Asian states. The Spratly Islands consist of more than 200 barren islets, coral reefs and shoals in the South China Sea over which six states (Brunei, China, Malaysia, Philippines, Taiwan and Vietnam) have made full or partial territorial claims (Figure 7.5). In addition to their geo-strategic position in the region, through which some of East Asia's prime sea-lanes of communication pass, there are alleged but unproven oil and gas riches in the Spratly Island area (Manning 2000, Senese 2005). Although there have not been any serious conflicts between the claimant states for some time – the last being a skirmish between China and Vietnam in 1988 – the lure of possible major oil and gas reserves in the Spratlys has the potential for raising tensions amongst those states from competitive quests to secure future energy supplies from within the region. The same applies to the Paracels, a smaller set of similar islands to the north of the Spratlys, which is claimed by China, Vietnam and Taiwan (Figure 7.5). In both cases parallels can be drawn with the East China Sea dispute between China and Japan. Moreover, contested claims over the Spratlys and Paracels highlight the wider strategic importance of the South China Sea zone, over which China claims 80 per cent as its territorial water and through which almost all of Japan's oil imports are shipped.

7.4.4.d North Korea's nuclear programme

North Korea has been trying to become a nuclear power for many decades. Given the often hostile nature of the North Korea state, under the leadership of Kim Jong-il, and the highly-charged security situation on the Korean peninsula, dealing with Pyongyang's nuclear power aspirations has become a critical security issue in East Asia. There is a fear that North Korea will use any developed nuclear power capacity to build weapons of mass destruction. In March 1995, the Korea Peninsula Energy Development Organisation (KEDO) was established by the US, South Korea and Japan as an international consortium devised to steer North Korea towards constructing light water reactor (LWR) plants, from which weapons grade plutonium could not be developed. Members of KEDO – which later expanded to include the EU, Australia, Canada, New Zealand, Indonesia, Argentina, Chile, Poland, Czech Republic and Uzbekistan – were to provide financial and technical assistance, while Pyongyang was obliged under the preceding 1994 US–North Korea Agreed Framework to curtail development of its Magnox type reactors at its long-standing nuclear power plant at Yongbyon.

However, delays over financing the construction of the new LWR plant meant that building work did not start at the chosen Kumho site until 2000. After the breakdown of the 1994 Agreed Framework in 2003, the KEDO project was seriously undermined. Even the new nuclear diplomacy framework of Six Party Talks (between North Korea, China, Japan, Russia, South Korea and the US) initiated the same year[17] could not revive KEDO's fortunes. With only a reported 30 per cent of the building work complete and

US$1.5 billion invested, KEDO announced in January 2006 that the LWR project was over although the organisation would continue to exist in some form. Around a year earlier in February 2005, North Korea announced formally for the first time that it had developed nuclear weapons, though this is yet to be verified. In the meantime, Six Party Talks (a sixth round was held in March 2007) have endeavoured to steer North Korea away from further developing its nuclear programme. Like many other Northeast Asian neighbours, though, North Korea lacks indigenous resources and is highly dependent on foreign imports of energy, especially oil from China. The US in particular has tried to use energy supply restrictions as diplomatic leverage on North Korea in Six Party Talks. There are thus special complexities involved regarding energy and security in relation to the North Korea question.

7.4.5 Regional co-operation on energy

East Asian states have begun to co-operate more closely with each other on both a bilateral and regional basis concerning energy matters. Japan and China have recently initiated a number of co-operative projects. One of the most important concerns new clean-coal research and development technologies. Japan has a direct incentive to do so as it would reduce acid rain levels in the Yellow Sea and East China Sea zones, mostly caused by China's numerous coal-fired power stations located in the country's northeast (Jaffe and Lewis 2002). In addition, Japan and China announced in January 2007 plans to further co-operate in the nuclear power sector, with Japanese companies helping to construct new nuclear power plants in China.[18] The two countries also agreed a few months later to launch an extensive co-operation programme on improving China's energy efficiency through Japanese technology transfers, joint energy conservation studies, training schemes and other means.[19] East Asia's more developed countries may consume higher levels of energy per capita but the region's developing countries are far less energy efficient. For example, in the late 1990s, China required nearly ten times the oil equivalent in energy consumption per $1,000 of GDP than Japan (Manning 2000). Improving energy efficiency has become a key area of energy sector co-operation in East Asia generally.

Transnational link-ups of energy infrastructure forms another important area of co-operation in the region, and this has largely centred on fuel pipeline and electricity grid connections. We previously discussed recent developments in Northeast Asia concerning a number of planned projects. Additional projects involving the region's states include the Vostok Plan (promoted by Russia), Energy Silk Route Project (China, Japan, Turkmenistan) and Irkutsk Gas Project (Russia, China, South Korea). Large ambitious infrastructure link-ups have also been proposed in Southeast Asia. The best known of these is the Trans-ASEAN Gas Pipeline (TAGP), first formally proposed in a memorandum of understanding signed in July 2002 whereby ASEAN governments agreed to build a regional-scale gas pipeline based on eight interconnection projects that would link up Southeast Asia's main natural gas distribution centres (Figure 7.4). The network would connect all ASEAN's natural gas producers, from the Philippines in the east to Myanmar in the west. However, the TAGP may not be completed until 2015 and will rely on Indonesia in particular, which holds around 70 per cent of the region's natural gas reserves, to further develop its own national gap pipeline system. While Indonesia may undertake this task it may prove intent on retaining larger shares of its natural gas production for domestic consumption as a means of reducing its dependency on imported oil. There are, in addition, a number of institutional-legal (e.g. regulating cross-border gas flows and trade), regulatory (e.g. transit rights through third countries, tax and tariff issues) and technical (e.g. harmonising design parameters and construction standards, co-ordinating operations) challenges to be met in realising the TAGP project (Amin 2002).

Regional-level energy co-operation in Southeast Asia dates back to the establishment of the ASEAN Council on Petroleum (ASCOPE) in 1976 as a forum for discussing oil and gas industry matters and later developing various analytical functions. In 1986, member states sought to foster closer co-operation on energy by signing the ASEAN Petroleum Security Agreement and ASEAN Energy Co-operation Agreement. Co-operation became further programmatic with the introduction of the ASEAN Programme of Action on Energy Co-operation (1995–9) and First ASEAN Plan of Action on Energy Co-operation (APAEC), 1999–2004. The ASEAN group then progressed to the Second APAEC (2004–9) in which the TAGP project forms one of six programme areas of co-operation. The first listed of these is the aforementioned ASEAN Power Grid project that aspires to establish a dozen cross-border interconnections amongst the region's national electricity generation systems. Other programme areas in the Second APAEC include co-operation on coal (e.g. wider application of clean coal technology), energy efficiency and conservation, renewable energy and regional energy policy and planning. These last four areas, though, lack detail on specific projects, deadlines, objectives and commitments generally.

The ASEAN group has also developed closer ties with outside energy partners such as the EU, Australia, multilateral institutions like the ADB, and with Japan, China and South Korea within the APT framework. It was at the twentieth ASEAN Ministers of Energy Meeting held in Bali in July 2002 that the first high-level consultations on how to advance energy co-operation within East Asia took place. In September 2002, APT Energy Ministers reached a common understanding on 'Energy Co-operation among Japan, China, Korea and ASEAN', which comprised a five-point initiative:

1) the creation of an energy emergency network;
2) development of a strategic oil reserve;
3) joint studies on the ASEAN oil market;
4) improvement of natural gas development; and
5) improvement of energy efficiency and renewable energy.

The ASEAN–China FTA also includes provisions on energy co-operation, while Japan's co-operation with the ASEAN group long pre-dates the formation of the APT framework.

Fostering co-operation and dialogue on energy security matters has become an increasingly prominent item on the APT and EAS agendas. In January 2007 at the second East Asia Summit meeting, leaders of the 16 member states signed a Declaration on Energy Security. The document committed the EAS group to similar sets of objectives previously agreed with ASEAN and APT, namely to reduce its dependence on conventional fuels, explore options for stockpiling oil and developing renewable energy capacity, improving energy efficiency, and so on. It remains to be seen whether this new agreement will lead to more substantial energy co-operation in the region. In the meantime perhaps its most significant immediate outcome outcome was the further enlargement of an East Asian 'energy community' by incorporating India, Australia and New Zealand into the regional dialogue process. At the January 2007 EAS meeting, Japan also announced a US$2 billion aid package to help Asian nations develop energy-efficient technologies.

Within the wider Asia-Pacific context, APEC's co-operation in this field has centred on its Energy Security Initiative (ESI). The ESI, established in 2001 and developed out of the organisation's Energy Working Group, consists of various short-term measures to respond to temporary energy supply disruptions (e.g. oil price volatility, occasional security threats to sea-lane supply routes), as well as longer-term policy measures aiming to address challenges concerning the region's security of energy supply, such as technology and infrastructure co-operation. The importance APEC member states attach to energy security continues to be referred to in Leaders Declarations at the organisation's summits.

In conclusion, while there is a clear intensification of dialogue on energy security matters at the regional level within East Asia and the Asia-Pacific, progress on serious co-operation in this area appears to have only just begun. It can be said with some certainty, however, that mounting economic, social and environmental pressures associated with East Asia's energy security predicaments will create increasingly stronger imperatives to co-operate more closely and effectively on regional energy issues over future years.

7.5 Conclusion

7.5.1 Summary overview

This chapter's analysis on three key transnational issues in East Asia has offered further insights into the dynamics of East Asian regionalism. In each of the three cases, it was shown that the transnational linkages studied have bound East Asian countries closer together in various ways, whether on a bilateral, sub-regional or regional basis. Furthermore, the associated environmental, labour/human security and energy related challenges presented to East Asian countries have compelled them to co-operate more closely in these areas, or at the very least manage the tensions arising amongst them as a consequence of these challenges.

In the first transnational issue, we saw how transboundary 'haze' pollution in Southeast Asia has been primarily caused by Indonesia's forest fire problem. Other affected countries – especially Malaysia and Singapore – have sought to work with Indonesia to address the causes, costs and broader effects of the haze pollution. This has not been easy given Indonesia's lack of capacity, ASEAN's cardinal principle of 'non-interference' of member states in the affairs of others, and how certain Singaporean and Malaysian companies have been implicated as partly culpable for the mass 'slash and burn' clearances of Indonesia's rainforests. The ASEAN group as a whole has endeavoured to find regional co-operation solutions to the problem with assistance also from countries outside the region.

The second transnational issue – international migration in East Asia – examined the increasing flows of migrant workers and refugees crossing over the region's national borders. Of these two trends, international *labour* migration, has become increasingly more important as people from one part of the region seek employment and settlement in another part. The various motives and other determining factors behind the rapid expansion of ILM flows in East Asia were discussed, as were the effects of this trend on certain socio-economic and political aspects of East Asia's regional affairs. Recent endeavours to advance international and regional co-operation in this area were also analysed.

Energy security in East Asia was the third transnational issue studied. We first considered the nature of East Asia's different energy security predicaments and the connections between them, and then examined the nature and location of the region's energy resources as well as relevant aspects of energy production and consumption. Many if not most East Asian countries have high dependency rates on imported sources of energy, and many are dependent on relatively few foreign sources (e.g. Middle East oil) and a narrow range of fuel types. This has made diversifying supply sources a critical energy security issue, and one that East Asian countries have together sought to address more collectively. At the same time, there are a number of potentially serious energy security conflicts that may arise in the region. These include the East China Sea dispute over seabed resources between Japan and China, and contested sovereignty disputes involving various countries over the believed energy-rich Spratly and Paracel Islands. Regional co-operation on energy related issues at the East Asia level was also studied, although this is still in its infancy.

7.5.2 International Political Economy (IPE) theoretical analysis

In evaluating the transnational issues studied in this chapter from a *neo-realist* perspective, we could start by making the general observation about the sensitive and strategic national interests at stake concerning all three issues. This has made East Asian nation-states particularly wary of entering into regional co-operative ventures that may in some way compromise those national interests. In the case of transboundary haze pollution, Indonesia has perhaps been reluctant to implement counter-measures that may compromise the objectives of national economic development. For example, cracking down on illegal logging practices in its rainforests would reduce the country's scope for generating timber export earnings and realising other economic benefits. According to neo-realists, this explains why Indonesia has only substantively acted to tackle the haze pollution problem when pressured to do so by neighbouring countries, especially those most affected, namely Singapore and Malaysia.

Regarding the expansion of international migration in East Asia, we saw various political and socio-cultural sensitivities arising from the social dislocations caused by this trend. The consequent strict regulations employed by many countries to limit the flow of peoples across their borders will ultimately narrow the scope for fostering an important element of social regionalisation in East Asia. Neo-realists would also argue that competition rather than co-operation between East Asian nations is the defining character of the region's energy security relations. There are few issues more strategically important to the national interest than energy security. Competition for energy resources between China and Japan has notable ramifications for the East Asia region, as do the contested sovereignty disputes over potentially energy-rich territories such as the Spratly Islands.

An initial observation from the *neo-liberal institutionalist* perspective concerns how the three transnational issues studied all reveal how interdependent relations in East Asia have become increasingly complex and widespread. This chapter has shown how various environment, labour and energy related linkages have grown stronger amongst East Asian countries over recent years. Thus, the problems of haze and additional forms of transboundary pollution (e.g. acid rain in the Yellow Sea zone and the South China Sea zone) can be resolved only by regional co-operation rather than the unco-ordinated independent actions of national governments and other agencies. In the case of Southeast Asia's haze pollution, ASEAN's non-interference principle does present a problem by offering Indonesia, like any of the other ASEAN member states, the right to significantly limit the extent of its regional community obligations in such matters. On a more general point of neo-liberal theory, we saw the multi-actor nature of the haze pollution problem, involving a range of actors from small-scale farmers to national governments, as well as the often complicated transnational nature of the relations between these actors, with special reference to multinational business activities.

In another line of neo-liberal thought, the chapter's study of international migration highlighted the importance of individuals in certain processes of East Asian regionalism. International migrants have become transnational actors in their own right, albeit in a generally non-collective and non-organised sense. Yet they have nevertheless forged their own kind of interdependent linkages amongst East Asian countries at the micro-level.

The trend looks set to continue as the region's more developed countries will need to increasingly import labour for mainly demographic and social reasons, while many labour-exporting countries will depend on the remittances these workers send back home. Meanwhile, energy is one of the most critical areas for East Asian countries to strengthen regional co-operation as the twenty-first century unfolds. Sustainable development in East Asia and elsewhere cannot be achieved without closer co-operation on energy security matters. East Asian countries need to more carefully manage the region's own increasingly scarce energy resources, as well as work with others outside the region to achieve the same objectives globally. East Asian governments and firms also need to work more closely together on both developing and dispersing new clean and efficient energy technologies. They must too collaborate in mitigating the effects of fossil fuel generated pollution across the region.

From a *social constructivist* perspective, all three transnational issues have in their own way raised the awareness of East Asian peoples of the growing inter-connections between them. As was specifically argued earlier in the chapter, haze pollution has affected a large number of Southeast Asians, providing stark evidence of common problems affecting the region. Such common experiences help create stronger associative ties and shared interests between the region's people from which a more developed sense of common regional identity may be achieved. Similar arguments apply to international migration in East Asia. The contribution this is making, albeit currently not that significantly, to social regionalisation in East Asia was noted above. Peoples travelling around the region are more likely to develop a sense of regional community than those who do not. Moreover, international migration can be an important transmission mechanism for spreading different social, cultural, political and economic values and ideas across the region, as well as help develop international social networks in East Asia. Likewise, all East Asians are confronted with energy security predicaments at some particular level or levels, whether this is coping with limits on energy fuel supply, unpredictable energy fuel prices or the environmental costs of energy fuel combustion. These problems, as with those relating to transboundary pollution and international migration, of course may be shared in a local, national, regional and global sense. It is, however, when they are articulated as common problems by regional organisations and frameworks that the conception of these as shared regional scale issues is more likely to occur. The East Asia Summit's Declaration on Energy Security made in January 2007 thus helped strengthen the social construction of the region's energy security predicaments, as it outlined some of the common challenges facing all East Asian peoples in this matter.

A general assessment from the *Marxist-structuralist* perspective on the studied transnational issues would attribute the main cause of their associated problems to the excesses of transnational capital. For example, transnational logging corporations have been primarily responsible for forest fire haze pollution in Southeast Asia, driven by their pursuit of profit. The Indonesian and other national governments have found it difficult to counter multinational enterprise power here. As was discussed, the Indonesian Government lacks the capacity to effectively regulate the practices of these companies. In addition, the Singapore and Malaysian governments appear to lack complete jurisdictional control over the foreign operations of MNEs originating from their countries. In sum, the haze pollution issue reveals some of the difficulties of governing the path and development of East Asia's regionalisation towards benign ends. The deepening trend of international migration in East Asia is meanwhile an aspect of the 'new international division of labour' created by MNEs. According to the Marxist-structuralist view, regional patterns of transnational capital primarily determine regional patterns of labour movements. Generally speaking, workers are compelled to find work overseas in zones where transnational capital is most concentrated in the region, these generally being in more developed 'core' economies. This further exacerbates core-periphery type divisions in the region as the best manual and professional workers from developing countries have increasingly looked for work in East Asia's more developed countries, further skewing the distribution of the region's resources towards the latter. As has been argued in other chapters, a worsening development divide makes regional community-building more difficult to achieve.

East Asia's energy security predicaments are, in addition, the outcome of the rapacious demands of global capitalism in the world's fastest growing economic region. This is just the latest episode in the long history of transnational capital's unlimited appetite for energy and other resources. Furthermore, the region's developing 'periphery' countries with relatively high energy reserves, such as those in Southeast Asia, are already under considerable pressure from developed 'core' countries like Japan to subordinate their energy supplies to the more developed capitalist zones of East Asia. Like neo-realists, Marxist-structuralists would predict that tensions amongst East Asian countries and firms will intensify owing to their anticipated increasing demands on a dwindling stock of energy supplies both inside and outside the region. All of the above factors are not conducive to fostering regional level co-operation on East Asia's energy security issues, and yet the imperative to co-operate can only get stronger. In the concluding chapter, we present an overview of the book's main findings and arguments in a new analytical framework for studying regionalism.

Chapter Study Questions

1. Why might forest fire 'haze' and other examples of transboundary pollution in East Asia be considered regional-scale problems with only regional-scale solutions?
2. Outline the problems faced by ASEAN as a regional group in tackling haze pollution.

3. What are the main determining factors behind the growth in international labour migration (ILM) flows in East Asia?
4. To what extent is the recent expansion of international migration part of a broader regionalisation process in East Asia?
5. Discuss the view that East Asia's energy security predicaments are more acute than those of most other regions.
6. What are the future prospects for deepening East Asia's regional co-operation on energy-related matters?

Notes

1 *Straits Times*, 23.01.2007.
2 Other general sources of haze can be farming activities (ploughing in dry weather), traffic, industry, and peat field fire.
3 *Agence France Presse*, 18.12.2006.
4 By March 2007 twelve AMMH events had been convened.
5 *Jakarta Post*, 27.08.2002.
6 *Singapore Institute of International Affairs News*, 28.02.2007.
7 *Xinhua Financial News Service*, 11.09.2006.
8 Hugo (2006a) observes that immigration of Asians to Anglo-Pacific countries of United States, Canada, Australia and New Zealand has risen for all countries since the 1960s. In the 1990s, 30.8 per cent of the total for the United States, 57.1 per cent for Canada, 29.4 per cent for Australia and 51.6 per cent for New Zealand.
9 Chia (2006) notes that up to 1980, this was the destination of 97 per cent of overseas contract workers from Thailand and 84 per cent from the Philippines.
10 Skeldon (2000) notes that in 1980, only 3 per cent of Thailand's migrant workers and 11 per cent of those from the Philippines went to other Asian nations. By 1994 these figures had changed to 89 per cent and 36 per cent, respectively.
11 Population Reference Bureau database, 2006 (www.prb.org).
12 From ASEAN Secretariat website: www.aseansec.org/16572.htm
13 *Jurnalo*, 26.04.2007.
14 *India e.News*, 23.03.2007.
15 The GCC comprises Bahrain, Kuwait, Oman, Qatar, Saudi Arabia and United Arab Emirates.
16 This was followed up by an understanding signed by the state-owned China National Petroleum Corporation (CNPC) and the Russian private company Yukos in May 2003 in which Russia would supply up to 30 million tonnes of oil a year through the Angarsk–Daqing pipeline.
17 This was an upgraded version of the antecedent Four Party Talks between North Korea, the US, China and South Korea which ran from 1997 to 1999.
18 *SEAPSNet News*, 24.01.2007.
19 *The Australian*, 12.04.2007.

Chapter 8

Regionalism in East Asia
A new framework of analysis

8.1 Introduction

This book has studied the various different aspects of East Asian regionalism primarily from an international political economy perspective. We began in Chapter 1 by studying the theories and concepts of regionalism, and its different manifest forms that have emerged within East Asia and the international system more broadly. Chapter 2 focused on the economic geography of regionalisation in East Asia, observing key developments in micro-level regionalism and sub-regionalism, and noting its network and zonal features. Chapters 3, 4 and 5 then studied the development of the main regional organisations and frameworks to which East Asian countries belong, namely ASEAN, APEC forum, APT and EAS. Chapter 6 examined the growth of bilateral FTA activity in East Asia and the Asia-Pacific, and considered the impacts of this deepening bilateralism on regional community-building in East Asia, and therein the relationship between bilateralism and regionalism. Chapter 7 provided another view on East Asian regionalism by case studying three key transnational issues – 'haze' pollution in Southeast Asia, international migration, and energy security – that have compelled East Asians to co-operate more closely with each other at the regional and other levels. This concluding chapter draws together the main findings of preceding chapters within a newly developed analytical framework devised to further improve our understanding of East Asian regionalism, and the nature of regionalism generally in the international system.

8.2 East Asian regionalism: different forms of its 'coherence'

8.2.1 Introduction

In Chapter 1, we generally defined regionalism as the structures, processes and arrangements that are working towards greater coherence within a specific international region in terms of economic, political, security, socio-cultural and other kinds of linkages. The key instrumental term in this definition is *coherence*, which itself concerns the uniting or unifying of different elements into new whole forms or entities. This book's study has shown overall that regionalism is essentially about the bringing together of different constituent elements within a region in a holistic and coherent manner. We may theorise that this coherence has taken three generalised forms, as outlined in Figure 8.1. The *conceptual basis* and *underlying attributes* of each form of coherence relates to its fundamental nature and characteristics, while *principal unifiers* relate to the prime forces or drivers (e.g. social, technological) in the formation of these different types of coherence. There are various main processes and prime manifest examples also to consider, as Figure 8.1 illustrates. Let us examine each of these forms of coherence in turn.

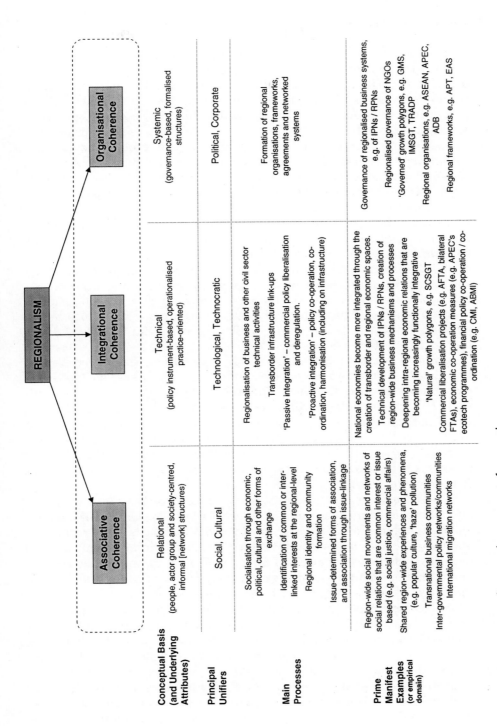

Figure 8.1 Regionalism as coherence: main framework

8.2.2 Associative coherence

This is essentially a relational concept that is primarily concerned with region-level links of association that form between agents or actors. It to some extent derives from the social constructivist strand of new regionalism theory discussed in Chapter 1. The principal unifiers of associative coherence are of a social and cultural nature as its prime focus is people, group and society centred. Regionalism cannot effectively advance without the strengthening of associative links amongst people, groups and societies within the region concerned. Regional community-building is grounded in the development of various region-wide socialisation processes that themselves stem from intensifying intra-regional economic, social, political, cultural and other forms of exchange. Previous chapters have observed how this is occurring across the East Asia region in numerous ways. For example, government officials from different East Asian countries are meeting with each other on a far more regular basis than in the past in regional and other international fora, further building up inter-governmental policy networks and communities within the region. The expansion of international production networks activity and other forms of transnational business operations in East Asia are more closely networking companies together on a regional basis (see Chapter 2). A similar trend is apparent in East Asia's civil society sector as NGOs seek to develop stronger associative ties with each other across the region (Curley 2007). In addition, Chapter 7 discussed how the growth of international labour migration was deepening inter-societal exchanges within East Asia. The growth of pan-regional social and cultural movements noted in Chapter 1 – especially developments in East Asian popular culture (e.g. Japanese cartoons and karaoke, Korean pop music, Star TV) – have too in their own way fortified associative links amongst the peoples of East Asia (Pempel 2005b). Together, these various processes have to varying degrees helped foster a stronger sense of East Asian regional identity.

Associative ties amongst East Asians can thus arise out of various but also inter-related processes and in different ways. The basis of association amongst people, groups and societies from different parts of the region has often originated from the identification of common or inter-linked interests amongst them (e.g. on matters of commercial practice, cultural behaviour, environmental concerns, political ideology, socio-religious belief, etc.). Similarly, associative links may be issue-determined. For example, actor-based networks can form based around particular region-wide issues, such as those related to matters of humanitarian missions (e.g. 2004 Asian Tsunami disaster), social justice, environment (e.g. as noted in Chapter 7 in relation to 'haze' pollution), consumer affairs, and so on.[1] Furthermore, issue-linkage has also established new associative connections amongst hitherto un-connected groups in East Asia. For instance, various NGOs (e.g. trade unions, environmental groups, agriculture associations) have become increasingly engaged in the region's trade policy agenda because of how trade policy decisions are seen to impact upon different areas of civil society interest. This can be seen concerning the region-wide trend of FTAs, where NGOs from different East Asian countries have often formed common or co-ordinated positions on various aspects of FTA policy (see Chapter 6).

While the associative coherence of the East Asia region has progressively strengthened over recent years, certain fundamental weaknesses remain that stem from a number of inter-related factors. First, and as outlined in Chapter 1, the region is highly diverse in terms of its economic development, political systems, socio-ethnic demography, and socio-cultural and religious characteristics. Such diversity is not naturally conducive to fostering closer associative links amongst peoples and societies across the region. Second, the diversity problem is compounded by strong nationalist sentiment that remains a feature of many East Asian societies. Closely tied to this are the historic animosities and mistrust that exist between particular nations in the region, as discussed in previous chapters. Third, the level of socialisation amongst East Asians themselves remains quite low. Most peoples within the region, especially those from developing countries, still have very limited interactions with each other. Organised civil society groups continue to be generally focused on national rather than region-wide issues, and many have yet to become regionally networked. International labour migration flows, whilst they have grown considerably in East Asia since the early 1990s, are still much lower than volumes of intra-national migration flows.

Overall, very few of the associative links examined in this book are of a pan-regional nature, being instead mostly localised on a relatively small sub-regional scale, e.g. Taiwan's *guanxi*-based business links with mainland China. Fourth, and owing largely to the above stated factors, the sense of an East Asian regional identity remains generally weak. Very few East Asians would actually call themselves 'East Asians' because their sense of association with other peoples from the region, as well as the region itself, remains under-developed (McNicoll 2005). There is thus much scope to develop the associative coherence of East Asian regionalism, primarily by more substantively developing various forms of inter-societal exchange across the region.

8.2.3 Integrational coherence

Our second form of coherence type, *integrational coherence*, is essentially a technical-related concept that considers the mechanisms and modalities by which integrative links are being forged within a region (Figure 8.1). The principal unifiers of integrational coherence are essentially technological and technocratic, and its underlying attributes are policy instrument-based and operationalised practice-oriented. Hence, the technical practices of both firms and governments are particularly relevant. For example, firms in East Asia are creating greater integrational coherence through developing numerous region-wide business mechanisms and processes. This was explored in some length in Chapter 2's discussions on the formation of IPNs and more 'natural' growth polygons (e.g. South China Sea Growth Triangle) at the sub-regional level in East Asia. Chapter 2 also highlighted how East Asia's regionalised integration should be understood from a geographic perspective in both networked and zonal terms concerning patterns of economic-related activity. We observed that IPNs were invariably rooted in industrial district zones, and therein created technical networked linkages between those zones across the region. However, these linkages were also facilitated by transborder infrastructural connections developed through both private and public sector endeavours. The development of region-wide infrastructure networks, also examined in Chapter 2, has made its own contribution to integrational coherence in East Asia by providing more generally the technical means for various forms of region-scale mobility and interaction for goods, services, people and capital. East Asia's 'world cities' have been the prime technical centres or hubs of these various regionalisation activities.

In addition, the *passive integration* (e.g. trade liberalisation) and *proactive integration* (e.g. policy co-operation, co-ordination and harmonisation measures) technical programmes of East Asian governments have also helped foster integrational coherence in the region. Passive integration measures are so called because they essentially involve the removal or reduction of barriers impeding economic exchange between East Asian countries. They do not entail the formation of common, congruent or co-ordinated technical policy elements amongst international or regional partners as such, unlike proactive integration measures. Previous chapters have studied the different forms that passive integration has taken in the region. In Southeast Asia, the AFTA project has eliminated or substantially reduced import tariffs on a comprehensive range of products, while one of its parallel schemes, the AIA, has made some progress on investment liberalisation. The objective of both AFTA and the AIA is to create a more coherent regional economic space in Southeast Asia by reducing the transaction costs of organising business on a transnational basis, e.g. IPN operations. The commercial liberalisation embodied in East Asia's various bilateral FTAs has also further opened up the region's economies to each other largely through passive integration effects, albeit in a patchy and ad hoc manner. To a much lesser extent and effect, APEC's commercial liberalisation schemes (e.g. the Individual Action Plans) have sought to achieve the same but on an Asia-Pacific trans-regional basis.

Meanwhile, East Asian countries have initiated an increasing number of proactive integration schemes at the regional level. Returning to Southeast Asia, the IAI entails a series of economic co-operation and development assistance projects that together aim to incorporate the sub-region's less developed countries (Cambodia, Laos, Myanmar, Vietnam) more effectively into regional integrational processes. Within the APT framework, we saw in Chapter 5 how the CMI, ABMI and ACU schemes have been devised to improve regional financial co-operation and policy co-ordination in East Asia. Although the level of policy co-operation and co-ordination involved in these schemes remains quite low, especially when compared to that achieved by the European Union, these schemes lay the foundation for far more substantive financial market integration to develop, as well as for more sophisticated regional financial policies such as exchange rate co-ordination.

All these technical developments noted above have strengthened the integrational coherence of the East Asia region, binding together its firms and national economies into more functionally integrative relationships. Intra-regional economic relations within East Asia have deepened in both quantitative and qualitative terms. East Asian countries are not only trading and investing more with each other but also in a more comprehensively integrative way. More generally, we can observe that certain aspects of integrational coherence possess material qualities and are often physically manifest. For example, we can actually see region-wide infrastructure networks in action, or the operationalised practices of regional business networks. From one perspective, these kinds of manifest examples may appear to take some form of organisational coherence, as we later discuss, but may at the same time be contrasted with the more abstract and intangible qualities of associative coherence.

The integrational coherence of East Asian regionalism remains weak, though, in a number of areas. The most significant factor here concerns the pronounced development divide that exists between relatively well developed 'core' zones of the region and much less developed 'periphery' zones. Chapter 2 identified how East Asia's most advanced economic development was concentrated along a particular 'development corridor' only a few hundred miles wide, roughly from Japan in Northeast Asia down to Singapore in Southeast Asia. Those parts of East Asia that lie outside this main development corridor (e.g. deep interior provinces in China, eastern Indonesia, Myanmar, Mongolia) have limited engagement with the region's integrational dynamics, as revealed by their poor business, market and infrastructural connections. East Asia's development divide is not just apparent at this macro-level but also at the more micro-level where capital or world cities dominate their home country's participation in regional trade, investment and other forms of economic exchange, leaving other areas of the country somewhat marginalised. The economic predominance of world cities is especially high in East Asia. For example, half of Southeast Asia's trade passes through the ports of the city-state of Singapore. In sum, patterns of integrational coherence in East Asia remain notably asymmetric but this is invariably the case for almost all macro-regions.

8.2.4 Organisational coherence

Our third and final coherence type, *organisational coherence*, may be broadly conceptualised in systemic terms. It relates primarily to how regionalism – and therefore its different aspects of associative and integrational coherence – may take some kind of organisational form. Thus, its underlying attributes are governance-based, while political (i.e. government or state) and corporate (i.e. private or civil sector, either acting separately or with the state) actions are the principal unifiers of organisational coherence. Regional organisations and frameworks of which East Asian countries are members (e.g. ASEAN, EAS, APEC, ADB) are more obvious examples of this, as are the region-wide governance structures created by NGOs such as Greenpeace and the governance and systemic development of regional production networks. East Asia is also host to a growing number of regional-level associations (e.g. Asian Network of Major Cities), regional NGO networks (e.g. Southeast Asia Rivers Network, Rivers Watch East and Southeast Asia) and regionally organised, multi-sector (i.e. public, private, civil) consultative mechanisms (e.g. East Asian Business Council[2] and Asian Bellagio Group[3]). These too contribute to the strengthening organisational coherence of East Asian regionalism.

Many studies on regionalism use regional organisations as the main focal point of their analysis. Three out of the eight chapters of this book have themselves been based on the study of regional organisations or frameworks. We have referred to both APT and EAS as regional frameworks, and ASEAN and APEC as regional organisations. This distinction has been made because ASEAN and APEC currently possess stronger formalised structures than either the APT or EAS arrangements. All four provide the following regional-level functions:

1) regularised meetings of political leaders, ministers, other government officials, business leaders and civil society groups;
2) co-operative and integrative activities and programmes;
3) improved socialisation amongst participating agents in these meetings, activities and programmes;
4) the capacity for envisioning and strategising future possible paths of regional community-building.

Not only do ASEAN and APEC have more developed and formalised structures regarding the above but they also in addition possess the following:

5) a secretariat, which although small in both cases nevertheless operates as a permanent co-ordinating agency for the organisation's activities;
6) the features of a defined organisational identity (e.g. with logo, website, etc.);
7) in ASEAN's case, an increasing capacity for unitary actions as an organisation interacting with other regional organisations (e.g. the EU), countries or other types of international partners.

The APT framework lacks such attributes and, it could be argued, is itself essentially a derivative of ASEAN-based diplomacy, hence an example of point 7. APT summits are tagged onto the end of ASEAN summits and only ASEAN countries are therefore eligible to host the meetings. The introduction of the EAS framework in 2005 was intended to bring greater organisational coherence to an East Asian grouping of states. It is too early to make predictions on the extent to which this objective will be achieved, if indeed at all.

One problem that both ASEAN and especially APEC have experienced over recent years is that organisational coherence can be significantly weakened by enlarged membership. Encompassing too much economic, political and socio-cultural diversity can hinder the progress of regionalist projects. A concluding point from Chapter 4 was that, in one sense, APEC was a regional organisation 'too far' in that reconciling the diverse interests of its large and diverse member economies had proved extremely difficult. In Chapter 5, we discussed how the EAS framework – by including hitherto perceived non-East Asian countries, India, Australia and New Zealand – could suffer a similar fate. We also examined in Chapter 5 how the APT framework, despite its aforementioned lack of organisational attributes, has made considerable progress in developing new structures of regional financial governance. In this respect, the CMI, ABMI and ACU schemes have substantially contributed to the organisation of financial policy co-operation amongst East Asian countries, with the assistance of the ADB. Thus, strong regional frameworks may achieve significantly more than relatively weak regional organisations. Notwithstanding the ongoing problems encountered by ASEAN, the raising of its organisational ambitions to create interlocking ASEAN economic, socio-cultural and security communities over forthcoming years, if realised, will represent significant steps forward in Southeast Asian regional community-building.

Overall, though, it could be argued that this aspect of organisational coherence will continue to be generally weak while East Asia's regional organisations remain under-institutionalised. This particularly relates to regional institutions charged with overseeing various common regional policy-making processes and structures, such as the EU's European Commission and European Central Bank. For reasons already considered in Chapter 1, it will be some time before East Asian countries prove ready to pool their sovereignty to the levels required to create these kinds of regional institutions. In addition, it was argued in Chapter 6 that bilateral FTAs could potentially undermine the integrity and coherence of East Asia's regional organisations and frameworks.

Advances in the organisational coherence of East Asian regionalism have been apparent in various micro-level regionalisation processes. Chapter 2 discussed the trend in IPN formation to the more regionally organised and integrated *type IV* form of international production (regional production network, or RPN) in East Asia. However, this is not yet the norm in East Asia, with many IPN activities often being organised on a relatively small transborder scale, or not that dynamically integrated as they involve mostly uni-directional production chain links. Yet firms operating generally in East Asia are increasingly thinking about the region in regionally integrative terms and organising their activities accordingly. The same applies to NGO operations based on the perception that East Asia is becoming an increasingly coherent regional entity overall. While the configuration of private and civil sector organisation activities may not exactly fit into the 'East Asia' box – rather being aligned instead to 'Asia' or the 'Asia-Pacific' parameters – East Asian countries invariably form the core focus of their regionalised operations. Finally, we may think of 'governed' types of growth polygons (i.e. those whose development is directly managed in some way by government agencies or regional organisations like the ADB) as also bringing some additional form of organisational coherence to East Asian regionalism at the sub-regional level.

8.2.5 Connections among the forms of coherence

The 'coherence' framework presented above offers different analytical perspectives from which we may observe and better understand the various aspects of regionalism. The different forms of coherence – associative, integrational and organisational – are not, however, mutually exclusive. Particular aspects of regionalism may connect across certain elements of the 'coherence' framework outlined in Figure 8.1. As already indicated, the empirical domains of each form of coherence (i.e. evidence of how they primarily manifest themselves) can overlap in some cases. Hence, the empirical elements shown at the bottom of Figure 8.1 under each form of coherence are referred to as 'prime' manifest examples: we should primarily locate these examples according to their coherence type but not necessarily consider them wholly compartmentalised to a singular coherence aspect of the analytical framework. This is discussed in illustrative detail below. More generally, some aspects of East Asian regionalism may connect at the conceptual basis level (e.g. relational and technical, technical and systemic) or concern sub-sets of principle unifiers (e.g. social and technological, technocratic and political) behind specific developments in regionalism.

Taking first the connections between *associative and organisational* coherence, both are concerned with the formation of regional groups (Figure 8.2). With respect to associative coherence, this may be conceived in people-centred terms that tend to be based on more informal 'un-governed' relational structures, such as international migration networks, inter-governmental policy communities and transnational business communities. Organisational coherence on the other hand entails the development of more formally structured and 'governed' regional group arrangements, such as regional organisations and frameworks involving groups of countries, and IPN-linked groups of firms. Of course regional group formation may fall somewhere in between these informal 'un-governed' and formal 'governed' categories, and the process of group formation itself may be highly dynamic. For example, a transnational business community grouping may evolve into a formally organised business association or coalition, e.g. the Asia Business Forum, the Asia-Pacific Business Forum, the

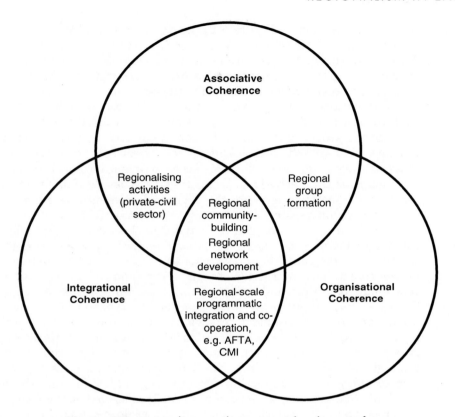

Figure 8.2 Regionalism as coherence: overlaps between forms

US–Thailand FTA Business Coalition. Our later debate on regional network development is closely related to these connections between associative and organisational coherence.

The connections between *associative and integrational* coherence mainly centre on the regionalising activities (or regionalisation) of private-civil sector activities (Figure 8.2). These were extensively studied in Chapter 2, which examined how such activities in East Asia were being primarily driven by a combination of socio-cultural, economic and technological factors. The technical development of IPNs or 'natural' growth polygons based on strong socio-ethnic ties, the existence of a transnational business community or other forms of socialisation are examples of this. As we later discuss, such developments may be co-determinant, in this case technological unifiers facilitating social unifiers and vice versa.

Connections between *integrational and organisational* coherence are primarily focused on regional-scale programmatic integration and co-operation schemes (Figure 8.2), many examples of which consist of regional agreements like AFTA and the CMI. These agreements tend to derive from regional organisations or frameworks (e.g. ASEAN and APT, respectively, in the aforementioned cases) and bring greater organisational coherence to regionalism by advancing the development of regional governance structures. Inter-governmental agreements and schemes such as AFTA and the CMI also embody elements of integrational coherence through the programmatic organisation of passive and proactive integration measures. In AFTA's case, this relates primarily to trade liberalisation (passive integration) and in the CMI's case to financial co-operation (proactive integration). International production networks also fall into this overlap category as they embody the technical elements of integrational coherence within a systemic or organisational framework.

There also exist two generic connections between all three forms of coherence (Figure 8.2). The first relates to regional network development. All three forms could lay claim over the role played by networks or networking in the construction of regionalism (Figure 8.1). Networks have relational, technical and systemic features. They generally comprise linkages forged amongst different actor types (people, groups, organisations) that are aided by technical or technologically facilitated processes and within a relatively loose and flexible organisational or governance structure. Inter-organisational networking that occurs at the regional level is common in the civil society and business sector alike. The second generic connection concerns regional community-building, which as Chapter 1 explained can be broadly conceived as the fostering of closer co-operative relations amongst the region's constituent states, peoples, organisations and other agencies with the aim of developing regional economic, political and social cohesion. Moreover, community-building and cohesion are closely related terms, both inferring how community members become increasingly beholden to each other. In this respect, advances in a region's associative, integrational and organisational coherence all contribute to regional community-building in their own particular ways and means.

Lastly, the different forms of coherence are co-determinant, in other words they can shape each other. For example, regionalisation derived from within associative and integrational coherence can provide a platform on which state-led forms of regionalism are built, leading to greater organisational coherence. Conversely, the systemic processes and outcomes derived from regionalism's organisational coherence may in turn spur activities within associative and integrational forms of coherence. For example, a number of spin-off groups and associations based on the ASEAN regional organisation have been created (e.g. ASEAN Chamber of Commerce and Industry, ASEAN People's Assembly, ASEAN Business Advisory Council, ASEAN Business Forum, US–ASEAN Business Council), and these have amongst other things cultivated further social relations on certain regional scales, e.g. sub-regional and trans-regional.

8.3 The extra-dimensional nature of East Asian regionalism

8.3.1 Introduction

In addition to understanding regionalism as 'coherence', we have seen throughout this book's study that there is almost always an expansionary or extra-dimensional nature to East Asian regionalism. For example, East Asian regionalism is embedded within wider economic, political and socio-cultural integrational forces and arrangements we typically associate with globalisation. Its development over time may also be understood as passes through different states of flux, in other words constantly evolving within dynamic parameters. The coherence of East Asia's regionalism can be maintained in relation to these processes because in most cases they tend to be involved in a mutually reinforcing relationship. For example, regional production networks maintain and further develop their integrational coherence in relation to their position within expanding global production networks. ASEAN has been able to maintain organisational coherence as a sub-regional group of Southeast Asian states within a deepening regional group formation (e.g. APT, EAS) at the East Asia macro-regional level. Other examples are discussed in the following section of the chapter.

8.3.2 Geo-spatial dimensions of regionalism

To preface our main discussion on the extra-dimensional nature of regionalism, it is helpful to first overview the geo-spatial dimensions to regionalism studied in previous chapters. As Figure 8.3 details, we can think of regionalist forms as broadly falling into four geo-spatial types of regionalism depending generally on how geographically concentrated or dispersed the activity embodied by the regionalist form is:

- *Sub-regionalism*: forming within a macro-region such as East Asia. These may involve contiguous sub-national areas from a number of countries or economies (e.g. South China Sea Growth Triangle) or sub-sets of countries within a macro-region, such as the Greater Mekong Sub-Region (GMS) project or ASEAN–China Free Trade Agreement. Larger sub-set group arrangements (e.g. ACFTA) may be considered *quasi-regionalist* forms on the geo-spatial scale in relation to a specific macro-region if they are approximating a comprehensive inclusion of all countries or economies within that macro-region.
- *Macro-regionalism*: concerned with recognised regional components of the global system, what may be referred to as 'macro-regions' or 'global regions'. There are no universal conventions of reference or definition as to what particular geo-spatial areas constitute macro-regions and which do not. Rather, it is a question of relative position between or amongst geo-spatial areas. For example, Southeast Asia and ASEAN

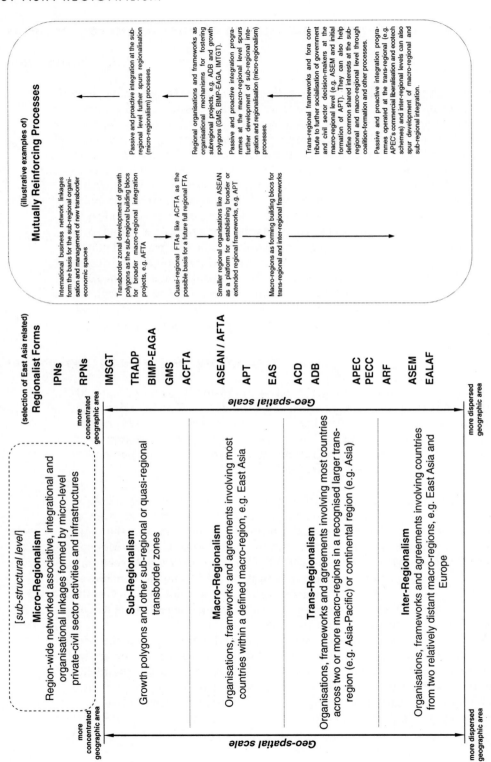

Figure 8.3 Geo-spatial dimensions of regionalism

may be considered macro-regional in their own right, or as sub-regional entities in relation to East Asia. Similarly, macro-regions may be sub-continental (e.g. East Asia as part of Asia, Central America as part of Latin America) or continental (e.g. Latin America, Africa) in geo-spatial scale.

- *Trans-regionalism*: relates to the coalescing of groups of countries across two or more macro-regions in a recognised larger trans-region, (e.g. Asia-Pacific and APEC) or continental region. Again, relative geo-spatial scales apply. Continental-based regional organisations and frameworks such as the Asian Development Bank (ADB) and Asia Co-operation Dialogue (ACD) may be considered 'trans-regional' arrangements from the perspective of different macro-regional level participation (i.e. East Asia, South Asia, Central Asia, Middle East).

- *Inter-regionalism*: organisations, agreements and frameworks involving countries or economies from two relatively distant macro-regions, e.g. Asia-Europe Meeting (ASEM) and East Asia–Latin America Forum (EALAF). In one sense, inter-regionalism is essentially about bringing together two regional groups into a co-operative or integrational arrangement rather than fostering regionalism *per se*. However, inter-actions of this sort may help deepen regionalism within the participating macro-regions themselves (see the 'mutually reinforcing processes' aspect of Figure 8.3). The number of participating member states or economies in inter-regional arrangements may be less than in trans-regional counterparts but in geo-spatial terms these arrangements tend to involve more dispersed or distant geographical linkages.

Underpinning the above at the sub-structural level are various forms of *micro-regionalism* that pervade the whole geo-spatial scale of regionalism's development. Micro-regionalism is synonymous with regionalisation, as we studied in Chapter 2, and also may be understood in relation to the 'coherence' analytical framework as it concerns region-wide networked associative, integrational and organisational linkages formed by micro-level private-civil sector activities and infrastructures across different regional geo-spaces. Examples of these from East Asia were previously discussed. Furthermore, and as discussed in Chapter 1, we must remember that regions may be viewed as 'constructed' economic, political, security and socio-cultural spaces rather than simply defined by distinct physical boundaries on a map, even though the social construction of regions still involves reference to geo-spatial entities such as East Asia. The key point here is that the various regionalist forms noted in Figure 8.3 have developed through an inter-play of economic, political, security and socio-cultural factors that have in turn ultimately determined their geo-spatial scale or demarcation.

Figure 8.3 uses a sliding scale of geo-spatially categorising these regionalist forms. Hence, the relatively small geo-spatial scale of the

Indonesia–Malaysia–Singapore Growth Triangle (IMSGT) places it towards the lower end of the scale in relation to geographically larger growth polygon arrangements such as the GMS. Similarly, ASEAN is placed before ASEAN Plus Three, which in turn is placed before the East Asia Summit grouping within the macro-regional scale. Some regionalist forms lie on the category cusps, such as APEC, PECC and ARF in relation to trans-regionalism and inter-regionalism. There is also the issue of how regionalist forms on different parts of the geo-spatial scale may be mutually reinforcing, with illustrations of this provided on the right-hand side of Figure 8.3. A number of co-constructive relationships between or amongst different regionalist forms have been studied in previous chapters, for example, whether or not quasi-regional FTAs such as ACFTA are positively contributing to regional community-building in East Asia.

8.3.3 Different extra-dimensional perspectives

The above geo-spatial analysis provides useful background reference and context when looking more closely at East Asian regionalism from extra-dimensional perspectives. The perceived boundaries or demarcations of regionalism – whether these are of a geo-spatial or other nature – are often blurred, contested or in a state of flux. Moreover, as noted earlier, the 'coherence' of East Asian regionalism is in some way constituent to other forms and processes of coherence occurring elsewhere within the world system. Six aspects of the extra-dimensional nature of East Asian regionalism are discussed below.

8.3.3.a Regionalisation and globalisation

In Chapter 2, we studied how the transnational business activities integrating East Asia together at a micro-level are often part of global production and distribution networks of firms originating from outside the region. Thus, much of East Asia's IPN/RPN activity is embedded within larger global production network (GPN) configurations (see Figure 8.4a, case [i]). This represents an important interface between regionalisation and globalisation for East Asia given the growing economic importance of IPNs in the region. We can apply the same principle to other forms of regionalised activity in East Asia that are embedded within wider globalised or globalising activities, be they of an economic (e.g. trade, investment and finance generally), socio-cultural (e.g. rise of middle-class consumerism and mass popular culture), socio-political (e.g. regional and global NGO network formation) or other nature. Further examples of the regionalisation–globalisation interface include regional networks of world cities in East Asia that exist within broader global networks of cities (Figure 8.4a, case [ii]). Likewise, East Asia's region-wide infrastructure network links form part of larger continental (e.g. the Trans-Asian Railway) and global infrastructure networks, as was discussed in Chapter 2.

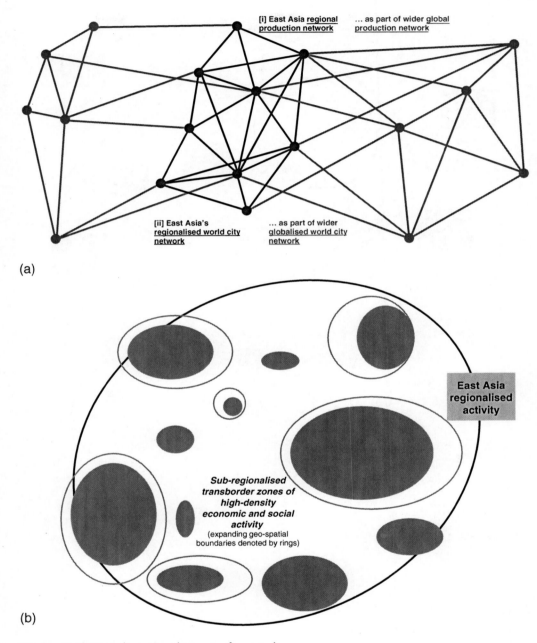

(a)

(b)

Figure 8.4 Extra-dimensional aspects of regionalism

(a) Regionalisation and globalisation

(b) Sub-regionalised zonal development within regionalised development

Note: Configurations in the above figures are based on arbitrary representations of the subject matter.

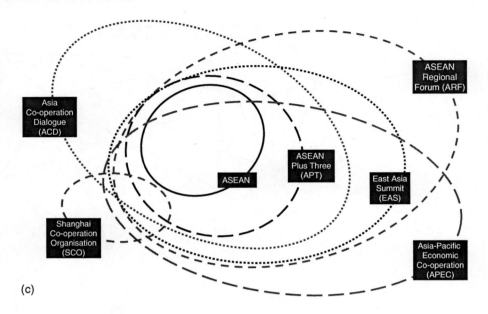

(c)

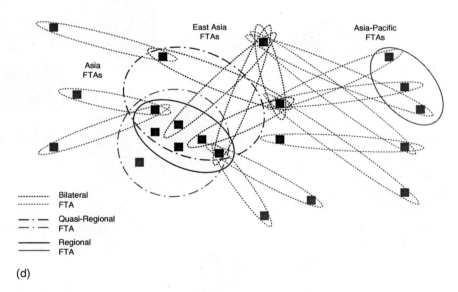

(d)

Figure 8.4 cont'd

(c) Regional organisations and frameworks

(d) Bilateralism, quasi-regionalism and regionalism

Note: Configurations in figure (d) are based on arbitrary representations of the subject matter.

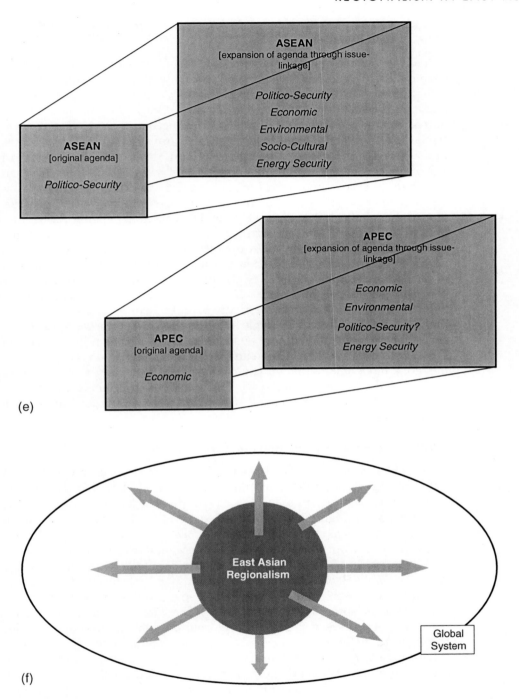

Figure 8.4 cont'd

(e) Regional issue-linkage and regional agenda expansion

(f) East Asian regionalism and its impacts on the global system

8.3.3.b Sub-regionalised zonal development within regionalised development

In addition to looking at the network features of East Asia's regionalisation, Chapter 2 also examined various zonal and sub-regional perspectives on the integration of the East Asia region at the micro-level. As discussed in that chapter, these closely connected with the networked dimension and we looked at how economic, social and political activities were often concentrated in sub-regional transborder zones within the region. Our analysis mostly focused on the recent emergence of East Asia's 'growth polygons'. In one sense, this is more of an intra-dimensional case of East Asian regionalism than an extra-dimensional one, as we are essentially looking at constituent micro-level developments in a broader regionalisation process. However, as indicated in Figure 8.4b and discussed in Chapter 2, the integrative activities of some growth polygons or other forms of sub-regional transborder activities may spill over into adjacent macro-regions such as South or Central Asia, thus further pushing out the geo-spatial boundaries of East Asia's regionalisation. We also discussed how the geographic scope of certain growth polygons has itself expanded over time, as indicated by the outer ring expansion denoted in Figure 8.4b. For example, the scope of the South China Sea Growth Triangle has expanded over time from the 'natural' outgrowth of transnational business activities between firms based in Taiwan, southeast coastal China and Hong Kong. Many 'governed' growth polygons have also extended their geo-spatial boundaries. As noted in Chapter 2, the Indonesia–Malaysia–Thailand Growth Triangle was the first to expand its arrangement, and new plans were announced in 2006 to further expand its reach.

8.3.3.c Regional organisations and frameworks

We first observed in Chapter 1 the involvement of East Asian countries in different regional organisations and frameworks, and how overlapping and concentric configurations of membership in these organisations and frameworks can arise (Figure 8.4c). As noted earlier, the APT framework may to some extent be considered derivative of ASEAN, and thereafter APT provided the basis from which the wider EAS regional framework was created (see Chapters 3 and 5). In Chapter 4, we also discussed the extent to which APEC, an Asia-Pacific based organisation, has both fostered closer ties amongst East Asian countries and helped advance East Asian regionalism itself, although sometimes more by default than design. In addition, Figure 1.3 in Chapter 1 showed that different sub-sets of East Asian countries belonged to different sub-regional, macro-regional, trans-regional and inter-regional groupings. These overlapping and concentric patterns of regional group membership are, however, mirrored in most other regions in the international system (see Figure 1.2, Chapter 1). Regional organisations and frameworks can help determine the perceived geographic boundaries of a macro-region like East Asia by way of presenting a collection of neighbouring countries in neat geo-spatial manner with a defined political border of the regional collective. Hence, notwithstanding East Timor's current omission from membership, ASEAN closely equates with Southeast Asia. The perception of an East Asia region by this formula is, as we know, more problematic because different organisations and frameworks are bidding to represent 'East Asia'. As discussed in Chapter 5, this mainly concerns the relationship between APT and EAS. Yet this extra-dimensional perspective on East Asian regionalism involves more than how the East Asia region should be organisationally represented or defined. As the ASEAN Regional Forum illustrates perhaps most clearly, managing a region's economic, political or security affairs may entail the assistance of outside partners. The United States in particular has been viewed by many East Asian states as a close regional partner over the past few decades, although this role has waned somewhat in more recent years. Likewise, the ADB as previously noted has played a strong supporting role in helping to advance APT-led regional initiatives such as the ABMI and ACU schemes. However, the membership of East Asian states in extra-regional frameworks and organisations (i.e. those clearly involving non-East Asian states, such as APEC, ACD and SCO) may undermine the work of those more clearly centred on the core East Asia region (n.b. APT and EAS) through orienting regional group formation away from this core. By the same token, the conventionally accepted membership set of a region's core states is itself often in flux. For example, we discussed in Chapter 7 how, as a consequence of energy security geopolitics, Russia (or at least the Russian Far East) may be increasingly incorporated into a future developed East Asia Community.

8.3.3.d Bilateralism, quasi-regionalism and regionalism

Chapter 6 examined how East Asia's new FTA trend formed part of a proliferation of FTA activity within the Asia-Pacific trans-region since the late 1990s, and furthermore as part of a global-level spurt of FTA activity from the early 1990s onwards. On all levels – macro-regional, trans-regional, global – it has been the growth of bilateral FTAs that has dominated the trend (Figure 8.4d). Some of these bilateral agreements, signed or being negotiated, involving East Asian states could be said to be 'quasi-regional' in nature when a regional group like ASEAN is partnering a singular neighbouring country (e.g. China, Japan, South Korea, India). As with 'extra'-regional organisations and frameworks, the formation of quasi-regional and bilateral FTAs involving both East Asian states and those outside the region could be argued to have either expanded or undermined the coherence of East Asian regionalism: expanded because they help incorporate hitherto extra-regional states (e.g. India) into the regional core or dynamic; undermined because such an inclusion may weaken the integrity of that core or dynamic through introducing greater diversity into East Asia's regional political economy. One thing is clear, namely that East Asia's new region-wide trend of FTAs is a constituent part of a trans-regional expansion of FTA activity across the Pacific, and moreover East Asian states have most recently extended their search for FTA partners to other regions, especially South Asia, the Middle East and Europe. Finally, and as also discussed in Chapter 6, the increasingly dense pattern of bilateral FTAs within just East Asia itself may or may not have a positive effect on regional community-building. Other forms of bilateralism in East Asia (e.g. the Chiang Mai Initiative system of bilateral currency swap agreements) may be discussed in the same context.

8.3.3.e Regional issue-linkage and regional agenda expansion

In certain parts of our study on East Asian regionalism, it was noted how the agendas of more long-standing regional organisations have expanded over time, mostly through imperatives stemming from issue-linkage. In Chapter 3, we saw how ASEAN was primarily focused on politico-security issues at its outset and during the Cold War period. In the context of changing geopolitical circumstances, ASEAN member states realised in the late 1980s and early 1990s that geo-economic factors would now play a greater part in the region's destiny, and that politics, economics and security would become increasingly inter-linked: economics would affect the region's security and political relations, and vice versa. The regional organisation's agenda expanded further during the 1990s and 2000s to more comprehensively incorporate social, cultural, environmental and energy security issues in particular (Figure 8.4e), as evidenced in ASEAN's programmes on regional co-operation. This came about from deepening socio-cultural (e.g. through international labour migration), environmental (e.g. forest fire 'haze' pollution) and energy security (e.g. addressing the problem of the region's depleting fossil fuel stocks) interaction amongst Southeast Asian countries, and from improved understandings of issue-linkage. As Chapter 7 discussed, there were complex and inter-related economic, political and socio-cultural factors behind the region's 'haze' problem, growth in international migration flows, and energy security predicaments.

This more multi-dimensional approach to advancing regional community-building in Southeast Asia has perhaps been most comprehensively revealed in the inter-constitutive ASEAN Economic Community, ASEAN Socio-Cultural Community, and ASEAN Security Community projects. Economic, socio-cultural and politico-security issues have to be addressed on linked programmatic fronts to best manage the processes of regionalism. Similarly, APEC began as an overtly economics focused trans-regional organisation but has come under pressure to incorporate security-related matters into its agenda after the 11 September 2001 terrorist attacks in the United States, as well as incorporate similar kinds of regional issues (e.g. environment) as ASEAN onto its agenda (Figure 8.4e). Other regional organisations around the world have also experienced a similar trend in agenda expansion through deepening issue-linkage. Consequently, the dimensions to regional co-operation in East Asia and elsewhere continue to expand.

8.3.3.f East Asian regionalism and its impacts on the global system

Our last extra-dimensional aspect considers the broader impacts of East Asian regionalism on the global system (Figure 8.4f). Many preceding aspects examined how regionalist developments in East Asia were in some way connected with, or were embedded within wider internationalised processes of integration and co-operation, and hence it is sometimes difficult to disaggregate the regional from the global. We can nevertheless assess East Asian regionalism's impact on the structure and general development of the global system in various ways. For example, the deepening of East Asian regionalism over recent years has significantly contributed to the global trend of regionalism. As discussed in Chapter 1, East Asia is one of the world's three most powerful economic regions (along with Europe and North America), and accounts for a quarter to a third of many forms of global economic activities (e.g. trade, production). An increasingly coherent East Asia region further consolidates the development of the global system into one comprising numerous regional communities and entities, especially in economic terms. Furthermore, if some form of 'regional power' emerges from East Asia – through single state leadership (e.g. Japan, China), co-leadership (e.g. Japan–China), or some other means of collective action (e.g. a formally represented East Asian Community) – as a consequence of deepening East Asian regionalism, this would have important geopolitical implications for the rest of the global community. There has already been much discussion on the impact of China's ascendancy upon those both inside and outside the region. The arrival of an East Asia 'regional superpower' on the international scene akin to the European Union may one day be a reality, but the world will very likely be a quite different place then to how we perceive it today. Moreover, by then the world system may be increasingly defined as one based on the interactions of various regional powers.

8.4 Final comments

This concluding chapter has considered how we may understand East Asian regionalism in terms of its associative, integrational and organisational coherence, and has therefore also presented a new analytical framework for studying regionalism *per se*. These different forms of coherence are not mutually exclusive but rather offer different analytical perspectives on how East Asian regionalism has evolved and developed over time. This book has generally argued overall that East Asia has become an increasingly coherent regional entity, especially in economic terms, and that there were extra-dimensional aspects to this coherence, this forming the second half of the chapter's analysis. East Asian regionalism has deepened but within a world system that in many respects is also becoming increasingly integrated. East Asia is a diverse and dynamic region of some considerable importance within that system for the various reasons discussed in this book.

Understanding how and why the region is becoming a more coherent entity is one of the critical emerging issues of the early twenty-first century.

Chapter Study Questions

1. Why might we consider regionalism as it has occurred in East Asia and elsewhere to be essentially about various forms of coherence?
2. Give examples of associative, integrational and organisational coherence that have arisen in the development of East Asian regionalism.
3. With reference to illustrative examples, discuss how different aspects of associative, integrational and organisational coherence in East Asian regionalism have interacted with each other?
4. For what main reasons can it be argued that there are extra-dimensions to East Asian regionalism as discussed in this chapter?

Notes

1   Hurrell (1995) refers to such processes of regional identification as 'cognitive regionalism'.
2   This explores how to deepen economic collaboration and investment amongst the APT countries.
3   A working committee of APT central bank officials, finance ministry bureaucrats and academics.

References

Acharya, A. (2004) 'How ideas spread: whose norms matter? Norm localization and institutional change in Asian regionalism', *International Organisation*, 58: 239–75.

Aggarwal, V.K. and Koo, M.G. (2005) 'Beyond network power? The dynamics of formal economic integration in northeast Asia', *The Pacific Review*, 18, 2: 189–216.

Aggarwal,V. and Urata, S. (eds) (2005) *Bilateral Trade Agreements in the Asia-Pacific*, London: Routledge.

Agnew, J. (2005) *Hegemony: The New Shape of Global Power*, Philadelphia, PA: Temple University Press.

Ahn, C., Kim, H.B. and Chang, D. (2006) 'Is East Asia fit for an optimum currency area? An assessment of the economic feasibility of a higher degree of monetary co-operation in East Asia', *Developing Economies*, 44(3): 288–305.

Aizenman, J. and Marion, N. (2003) 'Foreign exchange reserves in East Asia: why the high demand?', *FRBSF Economic Letter*, No. 2003–11, April.

Akamatsu, K. (1935) 'Trend of Japanese Trade in Woollen Goods', *Journal of Nagoya Higher Commercial School*, 13: 129–212.

Amin, M.F.M. (2002) 'Trans-ASEAN gas pipeline', presented at the *International Energy Agency Conference on Cross-Border Gas Trade*, Paris 26–27 March.

Amyx, J. (2004) 'A bond market for East Asia? The evolving political dynamics of regional financial co-operation', *Pacific Economic Paper*, No. 342, Australia–Japan Research Centre, Australian National University.

Ando, M. and Kimura, F. (2003) *The Formation of International Production and Distribution Networks in East Asia*, National Bureau of Economic Research Working Paper No. 10167, Cambridge, MA: NBER.

Arase, D. (1995) *Buying Power: The Political Economy of Japan's Foreign Aid*, Boulder, CO: Lynne Rienner.

Ariff, M. (1991) *The Pacific Economy: Growth and External Stability*, Sydney: Allen and Unwyn.

Arndt, S.W. (2001) 'Production networks in an economically integrated region', *ASEAN Economic Bulletin*, 18,1: 24–34.

ASEAN Secretariat (2003) *Declaration ASEAN Accord II (Bali Accord II)*, Jakarta: ASEAN Secretariat.

Asia-Pacific Economic Cooperation / APEC forum (1993) *A Vision for APEC: Towards an Asia-Pacific Economic Community*, First Report of the EPG to APEC Ministers, Singapore.

Asia-Pacific Economic Cooperation / APEC forum (1994) *Achieving the APEC Vision: Free and Open Trade in the Asia-Pacific*, Second Report of the EPG, Singapore.

Asia-Pacific Economic Cooperation / APEC forum (1995a) *Implementing the APEC Vision*, Third Report of the EPG, Singapore.

Asia-Pacific Economic Cooperation / APEC forum (1995b) *The Osaka Action Plan: Roadmap to Realising the APEC Vision*, Report of the PBF, Singapore.

Asia Pacific Economic Co-operation / APEC forum (2002) *Toward the Shanghai Goal: Implementing the APEC Trade Facilitation Action Plan*, APEC Secretariat, Singapore.

Asia Pacific Economic Co-operation / APEC forum (2004) 'Best Practice for RTA/FTAs in APEC', submitted at the *16th APEC Ministerial Meeting*, Santiago, Chile, 17–18 November.

Asia Pacific Economic Co-operation / APEC forum (2005) 'PECC Recommendations for Building on the "Best Practice" Guidelines on RTAs/FTAs in APEC', paper presented by PECC, *APEC Third Trade Policy Dialogue on FTAs*, Jeju, South Korea, 29 May.

Athukorala, P. (2003) *Product Fragmentation and Trade Patterns in East Asia*, ADB Working Paper No. 2003/21, Manila.

Athukorala, P. (2006) 'International labour migration in East Asia: trends, patterns and policy issues', *Asian–Pacific Economic Literature*, 20,1: 18–39.

Athukorala, P. and Manning, C. (1999) *Structural Change and International Migration in East Asia: Adjusting to Labour Scarcity*, Oxford: Oxford University Press.

Automotive World (2006) *Toyota Motor Company 2006*, London: Automotive World.

Ba, A.D. (2006) 'Who's socialising whom? Complex engagement in Sino-ASEAN relations', *The Pacific Review*, 19,2: 157–79.

Bairoch, P. (1981) 'The main trends in national economic disparities since the Industrial Revolution', in P. Bairoch and M. Levy-Leboyer (eds) *Disparities in Economic Development since the Industrial Revolution*, London: MacMillan.

Baker, J. (1995) *The Politics of Diplomacy: Revolution, War and Peace: 1989–1992*, New York, NY: Putnams.

Balassa, B. (1961) *The Theory of Economic Integration*, Boston, MA: Irwin.

Baldwin, R.E. (1999) 'A domino theory of regionalism', in J. Bhagwati, R. Krishna and A. Panagariya (eds), *Trading Blocs: Alternative Approaches to Analysing Preferential Trade Agreements*, Cambridge, MA: MIT Press.

Baldwin, R.E. (2001) 'The implications of increasing fragmentation and globalisation for the World Trade Organisation', in L. Cheung and H. Kierzhowski (eds) *Global Production and Trade in East Asia*, Boston MA: Kluwer Academic.

Beasley, W.G. (1987) *Japanese Imperialism, 1894–1945*, Oxford: Clarendon Press.

Beaverstock, J.V., Smith, R.G. and Taylor, P.J. (1999) 'A roster of world cities', *Cities* 16,6: 445–58.

Beeson, M. (ed.) (2006a) *Bush and Asia: America's Evolving Relations with East Asia*, London: Routledge.

Beeson, M. (2006b) 'American hegemony and regionalism: the rise of East Asia and the end of the Asia-Pacific', *Geopolitics* 11: 1–20.

Beeson, M. (2007) *Regionalism, Globalisation and East Asia: Politics, Security and Economic Development*, Basingstoke: Palgrave.

Berger, M. and Beeson, M. (2005) 'APEC, ASEAN+3 and American power: the history and limits of the new regionalism in the Asia-Pacific', in M. Boas, M.H. Marchand and T. Shaw (eds) *The Political Economy of Regions and Regionalisms*, Basingstoke: Palgrave Macmillan.

Berger, S.M. (2006) 'The US stake in greater Asian integration', *Global Asia* 1,1: 25–27.

Bergsten, C.F.(1994) 'Sunrise in Seattle' *International Economic Insights* 5,1: 18–20.

Bergsten, C.F. (1996) 'Globalising free trade', *Foreign Affairs*, 75,3: 105–21.

Bhagwati, J. (1993) 'Regionalism and multilateralism: an overview', in J. De Melo and A. Panagariya (eds) *New Dimensions in Regional Integration*, Cambridge: Cambridge University Press.

Bhagwati, J. (2004) *In Defense of Globalisation*, Oxford: Oxford University Press.

Bird, G. and Rajan, R.S. (2002)'Regional arrangements for providing liquidity in a financial crisis: developments in East Asia', *The Pacific Review* 15,3: 359–79.

Boas, M., Marchand, M.H. and Shaw, T. (eds) (2005) *The Political Economy of Regions and Regionalisms*, Basingstoke: Palgrave Macmillan.

Borrus, M., Ernst, D. and Haggard, S. (eds) (2000) *International Production Networks in Asia: Rivalry or Riches?*, London: Routledge.

Bowen, J.T. and Leinbach, T.R. (2006) 'Competitive advantage in global production networks: air freight services and the electronics industry in Southeast Asia', *Economic Geography*, 82,2: 147–66.

Bowles, P. (1997) 'ASEAN, AFTA, and the new regionalism', *Pacific Affairs*, 70,2: 219–33.

Bowles, P. and MacLean, B. (1996) 'Understanding trade bloc formation: the case of the ASEAN free trade area', *Review of International Political Economy*, 3,2:319–48.

Braudel, F. (1992) 'The perspectives of the world', in *Civilisations and Capitalism: Volume III*, Berkeley, CA: University of California Press.

Buzan, B. (1998) 'The Asia-Pacific: what sort of region in what sort of world?, in A. McGrew and C. Brook (eds) *Asia-Pacific in the New World Order*, London: Routledge.

Buzan, B. and Waever, O. (2003) *Regions and Powers: The Structure of International Security*, Cambridge: Cambridge University Press.

Buzan, B., Waever, O. and de Wilde, J. (1998) *Security: A New Framework of Analysis*, Boulder, CO: Lynne Rienner.

Byron, N. and Shepherd, G. (1998) 'Indonesia and the 1997–98 El Nino: fire problems and long-term solutions', *ODI Natural Resource Perspectives* 28 (April): 1–4.

Calder, K. (1997) *Asia's Deadly Triangle: How Arms, Energy and Growth Threaten to Destabilise the Asia-Pacific*, London: Nicholas Brealey.

Calder, K. (2006) 'China and Japan's simmering rivalry', *Foreign Affairs* 85,2: 129–36.

Chalongphob, S.(2002) 'East Asian financial co-operation: an assessment of the rationale', paper presented at the *East Asian Cooperation* conference, Institute of Asia Pacific Studies / Centre for APEC & East Asian Cooperation, Chinese Academy of Social Sciences, August 22–3, Beijing.

Chanda, N. (2006) 'When Asia was one', *Global Asia*, 1,1: 58–68.

Chang, L.L. and Rajan, R.S. (2001) 'Regional versus multilateral solutions to trans-boundary environmental problems: insights from the Southeast Asian haze', *World Economy* 24,5: 655–71.

Charrier, P. (2001) 'ASEAN's inheritance: the regionalisation of Southeast Asia, 1941–61', *The Pacific Review* 14,3: 313–38.

Chase-Dunn, C. (1989) *Global Formation: Structures of the World Economy*, Oxford: Blackwell.

Chen, E.K.Y. and Ho, A. (1995) 'Southern China growth triangle: an overview', in M. Thant, M. Tang and H. Kakazu (eds) *Growth Triangles in Asia: A New Approach to Regional Economic Co-operation*, Oxford: Oxford University Press.

Chen, X. (1995) 'The evolution of free economic zones and the recent development of cross-national growth zones', *International Journal of Urban and Regional Research* 19,4: 593–621.

Chia, S.Y. (2006) 'Labour mobility and East Asian integration', *Asian Economic Policy Review* 1: 349–67.

Chng, M. K. (1985) 'ASEAN economic co-operation: the current status', *Southeast Asian Affairs*, ISEAS, Singapore: 31–53.

Chowdhury, A. and Islam, I. (1993) *The Newly Industrialising Economies of East Asia*, London: Routledge.

Christie, C.J. (1996) *A Modern History of Southeast Asia: Decolonisation, Nationalism and Separatism*, London: Tauris.

Coe, N.M., Hess, M., Yeung, H.W.C., Dicken, P. and Henderson, J. (2004) 'Globalising regional development: a global production networks perspective', *Transactions of the Institute of British Geographers* 29: 468–84.

Cohen, S.S. (2002) 'Mapping Asian integration: transnational transactions in the Pacific Rim', *American Asian Review* 20,3: 1–30.

Collins, A. (ed.) (2007) *Contemporary Security Studies*, Oxford: Oxford University Press.

Cotton, J. (1999) 'The haze over Southeast Asia: challenging the ASEAN mode of regional engagement', *Pacific Affairs*, 72,3: 331–51.

Curley, M.G. (2007) 'The role of civil society in East Asian region building', in M.G. Curley and N. Thomas (eds) *Advancing East Asian Regionalism*, London: Routledge.

Cuyvers, L., de Lombaerde, P. and Verherstraeten, S. (2005) 'From AFTA towards an ASEAN economic community... and beyond', *CAS Discussion Paper No. 46*, Centre for ASEAN Studies, Antwerp.

Daquila, T.C. and Huy, L.H. (2003) 'Singapore and ASEAN in the global economy: the case of free trade agreements', *Asian Survey* 43,6: 908–28.

Das, D.K. (2004) 'Structured regionalism in the Asia-Pacific: slow but sure progress', *Asia Pacific Viewpoint*, 45,2: 217–33.

Dent, C.M. (1997) *The European Economy: The Global Context*, London: Routledge.

Dent, C.M. (1999) *The European Union and East Asia: An Economic Relationship*, London: Routledge.

Dent, C.M. (2001a) 'Singapore's foreign economic policy: the pursuit of economic security', *Contemporary Southeast Asia* 23,1: 1–23.

Dent, C.M. (2001b) 'The Eurasian economic axis: its significance for East Asia', *Journal of Asian Studies* 60,3: 731–59.

Dent, C.M. (2001c) 'ASEM and the Cinderella complex of EU–East Asia economic relations', *Pacific Affairs* 74,1: 25–52.

Dent, C.M. (2002) *The Foreign Economic Policies of Singapore, South Korea and Taiwan*, Cheltenham: Edward Elgar.

Dent, C.M. (2003) 'New economic and security co-operation in the Asia-Pacific: an introduction', in C.M. Dent (ed.) *Asia-Pacific Economic and Security Co-operation: New Regional Agendas*, Basingstoke: Palgrave.

Dent, C.M. (2004) 'The Asia-Europe Meeting (ASEM) and inter-regionalism: towards a theory of multilateral utility', *Asian Survey*, 44,2: 213–36.

Dent, C.M. (2005a) 'Taiwan and the new regional political economy of East Asia', *China Quarterly* 182: 385–406.

Dent, C.M. (2005b) 'Bilateral free trade agreements: boon or bane for regionalism in East Asia and the Asia-Pacific?', *European Journal of East Asian Studies* 4,2: 287–314.

Dent, C.M. (2006a) *New Free Trade Agreements in the Asia-Pacific*, Basingstoke: Palgrave Macmillan.

Dent, C.M. (2006b) 'The new economic bilateralism in Southeast Asia: region-convergent or region-divergent?', *International Relations of the Asia-Pacific* 6,1: 81–111.

Dent, C.M. (2007a) 'Economic security', in A. Collins (ed.) *Contemporary Security Studies*, Oxford: Oxford University Press.

Dent, C.M. (2007b) 'The International Political Economy of ASEAN economic integration and bilateral FTAs', *Journal of Current Southeast Asian Affairs* 26,1: 51–75.

Dent, C.M. and Huang, D. (eds) (2002) *Northeast Asian Regionalism: Learning from the European Experience*, London: Curzon Press.

Department of Statistics, Malaysia (2006) 'International migration in Malaysia', *Expert Group Meeting on ESCAP Regional Census Programme*, 26–7 November, Bangkok.

Desker, B. (2004) 'In defence of FTAs: from purity to pragmatism in East Asia', *The Pacific Review* 17,1: 3–26.

Deutsch, K. W. (1957) *Political Community and the North Atlantic Area. International Organization in the Light of Historical Experience*, Princeton, NJ: Princeton University Press.

Deutsch, K. W. (1966) *Nationalism and Social Communication: An Inquiry into the Foundation of Nationality*, Cambridge, MA: MIT Press.

Dicken, P. (2003) *Global Shift: Reshaping the Global Economic Map in the 21st Century*, London: Sage.

Dieter, H. (1997) 'APEC and WTO: collision or co-operation?', *Pacific Review* 10, 1: 19–38.

Dieter, H. (2006) 'Report on East Asian integration: opportunities and obstacles for enhanced economic co-operation', *Notre Europe Studies and Research Paper No. 47*, Paris.

Dobson, W. and Chia, Y.S. (1997) *Multinationals and East Asian Integration*, Institute of Southeast Asian Studies, Singapore.

Doner, R.F. (1991) 'Approaches to the politics of economic growth in Southeast Asia', *Journal of Asian Studies* 50,4: 818–49.

Doner, R.F., Noble, G.W. and Ravenhill, J. (2004) 'Production networks in East Asia's auto parts industry', in S. Yusuf, M.A. Altaf and K. Nabeshima (eds) *Global Production Networking and Technological Change in East Asia*, Oxford: Oxford University Press, for the World Bank.

Dosch, J. (2003) 'Sub-regional co-operation in the Mekong Valley: implications for regional security', in C.M. Dent (ed.) *Asia-Pacific Economic and Security Co-operation: New Regional Agendas*, Basingstoke: Palgrave Macmillan.

Dosch, J. (2006) *The Changing Dynamics of Southeast Asian Politics*, Boulder, CO: Lynne Rienner.

Drifte, R. (2006) 'Leadership issues for Asia in the 21st century', *Asien* 100: 33–7.

Drysdale, P. (1991) 'Open regionalism: a key to East Asia's economic future', *Pacific Economic Papers*, No. 197, Australia-Japan Research Centre.

Drysdale, P. and Elek, A. (1996) 'The APEC experiment: an open economic organisation in the Asia-Pacific', *International Journal of Social Economics* 23,4–6: 164–87.

East Asia Study Group (2002) *Final Report of the East Asia Study Group*, East Asia Study Group.

East Asia Vision Group (2001) *Towards an East Asian Community: Region of Peace, Prosperity and Progress*, East Asia Vision Group.

Eaton, S. and Stubbs R. (2006) 'The English School and ASEAN', *The Pacific Review* 19, 2: 135–55.

Elek, A. and Soesastro, H. (2000) 'ECOTECH at the heart of APEC: capacity-building in the Asia-Pacific', in I. Yamazawa (ed.) *Asia-Pacific Economic Co-operation (APEC): Challenges and Tasks for the Twenty-First Century*, London: Routledge.

Elliott, L. (2003) 'ASEAN and environmental co-operation: norms, interests and identity', *The Pacific Review* 16,1: 29–52.

Ernst, D. (2002) 'Global production networks and the changing geography of innovation systems: implications for developing countries', *Economics of Innovation and New Technology* 11,6: 497–523.

Ernst, D. (2004) 'Global production networks in East Asia's electronics industry and upgrading perspectives in Malaysia', in S. Yusuf, M.A. Altaf and K. Nabeshima (eds) *Global Production Networking and Technological Change in East Asia*, Oxford: World Bank / Oxford University Press.

Ernst, D. (2005) 'Searching for a new role in East Asian regionalisation: Japanese production networks in the electronics industry', in P.J. Katzenstein and Takashi Shiraishi (eds) *Beyond Japan: The Dynamics of East Asian Regionalism*, Ithaca, NY: Cornell University Press.

Estevadeordal, A. and Suominen, K. (2005) 'Mapping and measuring rules of origin around the world', presented at the *International Workshop on Identifying and addressing Possible Impacts of FTAs/RTAs Development on APEC Developing Member Economies*, Hanoi, 28–30 June.

Fairbank, J.K. (ed.) (1968) *The Chinese World Order: Traditional China's Foreign Relations*, Cambridge, MA: Harvard University Press.

Fawcett, L. and Hurrell, A.(1995) *Regionalism in World Politics*, Oxford: Oxford University Press.

Feenstra, R. (1998) 'Integration of trade and disintegration of production in the global economy', *Journal of Economic Perspectives*, 14,4: 31–50.

Fei, J.C.H. and Ranis, G. (1964) 'A theory of economic development', *American Economic Review* 51, 4: 533–65.

Felker, G.B. (2004) 'Global production and Southeast Asia's industrialisation', in K. Jayasuriya (ed.) *Asian Regional Governance: Crisis and Change* London: Routledge.

Ferguson, J. R. (2004) 'ASEAN Accord II: policy prospects for regional participant development', *Contemporary Southeast Asia*, 23,3: 393–415.

Frank, A.G. (1998) *ReOrient: Global Economy in the Asian Age*, Berkeley, CA: University of California Press.

Frankel, J.A. (1993) 'Is Japan creating a yen bloc in East Asia and the Pacific', in J.A. Frankel and M. Kahler (eds) *Regionalism and Rivalry: Japan and the United States in Pacific Asia*, Chicago, IL: University of Chicago Press.

Freeman, N.J. and Bartels, F.L. (eds) (2004) *The Future of Foreign Investment in Southeast Asia*, London: Routledge.

Fritz, B. and Metzger, M. (eds) (2005) *New Issues in Regional Monetary Co-ordination: Understanding North-South and South-South Arrangements*, Basingstoke: Palgrave Macmillan.

Frobel, F., Heinricks, J. and Kreye, O. (1980) *The New International Division of Labour*, Cambridge: Cambridge University Press,.

Fujita, M. (ed.) (2007) *Regional Integration in East Asia: From the Viewpoint of Spatial Economics*, Basingstoke: Palgrave.

Fujita, M., Krugman, P. and Venables, A.J. (eds) (1999) *The Spatial Economy: Cities, Regions and International Trade*, Cambridge, MA: MIT Press.

Furuoka, F. (2005) 'Japan and the flying geese pattern of East Asian integration', *Eastasia.at*, 4, 1 (October).

Gamble, A. and Payne, A. (eds) (1996) *Regionalism and World Order*, Basingstoke: Macmillan.

Garnaut, R. (2000) 'Introduction – APEC ideas and reality', in I. Yamazawa (ed.) *Asia-Pacific Economic Co-operation (APEC): Challenges and Tasks for the Twenty-First Century*, London: Routledge.

Garnaut, R. and Drysdale, P. (1994) *Asia Pacific Regionalism*, Pymble: Harper Educational.

Gehrels, F. (1956) "Customs unions from a single-country viewpoint", *Review of Economic Studies* 49: 696–712.

Gilpin, R. (1984) 'The richness of the tradition of political realism', *International Organization*, 38, 2: 287–304.

Gilson, J. (2002) *Asia Meets Europe: Interregionalism and the Asia-Europe Meeting*, Cheltenham: Edwin Elgar.

Giroud, A. (2003) *Transnational Corporations, Technology and Economic Development: Backward Linkages and Knowledge Transfer in South East Asia*, Cheltenham: Edward Elgar.

Giroud, A. (2004) 'Foreign direct investment and the rise of cross-border production networks in Southeast Asia', in N.J. Freeman and F.L. Bartels (eds) *The Future of Foreign Investment in Southeast Asia*, London: Routledge.

Glover, D. and Jessup, T. (eds) (1999) *Indonesia's Fires and Haze: The Cost of Catastrophe*, Singapore: Institute of Southeast Asian Studies.

Goldstein, L. and Kozyrev, V. (2006) 'China, Japan and the scramble for Siberia', *Survival* 48, 1: 163–78.

Greenaway, D. and Milner, C. (2002) 'Regionalism and gravity', *Scottish Journal of Political Economy* 49,5: 574–85.

Grimes, W. and Kimura, S. (2005) 'Japan, East Asia and the limits to financial regionalism', *RIETI Seminar Paper*, 27 July 2005, Tokyo.

Grundy-Warr, C. (2004) 'The silence and the violence of forced migration: the Myanmar–Thailand border', in A. Ananta and E.N. Arifin (eds) *International Migration in Southeast Asia*, Singapore: Institute of Southeast Asian Studies.

Grundy-Warr, C., Peachey, K. and Perry, M. (1999) 'Fragmented integration in the Singapore–Indonesia border zone: Southeast Asia's growth triangle against the global economy', *International Journal of Urban and Regional Research*, 23,2: 304–28.

Haggard, S. and Moravcsik, A. (1993) 'The political economy of financial assistance to Eastern Europe, 1989–1991', in R.O. Keohane, J. S. Nye and S. Hoffmann (eds) *After the Cold War*, Cambridge, MA: Harvard University Press.

Hall, J.W. (1970) *Japan: From Prehistory to Modern Times*, New York, NY: Delacorte Press.

Hamashita, T. (1997) 'The intra-regional system in East Asia in modern times', in P.J. Katzenstein (ed.) *Network Power: Japan and Asia*, Ithaca, NY: Cornell University Press.

Hamilton-Hart, N. (2004) 'Co-operation on money and finance: how important? How likely?', in K. Jayasuriya (ed.) *Asian Regional Governance: Crisis and Change*, London: Routledge.

Hamilton-Hart, N. (2007) 'Financial co-operation and domestic political economy in East Asia', in M.G. Curley and N. Thomas (eds) *Advancing East Asian Regionalism*, London: Routledge.

Harrison, S.S. (2005) 'Seabed petroleum in Northeast Asia: conflict or co-operation?', *Woodrow Wilson International Centre for Scholars – Asia Programme*, Washington, DC.

Hatch, W. and Yamamura, K. (1996) *Asia in Japan's Embrace: Building a Regional Production Alliance*, Cambridge: Cambridge University Press.

Hayashi, S. (2006) *Japan and East Asian Monetary Regionalism*, London: Routledge.

Hayes, P. and von Hippel, D. (2006) 'Energy security in Northeast Asia', *Global Asia* 1,1: 90–105.

Hellenier, G.K. (1973) 'Manufacturing exports from less developed countries and multinational firms', *Economic Journal* 83: 21–47.

Henderson, J., Dicken, P., Hess, M., Coe, N. and Yeung, H.W.C. (2002) 'Global production networks and the analysis of economic development', *Review of International Political Economy* 9,3: 436–64.

Henning, C.R. (2002) *East Asian Financial Co-operation*, Washington, DC: Institute for International Economics.

Herberg, M.E. (2004) 'The geopolitics of natural gas and LNG in Asia', paper presented at *Energy Security in Asia and its implications for the US* conference, Seattle, WA.

Herberg, M.E. (2007) 'Asia's national oil companies: international expansion and competitive implications', presented at Institute of Energy Economics Japan, Tokyo, 7 April.

Hettne, B. (2005) 'Beyond the new regionalism', *New Political Economy*, 10,4: 543–71.

Hettne, B. and Inotai, A. (1994) *The New Regionalism: Implications for Global Development and International Security*, World Institute for Development Economics Research, United Nations University, Helsinki.

Hettne, B. Inotai, A. and Sunkel, O. (eds) (1999) *Globalism and the New Regionalism*, London: MacMillan.

Hettne, B. and Soderbaum, F. (2000) 'Theorising the rise of regionness', *New Political Economy* 5, 3: 457–74.

Higgott, R. (1998) 'The Asian economic crisis: a study in the politics of resentment', *New Political Economy* 3,3: 333–56.

Higgott, R. and Stubbs, R. (1995) 'Competing conceptions of economic regionalism: APEC versus EAEC in the Asia-Pacific', *Review of International Political Economy* 2,3: 516–35.

Hiratsuka, D. (2006) 'Vertical intra-regional production networks in East Asia: a case study of the hard disc drive industry', in D. Hiratsuka (ed.) *East Asia's De Facto Economic Integration*, Basingstoke: Palgrave.

Hobday, M. (1995) *Innovation in East Asia: The Challenge to Japan*, Cheltenham: Edward Elgar.

Hu, T.S., Lin, C.Y. and Chang, S.L. (2005) 'Technology-based regional development strategies and the emergence of technological communities: a case study of HSIP, Taiwan', *Technovation*, 25: 367–80.

Hughes, C.W. (2000) 'Japanese policy and the East Asian currency crisis: abject defeat or quiet victory?', *Review of International Political Economy* 7, 2: 219–53.

Hugo, G. (2005) *Migration in the Asia-Pacific*, Global Commission on International Labour Migration, Geneva.

Hugo, G. (2006a) 'International migration in the Asia-Pacific region: emerging trends and issues', in D.S. Massey and J.E. Taylor (eds) *International Migration: Prospects and Policies in a Global Market*, Oxford: Oxford University Press.

Hugo, G. (2006b) 'Improving statistics on international migration in Asia', *International Statistical Review* 74,3: 335–55.

Hund, M. (2003) 'ASEAN Plus Three: towards a new age of pan-East Asian regionalism? a sceptic's view', *The Pacific Review* 16,3: 383–417.

Hurrell, A. (1995) 'Regionalism in theoretical perspective', in L. Fawcett and A. Hurrell (eds) *Regionalism in World Politics: Regional Organisation and International Order*, Oxford: Oxford University Press.

Inoue, R., Kohana, H. and Urata, S. (eds) (1993) *Industrial Policy in East Asia*, Tokyo: JETRO.

Institute of Energy Economics Japan / (IEEJ) (2006) *Asia / World Energy Outlook 2006*, Tokyo: Institute of Energy Economics Japan.

International Monetary Fund/IMF (2005) *Direction of Trade Statistics Yearbook 2005*, IMF, Washington DC.

Iredale, R. (2000) 'Migration policies for the highly skilled in the Asia-Pacific region', *International Migration Review* 34,3: 882–906.

Islam, I. and Chowdhury, A. (1997) *Asia Pacific Economies: A Survey*, London: Routledge.

Ito, S. (2004) 'The issues and prospects of international migration in East Asia', *The Japanese Economy* 32,2: 113–38.

Ito, T. (1993) 'The yen and the international monetary system', in C.F. Bergsten and M. Noland (eds) *Pacific Dynamism and the International Economic System*, Washington, DC: Institute for International Economics.

Ito, T. (2004) 'Exchange rate regimes and monetary co-operation: lessons from East Asia and Latin America', *Japanese Economic Review* 55,3: 240–66.

Jaffe, A.M. and Lewis, S.W. (2002) 'Beijing's oil dependency', *Survival* 44,1: 115–34.

Japan Economic Research Centre (JERC) (1966) *Measures for Trade Expansion of Developing Countries*, Tokyo: Japan Economic Research Centre.

Jayasuriya, K. (1994) 'Singapore: the politics of regional definition', *The Pacific Review* 7,4: 411–20.

Jones, D.S. (2006) 'ASEAN and transboundary haze pollution in Southeast Asia', *Asia-Europe Journal* 4: 431–46.

Jones, R. and Kierzkowski, H. (1990) 'The role of services in production and international trade: a theoretical framework', in R. Jones and A. Krueger (eds) *The Political Economy of International Trade: Essays in Honour of Robert Baldwin*, Oxford: Blackwell.

Kagami, M. (2003) 'ASEAN–Japan comprehensive economic partnership and Japan's FTAs with other countries including Korea and Mexico', presented at the *JEF/SIIA International Symposium*, Singapore, 7–8 March.

Kahler, M. (1995) 'Institution building in the Pacific', in A. Mack and J. Ravenhill (eds) *Pacific Cooperation: Building Economic and Security Regimes in the Asia-Pacific*, St. Leonards: Allen and Unwin.

Kanagawa, M. and Nakata, T. (2006) 'Analysis of the impact of electricity grid inter-connection between Korea and Japan: feasibility study for energy network in Northeast Asia', *Energy Policy* 34: 1015–25.

Katada, S.N. (2002a) 'Japan's two-track aid approach: the forces behind competing trends', *Asian Survey* 42,2: 320–42.

Katada, S.N. (2002b) 'Japan and Asian monetary regionalisation: cultivating a new regional leadership after the Asian financial crisis', *Geopolitics* 7,1: 85–112.

Katzenstein, P.J. (1996) 'Introduction: alternative perspectives on national security', in P.J. Katzenstein (ed.), *The Culture of National Security: Norms and Identity in World Politics*, New York, NY: Columbia University Press.

Katzenstein, P.J. (ed.) (1997) *Network Power: Japan and Asia*, Ithaca, NY: Cornell University Press.

Katzenstein, P.J. (2000) 'Regionalism and Asia', *New Political Economy* 5,3: 353–68.

Katzenstein, P.J. (2005) *A World of Regions: Asia and Europe in the American Imperium*, Ithaca, NY: Cornell University Press.

Kawai, M. and Takagi, S. (2005) 'Towards regional monetary co-operation in East Asia: lessons from other parts of the world', *International Journal of Finance and Economics* 10: 97–116.

Keohane, R.O. (1990) 'Multilateralism: an agenda for research', *International Organisation*, 45, 4: 731–64.

Keohane, R.O. and Nye, J.S. (1977) *Power and Interdependence*, Boston, MA: Little Brown.

Keynes, J.M. (1936) *The General Theory of Employment, Interest and Money*, Cambridge: Cambridge University Press.

Kim, J.Y. (2005) 'The formation of clustering of direct foreign investment and its role of inter-firm networks in China: case study of Qingdao development zones', in C. Karlsson, B. Johansson and R. Stough (eds) *Industrial Clusters and Inter-Firm Networks*, Cheltenham: Edward Elgar.

Kim, T.J, Ryou, J.W. and Takagi, S. (2005) 'Regional monetary integration in the presence of two large countries: what modality makes sense for East Asia?, *Japan and the World Economy* 17: 171–87.

Kimura, F. and Ando, M. (2004) 'The economic analysis of international production / distribution networks in East Asia and Latin America: the implication of regional trade arrangements', paper presented at the *APEC Study Centres Consortium Meeting*, Vina del Mar, Chile, 26–9 May.

Kimura, F. and Ando, M. (2005) 'The economic analysis of international production / distribution networks in East Asia and Latin America: the implications of regional trade arrangements', *Business and Politics*, 7,1: Article 2.

Kindleberger, C. (1973) *The World in Depression: 1929–1939*, Berkeley, CA: University of California Press.

Klaassen, G., McDonald, A. and Zhao, J. (2001) 'The future of gas infrastructures in Eurasia', *Energy Policy* 29: 399–413.

Knox, P. and Agnew, J. (1998) *The Geography of the World Economy*, London: Arnold.

Kohlscheen, E. and Taylor, M.P. (2006) 'International liquidity swaps: is the Chiang Mai Initiative pooling reserves efficiently?', *Warwick Economic Research Papers*, No. 752, Coventry: University of Warwick.

Kojima, K. (1977) *Japan and a New World Economic Order*, Boulder, CO: Westview Press.

Korhonen, P. (1994) *Japan and the Pacific Free Trade Area*, London: Routledge.

Kraft, H. (2000) 'ASEAN and intra-ASEAN relations: weathering the storm?', *The Pacific Review* 13,3: 453–72.

Krasner, S.D. (1976) 'State power and the structure of international trade', *World Politics* 28,3: 317–48.

Krauss, E.S. (2000) 'Japan, the US and the emergence of multilateralism in Asia', *The Pacific Review* 13,3: 473–94.

Krauss, E.S. (2004) 'The US and Japan in APEC's EVSL negotiations: regional multilateralism and trade', in E.S. Krauss and T.J. Pempel (eds) *Beyond Bilateralism: The US–Japan Relationship in the New Asia-Pacific*, Stanford, NY: Stanford University Press.

Kuchiki, A. (2006) 'An Asian triangle of growth and cluster-to-cluster linkages', *Institute of Developing Economies Discussion Paper No. 71*, IDE, Tokyo.

Kuchiki, A. and Tsuji, M. (eds) (2005) *Industrial Clusters in Asia: Analyses of the Competition and Co-operation*, Basingstoke: Palgrave Macmillan.

Kwan, C.H. (1994) *Economic Interdependence in the Asia-Pacific Region: Towards a Yen Bloc*, London: Routledge.

Lake, D.A. (1991) 'British and American hegemony compared: lessons for the current era of decline', in M. Fry (ed.) *History, the White House and the Kremlin: Statesmen as Historians*, London: Pinter.

Larner, W. and Walters, W. (2002) 'The political rationality of new regionalism: toward a genealogy of the region', *Theory and Society* 31: 391–432.

Lecler, Y. (2002) 'The cluster role in the development of the Thai car industry', *International Journal of Urban and Regional Research* 23: 379–95.

Lee, K.T. (ed.) (2002) *Globalisation and the Asia Pacific Economy*, London: Routledge.

Levine, J.S. (1999) 'The 1997 fires in Kalimantan and Sumatra, Indonesia: gaseous and particulate emissions', *Geophysical Research Letters* 26: 815–18.

Lewis, W.T. (1954) 'Economic development with unlimited supplies of labour', *The Manchester School* 22, 2: 139–19.

Lim, L.Y.C. (1995) 'Southeast Asia: success through international openness', in B. Stallings (ed.) *Global Change, Regional Response: The New International Context of Development*, Cambridge: Cambridge University Press.

Lipsey, R.G. (1970) *The Theory of Customs Unions: A General Equilibrium Analysis*, London: Weidenfeld and Nicolson.

Low, L. (1996) 'Government approaches to SIJORI', *Asia-Pacific Development Journal* 3,1: 1–19.

Luthje, B. (2002) 'Electronics contract manufacturing: global production and the international division of labour in the age of the internet', *Industry and Innovation* 9,3: 227–47.

MacLeod, G. (2001) 'New regionalism reconsidered: globalisation and the remaking of political economic space', *International Journal of Urban and Regional Research* 25,4: 804–29.

Mahani, Z.A. (2002) 'ASEAN integration: at risk of going in different directions', *The World Economy* 25,9: 1263–77.

Mahathir, M. (2006) 'Let Asians build their own future regionalism', *Global Asia*, 1,1: 13–15.

Manning, C. (2002) 'Structural change, economic crisis and international labour migration', *The World Economy* 25,3: 359–85.

Manning, R.A. (2000) 'The Asian energy predicament', *Survival*, 42,3: 73–88.

Mansfield, E.A. and Milner, H.V. (1999) 'The new wave of regionalism', *International Organisation* 53, 3: 587–627.

Marton, A., McGee, T. and Paterson, D.G. (1995) 'Northeast Asian economic cooperation and the Tumen River area development project', *Pacific Affairs* 68,1: 9–33.

Mason, M. (1999) 'The origins and evolution of Japanese direct investment in East Asia', in D. Encarnation (ed.) *Japanese Multinationals in Asia: Regional Operations and Comparative Perspective*, Oxford: Oxford University Press.

McKendrick, D., Doner, R. and Haggard, S. (2000) *From Silicon Valley to Singapore: Location and Competitive Advantage in the Hard Disk Drive Industry*, Stanford, NY: Stanford University Press.

McNicoll, G. (2005) 'Demographic future of East Asian regional integration', in T.J. Pempel (ed.) *Remapping East Asia: The Construction of a Region*, Ithaca, NY: Cornell University Press.

Meade, J.E. (1955) *The Theory of Customs Unions*, Amsterdam: North-Holland.

Means, G. P. (1995) 'ASEAN policy responses to North American and European trading arrangements', in A. Acharya and R. Stubbs (eds) *New Challenges for ASEAN: Emerging Policy Issues*, Vancouver: UBC Press.

Michaely, M. (1965) 'On customs unions and the gains from trade', *The Economic Journal* 75, 299: 577–83.

Milner, H. (1992) 'International theories of co-operation among nations: strengths and weaknesses', *World Politics* 44 (April): 466–96.

Milner, H. (1998) 'International political economy: beyond hegemonic stability', *Foreign Policy* 110 (Spring): 112–23.

Ministry of Economy, Trade and Industry (METI) (2005) *White Paper on International Economy and Trade: Towards a New Dimension of Economic Prosperity in Japan and East Asia*, Tokyo: METI.

Ministry of Economy, Trade and Industry (METI) (2006), *Japan's Global Economic Strategy: Economic Integration in East Asia and Japan's Policy Choices*, Tokyo: METI.

Miyashita, A. (1999) 'Gaiatsu and Japan's foreign aid: rethinking the reactive–proactive debate', *International Studies Quarterly* 43,4: 695–731.

Mori, M. (2002) 'The new strategies of vehicle assemblers in Thailand and the response of parts manufacturers', *Pacific Business and Industries RIM* 2,4: 27–40.

Morrison, C. (1981) 'American interests in the concept of a Pacific Basin community', in J. Crawford and G. Seow (eds) *Pacific Economic Cooperation: Suggestions for Action*, Selangor (Malaysia): Heinemann.

Narine, S. (1999) 'ASEAN into the twenty-first century: problems and prospects', *The Pacific Review*, 12,3: 357–80.

Narine, S. (2006) 'The English School and ASEAN', *The Pacific Review* 19,2: 199–218.

Naughton, B. (1999) 'The global electronics revolution and China's technology policy', *NBR Analysis* 10,2: 5–28.

Nesadurai, H. (2003) *Globalisation, Domestic Politics and Regionalism: The ASEAN Free Trade Area*, London: Routledge.

Nesadurai, H. (2006) 'APEC and East Asia: the challenge of remaining relevant', in L. Elliott, J. Ravenhill, H. Nesadurai and N. Bisley, *APEC and the Search for Relevance: 2007 and Beyond*, Canberra: Department of International Relations, Australia National University.

Ng, F. and Yeats, A. (2003) 'Major trade trends in East Asia: what are their implications for regional co-operation and growth?', *Policy Research Working Paper 3084*, Washington, DC: World Bank.

Nischalke, T. I. (2002) 'Does ASEAN measure up? Post-cold war diplomacy and the idea of regional community', *The Pacific Review* 15,1: 89–117.

Noppach, S. (2006) 'Supplier section in the Thai automotive sector', Discussion Paper No. 186, Hitotsubashi University Research Unit, Tokyo.

Ojendal, J. (2004) 'Back to the future? Regionalism in Southeast Asia under unilateral pressure?, *International Affairs* 80,3: 519–33.

Okamoto, J. (ed.) (2003) *Whither Free Trade Agreements? Proliferation, Evaluation and Multilateralisation* Japan: IDE-JETRO.

Okamoto, J. (ed.) (2004) *Trade Liberalisation and APEC*, London: RoutledgeCurzon.

Okunishi, Y. (1995) 'Japan', *ASEAN Economic Bulletin* 12,2: 139–62.

Olds, K., Kelly, P., Kong, L., Yeung, H. and Dicken, P. (eds) (1999) *Globalisation and the Asia- Pacific*, London: Routledge.

Organisation for Economic Co-operation and Development (OECD) (2006) *International Migration Outlook*, Paris: OECD.

Orru, M., Biggart, N.W. and Hamilton, G.G. (1997) *The Economic Organisation of East Asian Capitalism*, London: Sage.

Otsuka, K. (2006) 'Cluster-based industrial development: a view from East Asia', *Japanese Economic Review* 57,3: 361–76.

Ozawa, T. (1991) 'Japanese multinationals and 1992', in B. Burgenmeier and J.L. Mucchielli (eds) *Multinationals and Europe 1992*, London: Routledge.

Pacific Basin Co-operation Study Group (1981) 'Report on the Pacific Basin operation concept', in J. Crawford and G. Seow (eds) *Pacific Economic Co-operation: Suggestions for Action*, Selangor: Heinemann Asia.

Pacific Economic Co-operation Council (PECC) (2006) *State of the Region: 2006–2007*, Singapore: PECC Secretariat.

Pangestu, M., Soesastro, H. and Ahmad, M. (1992) 'A new look at intra-ASEAN economic co-operation', *ASEAN Economic Bulletin* 8,3: 344–52.

Paprzycki, R. (2005) *Inter-Firm Networks in the Japanese Electronic Industry*, London: Routledge.

Pempel, T.J. (1997) 'Transpacific Torii: Japan and the emerging East Asian regionalism' in P.J. Katzenstein (ed.) *Network Power: Japan and Asia*, Ithaca, NY: Cornell University Press.

Pempel, T.J. (2000) 'International finance and Asian regionalism', *Pacific Affairs* 13,1: 57–72.

Pempel, T.J. (2005a) 'Conclusion: tentativeness and tensions in the construction of an Asian region', in T.J. Pempel (ed.) *Remapping East Asia: The Construction of a Region*, Ithaca, NY: Cornell University Press.

Pempel, T.J. (2005b) 'Introduction: emerging webs of regional connectedness', in T.J. Pempel (ed.) *Remapping East Asia: The Construction of a Region*, Ithaca, NY: Cornell University Press.

Peng, D. (2000) 'The changing nature of East Asia as an economic region', *Pacific Affairs* 73,2: 171–91.

Perry, M. (1991) 'The Singapore growth triangle: state, capital and labour at a new frontier in the world economy', *Singapore Journal of Tropical Geography* 12,2: 138–51.

Petri, P. (1997) 'Measuring and comparing progress in APEC', *ASEAN Economic Bulletin* 14,1: 1–13.

Plummer, M.G. and Click, R.W. (2005) 'Bond market development and integration in ASEAN', *International Journal of Finance and Economics* 10: 133–42.

Pomeranz, K. (2000) *The Great Divergence: China, Europe and the Making of the Modern World Economy*, Princeton, NJ: Princeton University Press.

Poon, J. (2001) 'Regionalism in the Asia-Pacific: is geography destiny?, *Area* 33,3: 252–60.

Quadri, S.T. (2001) *Fire, Smoke and Haze: The ASEAN Response Strategy*, Manila: Asian Development Bank.

Quah, E. (2002) 'Transboundary pollution in Southeast Asia: the Indonesian fires', *World Development* 30,3: 429–41.

Quibria, M.G. (1997) 'Labour migration and labour market integration in Asia', *The World Economy* 20,1: 21–42.

Rafael, V.L. (1999) 'Regionalism, area studies and the accidents of agency', *American Historical Review* 104, 4: 1208–20.

Rajan, R.S. and Siregar, R. (2002) 'Private capital flows in East Asia: boom, bust and beyond', in G. de Brouwer (ed.) *Financial Markets and Policies in East Asia*, London: Routledge.

Rallu, J.L. (2002) 'International migration in Southeast Asia: the role of China', paper presented at the *IUSSP Conference on Southeast Asia's Population in a Changing Asian Context*, Chulalongkorn University, Bangkok, 10–13 June.

Rana, P.B. (2002) 'Monetary and financial co-operation in East Asia: the Chiang Mai Initiative and beyond', *Economic and Research Department Working Paper Series No. 6*, Asian Development Bank, Manila.

Rao, B. (1996), *ASEAN Economic Co-operation and ASEAN Free Trade Area: A Primer*, Singapore: Institute for Policy Research.

Rapkin, D. (2001) 'The US, Japan, and the power to block: the APEC and AMF cases', *The Pacific Review* 14,3: 373–410.

Ravenhill, J. (2001) *APEC and the Construction of Pacific Rim Regionalism*, Cambridge: Cambridge University Press.

Ravenhill, J. (2002a) 'Institutional evolution at the trans-regional level: APEC and the promotion of liberalisation', in M. Beeson (ed.) *Reconfiguring East Asia: Regional Institutions and Organisations After the Crisis*, London: Curzon Press.

Ravenhill, J. (2002b) 'A three bloc world? The new East Asian regionalism', *International Relations of the Asia-Pacific* 2: 168–95.

Ravenhill, J. (2003) 'The new bilateralism in the Asia-Pacific', *Third World Quarterly* 24,3: 299–318.

Ravenhill, J. (2006) 'Mission creep or mission impossible? APEC and security', in A. Acharya and E. Goh (eds) *Reassessing Security Co-operation in the Asia-Pacific: Competition, Congruence and Transformation*, Cambridge, MA: MIT Press.

Research and Information System for Developing Countries (2005) 'Towards an Asian energy community: an exploration', presented at *Asian Economic Integration: Towards an Asian Economic Community*, New Delhi, 18–19 November.

Rimmer, P.J. (1994) 'Regional economic integration in Pacific Asia', *Environment and Planning A* 26: 1731–59.

Risse-Kappen, T. (ed.) (1995) *Bringing Transnational Relations Back In: Non-State Actors, Domestic Structures and International Institutions*, Cambridge: Cambridge University Press.

Rocamora, J. (1994) 'The Philippines and competing Asian regionalism', *Politik* (Ateno University Manila) 1,1: 33–6.

Rose, C. (2004) *Sino-Japanese Relations: Facing the Past, Looking to the Future?*, London: RoutledgeCurzon.

Rudner, M. (1995) 'APEC: the challenges of Asia Pacific Economic Co-operation', *Modern Asian Studies* 29,2: 403–37.

Ruggie, J.G. (1993) 'Multilateralism: the anatomy of an institution', in J.G. Ruggie (ed.) *Multilateralism Matters: The Theory and Praxis of an Institutional Form*, New York, NY: Columbia University Press.

Ruland, J. (2000) 'ASEAN and the Asian crisis: theoretical implications and practical consequences for Southeast Asian regionalism', *The Pacific Review* 13,3: 421–52.

Ruland, J., Manske, E. and Draguhn, W. (eds) (2002) *Asia-Pacific Economic Co-operation: The First Decade*, London: RoutledgeCurzon.

Saha, P.C. (2003) 'Sustainable energy development: a challenge for Asia and the Pacific region in the 21st Century', *Energy Policy* 31: 1051–9.

Sakakibara, E. and Yamakawa, S. (2003) 'Regional integration in East Asia, challenges and opportunities: Part I – History and institutions', *Policy Research Working Paper 3078*, Washington, DC: World Bank.

Sakakibara, E. and Yamakawa, S. (2004) 'Market-driven regional integration in East Asia', in J. McKay, M.O. Armengol and G. Pineau (eds) *Regional Economic Integration in a Global Framework*, Frankfurt: European Central Bank.

Salameh, M.G. (2003) 'Quest for Middle East oil: the US versus the Asia-Pacific region', *Energy Policy* 31: 1085–91.

Saravanamuttu, J. (1988) 'The look east policy and Japanese economic penetration in Malaysia', in K.S. Jomo (ed.) *Mahathir's Economic Policy*, Kuala Lumpur: Insan.

Sassen, S. (1991) *The Global City: New York, London, Tokyo*, Princeton, NJ: Princeton University Press.

Sastry, N. (2002) 'Forest fires, air pollution, and mortality in Southeast Asia', *Demography* 39,1: 1–23.

Saxenian, A.L. (1999) *The Silicon Valley–Hsinchu Connection: Technical Communities and Industrial Upgrading*, Stanford Institute for Economic Policy Research, Stanford University.

Scholte, J.A. (2001) 'The globalisation of world politics', in J. Baylis and S. Smith (eds) *The Globalisation of World Politics*, Oxford: Oxford University Press.

Schwarz, A. and Villinger, R. (2004) 'Integrating Southeast Asia's economies', *McKinsey Quarterly*, No. 1: 1–10.

Scott, A.J. (1998) *Regions and the World Economy: The Coming Shape of Global Production, Competition, and Political Order*, Oxford: Oxford University Press.

Senese, P.D. (2005) 'Chinese acquisition of the Spratly Archipelago and its implications for the future', *Conflict Management and Peace Science* 22: 79–94.

Shambaugh, D. (2004) 'China engages Asia', *International Security* 27,4: 64–99.

Sharpton, M. (1975) International subcontracting, *Oxford Economic Papers* 27,1: 94–135.

Siddiqui, A.I. and Quah, E. (2004) 'Modelling transboundary air pollution in Southeast Asia: policy regime and the role of stakeholders', *Environment and Planning A*, 36: 1411–25.

Skeldon, R. (2000) 'Trends in international migration in the Asian and Pacific Region', *International Social Science Journal* 52,165: 369–82.

Skeldon, R. (2006) 'Interlinkages between internal and international migration and development in the Asian region', *Population, Space and Place* 12: 15–30.

Smith, D.A. (2004), 'Global cities in East Asia: empirical and conceptual analysis', *International Social Science Journal* 56,3: 399–412.

Soesastro, H. (1999) 'APEC after ten years', *Indonesian Quarterly* 27,2: 146–70.

Soesastro, H. (2003) 'An ASEAN economic community and ASEAN+3: how do they fit together?', *Pacific Economic Paper No. 338*, Australia–Japan Research Centre, Canberra.

Sonobe, T., Kawakami, M. and Otsuka, K. (2003) 'Changing role of innovation and imitation in development: the case of the machine tool industry in Taiwan', *Economic Development and Cultural Change* 52,1: 103–28.

Sonobe, T. and Otsuka, K. (2006) *Cluster-Based Industrial Development: An East Asian Model*, Basingstoke: Palgrave Macmillan.

Stares, P.B. (ed.) (1998) *The New Security Agenda: A Global Survey*, Tokyo: Japan Centre for International Exchange.

Storper, M. (1997) *The Regional World: Territorial Development in a Global Economy*, New York, NY: The Guildford Press.

Strange, S. (1994) *States and Markets*, London: Pinter.

Stubbs, R. (2000) 'Signing on to liberalisation: AFTA and the politics of regional economic co-operation', *The Pacific Review* 13,2: 297–318.

Stubbs, R. (2002) 'ASEAN Plus Three: emerging East Asian regionalism?', *Asian Survey* 42,3: 440–55.

Sturgeon, T.J. (2001) 'How do we define value chains and production networks?', *IDS Bulletin* 32,3: 1–10.

Sugihara, K. (1990) 'Japan as an engine of the Asian international economy, c. 1880–1936', *Japan Forum*, 2,1: 127–45.

Sum, N.L. (1996) 'The NICs and competing strategies for East Asian regionalism', in A. Gamble and A. Payne (eds) *Regionalism and World Order*, London: MacMillan.

Suriyamongkol, M. L. (1988) *Politics of ASEAN Economic Co-operation: The Case of ASEAN Industrial Projects*, Oxford: Oxford University Press.

Symon, A. (2004) 'Fuelling Southeast Asia's growth: the energy challenge', *ASEAN Economic Bulletin* 21,2: 239–48.

Tachiki, D. (2005) 'Between foreign direct investment and regionalism: the role of Japanese production networks', in T.J. Pempel (ed.) *Remapping East Asia: The Construction of a Region*, Ithaca, NY: Cornell University Press.

Taga, H. (1994) 'International networks among local cities: the first step towards regional development', in F. Gipouloux (ed.) *Regional Economic Strategies in East Asia: A Comparative Perspective*, Tokyo: Maison Franco-Japonaise.

Tan, A.K.J. (1999), 'Forest fire of Indonesia: state responsibility and international liability', *International and Comparative Law Quarterly* 48 (October): 854–5.

Tan, R.M., Pante, F. and Abonyi, G. (1995) 'Economic co-operation in the Great Mekong subregion', in K. Fukasaku (ed.) *Regional Co-operation and Integration in Asia*, Paris: OECD.

Tanaka, A. (2007) 'The development of the ASEAN Plus Three framework', in M.G. Curley and N. Thomas (eds) *Advancing East Asian Regionalism*, London: Routledge.

Tay, S. (2001) 'ASEAN Plus 3: challenges and cautions about a new regionalism', *Singapore Institute of International Affairs Reader* 1,1: 21–44.

Taylor, P.J. (2005) 'Leading world cities: empirical evaluations of urban nodes in multiple networks', *Urban Studies* 42,9: 1593–608.

Terada, T. (1998) 'The origins of Japan's APEC policy – foreign minister Miki Takeo's Asia-Pacific policy and current implications', *The Pacific Review*, 11,3: 337–63.

Terada, T. (2003) 'Constructing an East Asian concept and growing regional identity: from EAEC to ASEAN+3', *The Pacific Review* 16,2: 251–77.

Thambipillai, P. (1998) 'The ASEAN growth areas: sustaining the dynamism', *The Pacific Review* 11,2: 249–66.

Than, M. (1997) 'Economic co-operation in the Greater Mekong Subregion', *Asian-Pacific Economic Literature* 11,2: 40–57.

Thant, M., Tang, M. and Kakazu, H. (eds) (1995) *Growth Triangles in Asia: A New Approach to Regional Economic Co-operation*, Oxford: Oxford University Press.

Tongzon, J.L. (2002) *The Economies of Southeast Asia*, Cheltenham: Edward Elgar.

Tongzon, J.L. (2005) 'ASEAN–China free trade area: a bane or boon for ASEAN countries', *World Economy* 28,2: 191–210.

Tran, V.H. and Harvie, C. (eds) (2007) *Regional Trade Agreements in Asia*, Cheltenham: Edward Elgar.

Tsai, P.L. and Tsay, C.L. (2004) 'Foreign direct investment and international labour migration in economic development: Indonesia, Malaysia, Philippines and Thailand', in A. Ananta and E.N. Arifin (eds) *International Migration in Southeast Asia*, Singapore: Institute of Southeast Asian Studies.

Tsui-Auch, L.S. (1999) 'Regional production relationships and developmental impacts: a comparative study of three production networks', *International Journal of Urban and Regional Research* 23,2: 345–59.

Tuathail, G.O. and Agnew, J. (1992) 'Geopolitics and discourse: practical geopolitical reasoning in American foreign policy', *Political Geography* 11: 190–204.

Turner, M. (1995) 'Subregional economic zones, politics and development: the Philippine involvement in the East ASEAN growth area (EAGA)', *The Pacific Review* 8,4: 637–48.

Vernon, R. (1966) 'International investment and international trade in the product cycle', *Quarterly Journal of Economics* 80: 190–207.

Viner, J. (1950) *The Customs Union Issue*, London: Steven.

Wallace, W. (1994) *Regional Integration: The West European Experience*, Wessington DC: The Brookings Institution.

Wallerstein, I. (1978) 'World system analysis: theoretical and interpretative issues', in B.B. Kaplan (ed) *Social Change in the Capitalist World Economy*, Beverly Hills, CA: Sage.

Wallerstein, I. (1979) *The Capitalist World Economy*, Cambridge: Cambridge University Press.

Waltz, K. (1979) *The Theory of International Politics*, Reading: Addison-Wesley.

Weatherbee, D. E (2005) *International Relations in Southeast Asia: The Struggle for Autonomy*, Oxford: Rowman and Littlefield.

Webber, D. (2001) 'Two funerals and a wedding? The ups an downs of regionalism in East Asia and Asia-Pacific after the Asian crisis', *Pacific Review* 14,3: 339–72.

Wendt, A. (1992) 'Anarchy is what states make of it: the social construction of power politics', *International Organisation* 46,2: 391–425.

Whitley, R. (1992) *Business Systems in East Asia: Firms, Markets and Societies*, London: Sage.

Wong, J. and Chan, S. (2003) 'China–ASEAN free trade agreement: shaping future economic relations', *Asian Survey* 43,3: 507–26.

World Bank (2003a) *Major Trade Trends in East Asia*, Policy Research Working Paper 3084, Washington, DC.

World Bank (2003b) *Innovative East Asia: The Future of Growth*, Washington, DC: World Bank.

World Bank (2005) *Global Economic Prospects 2005: Trade, Regionalism and Development*, Washington, DC: World Bank.

World Bank (2006) *Global Economic Prospects 2006: Economic Implications of Remittances and Migration*, Washington, DC: World Bank.

World Trade Organisation / WTO (2002) *Coverage, Liberalisation Process and Transitional Provisions in Regional Trade Agreements*, Committee on Regional Trade Agreements, Document WT/REG/W/46, WTO Secretariat, Geneva.

World Trade Organisation (WTO) (2005), 'The changing landscape of regional trade agreements', *WTO Discussion Paper Series*, No. 8, WTO Secretariat, Geneva.

Yahuda, M. (1996) *The International Politics of the Asia-Pacific, 1945–1995*, London: Routledge,.

Yamamura, E., Sonobe, T. and Otsuka (2003) 'Human capital, cluster formation and international relocation: the case study of the garment industry in Japan, 1968–1998', *Journal of Economic Geography* 3,1: 37–56.

Yamamura, E., Sonobe, T. and Otsuka (2005) 'Time paths in innovation, imitation, and growth: the case of the motorcycle industry in postwar Japan', *Journal of Evolutionary Economics* 15,2: 169–86.

Yamawaki, H. (2001) *The Evolution and Structure of Industrial Clusters in Japan*, Working Paper 37183, Washington, DC: World Bank Institute.

Yasutomo, D.T. (1983) *Japan and the Asian Development Bank*, New York, NY: Praeger.

Yeoh, B. and Willis, K. (1997) 'The global-local nexus: Singapore's regionalisation drive', *Geography* 82, 355(2): 183–6.

Yeung, H.W.C. (2001) 'Organising regional production networks in Southeast Asia: implications for production fragmentation, trade and rules of origin', *Journal of Economic Geography* 1: 299–321.

Yoshimatsu, H. (2003) *Japan and East Asia in Transition: Trade Policy, Crisis and Evolution, and Regionalism*, Basingstoke: Palgrave Macmillan.

Yun, C. (2003) 'International production networks and the role of the state: lessons from the East Asian development experience', *European Journal of Development Research* 15,1: 170–93.

Yun, W.C. and Zhang Z.X. (2006) 'Electric power grid interconnection in Northeast Asia', *Energy Policy* 34: 2298–309.

Yusuf, S. (2003) *Innovative East Asia: The Future of Growth*, Oxford: Oxford University Press.

Yusuf, S., Altaf, M.A. and Nabeshima, K. (eds) (2004) *Global Production Networking and Technological Change in East Asia*, Oxford: World Bank/Oxford University Press.

Zhai, F. (2006) 'Preferential trade agreements in Asia: alternative scenarios of hub and spoke', *Economics and Research Department (ERD) Working Paper*, No. 83, Asian Development Bank, Manila.

Zhang, Y. (2003) *Pacific Asia: The Politics of Development*, London: Routledge.

Zhang, Z., Sato, K. and McAleer, M. (2004) 'Is a monetary union feasible for East Asia?', *Applied Economics* 36: 1031–43.

Zhao, Q. (2004) 'Japan's leadership role in East Asia: co-operation and competition between Japan and China', *Policy and Society* 23,1: 111–28.

Index

eBooks – at www.eBookstore.tandf.co.uk

A library at your fingertips!

eBooks are electronic versions of printed books. You can store them on your PC/laptop or browse them online.

They have advantages for anyone needing rapid access to a wide variety of published, copyright information.

eBooks can help your research by enabling you to bookmark chapters, annotate text and use instant searches to find specific words or phrases. Several eBook files would fit on even a small laptop or PDA.

NEW: Save money by eSubscribing: cheap, online access to any eBook for as long as you need it.

Annual subscription packages

We now offer special low-cost bulk subscriptions to packages of eBooks in certain subject areas. These are available to libraries or to individuals.

For more information please contact webmaster.ebooks@tandf.co.uk

We're continually developing the eBook concept, so keep up to date by visiting the website.

www.eBookstore.tandf.co.uk